THE
✠ CHRISTIAN CENTURIES ✠

THE

CHRISTIAN

CENTURIES

From Christ to Dante

ROBERT PAYNE

New York · W · W · NORTON & COMPANY · INC ·

FOR MY FATHER

On His Eightieth Birthday

✠ CONTENTS ✠

7

✠ ILLUSTRATIONS ✠

PLATES

Between pages 32 and 33

The young Christ, from a fourth-century ivory casket in the Museo Civico, Brescia. (Hirmer)

St. Luke, from a painting in the Catacomb of Comedilla in Rome. (Anderson)

The Virgin with the Christ Child, from a painting in the Catacomb of Priscilla in Rome. (Alinari)

John the Baptist, from Deësis panel at Hagia Sophia, Constantinople. (The Byzantine Institute)

Christ descending into Hell, from the Anastasis fresco in Kariye Kamii, Constantinople. (The Byzantine Institute)

St. Ambrose, from a mosaic in San Vittore in Ciel d'Oro, Milan. (Hirmer)

St. Basil and St. John Chrysostom, from a mosaic in the Cappella Palatina, Palermo.

St. Gregory of Nyssa, from a mosaic in the Church of Sophia, Kiev.

Between pages 64 and 65

John the Baptist, late tenth-century ivory in Victoria and Albert Museum, London. (Crown copyright)

The Archangel Michael, sixth-century ivory in the British Museum. (Hirmer)

St. Porphyrius, mosaic on the Rotunda of St. George, Salonica. (Hirmer)

St. Onesiphorus, mosaic on the Rotunda of St. George, Salonica. (Hirmer)

Four Apostles, from the dome of the Church of Hagia Sophia, Salonica.

Another Apostle from the same dome.

An Apostle gazing up at Christ, from the same dome.

Constantine the Great. Gold solidus, showing nimbus, from the Ashmolean Museum, Oxford. (Ashmolean Museum)

FIGURES

The greater number of the devices appearing at the ends of chapters are
derived from the sketchbook of Villard de Honnecourt prepared about
1235 A.D. The portrait of the young Christ comes from a glass fragment in
the British Museum dating from the third century. The last two drawings
are from Botticelli's designs for *The Divine Comedy*.

✠ PREFACE ✠

In THE following pages I have attempted to tell the story of the Christian centuries, those years when Christianity was a vivid and creative force in Europe, moving men's minds and working fiercely on their spirits. They were the years when faith was a simple thing, not to be squandered away in casual disputations of profit and loss, but kept as a treasure—the most sacred treasure a man possessed. In those years men lived in Christ; the shadow of the Cross loomed over them; and the promises made in Jerusalem and Galilee were accepted as the living words of a living God. For them Jerusalem and Galilee were only a stone's throw away. For us, coming so many centuries later, the vision has been dimmed by distance and we sometimes look back on those early years with a sense of bewilderment, wondering how it could have happened that a man from an obscure hill-town near the shores of an obscure lake became so powerful that he conquered the greater part of the known world.

The mystery remains; but we come closer to the heart of the mystery when we realize that it was precisely because Christ brought the element of sacramental mystery into human life that he succeeded in diverting the current of history. By giving a sacramental meaning to life, he gave to the lives of ordinary men a significance they had never previously possessed. The words *bread, wine, supper, love, birth, death* assumed the colors of majesty. Every meal became a divine feast, every birth took place in Bethlehem, every death occurred on Golgotha. All the events of his short life as they were chronicled by the Gospels and the apocryphal Gospels written in a later age touched on the lives of ordinary men and women. Marriage became a sacrament at Cana, suffering was sanctified by his torture and by the agony of the Crucifixion, and children were made sacred by his love of them. Under the Romans life had little purpose and was nourished on faint hopes. Under Christ life became full of hope and its purpose was known.

In this way the pragmatic, down-to-earth, eminently orderly conceptions of the Romans were ultimately exchanged for the other-worldly and mysterious conceptions of the Christians who refused obedience to the laws of Roman civilization. The Christians, in the phrase of St. Paul, had "turned the world upside down," and in the process they discovered themselves. What the Romans prized above all—loyalty to the state, martial valor, sobriety, conformity—all these were dismissed by the Christians as irrelevant to the main purpose of living. Their loyalty was to Christ, and they prized the valor of a martyr more than the valor of a soldier. Not sobriety but a holy joy; not conformity, but each man's leaping awareness of Christ. So it was inevitable that from the very beginning Christianity should be rent with heresies: the individual was continually making his own claims to salvation, which were not necessarily the claims of the Church. The winds of faith were often contrary, and the peace of God was often the cause of war.

Because Christ placed so much power and emphasis on the individual, the story of Christianity is very largely the story of individual Christians, who built the Church with their blood, sweat, and tears. Within the circumference of the Church the individual could move at will. Christianity never possessed a monolithic structure like Muhammadanism; it changed with the seasons, and like a tree it was continually putting forth new shoots and shedding new seeds. It was nervous and experimental, never still, seeking always for new wine to pour into old bottles. The Muhammadan, reciting the Koran daily and genuflecting in the direction of Mecca, found himself imprisoned in a clean-cut set of concepts as solid as the great cube of stone which Muhammad once thought of destroying and then retained because it represented the monolithic structure of his thought. There was nothing solid about Christianity, which was concerned with the movements of the individual human soul. "The wind bloweth where it listeth, and thou hearest the sound thereof, but canst not tell whence it cometh, and whither it goeth: so is everyone that is born of the

Spirit."

Until comparatively recently it was the custom to regard the medieval Christians with a curious mingling of pity and envy. We were told that medieval Christianity formed a closed system encircled by the walls of dogma, shadowy and ill-lit, filled with the accumulated detritus of centuries. In these Dark Ages men were placidly obedient to Rome, indifferent to the experimental sciences, and secure in the enjoyment of hallowed traditions. The world was superbly finite; the crystal heavens shone overhead; at the world's center lay Jerusalem, at the circumference were the lapping waters of Ocean. The priests ruled men's minds, cultivating in their flock a belief in the literal accuracy of the scriptures. Men went about looking for signs and wonders, and the unseen mysteries were more credible than the evidence set before their eyes. Hidebound and credulous, the medieval Christians trembled among shadows.

So we were told, but as the years pass it is becoming increasingly evident that the Dark Ages were a period of sustained brightness and extraordinary achievement. The medieval mind never completely submitted to authority. The Church, which played a major role on Sundays and feast days, succumbed to another authority during the remaining days of the week. Far from being subservient to authority, the medieval mind was rich in adventure and contradiction, and possessed a raw strength and vitality. Hot for certainties, always questing, it seems sometimes to be devoured by its own energy.

That energy, that sense of a continually expanding power which refused to acknowledge the existence of obstacles, was harnessed to a sacramental conception of the world; it was present even in the stillness and silence of prayer. So from the very beginning there was a dichotomy: a religion so personal and so intimate could scarcely bear the weight of organization. The organized church, as we shall see, emerged tentatively, at first with a small number of Jerusalem elders vested with authority, and then when they vanished from the scene authority was dispersed among the priests. There was never one central authority, nor could there be, since supreme authority lay with Christ, still living and eternally watchful. From him came the energy and the promise of ultimate blessedness, and the innumerable churches each represented themselves as the chosen vehicles of his peace.

Strange accidents and stranger designs went into the making of the churches. In A.D. 307 Diocletian, Galerius, and Licinius, meeting

in a solemn interview at Carnuntum on the Danube, dedicated a sanctuary there to Mithra, "the protector of their empire" (*fautori im-
perii sui*). The forward march of Mithraism was leading it to a position of formidable power and influence in the Roman world, when
Constantine emerged from England to destroy his rivals for the
throne. Not Mithra but Christ became the protector of the empire
only because Constantine willed it so. If it had not been for Constantine, Christianity in the West might have gone down to defeat.

Under Constantine Christianity was armed with imperial authority, and the Roman legions fought under its banners. Henceforth
Christianity in the West was to be colored by the religious practices
of pagan Rome. The robes of Christian priests, the shapes of Christian churches, the order of services, the offerings at the altars, the title
of the supreme pontiff, and the very language of Christian ceremonial
were derived from ancient Rome. And when the Roman court was
transferred to Byzantium, then all the more eagerly did the emperors
embrace Christianity and endow it with their own pomp and majesty
and armed power. For the Christian taught to render unto Caesar the
things that are Caesar's and unto God the things that are God's the
theocratic emperor served as a vehicle of both earthly and heavenly
honors. Yet there was nothiing in any of the four gospels to suggest
that Chirst approved of emperors.

Authority laid down the law, and emperors dictated to ecclesiastical councils. With exquisite finality doctrines were promulgated,
possessing the force of imperial edicts, only to be changed in another
century. Christianity accepted authority, but was never comfortable
in its presence. Since authority always stood for stability and Christianity was continually changing, the conflict between them could
rarely be hidden. The real strength of the papacy lay not in its doctrines and traditions but in its power to change them. Change, indeed,
lay at the heart of the mystery.

The essential work of Christianity had little to do with authority. Authority was a goad, a tyrant who demanded to be heard;
his voice could not be stilled, but it was not necessary for the fulfillment of the Kingdom. As in the days when they pursued their secret
lives in the catacombs, so the Christians continued to live secretly
even when the Cross became the symbol of an earthly triumph. It was
a religion of solitudes. In the imitation of Christ and in the study of
love, in silence and prayer, the Christian found himself. In the end

there was always the solitary soul confronting the solitary God on
the Cross, watching the blood fall and the eyes close.

So, writing about the Christian centuries, I have not dwelt overmuch with Christian potentates, although they too have their place. I
was concerned with the individual Christians, and how they adapted
themselves and kept their faith in a changing world. It seemed to me
that Christianity was like a river, now still, now turbulent, now
widening like a sea and then narrowing again between high cliffs,
changing color according to the colors of the sky and the seasons,
while here and there the waters were stained with blood, and sometimes there were abrupt turnings and stupendous waterfalls. Sometimes one can be deafened by the roar of that heroic river which had
its origins in the silence of Galilee.

Throughout the writing of this book I have been haunted by a
story written by the Danish poet Jens Peter Jacobsen. He tells of a
strange emaciated monk, "pale as linen, with black eyes glowing like
dying embers, with melancholy, pain-stiffened lines around the
mouth which seemed to have been carved with a knife out of wood,"
who appeared during a plague at Bergamo when all the survivors
were given over to despair. His purpose was not to encourage them,
but to expound a new, heroic, and more terrible gospel. He said:

*"They made Christ carry the Cross through the whirling dust,
they stripped his garments from him and left him naked in the sight
of all, and then they drove the nails in his flesh, and raised up the
Cross, and no one showed any sign of pity. They said: "If Thou be
the Son of God, come down from the Cross," and they reviled him.*

*Then he tore his feet free from the nails, and clenched his hands
round the heads of the nails and tore them out, so that the arms of the
Cross bent like a bow. He leaped down to earth, snatched up his robe
so that the dice rolled along the slopes of Golgotha, and then he
threw the robe round his shoulders with the wrath of a King, and
ascended to Heaven.*

*So the Cross stood empty, and the great work of redemption was
never fulfilled. There is no mediator between God and us. There is
no Jesus who died for us on the Cross."*

*Then one who heard him, a butcher, cried out: "Nail him on the
Cross again."*

There was no impiety in the butcher's words, for he was saying only that the Cross was necessary to human life, and there could be no mediator except the crucified Christ. Nor was there any impiety in the words of the strange monk, for he was describing one of the many aspects of the Crucifixion: Christ had indeed descended of his own will from the Cross, thrown his royal mantle over his shoulders, and ascended to heaven, leaving the Cross empty. A single event had taken place, and those who were present and those who contemplated it in their daily lives saw it under different aspects, under different skies, in different ages, knowing that the event took place in time and eternity, and that Christ absent was all the more present. And to many this paradox seemed no more than a simple statement of fact, while others would dispute it to the end of their lives.

Yet even the unbelievers were often enthralled by the majesty of the conception, the splendor of the dying and the risen Christ. In some mysterious way, beyond the edge of thought, his life and words gave meaning to human life, which seemed otherwise meaningless. Those who protested most fiercely against him found themselves helpless to destroy him. At the last turning of the last road he was always present, blood streaming down his face as he spoke of victory.

In this way he continued to live as an image in men's minds, a face, a presence, an emblem of man's hopes, a battle flag to be raised in the perpetual war fought against the outer darkness. If he could not be seen, for a silence and a stillness surrounds his earthly life, he could be felt and known, as men know that the sun will rise after the darkest night. He became the most private of possessions, while remaining the public property of all. The public Christ who entered the stream of history possessed powers that were strangely at variance with the powers of the private Christ men knew in their hearts. He became the ally of emperors and princes, who ruled in his name, revised his commandments, and punished those for whom he had died. Yet even in the darkest ages, when he was concealed by the pomp and panoply of the courts, he continued to speak to the humble and the merciful, to give solace to the poor and the dying. The emperors perished, but Christ lived on.

That life which was like no other life seemed to gain strength as the centuries passed. Christ answered the needs of each age, spoke with authority at every crisis, welcomed all that was new and cherished the old. He had lived so long on the earth that he had become a part of it; he was in the earth, in the rivers, in the woodlands; he was in the atmosphere men breathed, and in every landscape. He became a law of nature.

So in the Christian centuries we see him in many forms. He is the wanderer in Galilee prophecying the coming of the Kingdom, and the only beloved Son dying on the Cross. He is the consoler of martyrs and the councilor of emperors, the private possession of men's hearts, the public sovereign, the law of nature, the power pervading the universe. His forms are so various that there is no end to them. But always at the heart of the mystery there is a voice speaking quietly by the lakeside. The voice is heavy with the weight of the world's tragedy and joyful with certainty, and for those who hear this voice there is no more mystery.

THE
✠ CHRISTIAN CENTURIES ✠

1 ✠ THE CHRIST

N O ONE knows his appearance, or what language he spoke beside the lake, or how he conducted the greater part of his life in the morning of the world. A strangeness hovers over all his recorded actions and everything about his brief life on earth was attended with mystery. He comes to us across the centuries like a ghost, as insubstantial as the wind, and we have no sooner caught a glimpse of him than he vanishes into the blueness of a lake or the darkness of a tomb. Only once do we see him steadily. He is standing nailed on a cross in the gathering darkness, pathetically naked, choking in his own blood, his arms flung out as though to embrace the world.

While we remember most that last vision of him, it was not always so. The early Christians remembered the Last Supper more often than the Crucifixion, and they represented him not as a bearded and majestic king in agony but as a princely youth presiding gravely over a well-apportioned table, sitting among his friends. They saw him in the fullness of his power, kindly and sweet-tempered, with a splendor about him. They were not haunted by the gaunt and ravaged face; they saw him in his beauty, a young shepherd among the skipping lambs.

The early Christians, who painted his image on the walls of catacombs, seem never to have been aware that his earthly life was full of paradoxes. They read the Gospels before the words were drowned in commentaries, reading with the full breath, not halting, as we do, before every jolting word. He lived almost within living memory. Great-grandfathers and grandfathers had spoken with the apostles, and they had no need to ask themselves how he appeared to men as he walked through the cornfields. They saw him with innocent eyes: young, beardless, regal, the brother of Apollo and Orpheus. They knew that he died an agonizing death, but they rarely dwelt on his dying. They saw him living, not dying, and they were concerned to perpetuate the memory of his eternal youth.

The tradition of his youthful beauty survived across the centuries. St. John of Damascus, writing in the eighth century, says that Jesus "resembled his mother and was slightly stooping, with beautiful eyes, red hair which was long and curly, and he had a pale olive complexion and long fingers." Epiphanius, a monk who lived about A.D. 1150, speaks of him as being "six feet tall, red-haired, with dark eyebrows, a ruddy complexion, cheeks full but not so round as his mother's, his neck inclining a little so that the posture of his body was not quite upright." Nicephorus Callistus in the fourteenth century follows the same tradition and speaks of "his fair, curly hair with dark eyebrows, eyes shining with inexpressible compassion, shoulders stooping a little." But though the tradition of his youthful beauty survived long after he was being represented as a man of august middle age, many of the early Fathers of the Church were convinced that he was ugly and unprepossessing. Irenaeus described him as weak and inglorious—"*infirmus et ingloriosus.*" Clement of Alexandria wrote that "he had no comeliness or beauty, and was insignificant in appearance, inferior to the beauty of men." An ancient tradition, preserved in *Isaiah*, demanded that the Messiah should be a man of forbidding countenance, and no doubt the early Fathers found some comfort in the thought of a Saviour as an ungainly hermit who had deliberately set his back on the world, becoming as emaciated as the other hermits of their time. Tertullian places in the mouth of Jesus the words of the Psalmist: "I am a worm, and no man, a reproach to men, and despised of the people." So there were two traditions: one of his great beauty, and the other of his paralyzing ugliness.

In apocryphal literature these two traditions were curiously fused together. We are told in the *Acts of Peter* that Jesus was both beautiful and horrible to look upon—"*formosus et foedus.*" In the earliest of the apocryphal Acts known as the *Acts of John*, we are presented with a strange and awe-inspiring portrait of Jesus as he appeared to the two disciples John and James, the sons of Zebedee, as they were sitting in their fishing boats off the shore of the lake. Suddenly James saw Jesus beckoning to them:

"What does this youth want with us? Why is he calling us from the shore?" said my brother James to me. And I said, "What youth?" He answered, "He that is beckoning to us." I said, "My brother James, your eyes must be dimmed by the many sleepless nights we have spent on the lake. Do you not see that the man standing on the shore is a tall man with a joyful face of great beauty?" My brother said, "I do not see him like that, but let us row ashore and then we shall know."

When we hauled up the boat, Jesus himself helped us to make it fast. When we left the place to follow him, he appeared to me as an old, bald man with a thick flowing beard, while to my brother James he seemed a youth with but a faint down on his cheeks. And we could not understand and were amazed. And so it often happened, and he would appear to us in forms even more marvelous, sometimes small of stature, with crooked limbs, sometimes as a giant, reaching to the heavens.

(Acts of John, 85)

This account of the first meeting of James and John with Jesus has a hallucinatory quality, as of something seen and remembered with fearful clarity. Whoever wrote those mysterious lines was either a master storyteller, who knew exactly how to achieve his effects, or he was recording a living tradition, as it was once related by James or John. Origen, the most distinguished and influential of all the Fathers of the ancient Church, found no great difficulty in believing that Jesus changed his appearance according to the needs of the onlookers. There is a passage in the Talmud which describes Jesus as "cloud-like." It is perhaps the best of all adjectives to describe him as he moves silently across the land, belonging more to the sunlit sky than to earth, shining with a mysterious light. Cloud-like, he eludes us to the end.

Nevertheless, throughout the Christian centuries men have felt the need to form an image of his presence. Because he was dear beyond all telling, because the images men formed of him were of surpassing beauty or power, and because the Gospels provided a shadowy portrait which was curiously convincing though lacking in substance, the attempt to portray him has continued into our own age. Men felt that if a portrait could be drawn, then his character would be known. Who was this man who claimed to be the Son of God, the Bread and the Wine?

The authors of the Gospels were not concerned to give a portrait in depth, to describe him in minute detail. They believed the Second Coming to be at hand, and there was scarcely time enough to offer more than a brief summary, a catechesis, an outline of the most significant events of his earthly life. They were racing against time. Soon time would have an end, and all men's writings and all their thoughts would vanish like the morning mists in the new earth, where there would be no more time. So they wrote hurriedly, in brilliant fragments, without orderly progression, careless of details, sometimes combining events and discourses from different times and different places. They were not writing for perpetuity, but for the few years, the few months, that remained.

With the possible exception of the unknown author of the *Gospel according to St. John,* none of the Gospel writers had seen Jesus face to face. Mark drew from the reminiscences of Peter, Luke relied heavily on the mother of Jesus, Matthew relied on Mark and traditions surviving among the disciples. But though they had not seen Jesus, they knew him well. They write like men who are so saturated in their subject that they take much for granted. They took so much for granted that commentators and exegetes for eighteen centuries have been unable to construct a clear and consecutive narrative out of the fragmentary material provided for them. We see the events of the life of Jesus in lightning flashes. We can only guess what happens in the darkness.

In spite of all the difficulties which the Gospel writers have made for us, the human character of Jesus emerges with quite extraordinary authority. While the features are hidden, the shape of the mind is disclosed; and while the man eludes us, the voice rises clear. Nowhere is it more authentically clear than in the long sermon which covers three chapters of the *Gospel according to St. Matthew,* beginning with the Beatitudes:

Blessed are the poor in spirit: for theirs is the kingdom of heaven.
Blessed are they that mourn: for they shall be comforted.
Blessed are the meek: for they shall inherit the earth.

Blessed are they which do hunger and thirst after righteousness: for
they shall be filled.
Blessed are the merciful: for they shall obtain mercy.
Blessed are the pure in heart: for they shall see God.
Blessed are the peacemakers: for they shall be called the children of
God.
Blessed are they which are persecuted for righteousness' sake: for
theirs is the kingdom of heaven.
Blessed are ye, when men shall revile you, and persecute you, and
shall say all manner of evil against you falsely, for my sake.
Rejoice, and be exceeding glad.

(*Matthew* 5:3–12)

These opening words of the sermon, which were to be repeated
endlessly until they assumed at last the qualities of an incantation, implied a revolutionary reversal of accepted values. They were addressed to the humble, the poor, and the weak, and they spoke of a
promise reserved only for the humble, the poor, and the weak, a
promise so far beyond anyone's dreams that the sermon came as a
revelation of a new dispensation. In the past Jewish prophets had
spoken haltingly of the blessedness which would come to the poor, to
widows and the fatherless, to all the lost travelers in the world, but
always with a sense of a benediction taking place at some remote and
unimaginable time. But Jesus was saying: "Rejoice, for blessedness is
now."

These words were addressed to the common people who were
not expected to theorize on the theological implications of each word
or to play the scholar's game of reducing the meaning to incoherence
by demonstrating that the sermon was no more than a collation of
things previously said by philosophers and prophets at different times
and on different occasions. In the huge body of Judaic doctrine and
commentary such ideas had been hinted at, but they had never been
expressed with such freshness and urgency. To these common people
Jesus offered the crown of blessings. They were the salt of the earth
and the light of the world, the chosen of God, for they were simple
and gentle and careless of wealth and the great positions of the world,
and simplicity and gentleness, not the learned commentaries of the
scribes, were the roads to heaven. They were not to walk in dread of
divine mysteries, but with a quiet joy; and they were to pay no attention to the iron laws of conduct outlined by generations of law-

givers, but to bring freshness and spontaneity to life, to live fully and abundantly in the knowledge that they were under the protection of God, the father of all.

So Jesus went on to depict a world bound with loving-kindness to a God who was not remote, but near, not demanding, but generous with his gifts, and impatient of the sacrifices offered to him, and of public prayers. God demanded no elaborate rituals; it was enough if a man spoke to God in the silence of his own room. There was no need for a man to speak in the formal manner; he should open his heart quietly and say the things that were on his mind, "for your Father knoweth what things ye have need of, before ye ask him." God was not the stern law-giver, but the gentle shepherd who loves his flocks with compassionate tenderness.

In the Sermon on the Mount all those things which commonly exercised men's minds—the state, the observance of ritual, the accumulation of wealth, public honor and private grief, the ruin of one's enemies, the law's perplexities—are dismissed as being absolutely without importance in the economy of heaven. It is not only that they have no importance, but they are beyond the range of divine sympathy, and even perhaps of divine guidance. They have nothing to do with God, who is manifestly unconcerned with mammon and all its works. God is indifferent to wealth, and in his eyes the wealthy have no advantages over the poor:

Lay not up for yourselves treasures upon earth, where moth and rust doth corrupt, and where thieves break through and steal:
But lay up for yourselves treasures in heaven, where neither moth nor rust doth corrupt, and where thieves do not break through or steal:
For where your treasure is, there will your heart be also.

(*Matthew* 6:19–21)

To acquire wealth is to commit an act of treason against God, who provides for all with his bounty, for he has made the earth for all to live in peace together, helping one another. Implicit in the sermon's argument is the brotherhood of man under the fatherhood of God: in this brotherhood there was no room for contention and ambition, or for antiquated legal codes, or for private judgment. The law demanded an eye for an eye: God demanded mercy and forgiveness of sins. The law provided exact punishment for sins committed: God demanded that sins of thought should not go unpunished, or at least that they should be regarded as sins. The hypocrisies of law-givers, priests, and rich merchants were especially displeasing to God because in their different ways they were usurping his powers. They might show a public humility, but God was indifferent to public displays of righteousness: what he desired above all was the humble heart, man's naked innocence. If men relied humbly on the bounty of God, then all that they wanted would be given to them:

Therefore I say unto you, Take no thought for your life, what ye shall eat, or what ye shall drink; nor yet for your body, what ye shall put on. Is not the life more than meat, and the body than raiment?

Behold the fowls of the air: for they sow not, neither do they reap, nor gather into barns; yet your heavenly Father feedeth them. Are ye not much better than they?

Which of you by taking thought can add one cubit unto his stature?

And why take ye thought for raiment? Consider the lilies of the field, how they grow; they toil not, neither do they spin:

And yet I say unto you, That even Solomon in all his glory was not arrayed like one of these?

(Matthew 6:25–29)

With the Sermon on the Mount, Jesus stripped away the irrelevant pretensions of men and offered a new faith in which the poor and the dispossessed were placed especially under God's care. For the humble, the poor in spirit, he promised blessedness not at some future time but now: for theirs is the Kingdom of Heaven. And as in later days he continually spoke of the Kingdom, he seemed to be conveying the idea that it was already within men's grasp, and in a moment the material earth and all its splendors will be swept away to reveal the infinitely greater splendors of heaven. The Kingdom of Heaven was immanent; and he pointed to flowers and the faces of children as testimony of its presence on earth.

This sermon was central to the doctrine he announced at intervals during his brief ministry. There were to be modifications and amendments, but the essential beliefs concerning the bounty of the all-loving Father were to remain unchanged.

The new interpretation of God's purposes involved an attack on Jewish customs and traditions, and an even more sweeping attack on

the Romans, the conquerors of Palestine. Where the Romans demanded a pious veneration of the state, Jesus demanded indifference
to the state; instead of the rule of brute force he offered the rule of
loving-kindness; and instead of Roman *gravitas* there was to be
gaiety, a kindly joy. Not the strong, but the weak would inherit the
earth.

The novelty of the doctrine announced with such assurance
caused him to be venerated as a prophet, and the crowds gathering in
the hills overlooking the Sea of Galilee began to see in him the long-
promised Messiah. He healed the sick and calmed the storms. The
fishermen of Capernaum knew him well and protected him from the
too eager attentions of the crowd; he spent his days among them, or
in seclusion in some hidden fastness in the hills. His appearances in the
town were brief and tumultuous with the excitement of his healing
powers; he spoke in the synagogues, visited other towns around the
shores of the lake, and chose from among the fishermen the four disciples, Simon, Andrew, James, and John, who were to become his
closest companions. Already in this late autumn of A.D. 30 he had incurred the suspicions of the Sanhedrim, the Jewish ecclesiastical court
sitting in Jerusalem, which sent its agents to Capernaum to sound out
the views and beliefs of the new prophet, who had declared himself
the Son of God, spoke blasphemously of his God-given power to forgive sins, and consorted with a rabble of "tax-collectors and sinners."
He had healed a leper and then sent him to Jerusalem as a living proof
of the divine authority granted by the Father. In the eyes of the
Sanhedrim he was already convicted of blasphemy and necromancy.
They watched him closely and continued to watch him until they
had accomplished his death.

He lived the life of a wanderer and an outcast, always in danger
of arrest. When the crowds gathered, he sometimes refused to speak
to them, and slipped away on a fishing boat. When one of the scribes
sent by the Sanhedrim offered to follow him, he answered that no one
could follow him, for he was a wanderer over the land and never
knew from day to day where he would spend the night. "The foxes
have holes, and the birds of the air have nests; but the Son of Man
hath not where to lay his head."

Nevertheless, throughout many of his wanderings he was accompanied by his disciples. Simon, Andrew, James, and John kept close to

his side. Of the twelve disciples who were chosen by him only one, the mysterious Nathanael, appears to have been a man of any education. Jesus was not addressing himself to the educated but to the common people. His parables were simple stories of the countryside, many of them concerned with the gathering of the harvest. He likened the Kingdom of Heaven to the full harvest of a bountiful year, to a wedding feast, to a fisherman's net which gathers up the good fish, while the bad are cast away. Again and again he employed the image of the bridegroom, for the time of nuptial joys had come.

In those early days of his ministry he was continually speaking of the joys of the Kingdom. His presence at the wedding feast in Cana suggested a foretaste of the apocalyptic banquet, and the miraculous multiplication of loaves and fish were demonstrations of the bounty of the Kingdom. He had come, he said, not to destroy the law or the prophets, but to fulfill them. In the hour of fulfillment the earth would glow with all the lamps of heaven and the blessed would partake of the eternal wedding feast.

The joyful beginning was to be followed by a terrible ending. The ring was closing round him, as the agents of the Sanhedrim became more desperate to destroy the new faith. While the disciples were scattered over the land to preach the new gospel, Jesus himself became increasingly aware of his own tragic burden and began to withdraw more and more into himself, into the dark regions where he could converse alone with the Alone. He had proclaimed the coming of peace, and now he spoke of a war to the death in which he was an inevitable victim. He had said he had come to preserve, and now spoke of himself as the predestined destroyer. In the Sermon on the Mount he had called the people "the light of the world," and now he said, "I am the light of the world," and announced himself as the Saviour who had come to bring the world to repentance, the Anointed whose tragic destiny was prophecied in the sacred books, for had not Isaiah prophecied the passion, and Jonah the resurrection? His life, which had been spent in the open, now lay under the shadow of the messianic prophecies. For the remaining months of his life he stands amid the storm.

When he declared, "I am the light of the world," or proclaimed the words of divine revelation, "I am He" (in Aramaic, "*Ana hu*"), he was announcing quite simply that the light was destined to be blown out and that the Son of Man would perish. In the Sermon on the Mount he had spoken of the Kingdom of Heaven as close at hand. Now he saw that it could only be accomplished by his own death.

During those last months he still spoke of humility and love, reminding all men and especially the disciples that they should love God and love one another, but the voice was often harsh and discordant. He who had been gentle and compassionate now shouted in divine rage and cursed like the prophets, like Zephaniah who had spoken of "a day of wasteness and desolation," when men would walk like the blind, their blood would be spilled out like dust, and their flesh like dung. He spoke with the pitiless vengefulness of the prophets, in tones of anguish and defiance, threatening doom and destruction upon a faithless world. The "dark sayings" of Jesus are an uncomfortable reminder that his whole message was not contained in the Sermon on the Mount.

These sayings have a disturbing resonance, and cannot be wished away. They were uttered with the utmost solemnity, and there is no doubting their authenticity. He spoke of them as being told "in darkness," and even today, after the commentators have attempted to explain them away for twenty centuries, they remain as dark as when they were first uttered. Sometimes through the darkness there can be observed the flash of swords.

These dark sayings come in no discernible order; they strike like lightning out of clear skies, nearly always unexpectedly. They are colored by the sense of his own approaching doom, and appear to derive their strength from a very personal anguish:

I came to cast fire upon the earth; would that it were already kindled.

(Luke 7:49)

Think not that I am come to send peace on earth; I came not to send peace, but a sword.

For I am come to set a man at variance against his father, and the daughter against her mother, and the daughter-in-law against her mother-in-law.

And a man's foes shall be they of his own household.

(Matthew 11:34–36)

What is this then that is written, The stone which the builders rejected, the same is become the head of the corner?

Whosoever shall fall upon that stone shall be broken; but on whomsoever it shall fall, it will grind him to powder.

(Luke 20:17–18)

Seeing a fig tree afar off having leaves, he came, if haply he might find anything thereon: and when he came to it, he found nothing but leaves; for the time of figs was not yet.

And Jesus answered and said unto it, No man eat fruit of thee hereafter for ever.

(Mark 11:13–14)

The violence of these dark sayings can chill the soul. Death hovers over them; corruption and mortality are in them; and they cannot be reconciled satisfactorily with the promise of the Beatitudes.

At intervals, and most notably during the last weeks of his ministry, an unforgiving spirit moved in him. The theme of the chosen and the damned is pursued with unremitting force: no mercy is to be shown to the sheep outside the fold. He speaks in tones of finality and despair. It is not only that the voice is heavy with doom, but it is also strangely impersonal, and therefore all the more terrible. In its most simple form the theme is stated in the *Gospel according to St. John:*

If a man abide not in me, he is cast forth as a branch, and is withered; and men gather them, and cast them into the fire, and they are burned.

(John 15:6)

The stark theme receives a terrible embroidery in the history of the Middle Ages, when men were sent to the stake not because they failed to abide in him, but because they failed to abide in the precepts of the Church.

There were many other dark sayings, so many indeed that attempts to reconcile them with the gospel of mercy and tenderness are doomed to failure. The white thread and the dark thread are inextricably intertwined. We are confronted with an iron law which cannot be wished away. In what is perhaps the most terrible of his sayings, he repeats once more the theme of the reversal of human values, and then launches into a remorseless sermon on the fate awaiting the damned:

The young Christ, from a fourth-century ivory casket in the Museo Civico, Brescia. (*Hirmer*)

St. Luke, from a painting in the Catacomb of Comedilla in Rome. (*Anderson*)

The Virgin with the Christ Child, from a painting in the Catacomb of Priscilla in Rome. (*Alinari*)

John the Baptist, from *Deësis* panel at Hagia Sophia, Constantinople. (*The Byzantine Institute*)

Christ descending into Hell, from the Anastasis fresco in Kariye Kamii, Constantinople. (*The Byzantine Institute*)

St. Ambrose, from a mosaic in San Vittore in Ciel d'Oro, Milan. (*Hirmer*)

St. Basil and St. John Chrysostom, from a mosaic in the Cappella Palatina, Palermo.

St. Gregory of Nyssa, from a mosaic in the Church of Sophia, Kiev.

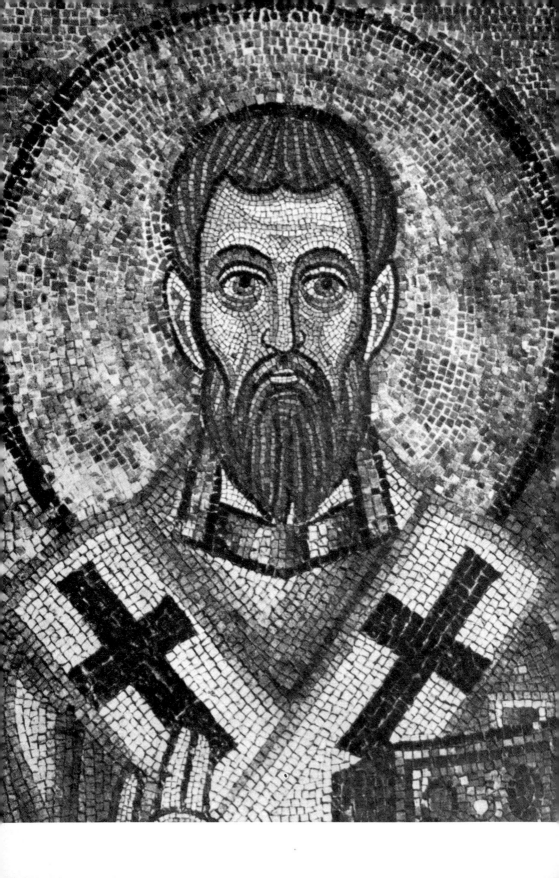

*Whosoever shall save his life shall lose it: and whosoever shall
lose his life shall preserve it.*

*I tell you, in that night there shall be two men in one bed; the
one shall be taken, and the other shall be left.*

*Two women shall be grinding together: the one shall be taken,
and the other left.*

*Two men shall be in the field: the one shall be taken, and the
other left.*

*And they answered and said unto him, Where, Lord? And he
said unto them, Wheresoever the body is, thither will the eagles be
gathered together.*

(Luke 17:33–37)

*Wheresoever the body is, thither will the eagles be gathered
together. . . .* In such stern terms, dismissing the damned as carrion,
he announced the division of the world. Then at last the rage is undis-
guised.

It is possible that the rage of Jesus was a passing thing, and that
the stern laws announced in the Gospels were not intended to be
taken literally, that the doors were never closed so dramatically, and
that the dark sayings were in the nature of dramatic hyperbole. Yet
there is nothing in the Gospels to warrant such a conclusion. The rage
was part of the man. It was there in the beginning when he was thrust
out of Nazareth, and again at Cana when he turned to his mother
and said: "Woman, what have I to do with thee?" It was especially
present during the last agonized journey through the streets of Jerusalem when he saw the women lamenting and turned on them, saying:

*Daughters of Jerusalem, weep not for me, but weep for your-
selves, and for your children.*

*For behold, the days are coming, in the which they shall say,
Blessed are the barren, and the wombs that never bare, and the paps
that never gave suck.*

*Then shall they begin to say to the mountains, Fall on us; and to
the hills, Cover us.*

*For if they do these things in a green tree, what shall be done in a
dry?*

(Luke 23:28–31)

In these words spoken in gall and bitterness there is no shred of
mercy; the voice is raucous; the air is stilled. Soon he would speak in a

different voice altogether from the Cross, and at Emmaus and on the shores of the Sea of Galilee he speaks with calm and authority. When we see him last, he stands on the edge of the lake cooking fish and waiting for the apostles to return to shore. Then once more he speaks the quiet words of blessing, the passion burnt out of him, only the peace remaining.

So he died and was born again, leaving to the world a mysterious knowledge and a strange certainty. The scholars would debate the meaning of every phrase, but the story of his life as it was related in the Gospels possessed an immediacy which the heart recognized, even if the intellect sometimes rebelled. The man of rage and the man of mercy became reconciled in a familiar presence of august power and gentleness, and while the events of his life could only with the greatest difficulty be placed in an intelligible order, the heart found reasons to ignore the incomparable disorder of the Scriptures. The heart saw him plain, for the heart needed him. He spoke to men in their sufferings and their joys, and in his presence the fear of death was quietened.

The philosopher Ibn Khaldun speaks of those moments in human history when for no apparent cause a blaze of divine energy appears on earth and the ensuing centuries reflect the glowing colors of the holy fire. A divine being appears, and the old orders of society collapse to form a succession of new orders dominated by new passions, a new humanity and a new brotherhood, charged with the energy of the incarnate divinity. Such divine beings appear rarely, and when they come they are not always recognized immediately. Sometimes many years may pass before they have established their empire among men: so it was with Jesus. The faith grew slowly, and many seeds fell on barren ground. It could hardly be otherwise, for to the worldly it was a hard and demanding faith, calling for a loving surrender to the Father and a rejection of the gifts of this world. It was not a faith to be embraced lightly; and if there was tenderness in it, there were sharp contours.

Out of the promise of the Kingdom of Heaven came the Christian centuries, the embattled years when men striving for perfection found themselves still at the mercy of their fears and lusts, and only a few saw the vision of paradise. "Be ye perfect as the Father in heaven is perfect," he had commanded them, but perfection escaped them. At

another time he said: "Take my yoke upon you, and learn from me;
for I am meek and lowly in heart: and ye shall find rest unto your
souls." In those centuries many bore the heavy yoke and found their
rest in him.

2 ✠ THE PLACE AND THE TIME

IN JERUSALEM, the divided city, and by the shores of a lake which lies below the level of the sea Christianity had its beginnings. From the lake there flowed down in the direction of Jerusalem a small stream which, then as now, a man could swim across in three strokes. Nearly all the events in the life of Jesus took place within that simple diagram: the city, the lake, the joining roads, the stream.

Along those dusty pathways, beside the flowering banks of the stream, beneath the towering walls of the city high in the Judaean hills, and on the shores of the enchanted lake he spent the greater part of his ministry, healing the sick and proclaiming the Kingdom; and there is a sense in which he took on the colors of the landscape. Jerusalem was the place of agony, Galilee of a calm measureless serenity. Between those two poles he swung like a pendulum which hung from the heavens. From the lowlands sprinkled with anemones he moves to the lonely heights, and then back again, restless always, like a man looking for something he has lost, something that is very precious to him, a signet ring, the lease of a house, a treasure chest, a kingdom. When he finds the lost paradise at last, he is on the Cross, in mortal agony and dying by inches.

For Jesus, Galilee was the place of preparation, the first tests of strength, the first songs. Not far from Galilee he first raised a child from the dead, and here, a morning's walk from the lake, he was raised to glory on Mount Tabor. He had grown up in the outskirts of the lake, and he knew all the pathways and the village inns. He was a Galilean to the core, possessing the Galilean characteristics of rebelliousness, ruthlessness, simplicity, and gentleness. Galilee was his home, his cradle, his familiar stamping ground. Fishermen, farmers, shepherds, carpenters, and olive-pickers were his friends; the hard ways of the cities were foreign to him.

When he came to Jerusalem he came almost as a stranger, unsure of himself or with an exaggerated self-assurance, as of one who has entered the enemy's citadel in disguise. He moves awkwardly and uncertainly even in his hours of triumph. When he is about to enter the city like a conqueror, riding on a colt, with a multitude of disciples spreading garments about his path, even then there is the realization that peace is denied to him. "And when he was come near, he beheld the city, and wept over it, saying, If thou hadst known, even thou, at least in this thy day, the things which belong unto thy peace! but now they are hid from thine eyes." A conqueror, he entered the city weeping.

Jerusalem was a city which had driven many men to despair. It stands in the Judaean wilderness amid the scarred golden rocks which resemble so many blistering volcanic bubbles. These hills are rounded, and have a savage unrelenting life of their own. Compared to this wilderness, the deserts of Arabia are consolingly gentle, for in the deserts at least even under the most pitiless sun there is the knowledge that one could crawl in a straight line toward the nearest oasis. Here there are only the skull-like mountains and the ash-colored canyons, the precipitous slopes down into the *wadis* where the flash floods roar in winter.

Intricately carved out on the top of one of those mountains, with steep and narrow streets, Jerusalem was more a fortress than a city. The modern traveler following the ancient trails and coming in sight of Jerusalem for the first time is surprised how small it is, like a child's toy lost in the immensity of the wilderness. The golden limestone weathers well under the eroding sun. The beauty of the city comes from the changing colors of the local stone, varying from yellowish-gray to pink-gold, russet-gold, and a deep reddish-bronze. This stone is admirably suited for building fortress walls and crenelated towers; it suggests power and endurance. Out of this stone are formed the immense, tumultuous waves of wilderness which surround the city on all sides.

When Jesus was entering Jerusalem in triumph, the Pharisees called out to him to rebuke the disciples for shouting: "Blessed be the

King that cometh in the name of the Lord: peace in heaven and glory in the highest." Jesus replied: "I tell you that if these should hold their peace, the stones would immediately cry out!" And by the stones he meant the whole wilderness of savage rocks.

But if the stones of the Judaean wilderness break men's hearts, the pure glinting skies bearing the sands of the Negev and of Arabia uplift their hearts. The sky over Jerusalem is a rich golden-blue, never at rest. It is the color of majesty, so ornate and shimmering that it seems artificial. There is the sense of a splendor beyond human comprehension. On a summer day God's face shines visibly in the heavens. The air breathes, and the light glancing off one mountain clashes visibly with the light glancing off another. In the trembling glare of that superb light all things seem possible; and in the presence of that light one no longer wonders why the prophets entered the Judaean wilderness and came out again with revelations of God's presence.

For the Jews and the Christian pilgrims who came after them, the journey to Jerusalem was always a journey to the heights. From the coastal plains the road mounts steeply into the raw upper air of the hills. A curtain of pines and cypresses crowds the lower slopes, but the curtain lifts at last to reveal the wilderness in its stupendous nakedness. Rock, sand, and gravel stretch out to the Dead Sea and far beyond.

The harshness of this landscape can chill the soul, and there are times when Jerusalem on its lonely eminence resembles one of those long-abandoned and crumbling cities in the foothills of the Himalayas. It seems to be outside history altogether, a place of legends which has long ago turned its back to the world. When men spoke about the heavenly Jerusalem and the crystal walls of Zion, they demonstrated how easily the earthly city could wear the colors of the heavenly city. Yet the city was real enough. It was caked with blood; violence haunted its streets; army after army has plundered and pillaged it or burned it to the ground. In barbaric splendor it always rose from the ruins.

Galilee seems to belong to another dispensation of time altogether. The sunken lake decorated a landscape of fertile plains and hills covered with dense vegetation. Nearby Nazareth clung to the lower slope of a hill beside a sweet-water spring. From the meadows of flowers growing near the spring the small town may have taken its name, for Nazareth comes from a root meaning "a flowering branch." It was so unimportant a town that the highway to the lake avoided it, and so obscure a place that no one ever thought to build fortifications. Perhaps a thousand people lived there in the time of Jesus. We hear of no armies attacking the forgotten town, and there were few who were concerned with its existence. Time and history swept over this small settlement in the shadow of the hills.

From these hills a man could see a vast panorama of the ancient world. He could see the Mediterranean, the blue waters flashing beyond Mount Carmel in the west, the grain fleets of Egypt and the Phoenician merchantmen from Tyre and Sidon plying up and down the coast. Mount Hermon with its snow-ribbed summit gleamed silvery to the north, and to the south amid bare hills stretched the plain of Esdraelon flowering with wheat. He could see the battlemented city of Sepphoris lying below, and Cana standing on a hill only two or three miles away. To the east lay Mount Tabor with its green and wooded slopes, shaped like a woman's breast, so gently shaped that one instinctively caressed it and wondered how a mountain could be so round and so beautiful. He could see the battlefield of Gideon and the mountains of Gilboa where Saul was slain, all lying before him as though they were on a map. For Nazareth was a hidden place, but from the heights above it all the traffic of the world was displayed.

Nazareth, then, was like a secret eyrie immune from the contagions of the world, strangely separate. Unencumbered by history, it was surrounded by history. It was a place where a boy could dream.

If he walked over the hills to the Sea of Galilee, he would see the traffic of the world in all its brilliant colors, in a setting of pure and perfect beauty. Here were large towns, busy streets, splendid highways beside the lake shore. There were forty thousand people in the town of Magdala; there were docks and shipbuilding yards and salting sheds and sheds where the fish were packed in baskets and dispatched in all directions by caravan. There were dye works and pottery shops, and there were some eighty shops of weavers of dyed wool and three hundred shops where the snow-white pigeons of sacrifice were raised and sold. Today there is scarcely a thornbush on the rocky slopes above Magdala, and of the town only a few crumbling walls remain, but in those days the slopes were green with oaks and the town was one of the richest in Galilee. The Emperor Vespasian found enough timber at Magdala to build a flotilla of warships. Magdala flourished; so did some ten or fifteen other towns around the small lake. Chorazin, Bethsaida, Capernaum, Beersheba, Hamath, Tarichea, Gergesa were all rich towns deriving their wealth from the lake and from the fertile valleys. In all the land there was no more fertile place than Galilee.

The lake itself was almost too perfect, being the color of sapphires and wonderfully indented, so that there was scarcely a view of it that was not breathtaking. In those days it was a richer, deeper blue than it is today, for the trees came down to the shore and there were no burned out barren mountains looking down on the lake, which was some seven hundred feet below sea level. There were sandy beaches, clumps of pink oleander growing out of the water, and thick papyrus groves, lushly green, crowding the northern shore. On the plain of Gennesaret between Magdala and Capernaum olives, fig trees, vines, and palm trees grew in profusion in fields watered by seven springs, and it was in this region, off the long-forgotten town of Beersheba, that the best fishing was to be found. Small delicately colored crab the size of pebbles scuttled along the shores, while white pelicans, silver grebes, and dark-feathered cormorants flew over the lake.

There was something mysterious about this lake. It was not only that it seemed to be artfully designed to show nature at her best, but it wore an air of remoteness while being actively engaged in the affairs of the world. Wealth gathered around the lake, but it was not like the wealth of Jerusalem. Galilee means "a circle"; it was as though someone had drawn an enchanted circle around this region to distinguish it from all the other regions of the earth. The air was a little heavier, the colors a little brighter in this deep hollow in the earth's surface. In this nearly tropical land everything grew quickly, perhaps a little too quickly for comfort.

Overnight in spring the meadows and hillsides would be covered with a brilliant carpet of anemones, scarlet and gold and blue, but in a few weeks they would have gone without a trace. The colors of the lake and of the lakeside were always changing. After April came the heat of summer, when the terrible *khamsin* wind turned the vegetation brown, but soon the winds would go, and the earth would be green again. Sometimes sudden storms would disturb the calm of the lake. In the long narrow *wadis* of the western hills, especially in the late afternoons between March and June, gusts of wind would spring up, sweep through the narrow gorges, and burst with terrifying force on the lake, churning it up and transforming it into a seething cauldron; and the wind hurtling against the eastern cliffs with the sound of an explosion would join forces with other winds from the east and stir up the waters to even greater heights. A storm on the Sea of Galilee is like a storm nowhere else, for it is contained in a small space. The storm subsides as suddenly as it arises; and when it is over, the air has a brilliance and purity which is strangely disturbing, for the earth seems to be almost too bright. At such times everything seems to glow as though lit with an inner flame.

The people who lived on the shores of the lake were of mixed descent. Jews, Greeks, Romans, Arabs, and Phoenicians had intermarried, and there were no clear blood lines. The hills of the Decapolis were almost wholly inhabited by Gentiles who were predominantly of Greek origin; and the cities of the Decapolis resembled the cities of Greece, forming a Greek enclave on the edge of the desert. Scythopolis, Hippos, and Gadara together with the other Decapolitan cities had been detached from Israel by Pompey, but they still traded with Galilee. On the shores of the lake Greek was the language of the traders, and Greek, too, was the language of culture. In architecture, in letters, even in dress, Greek ideas influenced the lives of the people living on the shores of the lake. In the theater at Scythopolis Greek plays were produced and acted by bands of traveling actors, who also performed in the theaters built by Herod the Great in Sidon, Damascus, Ptolemaïs, Tripoli, and Caesarea. The Greek poet Meleager was born in Gadara, and not far from the lake there was a famous sanctuary to Pan, the god of flocks and shepherds.

But while Greek influence was strong, there remained a hard core of Jewish feeling. These people regarded themselves as Jews, and they spoke a barbarous form of Aramaic, very guttural and difficult to understand even by those who normally spoke Aramaic. The ordinary language of the Galilean peasant was so distinctive that if he came to Jerusalem he had only to speak a few syllables to be immediately recognized.

The Galileans were recognized too by their quick tempers, their passion for independence, their continual revolts against authority. The most notable revolt occurred in A.D. 7, when Judas of Galilee stormed the armory at Tiberias, acquired enough arms to equip his small army of Zealots, and captured Sepphoris. The battle cry of the Zealots was: "No ruler but God." A Roman army descended from the hills above Gadara to put down the rebellion; the army of Zealots was destroyed; and on all the high places of Galilee crucifixes were set up to permit the people to watch the dying agonies of the rebels. So brutal and relentless were the exactions of the Roman power that the Jews were coming to believe that the end was near, that for them, and perhaps for all the world, there would come the Judgment long promised by the prophets. Now more than ever they awaited the coming of the Messiah who would usher in the new, divine age, and there were some who believed that the Messiah would appear on the shores of the Sea of Galilee.

In the year A.D. 26 a new governor, Pontius Pilate, was sent from Rome to the administrative capital at Caesarea. His task was to transform the rebellious Jews into obedient subjects of the Roman emperor, to crush all opposition, and to spare no effort in the endeavor. Almost his first act was to order the legionaries to march to Jerusalem bearing their standards, which contained medallion portraits of the Emperor Tiberius, and he seems to have been well aware that the appearance of the standards would be an affront to Jewish tradition and to the Mosaic law, which permitted no graven images. Crowds of Jews hurried to Caesarea in a desperate resolve to prevent the march of the legionaries. Pilate, who saw no advantage in precipitating a rebellion so early in his governorship, held his hand. He was a cautious man and could afford to wait. For five days and nights the crowd of Jews lay prostrate and motionless around his palace in Caesarea, refusing to leave until he had promised to remove the standards, and when he sent soldiers among them, they merely bared their necks and offered themselves as willing sacrifices. It was one of the first recorded examples of civil disobedience, and Pilate appears to have been impressed by the spectacle of so many people who preferred to die rather than see the standards flying in Jerusalem. Josephus, who is not an altogether reliable witness, tells us that Pilate was so impressed by their fanatical devotion that he ordered the removal of the standards, thus giving way to the wishes of the Jews.

But if the Jews thought Pilate was one of those who supported their interests, they were mistaken. To keep them in subjection, to see that they paid their taxes, and to ensure the continuity of Roman rule, he was prepared to employ all the weapons of cunning and brute force available to him. He would humor them, threaten them, cajol them; finally, if they refused to obey him, he would destroy them, or massacre so many that the rest would see the advantages of obedience.

Some years later, probably in A.D. 30, Pilate decided to build an aqueduct some fifty miles long to feed the diminishing water supply of Jerusalem. To defray the expense he raided the sacred treasury of the Temple and seized the corban money. Once more the Jews formed a ring around the palace of Pilate, who was then on a visit to Jerusalem. They were in a threatening mood, and seemed about to come out in open rebellion. This time Pilate refused to give way. Avoiding any outward show of force, he ordered his troops to appear in civilian clothes, not to use their swords, and to break up the demonstration with cudgels. At a given signal the troops in disguise drove into the mob. Josephus tells us that "large numbers of the Jews perished, some from the blows they received, while others were trodden to death by their companions in the ensuing flight." The survivors were cowed, and nothing more was heard of the demand to restore the money taken from the sacred treasury. Rome had shown that it was indifferent to the high priests and solemnly committed to producing a better water supply. For Jerusalem water was life and growth; without it, as Pilate well knew, the city would perish.

Under Pilate the Jews formed a sullen and exasperated community vowed at whatever the cost to maintain their ancient traditions. The war between Jews and Romans was being fought nakedly while both sides sheathed their weapons. In thus refusing to precipitate an open conflict, they succeeded only in increasing their mutual distrust, their suspicions, and their deep-seated hatred of one another. The last months of the life of Jesus were spent in an atmosphere of growing bitterness and resentment between the Jews and the Romans, who were rarely merciful toward subject nations. Their impulse, when they were thwarted, was to strike hard. In their long history they had never hesitated to destroy whole nations that opposed them.

Jesus was living in Bethany when he heard the news of the disturbances in Jerusalem. Not all the fighting took place around the palace of Pilate. A group of Galileans overcame the garrison and seized the tower of Siloam, which dominated the water supply from the pool of Siloam. The tower was the key to the possession of the Lower City, where the poor Jews lived and where the revolutionary ferment was strongest; and with the occupation of the tower the Galileans might have been able to encourage a *levée en masse* if the Romans had not acted quickly. They brought up battering rams and reduced the tower to rubble, eighteen of the defenders perishing in the debris.

That Jesus approved of the rebellious Galileans is made clear in a passage in *Luke.* Jesus proclaims that these Galileans, "whose blood Pilate had mingled with their sacrifices," were without blemish of sin:

And Jesus answering said unto them, Suppose ye that these Galileans were sinners above all the Galileans, because they suffered such things?

I tell you, Nay: but, except ye repent, ye shall all likewise perish.

Or those eighteen, on whom the tower in Siloam fell, and slew them, think ye that they were sinners above all men that dwelt in Jerusalem?

I tell you, Nay: but, except ye repent, ye shall all likewise perish.

(*Luke* 13:2–5)

With the fall of the Tower of Siloam the stage was set for the fall of Jerusalem.

The lean years had come, the years of disenchantment and foreboding, of anguish and doom. There was a strange shimmering in the air, as nearly always before some heaven-sent visitation or natural catastrophe. That in some way or other Jerusalem would be destroyed, that Jesus himself would be the agent of its destruction, and that its fall would coincide with the advent of a new dispensation of time: these were matters which were of deep concern to Jesus during the last months of his life. Sometimes the vision faded and he held back, uncertain of the tasks demanded of him; at other times he spoke of the fall of the city as something ordained by God, inevitable and desirable. So in one of the many parables of the fig tree, related by Luke immediately after the discussion of the Galileans, Jesus says:

A certain man had a fig tree planted in his vineyard; and he came and sought fruit thereon, and found none.

Then said he unto the dresser of his vineyard, Behold, these three years I come seeking fruit on this fig tree, and find none: cut it down; why cumbereth it the ground?

And he answering said unto him, Lord, let it alone this year also, till I shall dig about it, and dung it.

And if it bear fruit, well: and if not, then after that thou shalt cut it down.

(Luke 13:6–10)

There is little doubt that the fig tree represented Jerusalem, and that Jesus himself was the dresser of the vineyard, who was prepared in his great patience to dig about it and wait until it bore fruit, until the time came when he could wait no longer. We are told that he left Jerusalem and returned to Galilee to resume his ministry. There followed mysterious errands and strange hesitations, and these hesitations were to remain with him until almost the end. He spoke with extraordinary finality at the Last Supper, but a few hours later, looking out at a world given over to darkness at Gethsemane, he was once more the prey to doubts and to anguished prayers; and again on the Cross the doubts assailed him. Such was his life in those last days, while hope and despair, the utmost certainty and the gravest doubts, quickened in him. There was no fixed point around which he revolved; not even God's mercy was certain. "My God, my God, why hast thou forsaken me?"

God was forsaken by God: so it must have been when he wandered like a ghost over the land, a stranger even to the disciples who always in those last days seem to be following him at a distance, unable to keep pace with him, until at the Last Supper they suddenly found themselves confronting a man who was scarcely recognizable, endowed with powers which are not of this earth, terrible and majestic; and then again at Gethsemane there was a distance between them, and they vanished altogether at his trial, while only John among the disciples was visibly present at the Crucifixion. And afterward, when the stone was rolled back and Mary Magdalene entered the empty tomb, how tentatively the disciples went about proclaiming his triumph, how quickly they accommodated themselves to the ordinary work-a-day world. Nathanael and Cleopas met him by chance on the road to Emmaus. The fishermen saw him in the morning light as he cooked the fish by the lakeside. Only when Thomas demands proof was there any sense of urgency. We are left with the impression that his death and resurrection were almost beyond their comprehension, neither terrible nor pitiable, because it was so remote from anything they understood. Only later, after an interval of many days, did there come to them the full realization of what had happened.

No doubt the disciples were intended to be the witnesses of his acts and the inheritors of the spiritual power bequeathed to them by virtue of their loyalty and understanding. Their loyalty, however, was questionable, and it is far from certain that they understood him. Nothing is so curious in the Gospels as the behavior of the disciples as they attempt in those last hours to come to terms with the mystery. When they should be watchful, they fall asleep; and when the arrest is made, they brandish their swords and slip away under cover of darkness. The revolutionaries who died in the rubble of the Tower of Siloam were made of sterner stuff.

It was not only the disciples who showed evasiveness and hesitation. Pilate, alternately praising and reviling his prisoner, showed himself to be a man of straw. He appears to have condemned Jesus to execution only because this was the simplest and least onerous solution to the problem of judgment, for it is always easier to condemn than to liberate, to kill than to create life. Only the Sanhedrim, determined to destroy the man they regarded as a false Messiah and a troublemaker, acted with single-minded determination. In the end Jesus was confronted with the Jewish law, which killed him. The Crucifixion came about as the result of traditional legalistic abstractions which in the eyes of Jesus had lost their validity. In their place he would substitute the new law of love and loving-kindness, of mercy and brotherhood. No longer would the lambs be slaughtered in offering to an unappeasable Jehovah; he would offer himself as the final sacrifice and put an end to the sacrificial law once and for all.

While reason rejects the thought of redemption through the sacrifice of God, the human heart, accustomed to mysteries, accepts it more readily. The horror of the sacrifice of God remains the ultimate horror, and that Christ should have spoken so humanly from the Cross is a testimony to the humanity he shares with his fellow men. As told in the Gospels his death was at once an allegory and a divine fulfillment, a revelation and a warning. It was strange that it happened, but it would have been stranger still if it had not happened.

The place was a rocky knoll just outside the Ephraim Gate of

Jerusalem. The time was the afternoon of a spring day. But in fact the place and the time were no more than the accidents of history; it could have happened anywhere, at any time of day, in any age. For the Christians the Crucifixion happens at every moment of every day.

3 ✠ THE TEACHING

WHEN the dead and bleeding Christ was taken down from the Cross, his life had only just begun. The young Nazarene who announced that he was the long-awaited Messiah was condemned to death for having proclaimed himself the messianic King of the Jews, while his followers were to proclaim that this was perhaps the least of his titles. To them, he was the Lord of Lords, the King of the Universe, the Judge of the quick and the dead. His power embraced the past and the future, the seen and unseen worlds, and there was no end to it. He stood by the right hand of God in glory, and offered to all who believed in him the promise of eternal life. With a kind of stupor the disciples had watched the inevitable unfolding of the drama in Jerusalem, and they may have asked why he did not step down from the Cross, then pull up the Cross by its roots and wield it like a hammer against his enemies.

For the disciples there was no comfort in the Crucifixion, and perhaps they found even less comfort in the Ascension. Above all they were concerned with his living presence. He died, he was buried, he ascended to heaven; all these events were colored by their grief. In an Easter of uncertainty, all that was certain was that he had abandoned them, leaving them to their own resources, like sheep without a shepherd. He had left them no body of doctrine, no laws, only a few brief commandments and the memory of his strange presence, humble and commanding. His ministry was very short, no more than two years and a few months. In this brief period there was scarcely time to know him, for he had spent many of those months on solitary journeys in remote places of Palestine and Phoenicia. They could only

48

guess what his purposes were during his many absences, and now that he had risen from the dead and ascended to heaven they were compelled once more to ask themselves why he had abandoned them and what was demanded of them now that he was gone. "Men and brethren, what shall we do?" they asked Peter on the day of Pentecost. Peter answered: "Repent, and be baptized every one of you in the name of Jesus Christ for the remission of sins, and ye shall receive the gift of the Holy Ghost. For the promise is unto you, and to your children, and to all that are afar off, even as many as the Lord our God shall call." (*Acts* 2:38–39)

These, then, were the tasks which the early Christians assumed to be peculiarly their own. They were to repent and to receive baptism with its promise of everlasting life in the Lord, but there were no doctrines to be learned by heart and announced from the pulpit. There was no orthodoxy, no credo, no Church in the sense that we have come to know the Church. The Christians were still Jews, for they still worshiped in the Temple, and when Peter rose to address his small community, he called them "men of Israel," meaning that they were Jews indeed, although they were the followers of Christ and a new dispensation. What he said to them was rooted in Jewish tradition, and especially in the Psalms, for had not David prophecied the coming of the Saviour? From the seed of David had come the Christ. So Peter spoke when the eleven tongues of fire descended upon the Eleven, on that astonishing day when he delivered the first of all Christian sermons:

Jesus of Nazareth, a man approved of God among you by miracles and wonders and signs, which God did by him in the midst of you, as ye yourselves also know: Him, being delivered by the determinate counsel and foreknowledge of God, ye have taken, and by wicked hands have crucified and slain: Whom God hath raised up, having loosed the pains of death: because it was not possible that he should be holden to it.

(Acts 2:22–24)

There follows a long passage showing that David had foretold the resurrection in the Psalms, and then Peter continued:

This Jesus hath God raised up, whereof we are all witnesses. Therefore being by the right hand of God exalted, and having received of the Father the promise of the Holy Ghost, he hath shed forth this, which ye now see and hear. For David is not ascended into the heavens: but he saith himself, The Lord said unto my Lord, sit thou on my right hand, until I make thy foes thy footstool. Therefore let all the house of Israel know assuredly, that God hath made that same Jesus, whom ye have crucified, both Lord and Christ.

(*Acts* 2:32–36)

The archaic character of the sermon may be proof of its authenticity, but Peter was saying very little about the new dispensation. He reminds the Jews that David died and was buried in the tomb which lay just below the Cenaculum, but Jesus was raised up from the dead, and was immortal and incorruptible. And although he speaks of the triumph of Jesus, he says little about the triumph of his followers. The solemn profession of faith uttered by Peter six days before the Transfiguration was far more explicit. There, standing near the headwaters of the Jordan at Caesarea Philippi he said, "Thou art the Christ, the Son of the living God," and Jesus answered with a special blessing, saying that this knowledge could only have come to Peter from God. Now Peter speaks of "Jesus of Nazareth, a man approved by God among you" in the faltering tones of a man reading out a carefully prepared script which he can scarcely understand. The tomb of David is near. Christ is elsewhere. He is speaking in the shuddering awareness of a great loss.

And not only Peter: the entire Christian community seems to have been given over to fear and trembling mingled with joy. We learn from *Acts* that "fear came upon every soul," and that they sold their possessions, and went from house to house breaking bread, and held everything in common, and ate their meat "with gladness and singleness of heart." A kind of collective madness seemed to have settled on them, fear and joy contending for mastery: fear because he had gone from them, joy because he had promised salvation to those who called on his name. The *eschaton*, the end of history, had taken place, and all of life was now a waiting for the Second Coming.

The early Christians listening to the sermon of Peter in the first shock of Christ's departure knew themselves to be the inheritors of the Kingdom, but no more than Peter could they define the nature of the Kingdom which had been promised to them. The Kingdom would come with the Second Coming. Following the classic Jewish tradition he would descend with troops of angels into the Holy of Holies of the Temple, and somewhere within the sacred precincts he would announce his kingship over the earth; and the earth would be changed into Heaven. In this belief they were content to gather together, remembering that he had said: "Where two or three are gathered together in my name, there am I in the midst of them." We read in *Acts:* "All that believed were together, and had all things common."

In these early years of Christianity one perpetual cry can be heard like a chorus rising above all other cries: "Our Lord, come!" The Christians were impatient for the Second Coming. They did not know and could not have guessed that the Coming would be delayed.

As the days passed, and as they became accustomed to their grief, certain elements of faith began to clarify and separate into a body of doctrine. The lordship of Jesus, the presence of the Holy Spirit, the certainty of salvation, and the knowledge that eternal life had been granted to them through the intercession of the Lord were the cornerstones of their belief. Baptism and the solemn breaking of the bread in memory of the Last Supper are the only rites known to have taken place. Seven deacons were appointed to serve the communal tables, for the apostles regarded themselves as spokesmen of the word of God, too busy to minister to the needs of the flesh. The communal life, which was to be continued in the great monastic establishments of the fourth century, was accepted joyously by the early Christians: sometimes too joyously, for Clement of Alexandria complained that some members of the early Church, following the injunction to treat the flesh with contempt, took to sharing each others' wives and living in absolute promiscuity, and Nicolaus, one of the seven deacons, went so far as to offer his beautiful wife to the apostles, saying that anyone who wished might enjoy her. In this way he proposed to renounce the desires of the flesh and serve the community of believers. But the early Christians were rarely promiscuous; a holy asceticism was the rule; and the Mosaic commandment against adultery was still in force.

Without priests, without altars, without a liturgy, the early Christians waited for the Second Coming with no thought of an extensive doctrine. What they hoped for was almost too simple to be put in words. Not for thirty years were there to be Gospels; nor were they needed at the time, for the apostles were still alive. The doctrine would emerge slowly and painfully in the course of time.

The Teaching of the Twelve Apostles

IN the year 1873 in the library of the Monastery of the Most Holy Sepulchre in Constantinople there was discovered by Philotheos Bryennios, later to become Metropolitan of Nicomedia in Asia Minor, a manuscript written on small sheets of vellum which contained among many other writings a long lost work called *The Teaching of the Twelve Apostles*. Some fragments of the work were quoted in other texts, but for many centuries no one had set eyes on the complete text. Such a document was known to have been drawn up to guide the infant Church, and many had speculated about its contents. The copy found by Bryennios had been written by a certain "Leo, scribe and sinner" in A.D. 1056, nearly a thousand years after its original composition. No other complete copy has ever been found.

The Teaching of the Twelve Apostles is an astonishing document, compounded of many strands and bristling with complications for the scholar, but no other surviving document shows the color of primitive Christianity so well. Here, stated very simply and firmly, are the commandments, rites, and beliefs of the early Church stripped bare of ornament. The complex rituals have not yet made their appearance. There is baptism, which should be performed "in living water," by which the unknown author meant a stream or a river like the Jordan, with the water being poured thrice on the head of the believer in the name of the Father, the Son, and the Holy Ghost. There is no question of immersion. The baptism in this early rite takes place in much the same way as the baptism of Christ as it appears in the Byzantine mosaics, where John the Baptist is seen pouring water on the head of Christ while he stands waist-deep in the Jordan. Only the baptized could take part in the Eucharist, where the wine was offered and the bread was broken. In those early days they said a prayer of such exquisite beauty that one wonders how the Church could have forgotten it:

> *Now concerning the Eucharist, thus give thanks: First, concerning the cup: We thank thee, our Father, for the holy wine of David thy servant, which thou hast made known to us through Jesus thy servant; to thee be the glory forever. And concerning the broken bread: We thank thee, our Father, for the life and knowledge which*

thou hast made known to us through Jesus thy servant; to thee be the glory forever. Just as this broken bread was scattered over the hills and having been gathered together became one, so let thy Church be gathered together from the ends of the earth into thy Kingdom; for thine is the glory and the power through Jesus Christ forever. But let no one eat or drink of thy Eucharist except those baptized into the name of the Lord, for in regard to this the Lord hath said: Give not that which is holy to the dogs.

And after ye are filled, thus give thanks: We thank thee, holy Father, for thy holy name, which thou hast caused to dwell in our hearts, and for the knowledge and faith and immortality which thou hast made known to us through Jesus thy servant; to thee be the glory forever. Thou, almighty Master (despota pantokrator), *didst create all things for thy name's sake; both food and drink thou didst give to men for enjoyment, in order that they might give thanks to thee; but to us thou hast graciously given spiritual food and drink and eternal life through thy servant. Before all things we thank thee that thou art mighty; to thee be the glory forever. Remember, Lord, thy Church, to deliver it from every evil and to make it perfect in thy love, and gather it from the four winds, it, the sanctified, into thy Kingdom, which thou hast prepared for it; for thine is the power and glory forever. Let grace come and this world pass away.*

(Didache, IX, X)

Let grace come and this world pass away. . . . Such was the perpetual prayer of the early Christians who still hoped that the Second Coming of Christ would occur in their lifetimes. This visitation had been promised to them both by Christ himself and by the prophets who went before him, and for them the imminence of the Second Coming was as much a part of their belief as their faith in God, the all-powerful Lord, whose servant was Christ.

Throughout *The Teaching of the Twelve Apostles* the two themes of service to God and the expectation of the Second Coming are continually repeated. God is to be served by simple obedience to his commands, and the Second Coming is to be awaited with a quiet joy. The unknown author, writing about A.D. 95, was himself evidently a man with a high and perhaps commanding position in the Church, hating dissension, careless of points of dogma, aware of the abuses which were already prevalent in the Church. He was not concerned to lay down the whole law, but simply to state the essentials.

Thou shalt not kill, thou shalt not commit adultery, thou shalt not corrupt boys, thou shalt not practice magic, thou shalt not be double-minded. The catalogue of vices is a long one, expressed vigorously, nowhere more vigorously than where he demands that "thy speech shall not be false, or empty, but filled with doing." He demands action; and the Christian community he describes is one where idlers are given short shift, and those who hope to enter the Kingdom of God must work for their reward.

When Paul wrote to the brethren in Salonica the first of the epistles that have come down to us, he spoke of the last days when "the Lord himself shall descend from heaven with a shout, with the voice of the archangel, and with the trump of God; and the dead in Christ shall rise first." There was no grief for the passing world. God would arise in his majesty and his power to introduce the new dispensation of time, in the new clear daylight. "We are not of the night, nor of darkness," Paul wrote. "Therefore, let us not sleep, as do others; but let us watch and be sober." The same theme is stated even more boldly in *The Teaching of the Twelve Apostles:*

Watch for your life's sake; let your lamp not go out and your loins not be loosed, but be ready; for ye know not the hour in which our Lord cometh. But ye shall come together often and seek the things that befit your souls; for the whole time of your faith thus far will not profit you, if ye be not made perfect in the last time. For in the last days the false prophets and the corruptors shall be multiplied, and the sheep shall be turned into wolves, and love shall be turned into hate; for when lawlessness increaseth they shall hate one another, and shall persecute and shall deliver up, and then shall appear the world-deceiver as Son of God, and shall do signs and wonders, and the earth shall be given into his hands, and he shall commit iniquities which have never yet been done since the beginning. Then all created men shall come into the fire of trial, and many shall be made to stumble and shall perish. But they that endure in their faith shall be saved from under even this curse. And then shall appear the signs of the truth; first the sign of an opening in Heaven, then the sign of a trumpet's sound, and thirdly, the resurrection of the dead, yet not of all, but as it hath been said: The Lord shall come and all the saints with him. Then shall the world see the Lord coming upon the clouds of heaven.

(*Didache*, XVI)

We shall not understand the beginnings of Christianity unless we remember the sense of expectation, the almost certain knowledge of the Second Coming that informed the Christian communities. All life was but a waiting for the Coming. The rituals therefore were brief and scarcely of great moment except for the Eucharist, which resembled a foretaste of the Coming. The faithful were enjoined to fast on Wednesdays and Fridays, and to recite the Lord's Prayer three times a day, and on Sundays to confess their sins. Above all they were enjoined to be humble and quiet and long-suffering, never exalting themselves, faithful and obedient to Caesar, giving tithes to their priests, and if there were no priests, then the tithes were to be given to the poor. In those early days there were evidently whole communities where the priesthood had not yet emerged. The hierarchy of the priesthood had already come into existence—we hear of bishops, deacons and teachers of the law—but a village or small town might be devoutly Christian without a single priest in it. In *The Teaching of the Twelve Apostles* there is no suggestion of a patriarchate, of a central figure who embodies accepted tradition and who rules over the religious life of the communities. Christianity still belonged to the people.

So for a few more years it would remain: the faithful living in a kind of trembling quiet in the shadow of the Day of Judgment, not knowing from hour to hour whether the last day was about to come, but certain that it was near.

The Sayings

AT some very early period, perhaps in the weeks following the Crucifixion, a concerted effort was made to record the words spoken by Jesus in the course of his ministry. These records were composed by men who were barely literate and whose memories were colored by their own emotions. They remembered in fragments, in disconnected episodes, in confused sequences. They remembered what they wanted to remember and were not concerned with the fact that future historians would want to put order and coherence into their texts. Out of these crude gospels there later emerged the canonical gospels and many others that the Church Fathers consulted, though they were not accepted within the canon. Luke, writing to Theophilus, describes how many have composed accounts "of those

things which are most surely believed among us," and says he
has seen them; there is little doubt that he employed them in the compilation of his own Gospel. Luke cannot have written his Gospel
earlier than A.D. 65, and the earliest Gospels and collections of sayings
belonged to a generation before his own.

Only fragments survive of those early works. Many of them are
puzzling, because they do not seem to fit into any easily intelligible
construction of the life of Christ. A famous passage from the lost
Gospel of the Hebrews, quoted by Origen and Jerome, reads: "Just
now my mother the Holy Spirit took me by one of my hairs and carried me off to the great mountain Tabor." We have no clues as to
where or when the statement was made, though it is sometimes supposed to refer to the story of the temptation. Another fragment from
the same Gospel reads:

*And when the Lord had given his linen cloth to the servant of
the priest, he went to James and appeared unto him. For James had
sworn that he would not eat bread from that hour wherein the Lord
had drunk the cup until he saw him rising from the dead. Bring a table and bread, saith the Lord. He took up the bread and blessed and
broke it, and afterwards gave it to James the Just, and said to him, My
brother, eat thy bread, for the Son of Man is risen from them that
sleep.*

Such a fragment seems to live in its own right, possessing the vitality of something seen and accurately recorded, insofar as anything can be accurately recorded. St. Paul tells us that Jesus appeared
to James, but except for this fragment nothing is known of this appearance. Who was the servant of the priest? We are not told, and
cannot guess. There is still another account of an appearance by Jesus
to the apostles in the *Gospel of the Hebrews:*

*Then the Lord came to Peter and the apostles, and said, Lay
hold, handle me, and see that I am not an incorporeal spirit. And
straightway they touched him and believed.*

Here, too, we are confronted with an event recounted so simply
and effortlessly that it becomes perfectly credible. Ignatius, Origen,
Jerome, and Eusebius were all familiar with this fragment, and each
drew his own conclusions concerning its validity. What is certain is
that the early Fathers of the Church possessed an abundant literature

of sayings that is now lost, and they sometimes interpreted the stories of the Gospels in ways which seem strange to us, because we lack the texts which were familiar to them.

There are, for example, many differing accounts of the baptism of Christ. Here is the account as set forth in the *Gospel of the Ebionites*, which according to Epiphanius was identical with the *Gospel of the Hebrews*:

After the people were baptized, Jesus also came and was baptized by John; and as he came out of the water, the heavens were opened and he saw the Holy Ghost descending in the form of a dove, and it entered into him. And a voice was heard from heaven, saying, Thou art my beloved Son, in thee I am well pleased, and again, This day have I begotten thee. And straightway there shone about the place a great light, and when John saw it, he said, Who art thou, Lord? and again there was a voice from heaven, saying, This is my beloved Son, in whom I am well pleased. Thereupon John fell down before Jesus and said, I beseech thee, Lord, baptize thou me. But Jesus prevented him, saying, Suffer it, for thus it behoveth that all things should be fulfilled.

This version, which appears to have been compiled from two separate sources, has an amplitude absent in the Gospel version. A simpler version is given by Justin Martyr, who says that "When Jesus went down into the water, a fire was kindled in the Jordan, and when he came up from the water the Holy Ghost like a dove fluttered over him." That the Jordan blazed with fire was an early tradition, often repeated. Origen was only continuing an existing tradition when he wrote: "Christ does not baptize with water; this he leaves to the disciples. He reserves to himself the power to baptize with the Holy Ghost and with fire." It is a startling sentence, but no more startling than many of the early traditional sayings of Jesus. There are many of these sayings preserved in the works of the Fathers which speak to us with astonishing authority and authenticity:

He who is near Me is near the fire; he who is far from Me is far from the Kingdom.

Those who desire to see Me and seize my Kingdom shall pass through tribulation and despair.

He who seeks shall not cease until he finds, and when he finds he shall wonder, and wondering he shall reign, and reigning he shall rest.

Raise up the stone, and thou shalt find Me; cleave the tree, and I am there.

When thou seest thy brother, thou seest God.

Again, I am about to be crucified.

I come to destroy the works of women.

Behold my bridechamber is ready. Blessed is he who is found in it wearing the shining raiment, for he will receive the crown upon his head.

I stood in the midst of the world, and in the flesh was I seen of them, and I found all men drunken, and none found I athirst among them. And my soul grieveth over the sons of men, because they are blind at heart and see not their poverty.[1]

What is strange about these sayings is their immediacy, their finality, the sense we have that these words once uttered could never have been forgotten. The Fathers who pondered them, and believed them to be authentic, were closer to the wellspring than we shall ever be. Other fragments, even more striking, have been preserved. In the fragmentary *Gospel of Peter* Jesus says: "My Power, Power, thou hast forsaken me," and not, "My God, my God, why hast thou forsaken me?" Epiphanius records a saying which seems to sum up the entire relationship between Jesus and the Jewish Temple: "I am come to abolish the sacrifices: if you do not cease from sacrificing, the wrath of God will continue to threaten you." One of the most beautiful of the sayings is inscribed in Arabic within the gateway of a mosque at Fatehpur Sikri in India. It reads: "Jesus, on whom be peace, said, The world is but a bridge over which you must pass, but you may not linger in order to build a dwelling-place." This saying is not among the strangely colorless sayings of Jesus that survive in the Koran, and no one knows how it came to be written in that rose-red city long since abandoned to the empty skies. Yet there, too, we hear the authentic voice of Jesus.

[1] These sayings come respectively from: Origen, *in Jerem. Homil.* XX:3; *Barnabas,* VII:11; Clement of Alexandria, *Stromateis,* II:9, 45; *Oxyrhynchus-Logia,* 4; Clement of Alexandria, *Stromateis,* I:19, 94; Origen, *in Joann.,* XX:12; Clement of Alexandria, *Stromateis,* III:9, 63; *Acta Philippi; Oxyrhynchus-Logia,* 3.

The Gnosis

AS time passed, the simple sayings of Jesus were orchestrated, becoming vast with organ notes never heard by the apostles. History was to deflect Christianity into its own courses. Inevitably, as the Gospel traveled across the earth, it acquired the colors of the regions it passed through. Local habits, old mythologies, new ways of thought, national traditions, all these were to influence its development, subtly transforming it. When Christianity entered Greece, it was compelled to confront the whole body of Platonic and Neoplatonic doctrine, and henceforward would always wear the shimmering veil woven in Greece. The dusty roads of Galilee sometimes vanished, giving place to intellectual pathways. Instead of the voice by the lakeside there was heard the mysterious, reverberating *Logos*.

In a hundred different ways Greece left its imprint on the young religion which was still uncertain of its destination. The Platonic dialectic was to confront the doctrine of salvation at a later time; in the beginning there was the confrontation between the mystery of Christ and the religious mysteries of Greece, which were also concerned with resurrection and the immortality of the soul; and though these mysteries are still hidden from us and we can only guess at the rituals, we know that they contained a form of Eucharist which was not wholly dissimilar to the Eucharist of the early Church. At the Eleusinian mystery the ear of wheat, which comes to life only after it is buried in the earth, was displayed to the worshiper in an atmosphere of intense religious excitement. The bread of angels and the Eleusinian ear of wheat belonged to the same order of things; and when a Greek heard the words, "Except a corn of wheat fall into the ground and die, it abideth alone: but if it die, it bringeth forth much fruit," he must have felt that he was listening to an echo of words heard long before.

The Teaching of the Twelve Apostles nowhere suggests the influence of Greek thought; there is no intellectual dance; the complexities of Christian thought lie far in the future. The teaching is naked and raw, in the hush before the Second Coming. But elsewhere, about this time, the Greek passion for conceptual thinking was already imposing itself on the body of Christian doctrine. The speculative mind, feeding on legends and parables, was already demonstrating its ability

to transform legends into ideas and parables into dialectic. The living
Christ was to become devoid of human attributes. He who was powerful was to become the abstraction of power.

This process was hastened remarkably by the strange system of
philosophy known as Gnosticism, which derived at a great distance
from Plato. The Gnostics believed that God dwelt in the Pleroma, the
Fullness of Creation, in a vast and everlasting light, where He abode
for ages in solitude and silence until, obeying some secret impulse, He
produced intelligences called Aeons. According to some Gnostics
Jesus was an Aeon who returned to the Pleroma just before the Crucifixion. According to other Gnostics there were three separate Aeons
called Jesus, Christ, and the Holy Ghost. Some believed that there
were only twelve Aeons since the beginning of Creation, others that
there were thirty. The dance of the Aeons was choreographed by the
Gnostics with extraordinary delicacy and imaginative force, but it remained essentially a dance around a fixed point. Fertile in invention
and assimilation, the Gnostics built towering systems of Emanations,
Aeons, and Ogdoads which resembled vast clouds of abstractions piled
upon abstractions. There were countless Jesuses, all emanations from
a primordial Jesus. Heaven was to be scaled by infinite ladders; humanity itself became an abstraction, and life and death were also abstractions. Reading the Gnostic scriptures, the mind reels before the
mechanical multiplication of mysteries.

Nevertheless Gnosticism deeply influenced primitive Christianity, and colored the beliefs and rites of the early Church. St. Paul regarded the Gnostics as enemies of the faith, but he was himself in
their debt. To the Colossians, whom he hoped to save from Gnosticism, he preached the transcendence of the Son above all creatures
and above the angels, and in his turns of phrase he constantly imitates
the Gnostics who saw the godhead as lying far above the angels, principalities, and powers, in a transcendence beyond all knowing. St.
John, too, borrows the language of Gnosticism when he transmutes
the living Christ into the living Word.

The heresies which invaded Christianity in the second century
were largely dependent upon the texts of the Gnostics and of the ancient mystery religions. Orphic texts with their promise of eternal life
were especially relevant, for they were sometimes very close to the
words spoken by Christ, and very appealing. The Orphic hymns,
which must go back at least to the sixth century B.C., celebrate the

divine life shared by all those who have been initiated into the mysteries.

I am the child of earth and of starry Heaven,
But my race is of Heaven

sung the choristers on the island of Samothrace in those ancient days, and the same theme returns in the second century treatise known as the *Pistis Sophia*, where Jesus addresses Andrew and promises him a destiny beyond any he had imagined. "Know ye not that ye are all gods and lords?" he declares. "Ye are all angels and archangels, and all of creation is given unto you?" A little later Valentinus, the ablest of the Gnostics, orchestrates the simple words in one of his homilies:

From the very beginning have ye been immortal and children of life—such life as the Aeons enjoy; yet would you have death shared up among you, to spend and lavish it, so that death might die in you and by your hands; for inasmuch as ye dissolve the world and are not dissolved yourselves, ye are lords of all creation and destruction.

Valentinus went down to defeat, his works surviving only in the fragments preserved by the Fathers of the Church, who protested bitterly against his heresies and especially against his exotic theories of the emanations of light. The light boils over; the emanations flash, and then vanish, and return with changing colors. Christ, robed in his garment of light, reels across the universe, uttering sayings which are sometimes merely silly, sometimes profound, and there is no knowing where silliness ends and profundity begins. It was heady wine, and the Fathers of the Church were understandably on guard. About the year A.D. 180 Valentinus vanishes from sight, but his influence persisted. In the medieval German mystics, in Swedenborg, in Blake, his strange subterranean influence can be felt. At a very early age Gnosticism fed into the stream of Christianity, and it still endures.

4 ✛ ST. PAUL

WHEN the Byzantine artists portrayed St. Paul they followed an ancient tradition by giving him a lean face, hooked nose, high bald forehead, long thin beard tapering to a point. There was gray in the beard, and a curling lovelock decorated the white forehead. They made him short and bowlegged, with stooping shoulders, and they liked to show him standing beside St. Peter, the lean visionary beside the robust apostle with the thick curly white beard. St. Peter was the type of the virile down-to-earth saint. There is no nonsense about him. St. Paul has knitted eyebrows, a wrinkled forehead, a look of wild perplexity: in a moment he will become flame.

This portrait of Paul derived directly from the apocryphal *Acts of Paul and Thecla*, which was current at the time of Tertullian, who denounced it as a forgery. The Greek fathers, who liked to quote from it, were inclined to accept it as one of the minor works of the apostolic age. "He was small and bald, with crooked thighs, handsome legs, hollow-eyed, and his nose was crooked," reads the description in the *Acts of Paul and Thecla*. "He was full of grace, for sometimes he appeared as a man, and sometimes he had the countenance of an angel." The portrait rings true. Luther, who adored him, called him "a poor tough little mannikin." But if he was small and ungainly, he had a mind of towering audacity. Nothing quite like that mind had ever appeared before or was ever to appear again. Uncouth and gentle and winged and harsh and intolerant, he was one of those who dared to accomplish impossible things.

To Paul was given the grace of being the first to shape the Christian doctrine as we know it today. He poured himself into Christ; he poured Christ out into himself; and Christianity will always bear the traces of that continual process of distillation which occupied half his lifetime. There is rest with Christ; there is none with Paul. The fuses are always being blown, the electricity crackles, the blue light of doom and love burns overhead: so that when Paul says, "I am crucified with Christ; nevertheless I live; yet not I but Christ liveth in me; and the life which I now live in the flesh, I live by the faith of the Son of God who loved me and gave himself for me," we are compelled to believe him implicitly, and like Luther we are tempted to read with great vehemence the words *me* and *for me*. Yet something is lacking. Paul speaks about Christ, rarely of Jesus. The man who broke the bread and blessed the wine is always the Son of God on the right hand of the Father.

Perhaps it was inevitable, for Paul could never forgive himself for not having seen Jesus in the flesh. He believed himself to have been divinely appointed by Christ to bring salvation to the Gentiles; the command came in a vision; and the Christ he knew was a visionary Christ, a voice speaking in a great light, not to be touched. For Paul, Christ was almost an abstraction.

Once Erasmus described Paul as "thundering and lightning and talking sheer flame." It was a description which would have pleased Paul, who had no illusions about the source of his strength. He enjoyed his torrents of flame, marshalled them in good order, and sent them spinning across the Mediterranean world without the least compassion for the people they might burn. Once he had become a Christian there seemed to be no moment in his life when he was not in an urgent hurry to accomplish his purpose. Time is running out, the Judgment is approaching, the Kingdom is almost within reach, the Gentiles are ill-prepared. He is always hurrying from one small group of Christians to another, urging them to prepare themselves for the end of the world. Forever on his lips is the prayer of the primitive Church, uttered at the end of the celebration of the Last Supper: *Maranatha!* (Our Lord, come!)

His temper was authoritarian, and there was little humility in him. To him, and to him alone, the mystery has been revealed. His mind was savage with certainties, and moved, though on another plane, with the staggering speed of Shakespeare's. He is always the improviser, inventing as he goes along, seeing ever more exciting pros-

John the Baptist, late tenth-century ivory in Victoria and Albert Museum, London. (*Crown copyright*)

The Archangel Michael, sixth-century ivory in the British Museum. (*Hirmer*)

St. Porphyrius, mosaic on the Rotunda of St. George, Salonica. (*Hirmer*)

St. Onesiphorus, mosaic on the Rotunda of St. George, Salonica. (*Hirmer*)

Four Apostles, from the dome of the Church of Hagia Sophia, Salonica.

Another Apostle from the same dome.

An Apostle gazing up at Christ, from the same dome.

Constantine the Great. Gold solidus, showing nimbus, from the Ashmolean Museum, Oxford. (*Ashmolean Museum*)

pects, ever more intricate complexities. "It is not permissible to go beyond the things that are written," he wrote in one of the epistles, but he was continually going beyond them, interpreting the words of Jesus according to the impulses of his flame-lit mind. He evidently knew none of the Gospels, for the earliest of them was not written until about the time of his death. He seems to have known surprisingly little about the earthly life of Jesus. What interested him above all was the Crucifixion, which he saw not as something suffered, but as a blaze of divine energy, springing out of the shame of the human condition and a heavenly triumph. What the Gospels were to say later he sometimes denied; and his essential dogmas were those of a man who had contemplated one event to the exclusion of others.

There was muscle in his mind, and a hard determination to employ those muscles to the uttermost. His visions had sinews in them. That Jesus healed the sick, comforted the humble, and walked by the lakeside were matters of supreme unimportance to him; and the very human events in the life of Jesus were either unknown to him or set aside as being of merely human importance. He had little patience with the smaller miracles, and went to some pains to explain the Pentecost away, saying that we are not to understand by "speaking with tongues" any miraculous gift in the use of language: the uttered words were unintelligible. He was the first to introduce irony, that commonplace of lawyers and Church Fathers; and this dangerous weapon, which he sharpened to a fine edge, was to remain long after it had lost its usefulness. All was grist to his mill. "I am debtor," he wrote, "both to the Greeks and to the barbarians, both to the wise and the unwise." He was so immensely skilled that he drowned all opposition in his rhetoric and his poetry, so that sometimes the deafened reader longs for the silence of which St. Ignatius has spoken: "He that hath the word of Jesus can truly hear his silence." Sometimes, too, we hear the authentic accents of his pride:

I am the least of the apostles . . . but by the grace of God I am what I am. . . . I labored more abundantly than they all; yet not I, but the grace of God which was with me.

Paul was born in Tarsus, the son of a tent-maker, whose name is unknown. Tarsus was a cosmopolitan city, the home of a university which rivaled those of Athens and Alexandria, with a long tradition of culture and mercantile activity. Paul learned the trade of a tent-maker, working in goat-hair felts, while pursuing his studies of the law. He appears to have been neither rich nor poor. Born of the tribe of Benjamin, he was dedicated to the priesthood, and at the proper age he traveled to Jerusalem to study under Gamaliel. In Jerusalem he first showed his mettle as a religious leader by actively taking part in the persecution of the Christians. He did not simply preach against the Christians, but incited the Jews to murder them. He appears to have been an agent of the Sanhedrim, armed with extraordinary powers. We hear that "he made havoc of the Church," arrested and imprisoned the Christians, and on at least one occasion presided over the murder of a Christian, who was led out through the gates and ritually stoned to death. The persecution of the Christians led to the scattering of the faithful. To Paul fell the task of following the refugees and hunting them down. He was journeying to Damascus on his errand of persecution when he was suddenly blinded by heavenly fire and fell to the ground, while a voice asked him why he was so intent on persecuting the Christians. "Who art thou?" Paul asked, and the voice answered: "I am Jesus whom thou persecutest. Arise, and go into the city, and it shall be told thee what thou must do."

There are no less than three separate accounts of this vision in *Acts;* in one of them Jesus addresses Paul at length, commanding him to open the eyes of the Gentiles that they may receive forgiveness of sins and enter their inheritance. The three versions agree in essentials. Blinded, Paul made his way to Damascus where a Christian accosted him and gave him back his sight. Then, as he wrote in his epistle to the Galatians, he decided against returning to Jerusalem and instead visited Arabia. Three years later he went to Jerusalem to meet Peter, with whom he stayed for fifteen days. Of the other apostles he saw only James, the brother of Jesus. By reason of his blood relationship with Jesus, James appears to have assumed the leadership of the infant Church. He was a man of grave piety and strict orthodoxy, and it was said of him that he never took a bath, never let a razor come near his head, and never drank wine. "His knees," says Hegesippus, "grew as hard as a camel's from his continual kneeling in worship of God and in begging forgiveness from the people." For him, as for nearly all the followers of Jesus, the question of converting the Gentiles had never arisen; Jesus was the Messiah of the Jews, who had been crucified in obedience to prophecies and now sat on the right hand of the Father. It was on this rock that Paul broke his heart. He quietly left the Judaic Christians to their own beliefs and assumed the task of converting the rest of the world.

For the Judaic Christians, anchored in Jerusalem and the cities of Palestine, Paul felt a growing contempt. He was baffled by their exclusiveness, their ignorance and insensitivity to the revelation of Jesus, who was not only the Messiah of the Jews but the Lord of the World. James and the brotherhood in Jerusalem had cut to shreds the word of God "like hounds or bad workmen"; nothing was to be gained from them. According to his own account, he simply abandoned them to their own resources and went about preaching the Gospel among the Gentiles in Syria and Cilicia, and did not return to Jerusalem for fourteen years. It was then, at this second meeting with James, Peter, and John, the three pillars of the Judaic Christian Church, that he received their formal blessing, after being cautioned to remember the poor. Together with the blessing there came a charter of liberty addressed to the Gentiles, permitting them to worship in their own way without having to submit to circumcision; they must not eat meat offered to idols or the flesh of an animal that had been strangled or drink blood or commit fornication; in all other matters they might follow the customs of the Gentiles. The charter of liberty, which took the form of a decree, read:

The apostles and elders and brethren send greeting unto the brethren who are of the Gentiles in Antioch and Syria and Cicilia:

Forasmuch as we have heard, that certain which went out from us have troubled you with words, subverting your souls, saying, Ye must be circumcised, and keep the law: to whom we gave no such commandment: It seemed good unto us, being assembled with one accord, to send chosen men unto you with our beloved Barnabas and Paul, men that have hazarded their lives in the name of our Lord Jesus Christ. We have sent therefore Judas and Silas, who shall also tell you the same things by mouth.

For it seemed good to the Holy Ghost, and to us, to lay upon you no greater burden than these necessary things: That ye abstain from meats offered to idols, and from blood, and from things strangled, and from fornication: from which, if ye keep yourselves, ye shall do well. Fare ye well.

(Acts 15:23–29)

This document represented the triumph of Paul as the apostle to the Gentiles, the missionary into whose hands there had been placed the task of shaping the Church outside of Palestine. He could now claim to be the bishop of all those who were "aliens from the commonwealth of Israel, and strangers from the covenants of promise, having no hope, and without God in the world." He would travel across the world proclaiming the new dispensation, always at odds with the brethren in Jerusalem, quarreling violently with everyone who disagreed with him, and often quarreling with himself, certain of only one thing: that he had been blessed by Christ in a vision, and this vision gave him authority to do as he pleased.

Paul attached enormous importance to the charter of liberty. "Though it was but a human covenant, yet being ratified, it was neither to be annulled nor added to." For him it was final; and it added human authority to the divine authority he had already received.

He appears to have extracted his charter from the Jerusalem brethren with some difficulty, after long argument and many strained discussions on the right of the Gentiles to enter the fold. In *Galatians*, written a few weeks after receiving the charter, he returns again and again to the argument that for the Gentile nothing was to be gained by obedience to the Judaic law; circumcision added nothing to a Gentile; the freedom to love Christ was all. Abraham had received the promise: "In thee shall all nations be blessed," and he had produced two sons, one by a bondmaid, the other by a freewoman. In the eyes of Paul the allegory was clear. "Brethren," he said to the Galatians, "we are not children of the bondwoman, but of the free." In that strangely querulous letter, written with a heavy heart because in his absence the Galatians had been persuaded that they could follow Christ only by adopting the customs of the Jews, Paul announced his own charter of independence. It was as though he were reciting once more the arguments he had presented in Jerusalem.

They were arguments that needed to be upheld, for his authority was not yet complete. Returning to Antioch from Jerusalem, he was visited by Peter who had spent many years in the city after the Crucifixion. Peter ate with the Gentiles until some visitors from Jerusalem sent by James arrived. Then Peter "withdrew and separated himself, fearing them which were of the uncircumcision." Paul was incensed, though it is possible that Peter simply wanted to discuss private business with the visitors. "I withstood him to the face, because he was to be blamed," Paul relates, not without satisfaction, and went on to upbraid him at length in front of the Gentiles. Barnabas, the Cypriote Jew, who was Paul's companion, was also implicated in the quarrel, and soon Paul was continuing his missionary journeys accompanied by Silas, one of the elders of Jerusalem sent to Antioch to convince the Antiochenes that the charter of liberty had the backing of the council sitting in Jerusalem.

Paul's task during his missionary journeys was to found new churches and to hammer out an interpretation of Christ's message outside the law. Inevitably, since Christ had lived within the law, the interpretation was colored by Paul's judgment on the law, his own fears and exaltations, his sense of his own divine mission as "the apostle to the uncircumcised," sent to redeem the world from its sins. It mattered nothing to him that Peter had been among the most intimate companions of Christ and that on many different occasions Peter had been a witness of extraordinary events which few others had seen. Peter and John were the chief custodians of the mystery, and both were useless to Paul. He would hammer out his own interpretation of the Gospel in spite of them and if necessary against them. In all this he behaved with a breathtaking ruthlessness which he would excuse by recalling the blinding light that felled him in Damascus. In that light there was no room for the apostles, or for tradition, or indeed anything at all except the presence of Christ.

Paul's constant concern during his missionary wanderings was to safeguard the freedom that had been granted to him. His fiery temperament exulted in this newfound freedom; he rejoiced in the crossing of swords, and it pleased him to spend his skill in fierce debates against those who would dare to limit his freedom. As he grew older, he grew even more authoritarian and even more hostile to the elders of Jerusalem whom he had abandoned and long ago consigned to oblivion.

That Paul should have succeeded so dramatically in injecting his own passionate identity into early Christianity was due as much to Luke as to his own missionary activities and vehement letters. Luke, who became Paul's traveling companion, was in every respect his antithesis. As Luke reveals himself in the Gospel which bears his name and in his recital of Paul's voyages, he is a man of quiet and studious temperament, gentle, tolerant and conciliatory, a physician with an abiding sympathy for women, loving the humble and hating the proud. He appears to have been born in Antioch of Roman parentage; he was not a Jew, and remained largely unconcerned with Jewish beliefs. When he describes Paul in *Acts* he is the devoted observer, deeply aware of the blaze of genius but refusing to be burned by it. He stands a little aside, a skilled reporter with a notebook in his hand. He was evidently not interested in the growth of Paul's ideas, perhaps because he was so close to the man that there seemed to be no growth, only the continual blaze. At times he seems to have been a little amused by Paul, as when he recounts the story of Eutychus of Troas who fell into a deep sleep during one of Paul's long sermons. The Christians were meeting in an upper room, Eutychus was sitting at a window, and while he was asleep he suddenly overbalanced and fell "from the third loft." He was taken up dead, but revived when Paul embraced him. One has the feeling that Luke too must have sometimes fallen asleep during those sermons of stupefying length.

In the eyes of Luke, Paul's mission was the logical consequence of the vision at Damascus, which is described at varying length and under entirely different aspects on the three occasions when it is desired to remind the reader of the divine authority which made the mission possible. The effect of the three versions is to make the vision all the more credible. No doubt Paul was continually relating it, never wearying of the memory of the moment when he was carried up to heaven. From that moment Paul's future was already determined, and as he moves from city to city, from island to island, calling upon the Gentiles to put away their idols and assume the garment of the Holy Spirit, there is the sense of an inevitable progress. Prison doors fly open; storms are unloosed, but there is always a safe landfall; the treacheries of the world cannot assail him. With his slow and inevitable tread, like a conqueror, Paul marches on Rome.

Originally *Acts* was designed to tell the story of all the apostles. Half way through, the original plan was abandoned: there is only Paul. From *Acts* we learn very little about the fate of the apostles; they drift away into the obscurity which is reserved for the defeated. Luke has made his choice: Paul is the preordained successor, the herald of the Kingdom, as John the Baptist was the herald of the King.

In painting the portrait of Paul in his wanderings, Luke is concerned to depict a man who walks in holiness, calm and serene, and he seems to accomplish this by injecting his own quiet passions into the portrait. He avoids excess. As a literary artist he must depict the credible. But in fact Paul was very nearly incredible. So many emotions made war in him, so much furious energy poured out of him, that he seems to have existed for long intervals in a state of flaming intoxication. *Acts* is oddly at variance with the Epistles. Where *Acts* describes a man who is logical and purposeful, the Epistles describe a man given over to savage indignation, ferocious hopes, and a terrible consciousness of the weight of sin. Freedom was almost too much for him. He recoils before it, seeks to set bounds for it, loses himself in intricate arguments in which Gnosticism, Hellenistic philosophy, and the experience of Christ are oddly mingled. There is scarcely a statement uttered directly; he peels off layer upon layer of ideas in an effort to seek the hidden core. His sins overwhelm him and he castigates himself as the worst of sinners while remembering to his despair that he is Christ's apostle, the chosen of God. He batters his head against the walls of his cell, breaks through the walls, and observes to his astonishment that the stars have gone out and the world is evil. Then he returns to the darkness of his cell and celebrates a Christ who is pure abstraction scarcely to be distinguished from the all-encompassing Pleroma of the Gnostics:

Who is the image of the invisible God, the first-born of every creature:

For by him were all things created, that are in heaven, and that are in earth, visible and invisible, whether they be thrones, or dominions, or principalities, or powers: all things were created by him, and for him. And he is before all things, and by him all things consist. And he is the head of the body, the church who is the beginning, the firstborn from the dead; that in all things he might have the preeminence.

For it pleased the Father that in him should all fulness dwell.

(*Colossians* 1:15–19)

This Christ never walked the earth and never had nails driven into his flesh; he has become pure spirit. It is so far from being the Christ of the Athanasian Creed that it seems to exist in another world altogether.

Paul is uneasy unless he can stretch Christ to the uttermost. The flesh must become spirit, for all the world is guilty before God; the only salvation lies in the spirit. Against the sinners of the flesh he pours out the vials of his apostolic wrath with all the fury of an Old Testament prophet:

As it is written, There is none righteous, no, not one.
There is none that understandeth, there is none that seeketh after

God. They are all gone out of the way, they are together become unprofitable; there are none that doeth good, no, not one. Their throat is an open sepulchre; with their tongues they have used deceit; the poison of asps is under their lips: whose mouth is full of cursing and bitterness.

(Romans 3:10–14)

So he rages, only too aware of the law of sin in his members, crying out: "O wretched man that I am! who shall deliver me from the body of this death?" Tormented by sin, he curses the flesh. Tormented by his Hebrew past, he curses Israel, saying, "I could wish that myself were accursed from Christ for my brethren, my kinsmen according to the flesh, who are Israelites," and he explains that although they are the children of the flesh, they are not the children of God, for they are not descended from the freewoman but from the bondmaid, being subservient to the law. Again and again he rails against the Jews, the broken branch of the tree which has deliberately separated itself from the truth. The invective is curiously strained; the anger mounts; the voice becomes shrill, and then hoarse; and sometimes there is a sudden fearful note of pride as he discovers in himself the solution to the mystery. King David, too, had visited his anger on the Jews:

David saith, Let their table be made a snare, and a trap, and a stumblingblock, and a recompence unto them. Let their eyes be darkened, that they may not see, and bow down their back alway.

I say then, Have they stumbled that they should fall? God forbid: but rather through their fall salvation is come unto the Gentiles, for to provoke them to jealousy. Now if the fall of them be the riches of the world, and the diminishing of them the riches of the Gentiles, how much more their fulness?

For I speak to you Gentiles, inasmuch as I am the apostle of the Gentiles, I magnify mine office.

(Romans 11:9–13)

The note of pride, rarely absent in Paul, here achieves its most notable expression. The fall of the Jews seen as the triumph of the Gentiles was not likely to commend itself either to the Judaic Christians or to the Sanhedrim, and when Paul made his last visit to Jerusalem in the spring of A.D. 58 he must have known that he was in such grave danger that he had little hope of returning alive. Warned of the danger, he rejoiced in the thought that he might die like Christ. James, who received him, pointed out that Paul had preached the faith outside the law and must now show his obedience to the law by a ritual act of purification in the company of four men chosen by the elders. The ritual must be performed in the Temple precinct, thereby demonstrating that he still lived according to the law of his fathers. While he was fulfilling his vows, some Jews from Asia caught sight of him. There were rumors that he had brought a Gentile with him into the inner court, an area reserved on penalty of death to Jews alone. The Asian Jews knew him by reputation, and their long animosity flared up into white heat. They attacked him as an apostate and a blasphemer, dragged him outside the inner court of the Temple, and began to beat him unmercifully. He was saved only just in time by the Roman guards whose duty it was to preserve order.

The Roman guards had no intention of freeing him; they decided to throw him into prison for having disturbed the peace. Later they would put him on trial, and it would be necessary to see whether the charges made against him by the Jews could be upheld. As he was being dragged away to the fortress, he was given permission to speak to the bloodthirsty mob from the steps of the prison. They had expected him to speak in Greek, but he spoke to them in Hebrew, and they listened until he proclaimed that Christ during the vision in Damascus had spoken to him and afterward in the temple at Jerusalem he had received the summons to preach to the Gentiles. Then the mob broke out in fury and the captain of the guard could quieten them only by throwing the prisoner into the dungeon.

To obtain a confession, it was decided that Paul should be flogged, but the flogging was countermanded when they learned that he was a Roman citizen. The Sanhedrim met, determined to convict him, but the members of the court which consisted of Sadducees and Pharisees—Paul was himself a Pharisee—could come to no conclusion about him, and he was returned to jail. When the captain of the guard heard a rumor that Paul would be killed while being brought before the Sanhedrim for the second time, he decided to take the matter into his own hands. Paul was sent at night under heavy guard to the governor's headquarters at Caesarea, and there he remained. Two years later when a new governor came to take up his command, the Sanhedrim decided to press the charge. They demanded that Paul should be tried in Jerusalem. Paul, as a Roman citizen, demanded to be sent to Rome for a hearing before the highest tribunal. The governor agreed, thus relieving himseif of all responsiblity in a case that threatened to have disastrous consequences. So it happened that Paul arrived in Rome in the autumn of A.D. 60 in the reign of the Emperor Nero.

He was a prisoner of the Romans, living under guard, with few followers. It appears that his case was never brought to trial. He was not dangerous to the Romans. His friends had easy access to him, and the work of evangelization went on. At various times, according to the unpredictable whims of the court of Nero, the Christians would be rounded up, interrogated, and released, or there would be a massacre, as happened after the Great Fire in A.D. 64, but there was no concerted plan to destroy them. Like Paul, they lived quietly and did not attract attention to themselves.

The letters of Paul's last years are strangely muted. Gone are the exaltations, the quarrels with Israel, the involved parenthetical phrases. He writes very simply about the love of Christ, "who thought it not robbery to be equal with God," and sometimes he will speak mysteriously about the saints who are of Caesar's household, meaning perhaps that there were already Christians among the servants of Nero, and through them he hoped to avoid trial. When winter comes, he asks that a coat be sent to him from Troas; he salutes distant friends; he is at peace with himself, undecided only whether to live for the sake of the brethren or to die for Christ.

For me to live is Christ, and to die is gain. But if I live in the flesh, this is the fruit of my labour: yet what I shall choose I wot not. For I am in a strait betwixt two, having a desire to depart, and to be with Christ, which is far better. Nevertheless to abide in the flesh is more needful to you.

(*Philippians* 1:21–24)

History knows nothing about his death, and the traditions are disconcertingly conflicting. It is possible that he died in A.D. 67 during the last tumultuous months of the reign of Nero in the region of Tre Fontane, three miles out of Rome along the Ostian Way. The earliest dependable reference to his death was written between A.D. 75 and A.D. 110 by Clement of Rome:

Because of jealousy and strife, Paul showed the way to win the prize of endurance. Seven times he was in bonds, he was driven away as an exile, he was a herald both in the East and West, he won the noble glory of his faith. He taught righteousness to all the world, and when he had reached the limit of the West he gave testimony before rulers, and thus passed from the world and was taken up into the Holy Place, the greatest example of endurance.

(*Epistolae* I, iii)

It was a verdict that would have pleased Paul, who prized endurance above most of the virtues. Throughout his life as a Christian he saw himself as a man who fought the good fight and would fight on to the end.

5 ✢ THE EARLY FATHERS

In THE years when Paul was wandering over Asia Minor and Greece, and in those later years when he was a prisoner in Rome, the faith was still uncertain and unformed. The processes of crystallization were at work, but no one living in that age could foresee when the first crystals would be formed, when the faith would take on a deliberate color and shape. The faith was liquid, pouring through the hands of the poor. There was no Church, or rather nothing that corresponded to the Church as we know it today; the small group of Judaic Christian elders in Jerusalem still worshiped according to Jewish custom, and were regarded as the keepers of the true faith, which was not always to be distinguished from the Jewish faith. But as the bonds with Jerusalem grew weaker, the faith shook itself free from its Jewish character. The farther it traveled from Jerusalem, the less Jewish it became.

In those years there was only a small scattering of Christian communities along the shores of the Mediterranean. "The apostles scattered over the whole world," says Eusebius, but it was a very small world; many of the apostles vanished into obscurity, and nothing was heard of them again. Jerusalem, Antioch, and Ephesus were the centers of the emerging faith. Here and there, in obscure places across the Jordan and in Asia Minor, the faith took root and flourished briefly. We hear of one of the apostles traveling to Samaria and being received with enthusiasm, but it is unlikely that the Samaritans accepted Christianity for long. It was still a tentative faith, probing and seeking a way.

These small and scattered communities of Christians were often in danger, for neither the Jews nor the Romans looked upon them approvingly. It was a faith that drew its strength from danger and from the spoken word. Men gathered together and spoke of the revelations of Jesus of Nazareth and of the strange events which had taken place at the time of the Passover in Jerusalem. Soon the world would come to an end, and in purity and loving-kindness they awaited the Second Coming.

According to the prophets and to Jewish tradition, the Second Coming would take place in Jerusalem, the royal city sanctified by David. Here Christ had suffered his agony, and here the Judaic Christians were determined to remain, or at least to maintain a kind of official residence. James, the brother of Jesus, acted as the titular head of the faith for some thirty years. Suddenly in A.D. 62, in the reign of the Emperor Nero, during the interregnum between the death of one procurator and the appointment of a successor, James was arrested by order of the Sanhedrim and commanded to renounce his faith. There was no trial. He was lifted up onto the parapet of the inner courtyard of the Temple and questioned on a point of doctrine. He was asked to explain the words, "The door of Jesus," and he answered in words that meant plainly enough that Jesus was the door of salvation. Then the order was given that he should be cast down from the parapet, and when he fell he was still alive. A fuller armed with a club beat out his brains, and he was buried on the spot. His last words were a conscious echo of the words from the Cross: "I beseech thee, Lord God and Father, forgive them, for they know not what they do."

James was not the first of those who were intimately connected with the life of Jesus to suffer martyrdom. Another James—the brother of John—had been arrested some years previously and beheaded at the orders of Herod Agrippa.

With the death of James, the brother of Jesus, the bonds binding the faith to Jerusalem were loosened. A few years later, just before a great revolt broke out against the Romans in A.D. 66, the Judaic Christians abandoned Jerusalem altogether and settled in Pella, one of the small cities of the Decapolis in eastern Palestine, on the other side of the Jordan. Eusebius tells us that they were commanded to go to Pella "through an oracle revealed to acceptable persons living in Jerusalem," and he notes with some satisfaction that these Christians thereby escaped the terrible punishment visited by the Romans on the Jews in Jerusalem.

Little is known about the Judaic Christians in their exile. We hear of obscure wanderings, as they abandon Pella and establish themselves some miles away in Batanea, while the relations of Jesus went to live in Kokaba near Ashtaroth Carnaim, said to be the birthplace of Job. In this way, very quietly, living in towns that had received the full impact of Greek civilization, and never very far from Beth Shean, that large and luxuriant city known to its Greek settlers as Scythopolis, the elders of Jerusalem lived out the storm. Their exile, however, did little to benefit the cause of Christianity. They were a small private group living in the shadow of a vast upheaval, far from the center of things. While Jerusalem was sacked and plundered, and the Jews were massacred, the exiles awaited the Second Coming. Among the many prophecies connected with the Coming of the Messiah there was one which spoke of the reign of destruction which would be the prelude for his appearance in the Temple; and they may have expected that on the last day the Messiah would appear in the Holy of Holies amid the smoking rubble of Jerusalem. For them the destruction of the Temple by the armies of Titus came as no surprise, for it had been prophecied by Jesus.

When the Judaic Christians returned at last to Jerusalem, they elected a certain Symeon, a cousin of Jesus, to be head of their community. He was said to be the son of Clopas, the brother of Joseph, and suffered martyrdom at the age of one hundred and twenty in the reign of the Emperor Trajan. Thirteen more bishops "of the circumcision" were elected, but Symeon was the last to belong to the family of Jesus. Thereafter, except for a brief reference to the grandsons of Jude, said to have been a brother of Jesus, nothing more is heard of the family of Jesus. Hegesippus tells us they were peasants working a few acres of land. They were brought before the Emperor Domitian who inquired into their beliefs and when they said that Jesus would return on the last day to judge the quick and the dead, they were dismissed as harmless lunatics.

The Judaic Christians vanished from history. They had been the guardians of the law and the keepers of the tradition; among them was concentrated the greatest number of people who had known the living Jesus; and they were perhaps responsible for the first renderings of the Gospel story. Yet they proved to be impotent. Determined to maintain their Jewish traditions, they became merely one more of the many Jewish sects. In Jerusalem Christianity went to seed; in Asia

Minor, Greece, and Rome it took root and flourished.

Ignatius, the third bishop of Antioch, was the drummer of the new age. A man of remarkable violence and simplicity, he spoke in taut memorable phrases colored by a flaring religious imagination. "Grant me nothing more than that I be poured out as a libation to God," he declared. "Be diligent, be sober, be God's athlete, be like a beaten anvil," he says in another place. As he sees himself he is the pressed vine, the wheat ground to powder, the red-hot iron hammered into shape. Always there is the sense of a transformation of his being into the body of Christ. He shows not the slightest interest in or knowledge of Jewish ritual; he has stripped faith of everything except the presence of Christ. Of his surviving works only his *Epistle to the Romans* is undoubtably genuine: and that terse and triumphant letter describes a man leaping toward his own death. Like Paul he was arrested by the Romans; unlike Paul he had no desire to linger in Rome. Brought under escort from Syria to Rome, he begged the people he met on his journey to do nothing to prevent his martyrdom. For him Rome was Golgotha, the place of the skull, and where better could a man die? Hearing that attempts were being made in Rome to save him, he wrote urgently to the Romans:

For what value is all this world? Better to die for Christ than to rule over the farthest kingdoms. The pangs of a new birth are upon me. Do not hinder me from living; do not desire my death. Suffer me to receive the pure light, to become a man, to be an imitator of the passion of my God. Do not abet Satan against me. I write to you in the midst of life, yet lusting after death. You will not be showing love, but envy and hatred against me, should you procure the saving of my life.

(*Ad Romanos*, 5)

This strange saint was to leave an indelible mark on Christianity. All the wilder elements descend from him, from the terrible urgency of his smile. There was little charity in him. He implores the Romans: "Let me be given to the wild beasts, by whom I shall attain to God. For I am the Wheat of God, and I am ground by the teeth of wild beasts that I may become the pure bread of Christ. Encourage the beasts to become my sepulchre, leaving no part of me behind." So he goes on, the awful hammer-beat of his lines suggesting a manic crisis, and sometimes the words will come in a long spate as he celebrates his despair over the world, his love of death.

With impassioned eloquence he wrote of the blessedness of his coming death:

All the way from Syria, by land and by sea, by day and by night, I struggle against the wild beasts, those ten leopards to whom I am chained. I am speaking of the soldiers who guard me, and who behave all the more cruelly the more kindness is shown to them. Their atrocious conduct makes me more completely a disciple, but I am not thereby justified. May I have joy of the beasts that have been prepared for me, and may I find them prompt in action. I shall coax them to devour me promptly, unlike some whom they have refused to touch through fear. If they are unwilling and refuse, I shall compel them to it. Bear with me. I know what is best for me. I am beginning to be a disciple. Let no visible nor invisible power grudge me, that I may attain unto Jesus Christ! Come fire and cross, encounters with wild beasts, tearing apart of bones, hacking of limbs, crushing of the whole body, tortures of the devil come upon me, if only I may attain unto Jesus Christ.

(*Ad Romanos*, 5)

Such passionate cries for martyrdom were new to Christianity, and were heard with awe. The violence, however, is studied and deliberate: Ignatius is not writing only to the Christians in Rome, begging them not to intervene; he is writing to the entire Church, as Paul wrote when he addressed himself to the Corinthians. A new, terrible note had entered Christianity. "I lust after death," Ignatius writes, and his undying hatred is directed on those who will prevent it.

Of Ignatius himself very little is known, and nothing is known with certainty about his death. The *Antiochene Acts*, compiled many years later, recounts a brief conversation between Ignatius and the Emperor Trajan:

"Who are you, poor devil?" Trajan asked.

"I am not a poor devil but a God-bearer," Ignatius replied. "Unless perhaps you mean that because I am a bearer of Christ, the heavenly king, I am confounder of devils."

"What do you mean by God-bearer?"

"One who has Christ in his heart."

"Do you think we do not have our own gods in our hearts?"

"There is only one God, and Jesus Christ his Son."

"Then you carry Christ within yourself?"

"Yes, for it is written: 'I will dwell in them and walk with them.' "

"Then let Ignatius who says he carried the Crucified in his heart be fettered, taken to Rome, and thrown to the wild beasts to amuse the people."

According to Jerome, Ignatius was martyred in A.D. 109, but no one knows whether the martyrdom took place in Rome or in Asia Minor.

Violence lay at the heart of Christianity; it could hardly be otherwise since it celebrated the violent death of Christ. The agony in the garden, the treachery of Judas, the armed apostles, the Crucifixion, the rending of the curtain of the Temple, all these were violent events to be remembered and pondered over for generations to come. To die violently, as Christ had died, became the aim of the martyrs in the ages of persecution, but always there were Christians who wished to live in loving-kindness and humility in accordance with the Sermon on the Mount. They were the two faces of the same coin—peace and violence going hand in hand.

Clement of Alexandria

"ALL life is a holy feast," wrote Clement of Alexandria, and that quiet assertion, though untrue for most of mankind, was evidently true of Clement himself. He was a quiet scholar and teacher with a deep knowledge of Greek philosophy and pagan mysteries, a great traveler who wandered through southern Italy, Palestine, Greece, Asia Minor, and Egypt in search of Christian teachers. He was born in Athens about A.D. 150, his original name being Titus Flavius Clemens, thus curiously commemorating the Roman emperor who overthrew Jerusalem, an imperial Roman family, and the third successor of St. Peter as Bishop of Rome. It is just possible that he was descended from the Consul Flavius Clemens, whose sons were declared heirs to the throne, until he became a Christian and was martyred by his cousin, the Emperor Domitian. But all we know for certain about him is contained in his four surviving works, which reveal him as a humorous, saintly, gentle, and omniverous scholar. His supreme virtue was that he attempted to reconcile Platonism with Christianity, and he seems to have delighted as much in Greek philosophy as in the

Gospels.

We know the views of Clement on nearly every subject under the sun. He resembles Montaigne in his playful pedantry, his firm prejudices, his grave benevolence. Unlike Ignatius, he believed calmness to be the most prized possession of a Christian, and though he always retained his calm he was often impatient with the foibles and excesses of the human race. He did not endure fools gladly. He did not like the smells of the market place. He detested fops, rhetoricians, men who shaved off their beards, women who wore expensive garments, all men in authority. He was curiously fascinated by sex, and spoke about sexual matters at considerable length. He was like a squirrel in the way he collected tag ends of verses and inserted them in his writings, often with little excuse except his own pleasure in them. He read voluminously—there are more than 700 quotations from more than 300 authors in his surviving works. He had the academic mind, in the best and the worst sense, and he was profoundly in love with freedom, being the first Christian philosopher to assert the doctrine of free will. His piety was lyrical and contemplative, the piety of a man who never had to battle his way to Christ. Born a pagan, he seems to have become a Christian as effortlessly as one crosses a country road.

In that great rag-bag of miscellaneous ideas which he called *Stromateis*, from a word originally meaning "a quilted bag for stuffing bedclothes," Clement explained how he searched through most of the known world for teachers of philosophy. He found one in Greece, a second in Italy, a third in Lebanon, a fourth in Egypt, a fifth in Assyria, a sixth in Palestine. All except the last two were pagans. These men, the Assyrian and the Palestinian, had preserved traditions derived directly from Peter, James, John, and Paul, "and in this way the ancestral apostolic seeds were handed down to me." His inheritance involved both the Judaic Christians of Jerusalem and Paul who had pronounced severely against Judaic Christianity. For Clement, the great reconciliator, it was a simple matter to reconcile the two opposing traditions.

Clement believed that all the stages of the world's history led inevitably to Christ. For him Greek philosophy, the study of his youth, was the prelude to Christianity. The errors of the heathen pointed the way to Christian truth, and it was necessary to understand heathens and Jews before coming to an understanding of Christ. He believed in the cross-fertilization of cultures, saying that Plato had learned much from Moses and hinting that Christ owed a debt to Plato. He knew the Greek mystery cults so well that his writings are among our chief authorities on those ancient mysteries, and he was continually repeating one of the major themes of the cults: that men are of heavenly birth, plants nourished on heavenly soil. It did not surprise him that the pagan and Christian mysteries sometimes overlapped. What surprised him was that anyone could still believe in the power of the ancient gods after they had been dethroned by Christ. "Where is Zeus?" he asks. "Where the eagle? Where the swan? Zeus has grown old with his feathers. He is dead, as Leda is dead, and the swan also, and the eagle, and the lover, and the serpent."

With such poetic improvisations he dismisses the gods, and then because they still show some flickering signs of life, he continually returns to observe their deathbed agonies. Throughout five chapters of his *Exhortation to the Greeks*, written about A.D. 190, he surveys the departing gods as they sink into the shadows. He knows them all by name, their many names. He knows that in Oxyrhynchus men worshiped a fish, in Thebes a sheep, in Syria a dove, in the Troad a mouse, in Egypt a cat. He reminds us that men have been known to worship men; they even worshiped King Philip, the father of Alexander the Great, when his collarbone was broken and he was lame in one leg and one of his eyes had been knocked out. They worshiped Artemis the Strangler and Zeus the Averter of Flies, and they were capable of worshiping even more outrageous divinities. Happily, those times are past. The time has come to put childish things away and to worship "the Creator of the universe, who put a candle to the sun, whom I long for with all my heart."

Like many of the Fathers of the Eastern Church, Clement was inclined to place man higher than the angels. Man was an immortal vehicle of the Godhead, a good bridegroom, a good father, and a good son; such goodness was an attribute of divinity:

A noble hymn of God is man, immortal, founded upon righteousness, the oracles of truth engraved upon him. For where else save in the wise soul can truth be written? or love? or reverence? or gentleness? Those who have had these divine characters engraved and sealed upon their souls deem such wisdom a fair port of departure for whatever journey their course is trimmed to, and this wisdom is also a

haven of peace and fair return. By this wisdom those who have be-
taken themselves to the Father have proved good fathers to their chil-
dren, and those who have known the Son have proved good sons to
their parents, and those who remember the Bridegroom become good
husbands to their wives; and having been redeemed from absolute
slavery, they are good masters to their slaves.

(Protreptikos, X)

So Clement announces the New Song, which is calm and sober, delighting in the ordinary works of man and all the humble duties of life. Ignatius proclaimed: "I am the wheat of God." Clement, who was kindlier, proclaimed that the whole world was God's fruitful field. "The world is a field, and we are the harvest watered by the grace of God," he wrote in *The Instructor*, which is not so much a pedagogical treatise as a diary of all his likes and dislikes, uttered sometimes with a gay inconsequence and often bluntly. "The Christian is always friendly to solitude, and quiet, and tranquillity, and peace," he wrote in one of his lost works; the sentence survives because St. John Damascene remembered it. Such simple memorable sentences were characteristic of the man who was not afraid to assert in the face of sin and death that "all life is a holy feast."

Origen

THE name sounds like a rock, but it is softer in the original Greek, meaning "born of Horus." In his lifetime he was called "Adamantius," meaning "a man of adamant," and a rock-like, adamantine strength poured out of him. Of all the Fathers of the early Church this passionate scholar was the most saintly, though he never received the title of saint. He thought his own thoughts about God with no fear of the consequences, with the result that the Church has often regarded him as a heretic. Joyous, headstrong, foolish, incapable of compromise, helplessly at odds with the world, he was the founder of scientific biblical scholarship and possessed the most daring mind of his time.

He was born about A.D. 185, the eldest child in a large family. His father, Leonides, was Greek, his mother probably Egyptian. Leonides owned a library of rare manuscripts and was devoted to scholarship, and the boy grew up in his father's image. Eusebius, who wrote a brief life of Origen when it was possible to describe with reasonable accuracy much that would otherwise have been distorted or forgotten, speaks of the deep affection between father and son, and describes how Leonides bent over his sleeping son and bared his breast and kissed it reverently as though it were the temple of the divine spirit. The boy read widely in his father's library, learned long passages of the Scriptures by heart, and asked interminable questions, so many that he had to be rebuked. They were dangerous times. During one of the waves of persecution in the reign of Septimius Severus, his father was arrested and imprisoned, and the shock so worked upon the boy that he felt called upon to offer himself as a martyr, and he would have run into the streets and proclaimed himself a Christian if his mother had not hidden his clothes and compelled him to stay at home. He wrote to his father in prison: "Do not weaken for our sakes." The father became a willing martyr, and the widowed mother became the pensioner of a wealthy Christian lady. The property of Leonides had been seized by the imperial treasury, and the family was destitute.

Origen was sixteen when his father died; the memory of the dead father haunted him for the rest of his life.

To live he became an elementary schoolteacher, giving lessons in Greek philosophy, while at the same time conducting a school for teaching Christian doctrine in secret. The persecutions continued, and it was remembered that Origen continually risked his life to be among the prisoners, and he was especially careful to be present when they were being led out to execution. At such times he would find himself being watched by crowds of pagans, and sometimes they would surround and threaten him, so that he barely escaped with his life. He had a special reverence for martyrs who by dying for Christ became almost indistinguishable from Christ.

Origen's beliefs were those of a fundamentalist strictly obedient to the commands of Jesus. He carried no scrip, wore only one coat, went barefoot, and distressed his friends by enduring cold and nakedness to the furthest extremes of poverty. He went so far as to perform the act of self-mutilation, following literally the precept of *Matthew* 19:12 that "there are eunuchs who have made themselves eunuchs for the Kingdom of Heaven's sake." Later he appears to have regretted the act, as he regretted selling off his large collection of pagan writings. He needed the collection when he came to study the Scriptures, especially the translation of the Old Testament into Greek, which had been executed by seventy Jewish elders at some time in the third century B.C. Faith and martyrdom were his chief preoccupations, but learning and philosophy sometimes ran them close. Once he said to Gregory Thaumaturgus that a man can have no genuine piety unless he loves philosophy, "a gift which man alone of all the teachers of the earth has been deemed honorable and worthy enough to possess." He spent his hours in study and preaching and prayer, and slept little, and ate little. In his writing he gives the impression of a man perfectly content with his lot.

The early Fathers of the Church sometimes give an impression of uneasy immaturity. Clement of Alexandria is often childish and sententious, there are occasions when Augustine shows an adolescent's delight in licking his wounds, and more often than one would like Jerome displays a wounded pride, a vanity that leads us to suspect that he is concealing something of himself. Origen is the mature man, never vain, never sententious, never raising his voice. At all times he knows exactly what he is doing.

The most important and far-reaching of his works is *De Principiis* (On First Principles), which has come down to us only in the Latin translation made by Rufinus. In this work Origen wrestles with the ultimate beliefs of a Christian, demanding answers to hard questions. What is God? What is the Son? What is the Holy Ghost? What are the angels? Why was the universe created? Having answered these questions, he goes on to discuss the even more mysterious intricacies of the faith. There is no niggardliness in him: always there is a sweeping breadth of vision. Here, for example, he discusses the relationship between Christ on earth and God in Heaven:

Imagine there is a statue so vast that it fills the universe, and therefore no one can see it. Then imagine that another statue is formed, an exact model of the first in limbs and features, in form and material, all these reduced proportionately in size, so that those who cannot behold the vast, all-encompassing statue can still say they have perceived it, for the smaller statue retains all the features of the larger, in limbs and features and in form, and it is in no way distinguishable from the other except in size. So did the Son of God divest himself of His equality with the Father and show us the way to the knowledge of Him who is made the express image of His person, so that we are unable to look on the splendor of the shining of the Godhead but

*may yet behold His brightness, and so by gazing upon the shining
light we come to behold the divine vision.*

(*De Principiis* I, ii, 8)

Origen's mind moves in vast outlines; his subject is the whole of
Creation. For him there is nothing on earth that is not touched with
divinity. Rocks, stones, fish, tigers, angels, all have their place in the
divine economy, all celebrate the glory of God. The stars are living
and rational beings, and there will come a time when the sun may declare: "I desire to be dissolved, to return and be with Christ, which is
far better." That return to the spiritual state, which he calls *apocatastasis*, is not limited to man, but includes everything that has ever
been or ever will be. By reason of God's charity even the Devil will
one day return to his proper inheritance; Hell will be no more, and all
sinners will come at last to Heaven; and the world which has so long
trafficked with evil will enter into a state of grace where evil is unimaginable.

Origen held firmly to the belief in *apocatastasis*, and it is a mark
of his own charity that he refused to assent to any faith that did not
permit the ultimate redemption of evil. He believed that wherever
there was alienation from God, there was restoration through Christ,
who had shed his blood not only "for sin," but also "as a gift on the
high altar which is in Heaven." He believed, too, that the angels had
been sent to minister to all things. "The angels command all things,
earth, water, air, and fire, and all alike," he wrote. "The Word employs them as instruments to regulate the movements of animals,
plants, stars, and even the heavens." They are "the virtues who pre-
side over the earth and the seeding of trees, who see to it that springs
and rivers do not run dry, who look after the rains and the winds, the
animals that live on land, and those that live in the sea, and all that is
born on earth." Having these beliefs, he could not bring himself to
condemn the flesh or to deny free will. That men should suffer eternal torment for their sins was in his eyes a burden too intolerable to
be borne and inconceivable in the light of God's beneficence. Men
were punished for their sins, but their punishment was like the medicine given to a sickly child; when they were well again, they no
longer took the medicine.

Origen's ideas on the nature of God and the purpose of Creation
are scattered through his commentaries on the Scriptures. He was not
a systematic philosopher, and sometimes he hovers between two alter-

native beliefs. He will say that Jesus is God in human form, and in his powers and virtues indistinguishable from God, but in the next breath he will say with equal assurance that Jesus is not, like God, entirely free from darkness, for he bore our sins. To Origen the two statements are equally valid, for they portray Jesus under different aspects. In much the same way he will employ a text and derive different meanings from it according to the theme of his argument. So he will speak of the grain of mustard seed as though it were a very real seed, and a moment later it will become faith or the Kingdom of Heaven.

Some six years before his death he wrote his great defense of Christianity, *Contra Celsum*, in reply to a pamphlet by an intelligent and penetrating critic. He matched the wit of Celsus with his own, answering him point by point, with good humor and remarkably good sense. Celsus, a Platonist, portrayed Christianity as an educator's nightmare: it was directed at the rabble; it propounded ideas that were nonsensical when they were not childishly simple. Origen answered by using the weapons of Plato against him. He described Christianity as a mystery to which all were invited, and the simple ideas of Christ were in fact profoundly difficult unless one had absolute faith. Plato described God as inaccessible. Origen replied that Christ was kinder to men than Plato, for he showed that God was not inaccessible, but on the contrary, by becoming man, He made Himself accessible to all, even to the rabble. Origen has more difficulty countering the accusation that Christians suffer from self-admiration as the chosen vehicles of God. "They come flying like bats from their nests or ants running from anthills, like frogs sitting in council in the marshes, like worms holding assembly in the mud, and they declare: 'God has revealed everything to us, and we are His favorites. Earth, water, air, and stars—all these were created for us and are under our dominion.'" Origen answered the charge by reminding Celsus that the Christians shared with the Stoics and the Epicureans the belief that the world was made for the enjoyment of the human race, and it was precisely because the world was made for the human race that human acts possess value. If the world was not made for men, if God lived in inaccessible regions indifferent to the fate of mankind, then morality would be nothing more than a ridiculous invention and all acts would possess the same value. When Celsus accused the Christians of behaving like "chosen people," Origen replied that they had indeed been chosen by Christ, and they were justified in rejoicing in their exclusivity. And when Celsus goes on to ask why the Christians took no interest in the state—"If everyone did the same, then the king would be left high and dry, everything would fall into the hands of the barbarians, and your sect and true wisdom itself would vanish from the midst of men"—Origen answers that disinterest in the state belongs to the very nature of the religion and Christians who courted the king lost all claim to the Kingdom of Heaven.

So the relentless argument continues, and although Origen was writing against a book that appeared sixty years before, and Celsus was long dead, we seem to see the protagonists in actual debate, seeking out each other's weaknesses, never at a loss for an argument. Origen plays the game fairly, and it is a mark of his generosity that he permits his adversary every advantage.

The humanity of Origen breathes through all his writings, even in those interminable discussions of Old Testament texts that were the solace of his long life. He had hoped to die a martyr, but this grace was not given to him. Arrested during the Decian persecutions, he was tortured and threatened with death by fire, and finally released. Worn out by sufferings, he died in A.D. 253, in his seventieth year. He was buried in the Church of the Holy Sepulchre at Tyre, where nearly a thousand years later there came the body of the Emperor Frederick Barbarossa, who had sought to revive the splendors of the Roman Empire. The church has long since vanished. Today a man may walk through the streets of Tyre and gather in his hands some earth that may, for all he knows, contain the dust of two emperors.

6 ✠ THE MARTYRS

THE BLOOD of the martyrs is the seed of the Church," wrote Tertullian of Carthage, and in the long history of Christianity the blood was continually being spilt and the seed was continually flowering.

From the beginning Christianity was pitted against the massive power of the Roman Empire ruling by armed might with fearful weapons of coercion. There was no thought of compromise. If a conquered nation rebelled or a religious sect continued to exist against the will of the Romans, the punishment was extermination. But the Christians, living quietly and obscurely, cultivating their religion behind closed doors, outwardly no different from the other laboring folk except perhaps that they were more tranquil, gentle, and modest, did not at first attract very much attention to themselves. Christianity was still a secret mystery with its mysterious passwords which the faithful drew in the air or in the dust in order to recognize one another: the ship, the ark, the anchor, the dove, the fish. Ignatius was the exception; the chief characteristics of the Christians were patience and a quiet faith.

The first Christians to be martyred died at the orders of Nero. "Nero first bled the infant Church," wrote the Church historian Eusebius. "Then it was that Peter had his loins girded by another than himself, and both he and Paul were condemned as atheists." Tertullian claimed that Peter "suffered a passion like that of the Saviour and Paul obtained the same coronation as John the Baptist." Legend has embroidered on the manner of their deaths, and in the apocryphal *Acts of Peter* we hear how Peter was arrested, brought before the

Prefect Agrippa, and sentenced to be crucified. He asked to be crucified with his head downward, and in this position delivered a sermon
to the crowd, saying that he was following the command of Christ
that everything be turned upside down. The apocryphal *Acts of Paul*
describes an even stranger death, for it tells how Nero in a rage because Paul had converted a favorite cupbearer to Christianity ordered
him to be beheaded "in accordance with the Roman law." Paul was
taken to the place of execution:

> *Then turning toward the east, Paul lifted up his hands to heaven
> and prayed much; and after having conversed in Hebrew with the fa-
> thers during prayer, he bent his neck and spoke no more. When the
> lictor cut off his head, milk splashed on the dress of a soldier. And the
> soldier, and all who stood nearby, were astonished at this sight and
> glorified God, who had thus honored Paul. And they went away and
> reported everything to Caesar.*
>
> (*Acts of Paul*, 5)

The executions of Peter and Paul during the last tumultuous
years of Nero's reign went unrecorded by the Roman historians. Suetonius mentions the persecutions of the Christians casually, as though
it were something well-known, inevitable, and perhaps scarcely
worth mentioning. When the great fire of Rome broke out on July
19, A.D. 64, Nero was staying with the veterans of the praetorian
guard in Antium, but hurried back in time to admire the blaze. The
fire raged unchecked for five days, and Suetonius tells us that the emperor's household servants were seen fanning the flames. "To quieten
the rumors," says Tacitus, "Nero placed the blame on the Christians
and inflicted the most exquisite tortures on these people who were
hated for their abominations. He first seized upon those who confessed their guilt, and from the informers he went on to arrest a considerable number, not so much for the crime of firing the city as for
their hatred of humanity. To their agonies, mockery was added: men
wrapped in animal skins were dismembered by dogs, or nailed to
crosses, or they were set on fire like torches to provide illumination at
dusk. Nero lent his gardens for this spectacle, and gave circus games,
while he mingled with the people in the costume of a charioteer or
stood aloft in his chariot. A feeling of compassion arose for even those
criminals who deserved extreme and exemplary punishment; for all
this happened not, as it seemed, for the public good, but in order to

glut a single man's cruelty. So they were destroyed."

The sullen rage of Nero took many forms, and no one was ever able to count his private and public murders. The massacre of the Christians, like so many of his massacres, seems to have been an afterthought. The strange power of the Christians was already being felt, and their doctrines were known. Among the beliefs of the early Christians was the Second Coming of Christ, which would be attended by fire storms, the whole earth becoming a single searing flame; and it is possible that Nero believed or was convinced that the Christians had deliberately fired the city to fulfill the prophecy. The punishment reserved for the Christians depended upon the whims of Nero. Later it would assume a more formal and familiar character.

Four years later Nero killed himself, having committed so many atrocities that wherever he turned he found himself confronting avengers. Thereafter, for twenty-seven years, the Christians were left in peace. By A.D. 95 the Church was sufficiently powerful to demand the attentions of the government.

We have already seen Ignatius rejoicing in martyrdom for the wrong reasons, or at least for reasons that have nothing to do with calm sobriety. His fellow-bishop Polycarp of Smyrna showed a gentler temper, and embraced martyrdom hesitantly. At the annual games given by Philip of Tralles, the Asiarch, the pagans in order to punish the growing influence of the Church had called for the martyrdom of eleven Christians who were to be given over to the wild beasts. They demanded that the aged bishop, who had once sat at the feet of St. John, should also be executed. Three days passed before the police caught up with Polycarp in a cottage outside the city. It was evening when they reached the cottage, and he could have escaped under cover of darkness. Instead, he calmly offered food and drink to his captors and asked to be allowed to pray for a while, and then accompanied them to the city, where he was met by the captain of police, who asked: "What is the harm of saying 'Caesar is Lord,' and offering incense?" This simple formula in honor of the imperial cult had been devised to ensure that no Christians should escape from the net. By confessing that "Caesar is Lord," the Christians were compelled to accept that all sovereignity came from the emperor. Polycarp refused to obey, and was hurried to the arena. It was Sunday morning, and the crowds were waiting.

The governor of Smyrna, Titus Statius Quadratus, was present, and he seems to have hoped that at the last moment the old bishop would see the error of his ways. "Have respect for your age," he said. "Swear by the Fortune of Caesar, repent, and say 'Away with the atheists!'" The old man sighed, raised his eyes to heaven, waved in the direction of the crowds huddled in the arena, and said: "Away with the atheists!" In this way, ironically, he accepted the challenge of the governor.

"Swear, and I will set you free. Revile Christ!" the governor went on, and Polycarp answered: "I have served Him for eighty-six years, and He has done me no wrong. How can I speak evil of my King, who saved me?"

The governor tried again, begging him to reconsider his decision, but all Polycarp would say was: "I am a Christian! If you wish to learn what it is to be a Christian, you would have to listen to me for a whole day."

The governor said, "It is the people you must convince," and Polycarp answered, "I could reason with you, for we have been taught to give Caesar his due, but I do not believe the people are worthy to hear any defense from me."

"Then I will have to throw you to the wild beasts unless you repent."

"Bring them in! Repentance from the better to the worse is no change to be desired, but it is good to change from cruelty to justice."

"Well then, if you despise the beasts, I will have you consumed by fire, unless you repent."

"What is that to me? The fire burns for an hour, and is speedily quenched, but you know nothing of the fire of the coming Judgment and the eternal punishment reserved for the wicked. Why delay? Do as you will!"

In his troubled soul desiring and not desiring martyrdom, weighing all things in the balance, Polycarp had at last come to his conclusion. There had been no reasoned argument: only a cautious exploration of many issues, but all these explorations ended too abruptly for comfort. This conversation, as it was recounted later by Marcion, has all the marks of authenticity. There was no eagerness, only acceptance. At the end it was as though a last flare of pride had risen in him, and he was afraid the crown of martyrdom would be snatched from him. So he reached out for it, slowly, uncertainly, scarcely knowing what was happening.

When it became clear that Polycarp had no desire to address the crowd, and that he would continue in his ways, the herald was sent out to proclaim his sentence of death. He was taken to the stake, and when they were about to nail him to it, he said: "Leave me as I am, for He who enables me to abide the fire will also enable me to abide unflinching at the stake." Then he prayed, and the fire was lit. As he stood there, stripped naked, he resembled, says Marcion, "a loaf in the oven," a loaf that refused to burn, for the flames arched over him like a ship's sail, and he was untouched until the *confector* stabbed him; then he fell, and the flames consumed him. "Later," wrote Marcion, "we gathered up his bones, which were more valuable than jewels or gold, and we laid them in a safe place."

There is no very good reason to distrust these accounts of the early martyrs. Their replies to their inquisitors ring true. It was an age when shorthand was well-known and abundantly practiced, and the trial and testimony of the martyrs would quite naturally be preserved with their relics. The proper bureaucratic procedures were invoked; certificates were issued to those who abjured Christ, and reports on the executions were no doubt drawn up and kept in voluminous files. Persecutions however were intermittent. A governor with an eye for promotion would promote the imperial cult and punish all offenders, while another like Pliny the Younger, sent to govern Bithynia by the Emperor Trajan, would show a marked distaste for ordering the execution of inoffensive maid-servants who had embraced the Christian faith. Only in Rome does the cry, "*Christianos ad leones*," seem to have been heard continually. For the Roman mobs the Christians performed the same service as the gladiators: their deaths provided entertainment.

The practices of the inquisitors differed widely, according to their moods and the determination of the Christians to offer themselves up for martyrdom. *The Acts of the Scillitan Saints*, the earliest surviving document concerning Christian martyrs in Africa, dated July 17, A.D. 180, shows a governor earnestly pleading with the Christians to renounce their faith and offering them thirty days in which to reconsider their errors. The mood is tranquil and restrained. Ultimately the Christians refuse to renounce their faith and walk cheerfully to the execution ground. There is no torture. They are beheaded or stabbed to death.

About the same time the Christians in Lyons and Vienne were being hideously tortured. *The Letter from the Churches of Lyons and Vienne*, attributed to St. Irenaeus, describes a scene not unlike a concentration camp in Germany. Torture assumed a peculiarly modern form. It was not enough that prisoners should be flogged, then mauled by wild beasts, then roasted on an iron chair, but they must be submitted to every degradation that the imagination of the Roman prosecutors could evolve. The aim was not only to destroy the Christian physically, but in the process to destroy him spiritually as well, to reduce him to a state of screaming nothingness. Relays of torturers worked on the prisoners from morning to night; the torturers themselves were tortured by their long hours and the terrible conditions under which they worked; and the prisoners, exhausted beyond endurance and scarcely knowing what they were saying, sometimes disavowed their beliefs only to learn that apostasy offered them no advantages. Denied a public martyrdom, they were sometimes suffocated to death in their cells. Then their bodies were thrown to the dogs.

The Letter from the Churches of Lyons and Vienne is a terrifying document which could only have been written by a man who had seen these tortures at close hand. The heart trembles and the pen races as he describes with jagged nerves the outrages committed on the innocent. One torture follows another, one nightmare follows another, and the accumulative effect is to suggest that Roman officialdom suffered from a failure of nerve, a blind nihilism. "You have become man-eaters," cried Attalus, later to become a martyr. The bestial horror is only too convincing. When the letter was written, the ruler of the Roman Empire was the calmly meditative Marcus Aurelius.

In fact, it was among the "good" Roman emperors that some of the greatest excesses were committed against the Christians. The Antonine emperors, scrupulously observing the letter of the law, permitted the greatest massacres. Commodus, the degenerate son of Marcus Aurelius and one of the very worst emperors, proved to be one of the most tolerant to the Christians, being influenced by his Christian concubine and other Christians who flocked to his court. He is known to have given pardons to those under arrest and to have relaxed the rigid laws of summary persecution. With the death of Commodus and the rise to power of Septimius Severus, a new era of total persecution began. Septimius Severus was a "good emperor," capable and effi-

Mosaics of Ravenna

Christ the Redeemer, in the Basilica of Sant' Apollinare
Nuovo. (*Alinari*)

Mausoleum of Gallia Placidia, looking up from the entrance.
(*Italian Tourist Office, New York*)

Mausoleum of Galla Placidia, from a lunette in the entrance
wall. (*Italian Tourist Office, New York*)

Basilica of Sant' Apollinare in Classe. (*Italian Tourist Office, New York*)

Church of San Vitale. The Empress Theodora and her retinue. (*Anderson*)

Church of San Vitale. The Emperor Justinian. (*Anderson*)

Basilica of Sant' Apollinare in Classe. The Cross. (*Anderson*)

✝SANCTVS APOLENARIS

cient, intolerant of any power but his own; and the Christians, who
had lived tolerably under Commodus, were now hunted down like
wild beasts. One emperor would be tolerant, the next intolerant. So it
happened that the weak Alexander Severus, who is said to have worshiped Christ together with the pagan gods in his private chapel, was
followed by the ruthless Maximin, who issued orders to renew the
persecution. His example was followed by Decius under whom the
Christians suffered as they had never suffered before.

Confronted with the threatened total collapse of the empire,
Decius acted with great firmness. He declared total war on the Christians, regarding them as wanton destroyers of the empire, a fifth column sapping at the energies of the empire from within. He was
incensed, like other emperors before him, by their exclusivity, their
refusal to worship him, to bear arms, or to obey the orders of their governors. *"Non serviam"* (I will not serve), a cry that was to go down
the ages, was heard often during that terrible reign. Where Decius ex-
celled, and where other emperors had failed, was in his determination
to carry out his threats. Persecution in the past was sporadic, unor-
ganized, inefficient. Decius was the first to organize the mass slaughter
of Christians.

The Christians fought back; they were in no mood to assent to
their own extermination. We hear of armed groups of Christians res-
cuing prisoners destined for martyrdom, killing the guards, fleeing
by night to some stronghold where they could defend themselves.
There are no records of an organized Christian militia, but it is clear
that a loosely organized militia existed. The Decian persecution lasted
for three years, from A.D. 249 to A.D. 251. With the death of Decius
the persecutions were abandoned, not to be resumed until the closing
years of the reign of Diocletian half a century later. Then once more
there was a brief period when the Church confronted the full weight
of the terror. Like Decius, Diocletian was a frontier general, concerned above everything else to preserve the might of the army and
the authority of his government. There opened on February 23, A.D.
303, the large-scale massacre that the Christians called "the Great Persecution." Uncounted thousands were executed for refusing to drop
incense into the burners erected on the altars dedicated to the emperor. We hear of executioners who dragged their victims to the altar
and made them drop the incense by main force, and sometimes they
would fill dead hands with incense and then cast it on the sacrificial

flames. In this way the commands of the imperial edict were obeyed.

"The Great Persecution" ended abruptly when Diocletian re-nounced the throne and retired into the immeasurable solitudes of his great palace at Spalato on the Dalmatian coast. At the time, Diocletian was the emperor of the East and Maximian the emperor of the West. By agreement they decided to retire at the same time, leaving the thrones of the empire to Galerius and Constantius Chlorus, the one a ruthless Thracian general concerned only with the army and the ag-grandizement of his own person, the other a Roman nobleman toler-ant and gentle in his dealings with his subjects. "He was a good and kindly man who strove to improve the fortunes of provinces and in-dividuals and was indifferent to enriching the treasury," wrote Eutro-pius of Constantius Chlorus. "He liked to say that it was better for wealth to be in the hands of individuals than stored in a guard-house." Galerius ruled the East, continuing to persecute Christians. Indeed, he had been the instigator of "the Great Persecution" and the chief agent of its success. Constantius Chlorus contented himself with burn-ing down a few churches as a token of his determination to root out a dangerous sect. He was the ruler of the West, his empire stretching across Britain, Spain, and France, and all of Italy. He died in Britain in York in A.D. 306, and his soldiers promptly elected his son Con-stantine to the purple. At that moment the long awaited turning-point in the fortunes of Christianity took place.

Constantine had no hereditary right to the throne. He received the purple by acclamation, but the decisions of the legionaries in York were not binding in Italy, Spain, or France. Maxentius, the son of Maximian, seized Italy, Africa, and the Northern Alpine provinces. Maximian emerged from retirement to lead his armies into France, to halt the southward march of the legions of Constantine, and was defeated and killed near Marseilles. Constantine drove on to Rome.

Handsome, arrogant, efficient, in love with power and his own glory, Constantine was to give an ineffaceable shape to Christianity. He gave it earthly power, wealth, and official sanction. From being persecuted, the Christians became rulers. The most dangerous of gifts was granted to them—official protection.

7 ✠ CONSTANTINE

I N THE mind of Constantine, as
in the minds of many of his contemporaries, the pagan past fought an
unrelenting war with the Christian present. Though he spoke sometimes in the authentic accents of Christianity, and attended Christian
ceremonies, and presided over the debates of his bishops, he was never
completely reconciled to the Christian faith. He saw Christ as the
victor over death, and himself as the victor over the living: victory
was never far from his thoughts. Because Christianity was triumphant, he attached himself to it, but he seems never to have felt the
need to inquire deeply into the Christian mysteries. He used the faith,
as he used his armies, to ensure his own triumph.

Constantine remains an enigma, for it is always enigmatical when
a man professes two faiths simultaneously. Long after his official conversion he was minting coins bearing the image of Apollo, and long
after he had proclaimed himself a Christian emperor he was still praying to the pagan gods of Rome. Across the arch of triumph which he
erected out of the remnants of the arches of three previous emperors
he wrote an inscription ascribing his victories to "the inspiration of
the divinity"—*instinctu divinitatis*. Churchmen have amused themselves by asking the inevitable rhetorical question: which divinity?
Apollo or Christ? Yet the answer is plain. Constantine's happy formula was carefully designed to avoid the issue, and by avoiding it he
made it all the more certain that he meant exactly what he said. By
"the inspiration of the divinity" he meant "the inspiration of all divinities." If Mithraism could have served his purpose, he would have embraced it with the same solemnity.

As he appears on the coins and medallions struck during his reign, and in his innumerable statues, he was one of the few Roman emperors who looked the part to perfection, well-built and sturdy, with a broad forehead, fine eyes, a straight nose, full lips, and a heavy rounded chin. When the Church historian Eusebius first saw him as a young man during his travels in Palestine before his accession, he was struck by Constantine's air of quiet dignity and abundant health. His eyes were remarkable for their brightness and their leonine glare, and he was proud of his strong, thick neck; he had a habit of throwing back his head in a contemptuous gesture to show off the powerful cords of his throat. He was a man who exulted in kingship.

Constantine was to leave on Christianity the impress of his vigorous and ill-disciplined mind. He was to receive many titles and many names, and the panegyrists were to celebrate him with tributes which were not notably different from the tributes paid to the mad emperors Nero and Elagabulus. He was the divinity whose light was so blinding that men averted their eyes; he walked in solemn radiance, and his divine intelligence sent the shadows of perplexity hurrying away. To the church historian Eusebius he was "the preeminent possessor of all the virtues that true religion can confer." In his lifetime he was addressed as *rector totius orbis*, ruler of the whole world, and after his death he became *isapostolos*, equal to the apostles, and accordingly a half-circle of cenotaphs representing the apostles was arranged around his sarcophagus in the Church of the Apostles. The half-circle was deliberately and carefully contrived; if there had been a full circle he would have been the equal of Christ.

The Christians who greeted with such triumphant acclaim the half-barbaric emperor knew what they were doing. They had reason to rejoice. For nearly three centuries they had suffered under the Romans, and now at last there appeared an emperor who was not only prepared to protect the Church, to offer substantial donations to the bishops, and to defend orthodoxy against the heretics, but he was also prepared to claim that the victory which brought him to the throne was blessed by Christ who had granted him a special token of affection.

As Constantine told the story to Eusebius many years later, he was marching with his army one afternoon when he saw a Flaming Cross superimposed upon the sun, and there were the words: "By this conquer," written in Greek across the heavens. That night Christ appeared to the emperor in a vision or in a dream. Once more there were the Flaming Cross and the words written in Greek, but in addition he heard Christ commanding him to make the Flaming Cross his battle standard; and as he heard these words, and wondered what was meant by them, the thought came to him to exchange the Roman eagle for a standard bearing the sacred monogram ☧ forming the first letters of Christ's name in Greek. Constantine awoke and immediately ordered his metalsmiths to construct the Christian battle-standard, known as the *labarum*. The *chi-ro* was also engraved on the shields of his soldiers.

Many years later Constantine, who was on friendly terms with Eusebius, permitted the bishop to see the original *labarum*, then stored in the imperial treasury. It was a highly ornate and Christianized version of the Roman cavalry standard, consisting of a long gilded spear with a crossbar from which hung a square of purple cloth bearing the portraits of the emperor and his two sons. Above the crossbar there was a golden wreath set with jewels enclosing the sacred monogram. The general shape did not differ remarkably from the eagle, the *chi* forming the wings, the *ro* forming the body and the head. A special tent and guards were assigned to the imperial *labarum*, and the emperor would sometimes enter it and commune in secret with his mysterious treasure.

Many attempts were made to explain the vision of the Flaming Cross in broad daylight. It was suggested that Constantine saw the rare "halo phenomenon" which occurs when the sun's image is refracted through suspended ice crystals, and a shining cross is formed with the sun at the center. It is more difficult to explain the Greek words written across the heavens. Nevertheless there is no doubt that Constantine believed in his vision. From this moment he deflected the current of western history. Christianity, so long the religion of the poor and dispossessed, of those who held the state in abhorrence, regarding all kings and rulers as irrelevant tyrants owing their position to chance or unbridled force, became a state cult supported by military and bureaucratic power. The pale Galilean had conquered the Roman Empire at the point where it was outwardly strongest: the apex of power.

For Constantine himself the change of battle standards was perhaps less startling than it appears to us. The Roman army was even more tolerant of oriental religions than the Roman state, and the cult of Mithra, the Persian god of the heavenly light, champion of truth and justice, and resolute enemy of the dark forces of evil, was widespread among the Roman soldiers. Mithraism was a religion with a carefully worked out structure of legends and sacramental offices, with hierarchies of priests and solemn rites of initiation. It was rounded and complete, and had lost nothing of its vigor since it was first introduced into the Roman army by Cilician pirates captured by Pompey. In Constantine's eyes Mithraism and Christianity cannot have been very dissimilar.

The similarities between the two religions were often so close as to cause confusion between them. Mithraism involved an atoning sacrifice, a sacramental meal of bread and wine shared by the faithful, the ascension of the god, the resurrection of the flesh, the ultimate destruction of the world in a fiery deluge. It promised the gift of immortality and the redemption of sins through baptism. In Mithraism the infant god was worshiped by shepherds. The Flood, the Ark, the Fiery Chariot, the drawing of water from the rock, all those symbols which the Christians drew from the Old Testament and adapted to specifically Christian ideas, also had their place in Mithraic legend. The ringing of bells, the lighting of candles, the sprinkling of holy water were common to both religions. The followers of Mithra were devoted to the cardinal virtues of purity, loyalty, and obedience. Yet, though they both worshiped a god whom they identified with the unconquered sun, Christians and Mithraists differed in their understanding of the sun's nature. For the Mithraists the sun represented power in its ultimate manifestation, and for the Christians the sun was merely the ornament of Christ, who was more powerful than all the suns.

To the very end a curious heaviness weighed down the cult of Mithra. The central legend, depicted on countless Mithraic sculptures, involved the sacrifice of a bull by the youthful sun-god. The bull kneels, the sun-god plunges a dagger into the bull's throat, and the blood pours out, sometimes taking the form of grains of wheat. The sun-god wears a Persian dress, his gown billows in the heavenly winds, and he turns away from the dying bull as though he sees no reason to contemplate so earthy an object, since he belongs to heaven. From the bull's tail sprout more grains of wheat, a dog leaps to drink the blood, a scorpion gnaws at the bull's genitals, while a prophetic raven hovers overhead. This mythological scene was imitated during the Mithraic baptism when the initiate, crouching in a pit, was washed in the steaming blood of a freshly killed bull. The stench of blood hung heavily over Mithraism.

The intricate mind of Constantine delighted in theological problems, and he took pleasure in all religions. He lived in an otherworldly age when men were more than ever groping toward a sense of communion with the gods. They thirsted for assurance of immortality and salvation. In such an age the very earthiness of Mithraism was suspect, and Christianity answered more closely to men's needs. In Mithraism a garland of flowers, flung from the tip of a whirling sword and caught by the initiate, symbolized that he had received some portion of the power of *sol invictus*, the unconquered sun. Among the Christians a garland of flowers placed on a martyr's tomb symbolized that he had entered eternal life. In both religions the garlands represented a divine promise, a sacramental union with the supreme God of the universe. Yet these promises answered different needs, and the Christian need was the more compelling.

Having won the battle against Maxentius with the help of the *chiro*, Constantine showed himself to be an indifferent Christian. He wrote a number of letters which have been preserved by Eusebius granting protection and exemption from public duties to high officers of the Church, and restoring by imperial edict properties which had formerly belonged to the Church, but it would appear that very similar letters were addressed to the high priests of Mithraism. He continued to celebrate the pagan festivals, minted coins in honor of Hercules, Mars, and Jupiter, and to the end of his life represented himself on his coins wearing the spiked crown of *sol invictus*. Tolerant of all religions, he showed no marked partiality for Christianity. Eusebius tells the story of how Constantine erected a statue of himself in a public place in Rome, showing him with a cross in his right hand, and the inscription: "By this sign of salvation, the true testimony of valor, I saved your city and freed it from the yoke of the tyrant, and having freed the senate and people of Rome, I restored them to their ancient honor and glory." There is no reason to disbelieve the story, but there is every reason to believe that Constantine caused statues of himself to be erected in other public places wearing the Mithraic crown and the emblems of pagan gods. When his sister Constantina died, he built for her a mausoleum decorated with mosaics depicting Cupids wandering among vines, the harvesters returning home, brilliantly colored birds frolicking in the branches of trees. Nine hundred years later this small and exquisite mausoleum with its two circular ambulatories was transformed into a church, and the pagan Constantina was transformed into Santa Constanza. Today the visitor to the Church of Santa Constanza finds himself in an atmosphere as purely pagan as the Pantheon.

Under Constantine both Christianity and paganism triumphed. The new emperor attached great importance to the externals of religious conduct, insisting that all services should be conducted with propriety. A religion in his view should be tidy, with clear contours, and well-defined lines of command. He detested quarreling ecclesiastics, of whatever faith, and he was especially annoyed by the quarrels between the Christian sects. Shortly after his decision to transfer the capital to Constantinople, he summoned all the Christian bishops to attend a council at Nicaea, a small city in Bithynia. It was to become the most famous of all the church councils, and Constantine himself was to play the decisive role in its proceedings.

At this council, held in the early summer of A.D. 325, the Church and the empire met nakedly face to face. There had been councils before, but never before had any council possessed imperial authority; nor indeed had such authority been desired by a Church. "The Great and Holy Synod" held at Nicaea accomplished many things, and not the least important was that Caesar entered into alliance with the servants of Christ. The alliance endured under the Byzantine Empire for more than eleven hundred years.

By Constantine's orders messengers were sent to all parts of the empire with invitations to the bishops to attend. Each bishop was permitted to bring two presbyters and three slaves in his retinue, and the services of the public post stations were offered free. It was not a good time for traveling, for the rivers in the East were flooded with the rains of a late spring, and though the empire was nominally at peace, there were marauding soldiers and bandits along the roads. Less than two hundred bishops appear to have answered the summons, although figures of 250, 270, and 318 were given by contemporary authors. Only six bishops came from the West, and the bishop of Rome merely sent two presbyters to represent him. Yet the number of people who attended the Council may have amounted to nearly a thousand, for presbyters, deacons, subdeacons, and laymen crowded into the hall where the Council met.

From the East came bishops who had suffered persecution. There was Paul, bishop of Mesopotamian Caesarea, with his hands scorched by flames. Paphnutius of Upper Egypt, famous for the austerity of his life, had been blinded in his right eye during the Diocletian persecution, and the sinews had been cut in his left leg. Some bishops had traveled vast distances in order to be present. Theophilus the Goth had journeyed through what is now Southern Russia in order to be present, while John, Bishop of Persia and Metropolitan of India, had journeyed across burning deserts. Some of these visitors brought their own strangeness to the Council. Among them was a certain Bishop Spyridion, a saintly shepherd who refused to give up raising sheep when he was elevated to the episcopate. He came from Cyprus, and it was remembered that he pleased the Cypriots by performing miracles and to their further delight he thundered against virginity. In Bishop Spyridion's opinion married couples should enjoy themselves in their beds.

This motley crowd of bishops represented all the varying traditions of Christianity. Among them were sharp-featured intellectuals, men of abstruse book learning who were capable of splitting hairs by the yard, but there were also old hermits who spent their days clothed in goatskins and living on roots and berries. There were men so saintly that it was almost expected of them that they would perform miracles during the Council. There were also cantankerous men riddled with heresy, and others who rode to Nicaea only in the hope of preferment from the hands of the emperor. Some came peacefully, intending only to observe and then report to their flock, and others came determined to wage war on the Council itself. Yet in the last instance none of the bishops except Hosius of Cordova, the friend and adviser of the emperor, had any great and final influence on the deliberations. The two chief antagonists were Arius and Athanasius, one a presbyter, the other a deacon. In theory they came to the Council to put an end to the heresies which were splitting the Christian Church apart; in fact the warring factions were at each others' throats.

Arius and Athanasius were men of mettle, determined not to withdraw from their fixed positions. Arius was over sixty, with the emaciated appearance of a martyr who had suffered all the agonies of martyrdom except the last. He was tall and lean, and spoke fierily, so fierily indeed that his name was sometimes linked with Ares, the Greek god of war. His matted hair, his ghastly pallor, and his great height attracted attention. His opponent, the deacon Athanasius, was a puny dark-faced man who could be savage when provoked but was more inclined to laugh his enemies away. His eyes were unusually bright, and when he was excited his face would take on an angelic look. Presbyter and deacon were well matched.

Although four fragmentary accounts of the Council have been handed down by eyewitnesses, and there are eight more accounts written by historians of the generation immediately following Nicaea, we do not know exactly where the Council took place, whether it was in a building specially erected for the purpose or in one of the imperial palaces. Tradition points to a site on the edge of the lake, suggesting perhaps the presence of Galilee. In the center of the hall was a throne on which an ornamented copy of the Gospels was placed. At the far end was another throne for the emperor, carved in wood, richly gilt, and set above the level of the unpainted thrones of the bishops. In this hall, early in the morning of Ascension Sunday, the bishops awaited the arrival of the emperor.

Few of the bishops had set eyes upon the emperor who had singlehandedly raised himself to a position of supreme power. They waited expectantly, and soon an avant-courier was seen raising a torch, the signal that the emperor was on his way. Human majesty in the person of the fifty-year-old Constantinus Victor Augustus Maximus was about to appear, and in the history of the world only the Emperor Augustus, who ruled the Roman Empire during the early life of Christ, had been the master of so vast an empire.

Constantine wore high-heeled scarlet buskins, a purple robe blazing with jewels and gold embroidery, and there were more jewels embedded in his tiara. With his high color and the strange glitter of his fierce, lion-like eyes, his long hair falling to his shoulders, his beard cut short, he was a commanding presence who inspired fear and awe. The Christian commentators are inclined to depict him as a man who was himself inspired with awe as he surveyed the congregation of bishops, and the ecclesiastical historian Theodoret describes how the emperor sat on a low footstool in the middle of the assembly, having first asked the bishops for permission to sit down. There is nothing in the recorded actions and utterances of Contantine to suggest that he acted with humility toward any man. It is unlikely that he sat on a low footstool, and equally unlikely that he would ask the permission of the bishops. He was the master of the Council, and he knew it.

Bishop Eusebius of Caesarea was the first to speak his welcome to the emperor, and this speech was followed by a chanted hymn of thanksgiving for the emperor's victories. Then the emperor spoke, very gravely, in a voice which seemed strangely soft and gentle for a man so commanding, bidding the bishops remember that it was the power of God which brought about the fall of tyrants, and worse than any battlefield was a civil war between factions of the Church.

"It is my desire," he said, "that you should meet together in a General Council, and so I offer to the King of All my gratitude for this mercy which exceeds all the other mercies granted to me—I mean the grace of seeing you assembled together, and the knowledge that you are resolved to be in complete harmony."

But this was flattery, for the very purpose of the convocation was to resolve a bitter conflict, and Constantine knew well enough from the petitions he had received from the bishops that they were in a bitter mood.

He continued: "When I gained my victories over my enemies, I thought nothing remained for me but to give thanks unto God and to rejoice with those who have been delivered by me. But when I learned, contrary to all expectations, that there were divisions among you, then I solemnly considered them, and praying that these discords might also be healed with my assistance, I summoned you here without delay. I rejoice to see you here, yet I should be more pleased to see unity and affection among you. I entreat you, therefore, beloved ministers of God, to remove the causes of dissension among you and to establish peace."

What Constantine wanted to do with his bishops was exactly what he had done with his empire: he had established his own peace among his subjects and he was determined to establish it among his bishops. There was no mistaking the threat behind his words, and as though to make his threat more clear, he summoned one of his attendants and silently produced the parchment rolls and letters containing complaints and petitions written by the bishops. A brazier was set up, and the emperor tossed them into the flames. While they were still burning, he explained that these petitions would no doubt be revealed on the Day of Judgment, and then the dreaded Judge of the Universe would pass judgment on them; for himself, he was content to listen to their public deliberations, setting aside their secret protestations.

The conference was now open, and at once it became evident

that the Arians, the followers of Arius, and the orthodox were at each others' throats. Denunciations and angry accusations flew across the hall. Everyone was suddenly arguing. "It was like a battle in the dark," wrote the historian Socrates. "Hardly anyone seemed to know the grounds on which they calumniated one another." Constantine did his best to restore order. Regarding himself as the presiding judge empowered to intervene in all the debates, he rebuked those who spoke too angrily and sternly silenced those whose arguments seemed to him fallacious. Arius, who believed that the Son was subordinate to the Father, declared his faith in a hymn that he sang to the assembled bishops. It was a long hymn, but the essence of it was contained in the words:

> *The Son is not equal to the Father,*
> *Nor does He share the same substance.*
> *God is the all-wise Father,*
> *And the Son is the teacher of His mysteries.*

By relegating the Son to an inferior position in the economy of heaven, Arius was maintaining a belief widely held in eastern countries, particularly in Egypt. To the orthodox, the statement that the Son was not equal to the Father implied that he was lesser than the Father, and there must have been a time when the Son was nonexistent. The statement that he did not share the same substance implied that he was of some lesser substance, less potent, and therefore flawed. This was also the view of the Arians, who saw no harm in the Son being born to an all-powerful God and living in God's shadow. They would admit that the Son was similar to God, but not that he was God's equal, and since the Greek words for *similar* and *equal* (*homoiousios* and *homoousios*) differed only by an *iota*, the battle raged around a single letter of the alphabet. Attempts to satisfy the Arians failed, and the final Creed took the form of a triumphant statement of the orthodox position. Arius was dismissed from the assembly and the Arians were anathematized.

The Nicene Creed left much to be desired. The language was tortured, repetitive, without poetry or rhythm, and curiously disorganized. It was a hammer blow directed at a powerful adversary, who was forced to withdraw from the battle because the weight of imperial authority was against him. Constantine himself took part in drawing up the Creed, his subtle mind delighting in the complexities of the faith and the Byzantine intricacies of their statement. The version authorized by Constantine read:

We believe in one God, the Father Almighty, maker of all things visible and invisible.

And in one Lord Jesus Christ, the Son of God, begotten of the Father, only-begotten, that is, from the substance of the Father, God from God, Light from Light, very God from very God, begotten not made, from the same substance as the Father, through whom all things were made, both things in Heaven and things on earth; who for us men, and for our salvation, came down and was made flesh, was made man, suffered and rose again the third day, ascended into Heaven, and shall come to judge the quick and the dead.

And in the Holy Ghost.

And those who say "There was a time when He was not" and "He did not exist before He was made" and "He was made out of nothing" or those who pretend that the Son of God is "of other hypostasis or substance" or "created" or "alterable" or "mutable," the Catholic Church anathematizes.

Such was the Nicene Creed as approved by the emperor in council, a weapon forged on abstractions, possessing little merit except the merit of keeping the Arians at bay. Fifty-six years later, at the Council of Constantinople, the assembled bishops, dissatisfied with so many abstractions, fleshed out the Creed with their own more enduring version; and at last the Creed assumed its familiar poetic shape:

We believe in one God, the Father Almighty, maker of all things visible and invisible.

And in one Lord Jesus Christ, the only-begotten Son of God, begotten of the Father before all worlds, Light from Light, very God from very God, begotten not made, being of one substance with the Father, through whom all things were made; who for us men and for our salvation came down from the heavens and was made flesh of the Holy Ghost and the Virgin Mary, and was made man, and was crucified for us under Pontius Pilate, and suffered and was buried, and rose again on the third day according to the Scriptures, and went up into the heavens, and sits on the right hand of the Father, and is to come again with glory to judge the quick and the dead, and of His Kingdom there shall be no end.

In this way by the slow processes of trial and error there came into existence a summary of the faith more memorable and more colorful than the original version issued under imperial authority.

Almost to the end Constantine remained the eclectic philosopher, devoted to the worship of the unconquered sun, whom he identified with God the Father, the power of powers; he paid homage not to Christ, but to the all-powerful Father.

When he was dying, shortly after Easter, A.D. 337, he seems to have decided that there were advantages in accepting the faith he had protected, and he put aside the purple cloak of an emperor and wore the white robe of a catechumen and prepared for a holy death. If we can trust the chroniclers, he spoke of his desire to receive baptism in the River Jordan and promised that if his life were spared he would make a pilgrimage to the holy places. His life was not spared, and he died quietly in the faith.

Nevertheless he was not a Christian in his life, and he was wholly lacking in the Christian virtues. A man of raw energy and courage, harsh, unforgiving, terrible in his wrath, sweet-tempered only when sweet temper was to his own advantage, he stands at the opening of the ways. A new dispensation of time came into existence. With him the thousand-year history to pagan Rome comes to end, and the Church was henceforth to be sanctioned by emperors and caesars.

The story was told that when Helena, the mother of Constantine, found the true Cross and the holy nails, she presented one of the nails to her son. For a long time he did not know what to do with it. Then at last he decided to erect in Constantinople, his new capital, an equestrian statue of himself. The holy nail became the bit between the horse's teeth.

8 ✙ THE EARLY SONGS

SCHOLARS have shown that many of the sayings of Jesus when translated from Greek into Aramaic fall into rhyme. The Beatitudes are verses, little songs meant to be sung or chanted, and therefore all the more memorable. The Lord's Prayer is a song, and so is "Consider the lilies of the field." There are perhaps fifty songs in the four Gospels, and it is one of the greater merits of the King James version of the New Testament that it preserves, however faintly, the voice of song.

The rich and heavily guttural Aramaic spoken in Galilee was admirably suited for these short and forceful lyrics, which have the effect of incantations glowing with energy. Lyrical poetry often takes the form of impetuous command, and the tone of command is rarely absent from these Galilean lyrics. The translation of Semitic languages into modern European languages usually involves a lightening of the texture, a weakening of heavy fiber; we lose the harsher sounds from the back of the throat and the roll of thunder. Here for example are four verses of the Beatitudes as they were originally spoken by the lakeside, with the accented syllables in italics:

> *Tube*hon *misk*nayya
> *dedile*hon *malkuta* dismayya.
>
> *Tube*hon *demitabbe*lin
> *dehin*nun mit*nahha*min.
>
> *Tube*hon *inwa*nayya
> *dehin*nun *yeretun* leara.

Tubehon dekaphenin wesahayin
dehinnun mitmelayin.

Blessed are the poor in spirit:
for theirs is the kingdom of heaven.

Blessed are they that mourn:
for they shall be comforted.

Blessed are the meek:
for they shall inherit the earth.

Blessed are they that hunger and thirst after righteousness:
for they shall be filled.

The Aramaic thunder has gone; the English words are muted. With us the words are delicate, hinting at unfulfilled aspirations. In the original they come with heavy hammer beats, and we hear the sound of ringing metal.

At the heart of the Christian mystery there were always songs. Christ spoke in song, and the early Christians followed his example. We find St. Ignatius writing about A.D. 107: "When you have formed yourselves into a choir, you may sing praises to the Father through Jesus Christ." At about the same time Pliny the Younger wrote to the Emperor Trajan about the strange behavior of the Christians in Bithynia in northern Asia Minor, saying that "they were accustomed to assemble on a fixed day before daylight and sing by turns a hymn to Christ as a god." He did not record what songs they sang, but there appears to have been a considerable body of hymns even in apostolic times. These early hymns affirmed the glory and power of Jesus, and his Coming. An early hymn attributed to St. James describes the fearful silence that descends upon the earth just before the angelic hosts appear in the heavens in the company of Christ. Here and there we find the remembered fragments of hymns in the letters of St. Paul. Some twenty fragments of hymns and songs appear in his letters. Mostly these verses are concerned with the power of love, or they celebrate the divine glory:

> *Who is the blessed and only Potentate,*
> *The King of kings, and Lord of lords;*

Who only hath immortality,
Dwelling in the light which no man can approach unto;
Whom no man hath seen, nor can see;
To whom be honor and power everlasting.

(I Timothy 6:15)

Like Jesus, Paul was a poet who could fall into cadenced verse in the middle of a sermon. Jesus spoke in Aramaic and was familiar with the *koine*, the simplified Greek which had become the common language in the lands conquered by Alexander the Great. Paul, raised in Tarsus, spoke a Greek saturated with Jewish turns of phrase and Jewish feeling; his prose has the clarity of Greek and the vigorous complexity of Hebrew. The very vigor of his prose sometimes sends it spinning into poetry. So Paul sings his hymn of love:

Though I speak with the tongues of men and of angels,
And have not love
I am become as sounding brass
Or a tinkling cymbal.

And though I have the gift of prophecy,
And understand all mysteries and all knowledge,
And though I have all faith,
So that I could remove mountains,
And have not love,
I am nothing.

And though I bestow all my goods to feed the poor,
And though I give my body to be burned,
And have not love,
It profiteth me nothing.

Love suffereth long, and is kind;
Love envieth not;
Love vaunteth not itself,
Is not puffed up,
Doth not behave itself unseemly,
Seeketh not her own,
Is not easily provoked,
Thinketh no evil,

Rejoiceth not in iniquity,
But rejoiceth in the truth,
Beareth all things,
Believeth all things,
Hopeth all things,
Endureth all things.

Love never faileth.
But whether there be prophecies, they shall fail;
Whether there be tongues, they shall cease;
Whether there be knowledge, it shall vanish away.
For we know in part,
And we prophesy in part:
But when that which is perfect is come,
Then that which is in part shall be done away.

When I was a child,
I spake as a child,
I understood as a child,
I thought as a child,
But when I became a man
I put away childish things.

But now we see through a glass, darkly,
But then face to face:
Now I know in part,
But then shall I know
Even as I also am known.

And now abideth faith, hope, love,
These three,
But the greatest of these is love.

(I Corinthians 13)

Though the hymn has a deceptively simple air, it is in fact astonishingly complex. Many different themes are interwoven in it. He
makes a voyage around the idea of Christian love, examines it, declares what it accomplishes and what it fails to accomplish, and
confronts love with the ancient mysteries and the more recent mysteries of the Christians. Love reigns supreme, for love alone can shatter

the partial world in which we live and bring about the total world of Christ.

Though the name of Christ is never mentioned in the hymn, Christ is all the more present. When Paul speaks of himself as a child who has put away childish things, he is speaking of the time before he "assumed the body of Christ." For him, love is a state of holiness and power.

Henceforward it was to become the central theme of the Church, to be endlessly celebrated.

We are so accustomed to the sound of these words that we no longer realize how surprising they must have been to the Corinthians. Such joyous love with its intimations of immortality had sources deep in Greek thought and poetry, but no one had ever expressed so simply or so passionately the supremacy of love over all the other articles of Christian faith. It was as though in the mind of Paul the whole of Christ could be included within a single word.

Of the many hymns that were sung in the early Church scarcely any have survived except those which appear in Paul's epistles. Some fifty years after Paul's death, an unknown author availing himself of the reminiscences of the Beloved Disciple wrote the *Gospel according to St. John*, where for the first time in Christian literature we come upon an antiphonal hymn where the priest chants one line that is answered with a response from the faithful, and the process is repeated until the end of the hymn:

> *In the beginning was the Word,*
>   And the Word was with God.
> *The Word was God,*
>   Who was in the beginning with God.
> *All things were made by him,*
>   And nothing made was made without him.
> *Whose being was Life,*
>   And Life was the light of men.
> *The light shineth in darkness,*
>   And the darkness comprehended it not.
> *This was the true light*
>   That lighteth all who cometh into the world.
> *He was in the world, and the world was made by him,*
>   And the world knew him not.
> *He came unto his own,*

And his own received him not.
The Word was made flesh and dwelt among us,
    And we beheld his glory.
Glory as of the Only-begotten of the Father,
    Full of grace and truth.
For of his bounty have we all received,
    Grace added to grace.
For the Law was given by Moses,
    But grace and truth came by Jesus Christ.

This hymn, which forms the prologue to the Gospel, may very well have been composed by St. John at Ephesus, where he is said to have lived to a great age, dying in the reign of the Emperor Trajan. We know that the Christians were singing antiphonal hymns, for Pliny mentions them in his letter to the emperor. Already we are far from the simple songs of the early Christians. The poet looks to the past, to the glory once beheld and the light that shone long ago. In the beginning was the Word. But nothing is said about the end of the world; there is no hint of the Second Coming. It is as though already the hope of the Second Coming were beginning to fade. The hymn glorifies the Word, the Gnostic abstraction of the living Jesus. In an earlier age the voice was more urgent:

> *Awake thou that sleepest*
> *And arise from the dead,*
> *And Christ shall give thee light.*
>
> (*Ephesians* 5:14)

These brief verses embedded in Paul's epistle to the Ephesians speak of a fiercer hope and a more commanding faith. Here there is no looking back; the time is now.

Nevertheless the Word remained. The authority of the *Gospel according to St. John* was so great that it could sustain the weight of Gnosticism. In time the Word would seek to descend from the abstract world and put on flesh, so that we find Christ saying in the apocryphal *Acts of John:* "In me is the piercing of the Word, the blood of the Word, the wound of the Word, the passion of the Word, the nailing of the Word, the death of the Word." But always among the Gnostic sects which embraced Christianity there is the sense of a ghostly, unreal Jesus who has in some mysterious way separated himself from his manhood. The Gnostics were aware that they were on dangerous ground, and the *Acts of John* attempts to reverse the process by making Christ say: "Think first of the Word, and then thou shalt perceive the Lord, and afterward thou shalt perceive the man, and what he suffered." But for the ordinary Christian it must always have been difficult to contemplate suffering through an abstraction.

The *Acts of John* were written about A.D. 140, when the traditions about the life of Jesus were still current. This strange and beautiful work was known to the Fathers, who sometimes quoted from it. At the second Council of Nicaea, held in A.D. 787, the Iconoclasts appealed to it; portions of the *Acts* were read aloud, and it was judged to be heretical because it describes Jesus as wholly spiritual, so that when John touched Jesus he was aware of no physical presence. This heresy, know as Docetism, was to survive in various forms for many centuries.

Among the fragments of the *Acts of John* known to St. Augustine was a hymn said to have been composed by Jesus before the Passion. "Before I am delivered up," Jesus said, "let us sing a hymn to the Father, and then go forth for whatever awaits us." Then he told them to hold hands and form a ring, and he stood in the middle of the ring and began to sing:

> *Glory to Thee, Father!*
> *Glory to Thee, Word!*
> *Glory to Thee, Grace!*
> *Glory to Thee, Holy Spirit!*
>
> *Glory to Thy Glory!*
> *We praise Thee, O Father!*
> *We give thanks to Thee, O shadowless Light!*
>
> *I would be saved, and I would save.*
> *I would be loosed, and I would loose.*
> *I would be pierced, and I would pierce.*
> *I would be born, and I would give birth.*
>
> *I would eat, and I would be eaten.*
> *I would hearken, and I would be heard.*
> *I would be wise, and I would grant wisdom.*

I would be cleansed, and I would cleanse.
Grace is dancing!

I would pipe, and all must dance!
I would lament, and all must lament!
The Heavenly Spheres make music for us!
The Holy Twelve join the dance!
All things are dancing!
Ye who dance not have no knowledge of wisdom!

I would flee, and I would stay!
I would give garlands, and I would be garlanded!
I would be united, and I would unite!
I have no dwelling, but I have mansions!
I have no resting-place, but I have the whole earth.
I have no temple, but I have the whole of Heaven.

I am the lamp to thee that beholdest me.
I am the mirror to thee that perceivest me.
I am a door for whoever knocks.
I am the Way for the wayfarer.

(Acts of John, 95)

The exuberance of the hymn survived its translation from Greek into Latin, and we have the Latin text that passed into St. Augustine's hands with a letter from an eastern bishop suggesting that he should write a commentary on it. St. Augustine replied by saying that the doctrinal truths contained in the hymn were better expressed in the canonical writings. He saw no reason to enter into a discussion on the Gnostic influence on Johannine mysticism. Yet the hymn cannot be disregarded, for it reflects preoccupations and attitudes that were common among Christians of the eastern Mediterranean. The sacred dance derived from origins more ancient than the mystery religions, and to this day some trace of the dance remains in the Mass.

The Greek and Hebrew bridal hymns also colored the hymns of the early Church, for the bride represented the adornments of virtue, or the devout Christian, or the Church itself, while the bridegroom represented Christ or the Coming of the Kingdom. The iconography of the soul's marriage with God, beloved by the medieval mystics, has a long ancestry going back to Sumerian times, but its ancient origins do not detract from the immediate splendor. The bridal hymn in the apocryphal *Acts of Thomas* survives in Greek and Syriac versions, but appears to have been sung originally in Hebrew:

My bride is the daughter of light,
On whom rests the majesty of Kings.
Proud and charming is her countenance,
Adorned with a pure grace and beauty.
Her garments are like flowers of spring,
And have a sweet and pleasant fragrance.
On the crown of her head the King is enthroned,
Nourishing with nectar those who live beneath him.
Truth is enthroned on her head,
And joy is stirred up in her feet.
Her mouth is open, and becomingly
Does she sing her hymns of praise.
Thirty-two attendants glorify her.
Her tongue is the door-curtain
Drawn back for those who enter.
Her neck is a stairway
Built by the first Creator.
Her two hands prophecy the choir of the blessed ages,
And her fingers are as the gates of the city.
Her bridal chamber is full of light,
Pouring forth the scent of balsam and unguents,
Sending forth the perfumes of myrrh
And all manner of sweet-smelling flowers.
The gates are adorned with calamus.
Her groomsmen attend her,
Seven in number, invited by her,
And seven bridesmaids attend her,
Leading her in the dance.
Twelve are those who minister to her,
Attending to her demands,
All gazing attentively at the Bridegroom
That they may be illumined by His glory
And with him attain the Eternal Kingdom,
Taking part in the Eternal Wedding Feast
To which all the righteous shall come,
And attain to the bliss

Into which they singly will enter,
That they may put on the garment of light
And be clothed with the glory of their Lord,
And praise the living Father
Because they have received the glory of the light
And have been illumined by the Lord's brightness,
And have received His nectar
Whose abundance never fails,
And have drunk also from His wine
Wherefore they neither crave nor thirst.
Praise the Father the Lord and the Only Begotten Son
And give thanks to the Spirit in His wisdom.

(Acts of Thomas, 6)

Such passionate hymns conceal the arid complexities of the Gnostics, who dwelt at great length on the virtues of numbers. No doubt the seven bridesmaids are the seven planets, and the twelve ministrants are the months; the dancers no longer revolve around Jesus, but around the sun who is Christ enthroned. No doubt, too, the passion derives from remembered fragments of the *Song of Solomon*. But what is unmistakable is the fusion between the ancient celestial mythologies and the contemporary feeling for the Second Coming. The long hymn embroiders on the single word: *Maranatha* (Our Lord, come).

The *Acts of Thomas* is one of the more extraordinary documents of early Christianity, for the purest fantasy is combined with careful explanations of ritual. Thomas's wanderings in India take the form of a fairy tale for children, full of mysterious adventures with dragons and beautiful women and prophetic dreams: the dragons brandish their tails, die atrociously, and great chasms appear at the place of their deaths; the women possess an impossible beauty; and all the dreams come true. At intervals the unknown narrator will break away from the fairy tale and describe a Christian ceremony as though he had only that moment left the church, or he will sing a long poem out of context for no better reason than that it appealed to him. Three times altogether he sings a hymn of *Maranatha*. At the midnight baptism of King Gundafor of India, Thomas sings:

Come, holy name of Christ,
Come, power of the Most High and perfect compassion,
Come, greatest of gifts,

Come, communion of blessing,
Come, revealer of mysteries,
Come, Mother of the seven houses, which has found rest in the eighth
*   house,*
Come, thou messenger of reconciliation,
Speak with these young ones!

(Acts of Thomas, 27)

In this way the baptism of the king was accomplished, "and when the dawn came, they broke the bread and were partakers of the eucharist of the Messiah, and rejoiced, and exulted."

This exaltation, this sense of the youthfulness of the worshipers who are "made young in Christ," recurs repeatedly in the early hymns. A third century fragment from the Amherst papyrus resembles a sudden joyful shout:

Tell the glad tidings unto children:
Tell them the poor have received the Kingdom:
The children are the inheritors.

Soon enough these sudden joyful cries were to be exchanged for formal hymns. Soon the scholars and bishops were to impose order and authority on a childlike faith; the formal ode would replace the triumphant cry. Instead of the *Maranatha*, there came the recital of Christ's titles in elegant versifications which are moving only because they retain, embedded within them, a sense of wonder and awe. The childlike faith was not forgotten. The first of the great formal hymns, composed by the scholarly Clement of Alexandria, recites the titles at length while remembering the holy children:

O bridle of colts untamed,
Wing of the hovering birds,
Steady helm of the ships,
Shepherd of royal lambs,
Gather thy chaste children
So they may sweetly sing
From holy and innocent lips
Christ the Protector of children.

O King of the holy saints,
All-conquering Word

Of the Most High Father,
Thou who art Prince of Wisdom
And Comforter of Sorrows,
Ever rejoicing Jesu,
Saviour of the human race,
Our Shepherd and Husbandman.

O Helm, Bridle, Heavenly Wing,
Soaring over the holy flock,
Fisher of those who are saved,
Luring with sweetest life
Pure fish from the evil sea,
Lead us, O holy King,
O Shepherd, guide thy sheep,
Thy sheep who belong to the world.

Lead thy innocent children
In the footsteps of Christ
Along the way to Heaven,
There for immeasurable ages
To bathe in eternal light
Amid fountains of mercy,
With thy eternal work
Following the paths of virtue.

O God of the hymn-singers,
The heavenly milk is pressed
Out of the bride's sweet breast:
Babes with their tender mouths
Are nourished by the virtue
Of the early dew
Flowing from the breast of the Word:
So let us sing simple hymns!

All honor to Christ the King!
In holy fee for his teaching
Let us sing in simplicity
Praise of the mighty child.
May the chaste children of Christ

Sing in the peaceful choirs,
Uttering with candid voice
Hymns to the God of Peace.

Clement's hymn reeks of the lamp. It is lyrical, but also formal. Christ is addressed with a list of titles arranged in proper order. He is the Helm, the Bridle, the Wing, the Fish, the Comforter, the Shepherd, and more titles are added as the occasion demands. The nervous, springing rhythm of the early songs gives place to the formal and contrived meter of the official ode. It is no longer the voice of a child crying out his joy, but the grave and detached voice of the scholar.

We see the same process at work on the epitaph of Abercius, Bishop of Hieropolis, which he wrote about A.D. 150. It was known from a fourth century text, and for many years was thought to be spurious because it spoke in such mysterious tones of strange journeys and nothing like it had ever been seen before. In 1883 Sir William Ramsay, traveling in Phrygia, discovered the original gravestone, which was then offered by the Sultan of Turkey to the pope. The stone, which is now in the Lateran Museum in Rome, is written in an archaic poetical language:

I am Abercius, disciple of the Holy Shepherd,
He who watches with all-encompassing eyes
And feeds his flock on the mountains and valleys,
Who taught me the true alphabet of life
And sent me to Rome to gaze upon the Kingdom,
Where the queen appeared to me in her gold robe and sandals.
There I saw the people possessing the splendid Sign,
And I wandered through the cities and fields of Syria,
And Nisibis also beyond the Euphrates,
And everywhere the companions welcomed me.
I followed Paul. Faith led the way.
They bade me eat the pure and mighty Fish
Out of the fountain. This was the Fish
Which a blameless Virgin took into her hands,
Offering it as eternal food for the brethren;
There was wine also, mingled with water, and bread.
While I stand here, these words were dictated
By me, Abercius, so that they may be written down,
When I was in the seventy-second summer of my age.

May every believer who understands these things
Pray for Abercius and those who share his faith.

The accent is formal, and never quite rises into poetry. Yet somehow Abercius suggests a whole life of devotion, a firm faith, and a delight in the mysteries of Christ. He is not hidebound by tradition, but says directly what is on his mind.

The great hymns came later, following the literary revival of the fourth century when the metallic Latin of the imperial age was hammered into a new shape, and Greek in the hands of the eastern Fathers began to sing more melodiously than ever. Augustine related how the first hymns arose in the West during the time when Ambrose of Milan was under the ban of the Empress Justina and the faithful gathered around the church to protect him. "Then," says Augustine, "it was first appointed that hymns and psalms should be sung after the manner of the eastern churches, lest the people should grow weary and faint through sorrow; and this custom has ever since been retained, and has been followed by almost all congregations elsewhere." In moments of crisis Augustine would find himself singing the hymns of Ambrose, and he especially delighted in the hymn, *Deus creator omnium*, which he sang to himself soon after his mother's death:

> *Creator of all that is,*
> *Ruler of starry spaces,*
> *Clothing the day with robes of light,*
> *Blessing with gracious sleep the night,*
>
> *That quiet may comfort weary men*
> *To face their useful toil again,*
> *And soothe awhile the harassed mind*
> *And sorrow's heavy load unbind.*

The hymns of Ambrose were nearly always equally simple; there are no glittering flashes, no attempts at grandiloquence. Written in iambic dimeters without rhyme, they resemble ancient inscriptions carved on marble with a simplicity more Greek than Roman. Told that his enemies were complaining against the enchantment of his verses, he answered: "I do not deny that these songs are incantations, and very potent. What could be more potent than a confession of the Trinity which is now pouring forth daily from the lips of people? In this way all are made teachers, where previously there were only learners."

The hymns of Ambrose moved with a kind of light solemnity, and were never overburdened with intricate theology. They were sensuous and passionate; he wrote them so easily that he would have been surprised to discover how long they have endured. The best of them, *Aeterne rerum conditor* and *Splendor paternae gloriae*, and many others, are still being sung.

No hymns came from Augustine. He was too busy hammering out his prose to give vent to song. Only once did he include a verse of his own composition in his writings:

> *Haec tua sunt, bona sunt, quia tu bonus ista creasti.*
> *Nil nostrum est in eis, nisi quod peccamus amantes,*
> *Ordine neglecto, pro te quod conditor abs te.*

> *There are thine, they are good, because Thou has made*
>   *them good.*
> *Ours is the sin, the degrading disorder which arises*
> *By loving them more than we love Thee, who created them.*

It is not verse of a very high quality, and he seems never to have attempted verse seriously; nor did he have any need to write verses, since there was so much poetry in his prose. The mainstream of Christian verse was fed by the Spanish poet Prudentius, who wrote hymns for all hours of the day in a remarkable profusion. They are simple and sweet-tempered, not unlike the verses of Ambrose, and he wrote them just as easily. The tragic fire is absent. It is absent, too, in the prodigious epic called the *Psychomachia*, which became the most popular of his writings and was quoted and requoted throughout the Middle Ages. Here the Christian virtues fought the pagan vices, winning their immense battles too easily for comfort.

With Venantius Fortunatus, for the first time we hear the deep organ note, the storm overhead:

> *Vexilla regis prodeunt,*
> *Fulget crucis mysterium,*
> *Quo carne carnis conditor*
> *Suspensus est patibulo . . . .*

The King's advancing banners wave:
The Cross gleams out its Mystery,
Where He who made the body gave
His body to the gallows-tree.

With savage nails His flesh was torn,
And torn His outstretched feet and hands:
For our salvation was He born;
His sacrifice perfected stands.

The dreadful spear which pierced His side,
As He upon the gallows lay,
Let loose the bloody tide
Which washes all our sins away.

Now is the truth fulfilled
Which David sang in prophecy
To all the nations of the world:
"God reigneth from a tree."

This lovely and light-bearing tree
Wears a royal purple dress,
Wherefore He chose it worthily
As setting for His holiness.

O blessed Tree, the ages lay
In ransom on the holy Cross,
And took from Hell its natural prey
And weighed the profit and the loss.

Around Thee now sweet spices pour,
Surpassing nectar's sweetest scents.
Rejoicing in their saving odor,
Thou dost applaud magnificence.

Altar and victim, sweet felicity!
O glorious was thy utmost pain!
Life endured its death in thee,
And life in death is made our gain.

As well as anyone Fortunatus could write the limpid verses expected of Christian poets, and indeed there are whole stanzas of the *Vexilla regis prodeunt* that are unworthy of its great beginning. The poem was composed to celebrate the coming of a fragment of the Holy Cross to Poitiers, and five hundred years later it became the marching song of the Crusaders.

Gravity, decorum, kindliness were the marks of early Christian poetry, but with Fortunatus a new element emerges. Henceforward it would be the task of the Christian poets to convey the energy, terror, and wonder of the faith.

9 ✛ ST. AUGUSTINE

THE SAINT with the august name comes to us across the centuries with a peculiarly modern mind. He is all fire and intricacy; he is concerned as much with the soul's enigmas as with the splendor of God. The most wanton of the saints, the man with the clearest mind, the most exalted opinion of himself, the subtlest knowledge of himself, he speaks directly to our own age. He has no patience with miracles: it is enough that there should be the miracle of the divine Saviour. He has little patience with the opinions of others; he must hammer everything out on the anvil of his own mind. His contemporaries were Ambrose, Jerome, Chrysostom, Basil, Gregory of Nyssa, and Gregory of Nazianzus, but he was as clearly their intellectual superior as he was their inferior in humility. He was a world in himself, the greatest of all the Fathers of the Church.

Augustine belongs to the times of crisis, when men's minds go wheeling after final purposes and dreadful certainties. He burns himself up with the fury to know all things, to determine all things. He speaks a language we know only too well, and if we set him beside Marcel Proust or Dostoyevsky, they would talk together as equals. Like the great modern psychological novelists he is armed with a scalpel and is prepared to knife the soul until it reveals its secrets. "Where is it?" he proclaims. "Where is the heart of the mystery?" He performs the surgical operation with ferocious self-control, his hands steady. Where is God? Why is there evil in men's hearts? What is love? Why do the stars go round? How did the angels fall? Where wast thou in the morning of the world? The words "why" and "how" were never far from his lips. He was continually asking questions and testing them against his knowledge and experience, and he found—he was never absolutely certain what he found: himself and God, a world almost too beautiful to contemplate, an uneasy alliance between the soul and blessedness. Of all the Fathers he was the only one who wrote his confessions, a justification and defense of his own earthly life.

There are no authentic portraits made in his lifetime, nor is there any fixed iconographical tradition. A manuscript painting made not long after his death shows him as a squat, black-bearded, dark-skinned man who seems to be uncomfortable in his halo. Botticelli's famous portrait in the Ognissanti church in Florence, where he sits in contemplation beside an astrolobe and a volume open at the theorems of Pythagoras, shows him in old age with a grizzled beard, a cruel mouth, a look of intense absorption. Botticelli gives him a low forehead and enormous hands, as though to emphasize the peasant in him, and piercing eyes looking up through shaggy eyebrows to emphasize his spirituality. It is not a calm face: almost as we watch we can see the quick thoughts passing in succession across his features. Botticelli had read deeply, and what he painted was the nervous, restless man of the *Confessions*, curious about all things and always dissatisfied with easy answers. "Our hearts are restless till they rest in Him," Augustine once wrote, and even in his most fervent and prayerful writings restlessness remains.

He was born on Sunday, November 13, 354, in the town of Thagaste in the Roman province of Numidia in what is now Algeria. It was a pleasant town with high white walls, set among wooded fields of ilex and pine. Lions roamed in the forests, while boar, hare, redwing, and quail were to be hunted a stone's throw from the city walls. The Roman town boasted a theater, a forum, baths, long marble colonnades, a great market place. Among the wealthy patricians who ruled over the destiny of the town was a certain Patricius, a senator and landowner. He was a pagan, happily married to a Christian. Patricius was stern and commanding, Monnica was gentle and withdrawing. Patricius was never quite reconciled to having Augustine as a son.

There were good reasons for this: the boy combined the characteristics of his father and mother. He could be sweet-tempered, but he was also given to ungovernable rages. Like Luther he was beaten at school and seems never to have forgotten his stripes, feeling them all

the more painfully when his parents merely laughed at them and refused to console him. Patricius, the stern old member of "the very
splendid council of Thagaste" (*splendidissimus ordo Thagastensis*),
possessing all the privileges of the minor nobility, desired above
everything that Augustine should become a rich lawyer. Beyond this
he had little interest in the child, allowing the boy to do as he pleased
and caring nothing about his morals, and when much later Augustine
drew up the balance sheet of his father's behavior, the greatest crime
of Patricius was precisely that he allowed the boy to be as immoral as
he pleased. It was hardly fair. The scales were loaded from the beginning. Augustine rejoiced in his small immoralities: he cheated at
games, stole, and told lies. On one celebrated occasion he joined a
gang of schoolchildren and stripped an orchard of its pears without
any desire to eat them, simply because it pleased him to be destructive.
He loathed mathematics and was too lazy to learn Greek, but he enjoyed Virgil and wept contentedly over the death of Dido, Queen of
Carthage.

Monnica was twenty-two or twenty-three when Augustine was
born. There was an older son, Navigius, of whom almost nothing is
known, and a daughter who eventually became an abbess. It is possible that Augustine deliberately omitted to record the name of his mistress and of a young man he once bitterly grieved over: in some deep
way they may have hurt him. He was easily hurt. He quarreled incessantly, and he lived in a house where quarrels were frequent. Monnica kept order with a smooth tongue, with a mother-in-law in the
house and a brood of lying slaves. The tempest began in the cradle,
for when Augustine tells the story of a baby gazing at the world with
withering hate, it is reasonably certain that he was talking about himself. But such tempestuous households are not necessarily unhappy.
Monnica was the sheet-anchor; the father was rarely seen; Augustine
was left to his own resources.

At twelve he was sent to a school at Madaura, proud of its ancient history as one of the great centers of Numidian culture. It was a
well-built city well-provided with statues, and he liked to remember
later the heroic proportions of the naked statue of Mars in the market
place, and another and perhaps even more intriguing statue of a man
stretching out three fingers to offset the evil eye. His senses were
keen, and in this hot city his first experiments in sensuality took place.
It was not love, but lust. He speaks about these things openly, with

little compassion for his own wayward youth. "I dared to roam the woods and pursue my vagrant loves beneath the shades," he says, perhaps referring to the woods surrounding Madaura or perhaps referring to no woods at all: only the shelters where lovers lie. "Lord, how loathsome I was in Thy sight," he says in the *Confessions*. "It stormed confusedly within me, whirling my thoughtless youth over the precipices of desire, and so I wandered still further from Thee, and Thou didst leave me to myself: the torrent of my fornications tossed and swelled and boiled and ran over."

Perhaps they did, but he seems to protest too much. It is possible that Augustine committed no very grave sins, and though he depicts himself as the worst of sinners while he was a schoolboy and a student, Bishop Vicentius of Carthage remembered him at this time as an earnest scholar and a man of quiet and honorable demeanor. A distinguished citizen of Thagaste called Romanianus thought well enough of him to finance his career at the university, when his father died. He was able and talented, already showing signs of a lawyer's ability to argue cases and a flair for writing. The university was at Carthage, then the greatest seaport on the western Mediterranean. To the Romans Carthage was known as *Carthago Veneris*, a softly shining city between the lakes and the sea, with her Capitol and Palatine and teeming colleges. "Carthage," wrote Apuleius, "is the heavenly muse of Africa, the inspirer of the Roman people," and so it was. All the races mingled there. Learning was encouraged in this pagan city where supreme honors were paid to the ancient Carthaginian goddess Tanit, whose Roman name was *Virgo Coelestis*, the Virgin of Heaven. Augustine attended the ceremonies performed in her honor. "Our eager eyes," he said, "rested in turn on the goddess and on the girls, her adorers." There were also ceremonies for Isis and the Phrygian Mother Goddess. Talking in Punic, mingling with the crowds, his blood rising to fever heat, his father dead and his mother far away, Augustine threw himself into the delights of the city, committing those sins which it pleased him to remember in the *Confessions* with bated breath. As furiously as he pursued women, he pursued scholarship. "My unquiet mind was altogether intent to seek for learning," he wrote. He read the book of Cicero called the *Hortensius*, which survives only in fragments, and was so impressed by the message that only the philosophical life was worth living that he was to say later that it was this book which turned him to God. At the time he had not read the Gospels, and when at last he began to read the New Testament, he came to the conclusion that there was nothing in it which was not better expressed by Cicero.

As Augustine describes his slow progress toward the Christian faith, we are made aware of hesitancies, sudden alterations of feeling, a deliberate effort to test religions by their works. He speaks of joining a group of sun-worshipers, but without conviction. "I thought they concealed something of great importance, which afterward would be revealed to me," he wrote, and it is clear that the revelation never came. Meanwhile the problem of evil fascinated and tormented him, and he turned to Manichaeism because it seemed to offer in its simple faith of a world divided between the forces of light and darkness a solution to the problem. He persisted in this faith for nine years. At last he returned to Thagaste, only to discover that Monnica, who had grown even more fervently Christian during his absence, regarded him now as a sinner fallen beyond redemption. She threw him out of the house. Augustine simply walked to the house of Romanianus, who also belonged to the Manichaean faith, and remained there as the tutor of the rich man's son. There followed a long period of preparation. Dimly he seems to have discerned that the Church was waiting for him at the end of the road. Meanwhile, as the adopted son of one of the most important men in the province, with money at his command and intelligent pupils sitting at his feet, he could amuse himself by applying his keen brain to such philosophical problems as he chose to consider. He taught his pupils law, and insists that he conscientiously trained them to become good lawyers, "not that they might injure the innocent, but might sometimes defend the guilty." He regarded himself tolerantly, knowing perfectly well that in all Thagaste there was no one so brilliant, so promising as Augustine.

Then the bubble burst. It burst in a way which is not uncommon among clever and talented youths. His closest friend, who had gone to school with him and who had studied with him at the university, "the youth who was sweet to me above all sweetness of this life," suddenly died. What was worse: shortly before he died, he received the sacrament. Augustine, the fervent Manichee, was appalled. Confronted with death, he gave way to a wild grief. "Darkness lay upon my heart, and wherever I looked there was only death," he wrote. "My eyes sought him everywhere, and found him not. Tears were my only comfort." He gave way to an unrestrained, self-tormenting grief.

This grief opened the way for his conversion.

Not, however, immediately; the shock of his friend's death left him open to doubts and troubled thoughts, but it did not convert him. He was twenty-nine when he left Carthage for Rome, intending to become a teacher. He still held to the remnants of his belief in Manichaeism, and he was still wonderfully self-assured. He gave exhibitions of eloquence, which he later described as exhibitions of the most wretched and feverish loquacity—*miserrima et furiosissima loquacitas*. But the Romans were less impressed by his eloquence than he had hoped. He fell ill, and he came to regard this illness as the third stage on the road to Christianity, following Cicero's *Hortensius* and the death of his childhood friend. From the misery of poverty and hopelessness in Rome he was rescued by the great statesman and scholar Symmachus, who had been proconsul in Africa and who may have heard of the brilliant young law professor. When the University of Milan asked Symmachus to select a promising candidate for the post of professor of rhetoric, he chose Augustine.

By the time he reached Milan, Augustine was beginning to question seriously his belief in Manichaeism. The arguments of the Manichees were arbitrary, too arbitrary, and he began to argue the case against them with increasing fervor. Since everything in the world was either light or dark, evil or good, the Manichees had found it necessary to prepare a vast catalogue of good and evil. "They say the golden melon comes from God's treasure house, but the golden fat of the ham and the yoke of an egg are evil? How so? And how does it come about that the whiteness of a lettuce proclaims divinity, while the whiteness of cream proclaims only evil? And why this horror of meat? For does not roast suckling pig offer us a brilliant color, an agreeable smell, an appetizing taste—sure signs, according to them, of the divine presence." Manichaeism was rooted in materialism; Augustine's spirit, like his wit, was already taking wings.

Everyone in Milan called on the saintly Bishop Ambrose, and Augustine was not long in calling upon the man he later described as "the polestar." "He received me," wrote Augustine, "like a father, and was pleased enough at my coming in a bishop-like fashion." It seems to have been a perfunctory meeting. Augustine did not come to him as a Christian; he went to the bishop's palace because it was the thing to do, because Ambrose was universally revered, because he was a confidant of the boy-emperor Valentinian II, and because he was the most powerful figure in Milan. Augustine's work made few demands on him. His earnings already made him comparatively wealthy: he owned a villa and he could afford to pay for the passage of his Carthaginian mistress and their son Adeodatus. There were a number of friends to make him feel at home: his brother Navigius, two cousins, Rusticus and Lastidianus, and Alypius, his bosom companion with whom he shared all his secrets. Soon he was inviting Monnica to come and stay with him. Monnica came, only to accuse him of wantonness for keeping a mistress. He could keep his son, but the woman must go. She argued with such force that he finally consented to do as she wished. When he wrote the *Confessions*, he could still remember the pain of the parting. "When they took from my side her with whom I had slept for so long, my heart was torn at the place where it stuck to her (*cor ubi adhaerebat*), and the wound was bleeding."

Without his mistress, and in the presence of the formidable Monnica, he was now more than ever ripe for conversion. As Augustine tells the story, the conversion began in the most humdrum way possible—with the visit of a Roman officer—and ended with a child's babbling. He was staying in the villa with his mother and Alypius when Pontitianus, an officer of the imperial household, an African and a Christian, came to call on them. On the table, which had been marked out for a game of dominoes, Pontitianus found a volume of the epistles of St. Paul. Augustine had been studying them, but without any deep interest. Pontitianus expressed his surprise at finding the volume and told the story of his own conversion, describing at some length the untroubled delights of the Christian, his sure faith, his certain knowledge of the path to be followed. He spoke of St. Antony of Egypt and of the contentment to be found in monasteries, to such effect that when he was gone Augustine was in a kind of trance and went wandering out of the house to debate with himself whether he should maintain his pride or submit to the Church. He was still debating when he heard a child chanting: "*Tolle, lege*" (Take up, read). The child was perhaps chanting for the sake of chanting, but Augustine felt he had received a divine command; he rushed back into the house, opened the epistles of St. Paul, and read the words: "Not in rioting and drunkenness, not in chambering and wantonness, not in strife and envying, but put ye on the Lord Jesus Christ, and make not provision for the flesh, to fulfill the lusts thereof." He put his finger on the page, calm at last. Alypius pointed to the words that followed: "Him that is weak in the faith receive ye." These words came to him as the ultimate confirmation that he must embrace Christianity.

In this way, at the age of thirty-three, with nearly half his life over, he became a Christian. For the remainder of his life he made up for lost time.

The character of Augustine, as it comes to us in his voluminous writings, combines a cold brilliance with the warmth of his African blood. He wrote sometimes with a direct earthy passion even when he was discussing complex theological ideas; and though he professed obedience to God, there was scarcely a moment when he was not guilty of self-will. His inflexibility, his furious rages remained, to color his thoughts and to give dramatic expression to his faith. His hot African blood was not stilled by his conversion: like many others he would have to wait until he was old before the fleshly demon was ultimately extinguished: his senses remained keen, and the texture of his prose, urgent and demanding, mirrored his sensuality as it mirrored his violence. He was the least calm of the saints, the most impetuous. He had loved "the perishable beauty of the body, the brightness of the light, the soft melody of the *cantilenae*, the delicious scent of flowers and the limbs made for the embracing of the flesh." He loved them less when he became a Christian, but there seems never to have been a time when the world's beauty did not affect him.

The great crisis in Augustine's life was now over, but there were other crises to come, to be fought with anguish and impatience. He fell into a long fever, had difficulty in breathing, and wondered whether there was blood in his lungs. He decided to resign from his professorship and disappear to some quiet place where he could think out his problems in seclusion. Verecundus, a grammarian at the university, offered him the use of a small country house near Lago Maggiore among olives and vineyards, and there Augustine spent the autumn in the company of Monnica, Alypius, Navigius, and his son, Adeodatus, as well as his two cousins, Lastidianus and Rusticus. With them was Licentius, the son of Romanianus, who underwrote the expenses of the holiday. Licentius became Augustine's confidant.

The days passed quietly; the nights were a torment. Augustine had a remarkable facility for summoning up the images of the past: the very smells, the very texture of things he had touched returned to plague his dreams. There passed before his eyes the women he had known, and in the silence of the night he heard their clear music. "Am I not," he cries, "am I not in dreams the man I am, O Lord my God? Does my reason slumber as well as my senses? Cannot Thy mighty hand purify the weakness of my soul, and with rich grace exterminate the guilt within my dreams?" To avoid the snares of dreams, he would lie awake to the point of exhaustion, taming himself to watchfulness, searching in his mind for some problem to solve, finding in incessant argument the solvent to desires.

As winter came on, he began to write his *Soliloquies*. The word, like so many others that have entered theology, was invented by him, and he was a little ashamed of it, wondering whether it would be understood. They take the form of lecture notes, diary entries, reports on his discussions with his friends, explorations of the spiritual landscape, a continuing dialogue with the soul. He cries out: "It is my guilt that causes Thy sufferings." At another time he says: "I have nothing else but my will." God and the will are held in a curious suspension, as when he declares: "God, who art always the same, let me know myself, let me know Thee." Sometimes "Thee" comes perilously close to "me." Sometimes, too, he employs the language of lovers in order to celebrate God, never more brilliantly than when he wrote later in the *Confessions* his perfect description of the moment of truth: *Mens mea pervenit ad id quod est in ictu trepidantis aspectus.* "My mind reached that which is in the thrust of a trembling glance."

In the spring he was baptized, together with Alypius and Adeodatus. Then, because his mother was growing old and wanted to die in her own country, he decided to return to Africa.

At Ostia, the port of Rome, Monnica fell ill, and there was no more thought of continuing the journey. She had no fear of death, and when Navigius complained that it would be better to die in Africa, hoping she would live long enough to reach Thagaste, she answered: "Nothing is far from God; I have no fear that He will not know where to find me at the world's end when He will raise me from the dead." She died a few hours later on the ninth day of her sickness. She was fifty-six and Augustine was thirty-three.

The death of Monnica was the most shattering experience of his life, and there is a sense in which he never recovered from his grief. His faith had run deep; now it ran deeper. He had been authoritarian before; now, armed with the authority of his faith, he became more authoritarian, more relentless, more determined than ever to justify the ways of God to man. For a few more months he remained in Italy, and then sailed for Carthage. At Thagaste he sold his paternal estate, giving the money to the poor and reserving nothing for himself, determined to live the religious life. Soon he formed a small community devoted to the reading of the Scriptures and long philosophical colloquies, which provided the basis for his written discourses on the nature of language, on music, and on *Genesis*. But when, for example, he wrote on music, what he was most concerned about was to search in his own memory and understanding and will for the impression that music made on him; he asked himself interminable abstract questions; he forced himself to reach deep within himself; and he rarely escaped from himself. Sometimes he resembles a man gazing into a mirror, losing himself in the contemplation of his own gaze.

That authoritarian, self-centered vision was always in conflict with a very real humility in the sight of God. When the aging Bishop Valerius retired from the episcopal throne and called upon the people to elect Augustine as his successor, Augustine flew into a rage. He had not wanted to be a bishop; he wanted to be a student of Christ, living quietly with his friends and enjoying an endless conversation on the divine verities. Once made bishop, he knew he would be molested by office-seekers and the usual humdrum devotees. He did not suffer fools gladly, and he would bark at them: *"Discedite a me, maligni!"*—Go away, you devils! Suffer me to study in peace the commandments of my God!

If he did not study these commandments in peace, at least he wrote about them. Before he died, he had composed two hundred and thirty books on subjects ranging over the whole gamut of divine and secular knowledge. He wrote about quicklime, salamanders, Jebusites, Mount Etna, widowhood, patience, the magnitude of the soul, the divine vision. He liked to discuss the meanings and origins of words, customs, even letters of the alphabet. He defines a single dogma through a thousand pages, and will write a commentary thirty pages long on a single sentence of the Bible. But these are small faults when set against the inordinate brilliance of his mind. It was characteristic of the man who wrote so much that he confessed he preferred reading to writing.

The collected works of Augustine fill fifty large volumes. It is to be doubted whether anyone has read them all, or ever will. But lost in the huge volumes are many things that should be remembered, for hardly anyone else has possessed in a single mind a superb poetic gift and a singular skill in dialectics. He can say difficult things with ease, and he will wrap easy things in endless difficulties of his own making. Often, as when he said: "You are not to suppose, brethren, that heresies are produced by small minds; on the contrary, only great minds can produce them," he says what needed to be said with exemplary precision. "We are all God's beasts," he wrote. He defined man as "a soul using a body." He spoke of "humility raised to the heights, drunkenness sober," and it was in this temper that he wrote his books, in a divine drunkenness and a divine pride. Sometimes he could be willfully aphoristic, as when he wrote in *On the Trinity:* "God always is, nor has He been and is not, nor is but has not been, but as He never will not be, so He never was not." The ideas disentangle themselves in the end, but the happy complexities remain.

Some of his lesser known passages should be quoted here, because they give the measure of the man, his poetry, his melancholy, his settled joy, and his pervading sense of an attainable peace. He liked to write of his joy in God, and he liked to declare the goodness of the earth which was created by God:

In creation I find the sky good, the moon good, the stars good, the earth good, the things which are brought forth from the earth and are rooted there, all good; and all that walks and moves is good, and all that flies in the air and swims in the waters is good; and I say that man is good, for "the good man out of the good treasure of his heart bringeth forth good." I say, too, that the angels are good, if they have not fallen by reason of their pride and become devils—they are good if they remain obedient to Him who made them. I say all these things are good, and when I turn toward God I think I can describe Him in no other way than by saying He is good, and I remember that the Lord Jesus said: "No one is good, save God alone."

(*Ennarationes in Psalmos*, CXXXIX, 4)

The *Ennarationes in Psalmos* comprised his longest and most formidable work. In effect it was his diary, the priestly journal in which he wrote down his daily contemplations on the Psalms during the greater part of his religious life, the source of many of his sermons, tracts, and philosophical investigations. There, if one searches, one can find his whole life.

There was violence in Augustine, and he had no pity for those who disagreed with him. He was the first to misuse the words of the parable: "Compel them to come in," and generations of tyrannical priests have thanked him for his defense of priestly tyranny. Tertullian, Ambrose, and Athanasius all inveighed against shedding the blood of heretics; Augustine, while admitting the grandeur of heresiarchs, thought them better dead. The Donatists especially incurred his wrath; he declared that they deserved to die. The Donatist bishop Gaudentius replied: "God appointed prophets and fishermen, not princes and soldiers, to spread the faith." It was an argument which never appealed to Augustine, who regarded himself as a prince of the Church and a mighty soldier in defense of the faith.

When he writes his polemical tracts Augustine is rarely convincing. When he writes of his childhood and youth, or his conversion, or the death of his mother, or God's majesty, he is overwhelmingly convincing. He will set a rhythm to work, making it reproduce in music the image he intended to convey. So here, speaking of Christ's newness, he reproduces the same image many times, but the effect is to give astonishing weight and dignity to a single idea:

Christ came when all things were growing old: He made them new. As something fashioned, created, perishable, the world was declining to its fall. And so it was inevitable that there should be miseries. He came to console thee in present troubles and to promise an everlasting rest. Choose, therefore, not to cleave unto this ancient world, nor be unwilling to grow young in Christ, who said to thee: The world is perishing, the world is growing old, the world is failing, the world has the labored breathing of old age. Fear not. "Thy youth shall be renewed as an eagle's."

(*Sermones de scripturas,* LXXXI, 8)

It is a theme which Augustine likes to repeat, for it was essential to the continuing argument he maintained between himself and God. It was a complex argument, for his insistent self sometimes got in the way, and sometimes one has the impression that it is being carried on in a strange no man's land, in the half darkness, to the sound of drums. Here, for example, he explains why he loves God, in an abstruse argument that involves all the senses and the denying of the senses:

What do I love when I love Thee? Not beauty of bodies, nor the fair harmony of time, nor the brightness of the light, so lovely to the eye, nor the soft melodies of many songs, nor the sweet smell of flowers and ointments and spices, nor manna and honey, nor the limbs acceptable to embraces by the flesh. None of these I love when I love my God. Yet I love a kind of light and melody and fragrance and meat and embracement when I love my God, and these are the light, melody, fragrance, meat and embracement of my inner man: where there shineth unto my soul what space cannot contain, and there soundeth what time beareth not away, and there smelleth what breathing dispelleth not, and there tasteth what eating diminisheth not, and there clingeth what satiety divorceth not when I love my God.

(*Confessiones* X, 6)

In this way Augustine will talk for page upon page, saying little but rejoicing in the music of adoration, simultaneously in love with the world of the flesh and with heavenly things. Sometimes the agonized cry breaks out: "Up, Lord, and do; stir us up, and recall us; kindle and draw us; inflame, grow sweet unto us; let us not love, let us run." Or again: "Too late have I loved Thee, O Thou Beauty of ancient days!" Then he remembers that the mercy of Christ is never too late, and in the end there is peace.

In his writings there are always these sudden passages of illumination, the argument vanishing into poetry. Even in *The City of God*, ostensibly a learned discussion on the misery of the earthly city in comparison with the heavenly city, he will fall into poetry and abandon the argument altogether; and indeed he rarely keeps to the argument. Earthly things attracted Augustine and he liked to discuss the affairs of the earth. "Alas, alas, how much of Babylon there is in his best book, *De Civitate Dei*," wrote the puritanical Cotton Mather. He pours into the book his hopes, his memories, his passions, everything he has thought and everything he has read, and his horror of the earthly city is only equaled by his affection for the historical Rome and all its traditions. He continually quotes Virgil in defense of Christ. As he travels back through all past history and shows that history is simply the road leading to the Heavenly City, he sometimes appears to be peering into the faces of the ancients in the hope of finding himself. Here again, in this immense and haphazard book as in so many of his writings, there looms the giant figure of Memory.

There was something of the Marxist in Augustine. He passionately denounced the city-dwellers, the *bourgeoisie*. "The world," he wrote, "is a sea in which men devour one another." The *pax civica* is based on naked fear, and the lords of the earth are rapacious demons. Like Marx, Augustine prays for the day when the state will wither away. Unlike Marx, Augustine believes the state will be replaced by the City of God, although he is never quite clear how the transformation will be brought about. In a moment, in a lightning flash, the sabbath peace will descend and the new landscape will unfold. "There we shall rest and see, we shall see and love, we shall love and we shall praise!" But the City of God is sketched in lightly; it is too bright to have firm outlines; and Augustine consoles himself as best he can by appealing to its inevitability, its beauty, its essential place in the grand design.

Rome fell to the armies of Genseric, and soon North Africa fell to the Vandals. In his monastery Augustine was quietly preparing to die, with the Vandals at the gates. He was seventy-five, his brain was clear, and he still sent out letters appealing for help to all those who might listen; and when the Vandals were so close that the sound of their hammering could be heard, he said: "I ask God to deliver this city from its enemies, or if that may not be, that He may give us strength to bear His will, or at least that He take me from this world and receive me into His bosom." As he lay dying, his eyes feasted on a text written above his bed: "Man goeth forth unto his work and to his labor until the evening." He died on August 28, 430. He had said once, "Thou hast made us for Thyself, and our heart is restless until it finds repose in Thee," and perhaps of all his writings these were the words closest to his heart.

THE YEARS pronounce their verdict, and from the vantage point of the twentieth century Augustine appears to tower over his age. He brought to Christianity a sense of African urgency and excitement and argument, but in his own time, before the sheer weight of the *Confessions* and *The City of God* had worked upon men's consciousnesses, he was less prominent than Ambrose and Jerome, who were his contemporaries. For nearly forty years Augustine remained Bishop of Hippo, writing endlessly, quarreling vehemently, and abusing everyone who disagreed with him; he was like a flame which burned everyone it touched. There were some, Jerome among them, who wondered sometimes whether it would not be better if the flame burned with a less brilliant light. In a famous letter Jerome even accused him of spiritual pride, the desire for praise and celebrity, the hope of astonishing people with his brilliance. "Stop annoying me," Jerome wrote. "I have only one desire—to seek the peace of my monastic cell."

To the end Augustine was a man who enjoyed the sounds of battle, and the peace of his monastic cell was constantly interrupted with battle cries, with alarms and excursions. There was no modesty in him. He saw himself always in some commanding position in the midst of the battle, the hero heroically defending the faith. But in fact Ambrose and Jerome between them did more to advance the Christian cause. They shouldered the heavier burdens, fought the more dangerous battles, and showed throughout their lives an essential austerity foreign to Augustine's nature.

While Augustine made war with ideas, Ambrose fought against

principalities and powers. For a long period of his life he was the arbiter of the western Roman Empire. He humbled emperors, lived in visions, and thirsted for righteousness. In him there was combined the firm dignity of a Roman senator and the fire of a Hebrew prophet, and a great humility.

There are mysteries about Ambrose, as there are about all the great Fathers of the Church, but he was the least mysterious. He seems never to have been wounded in the side, and never needed to fight for position or power. He was born into the purple. His father, Aurelius Ambrosius, was Prefect of Gaul, who from his palace at Treves administered Britain, France, Spain, and Portugal, as well as part of Germany and the islands of Sardinia, Corsica, and Sicily. Both his parents were Christians; a great-aunt had suffered martyrdom in the Diocletian persecutions; for him Christianity was a way of life, not a matter of debate. His ancestors had been consuls and praetors, and in the normal course of events he would obtain a high administrative post in the government. But even as a child he seems to have known that he would become a bishop. Paulinus, his secretary and biographer, tells the perfectly credible story that when Ambrose was a child staying in his mother's house in Rome, papal dignitaries came to visit her, and there was much kissing of clerical hands. Ambrose stretched out his hand to his sister and said: "You should do the same to me, since I am going to become a bishop." His sister refused the offer, but Paulinus observed sententiously that "the spirit of the Lord, who was nurturing him for the priesthood, was already speaking in him."

Perhaps the Lord was speaking in him, but it is more likely that Ambrose was merely amusing himself with mimicking the ostentatious gestures of the dignitaries. He seems to have felt no vocation for the priesthood. He studied the law, read deeply in Latin and Greek literature, and prepared to enter government service. His brother Satyrus had risen to become one of the most noted lawyers of his time, and for a while Ambrose practiced as a lawyer at Sirmium in Illyria. But law held no great attraction for him, and when Probus, the Praetorian Prefect of Italy, offered to make him an assessor, he accepted the post with alacrity. An assessor was the equivalent of a high court judge, but he also possessed administrative duties; and while Ambrose seems to have had little liking for judicial matters, he enjoyed helping to administer a vast province. He was so able an administrator that Probus recommended him for the post of governor of the provinces of Liguria and Aemilia. His predecessors had acted oppressively, and there is a legend that Probus bade him farewell with the words: "Go, and act not as a judge but as a bishop." This story, too, is perfectly credible, for Probus, though he had acquired immense wealth by questionable methods, was remarkable for his generosity of spirit. In this way Ambrose came to Milan, where except for brief excursions outside the city he spent the rest of his life. At the time of his appointment he was about twenty-nine.

In those days Milan was the principal seat of the imperial government of the West, and the governor of the province was therefore in a quite extraordinary position of power. Inevitably he would come in contact with the western emperor. Still more inevitably, since Valentinian I was a brutal bigot, the new governor would find himself in conflict with the emperor. With his steel-blue eyes, his flaxen hair, and his diabolical temper, Valentinian was everything that Ambrose was not. He came from the people, delighted in violence, and was accustomed to say: "Authority must be enforced with severity." He was not simply stating a commonplace. His severity took the form of outrageous punishments and sadistic tortures. His brother Valens, swarthy and pot-bellied, was the emperor of the East.

It was a time when the Roman Empire was being shaken to its foundations, with the barbarians continually breaking through the frontiers. The emperor commanded his armies in the field, abandoning civil matters to his local governors. It was Ambrose's opportunity. He ruled wisely and firmly. When Auxentius, the Arian bishop of Milan, died in 374, Ambrose quietly used his influence to see that an Arian bishop would no longer rule over the diocese. He did not know that he would himself become the bishop of Milan. During the near riots which followed the death of Auxentius, Ambrose spoke soothingly to the people on the duty of maintaining order. The crowd would have gone quietly away if a child had not suddenly cried out: "Ambrose for bishop!" The cry was taken up by the people, and Ambrose, confronted by the popular verdict, seems to have acted like a man confronted by unruly children. He decided to show that he was not to be trifled with.

He had no desire to be a bishop. He was not an ecclesiastic; he had not even been baptized. He was only a catechumen, a candidate for baptism at some future time. He was thirty-four, with a brilliant government career in front of him. Why exchange a governorship for a bishopric? The crowd was convinced of his sanctity. Then let them know that he could be brutal, evil, even sinister, like his imperial master. He ordered torture to be applied to some prisoners, hoping to persuade the people that he was as cruel as Valentinian. The crowd shouted: "Your sin be upon us!" He ordered loose women to come to his palatial apartments, and the crowd again shouted: "Your sin be upon us!" Sickened by their fervor and their display of emotion, he decided to take refuge in flight. He left his palace by a side door at midnight, intending to make his way to Pavia, but it was a moonless night and he took a wrong road; in the morning he found he was once again in Milan, entering by the Roman Gate. Paulinus is not always trustworthy, but his description of Ambrose's attempts to escape have the ring of authenticity. He fought against becoming bishop with all his strength, but he may have known that it was inevitable. The people sent a message to Valentinian, urging the appointment. Valentinian, who may have had his own reasons for removing Ambrose from the government, replied that he agreed with the verdict of the people. When news of Valentinian's reply reached Milan, Ambrose had already disappeared. Now there was no governor and no bishop.

Ambrose had not gone far. He was merely staying in a country house not far from Milan. No one except his friend Leontius, the owner of the house, knew where he was. Ambrose had not, however, counted on the pope, who ordered that anyone harboring Ambrose should immediately give him up upon pain of severe penalties. Leontius, frightened, betrayed the secret. Ambrose was led in triumph to Milan.

The people insisted that Ambrose should become bishop at once. Ecclesiastical authorities argued that he must follow established procedure, mounting stage by stage the ranks of the ecclesiastical hierarchy. There were eight ranks separating the non-baptized Christian from the bishopric, and accordingly it was arranged that Ambrose must spend at least one day in each rank. On the first day he was baptized. On the second he was appointed doorkeeper; then, on succeeding days, he was made reader, then exorcist, then subdeacon, then deacon, then presbyter, then bishop. No one had ever gained such high ecclesiastical rank with such speed.

Almost the first act of Ambrose as bishop was to write to the great Basil of Caesarea requesting that some holy relics should be given to the Cathedral at Milan; and Basil, who knew Ambrose by repute as a man of noble birth, high office, and astonishing eloquence, was only too happy to comply. They had much in common; they were both grave, austere men dedicated to administering the affairs of the Church. Ambrose was the kinder and more tolerant, but he could be firm when the occasion demanded. "If he says to the sun, 'Stand,' it stands," they said of him, and he rarely changed an opinion or countermanded an order. He was one of those who succeeded in combining inflexibility with kindness.

He gave his estates to the Church and sold his gold and silver vessels for the benefit of the poor, obeying Christ's instructions to rid himself of earthly possessions. He fasted every day, taking only one small meal in the evening, and spent half the night in prayer. He wore himself out with the business of the Church. He gave orders that his door should be kept open permanently; no one must be refused admittance into his presence. Augustine has left a pleasant account of him sitting in his office while a continual stream of visitors passes in front of his table. At odd moments the bishop takes up a book from the table and reads for a brief interval; then once more the stream of visitors descends upon him.

Ambrose enjoyed his nights more than his days: then he could read quietly and give himself up to uninterrupted prayer. He had a special fondness for Plato and for the writings of Origen, Basil, and Gregory of Nyssa. He preferred to write alone, without the help of secretaries.

In the small church of San Vittore in Ciel d'Oro in Milan there exists a mosaic portrait of Ambrose. He appears as a slight man with large, melancholy eyes, a broad forehead, a long nose, a thin beard, and drooping mustaches; his head is bent forward; he has the look of one who deeply cares and suffers deeply. It is not the face of a patrician or of a high ecclesiastical dignitary, but of a man who is humble and urgent in his humility. He stands there with his feet firmly planted on the ground, swathed in a voluminous gown, his hand placed over his heart, not in the attitude of blessing, but in the attitude of a man who begs for God's forgiveness and shares the sorrows of the world. It is a portrait of Ambrose done from the life or when his memory was still fresh, before he became a monumental figure in the history of the Church. While Augustine has his flaming core of individuality, Ambrose demonstrates his humanity, his gentleness, his desire to follow in God's pathway.

How deeply sensitive Ambrose was we know from his devotion to his brother Satyrus, who gave up a governorship to become the bishop's chief adviser and manager of episcopal affairs. The affection between them was like love; they dreaded being parted from one another. They were so close to one another that they could read one another's thoughts. When Satyrus fell ill in Africa after being shipwrecked in ice-cold water, Ambrose fell into a kind of stupor as soon as he heard the news. His sister Marcellina hurried to Milan to be near him, fearing he would die of grief or shock. Satyrus recovered sufficiently to make the journey back to Milan, only to suffer a relapse some days later. He died in Ambrose's arms, and for days Ambrose remained mute with sorrow, inconsolable. At last he roused himself and delivered the funeral oration over his brother's uncovered body. Grief for a dead brother has rarely been expressed so vividly as in that famous oration:

Thou art present, I say, and art always before me, and with my whole mind and soul do I embrace thee, whether in the quiet of the night or in the daylight, when thou didst vouchsafe to visit me and comfort me. And now the very nights which, while thou wast living, seemed so wearisome, because they denied us the power of seeing each other, and sleep itself, once hated as an interruption of our intercourse, have begun to be sweet, because they have restored me to thee. . . .Therefore I hold thee, my brother, and neither death nor time shall tear thee from me. Tears themselves are sweet, and weeping itself is pleasant, for by these the ardent longing of the mind is assuaged, and affection is soothed and quieted. For I cannot be without thee, or ever forget thee, or remember thee without tears. O bitter days which show that our union is broken! O nights of tears, which reveal the loss of the gentle partner of my rest, of my inseparable companion! What agonies would thou cause me, were it not that the image of my ever-present brother comes to me, were it not that the visions of my mind bring vividly before me him whom in the body I may look upon no more.

(De Excessu fratris sui Satyri, I, 19)

Ambrose pretended to find comfort in his brother's death, but he found none. To distract a mind made almost insane with grief he

turned once more to work, to reading, to study, to long nights spent
in prayer. He quoted from St. Paul, "This incorruptible must put on
incorruption, and this mortal must put on immortality," but he seems
not to have been completely convinced. Satyrus left no will. His
immense fortune descended to Ambrose and Marcellina, and they
gave it to the poor.

Not many months later, Valentinian I died in his camp in central
Europe. He had crossed the Danube and was arguing the terms of
surrender with one of the chieftains of the revolting tribe of the
Quadi when he suddenly turned purple, choked, and dropped dead.
He was succeeded by his sixteen-year-old son Gratian, who possessed,
according to his tutor Ausonius, all the gifts that kingship demanded.
He was handsome, and rode well. He was popular with the soldiers,
and led them brilliantly. He seemed to be another Augustus destined
to bring peace to the empire. Ambrose loved him, treasured his few
letters, and pronounced him perfect. He wrote books for the young
emperor, including one on the subject of the Holy Ghost that
Jerome, in an irascible mood, described as "a weak, feeble, spiritless,
pretty thing, full of purple passages, and lacking in logic." When
Gratian was murdered Ambrose knew the same desolation that
afflicted him when Satyrus died; now it was a son who had perished.

The death of Gratian was to have a profound effect on the fortunes of Ambrose. The young emperor had been killed at the orders
of the usurper Maximus, who had conquered most of the Roman Empire north of the Alps and threatened to invade Italy. The task of
Ambrose was to safeguard the peace and to protect the twelve-year-
old brother of Gratian, now elevated to the throne under the name of
Valentinian II. The boy's mother, the empress Justina, was an Arian,
and surrounded by Arian advisers. She came to Milan to seek the protection of Ambrose, and especially to arrange that Ambrose should go
on an embassy to Maximus in his capital at Treves, for she feared
most of all an attack on Italy. Ambrose, a man of peace, alone seemed
capable of ensuring that there would be no invasion. Accordingly he
made the dangerous journey to Treves and exacted from Maximus a
promise that he would keep the peace. When he returned to Milan, he
discovered that the Empress Justina had been undermining his authority by giving preference and benefices to the Arians in her court. Between the Arian empress and the Catholic bishop there could be no
peace.

In the eyes of Ambrose the Church was in peril, and he thundered against the empress with all his oratorical power. In revenge the empress called out the soldiers and ordered them to surround the church, not with the intention of killing Ambrose but in the hope of demonstrating to him that she was in a position of authority. In this state of siege, with the congregation growing restless, the church surrounded by armed men, all the entrances guarded, Ambrose hit upon the pleasant device of instituting in the western Church the antiphonal singing which had long been customary in the East. He divided the congregation into two choirs singing alternate verses of the Psalms. Augustine, who was present in the embattled church, wrote that these antiphonal chants had the effect of restoring a divine calm to the congregation, and like them he wept tears of joy. At last, realizing that nothing was to be gained by surrounding the church, the empress ordered the withdrawal of the soldiers.

Soon another event added to the triumph of Ambrose. A new basilica was being consecrated, and in a mood of prophetic ardor Ambrose called upon the martyrs to protect the church from her enemies. It was such a prayer as he might utter quite normally at any church service, but on this occasion the voice was charged with violent emotion. He seemed like one inspired, speaking to the dead across the centuries. The martyrs were clamoring to appear; they were present; the church was full of their ghostly voices. Suddenly Ambrose heard himself saying: "You must dig before the railing of Saints Felix and Nabor." Excavations were begun almost immediately, but no trace of the martyrs was found. Nevertheless, when the blind, the halt, and the lame were led to the place, they were immediately cured. Then they dug deeper and found the bodies of two men. "They were," said Ambrose, "of surprising stature, like those of the old legends. All the bones were perfect, and there was much blood." The heads had been severed from the trunks. The bodies were taken up, placed on biers, and brought to the new basilica, where more miraculous cures took place to the discomfiture of the empress and the Arians. No one knew who the martyrs were, until some old men came forward and remembered that they had once heard the names of Gervasius and Protasius, who had suffered martyrdom in the reign of Nero. Accordingly the crimson bones were given the names of these two long forgotten martyrs, and Ambrose pronounced that the saints of old were rising in defense of the Church.

In the summer of A.D. 390 a curious incident took place in Salonica. A young and beautiful charioteer, accused of homosexual practices by his cupbearer, was thrown into prison by Botheric, the
governor of Illyria. The townspeople rose in revolt, murdered Botheric, and dragged his body through the streets. Theodosius, emperor
of the eastern Roman Empire, who was then in Milan, was incensed
and threatened dire punishment on the people of Salonica, who had
preferred a favorite charioteer to the legally appointed governor. Ambrose, knowing the emperor's rages, intervened, but he had no sooner
left the imperial presence and obtained a promise of clemency than
Rufinus, the Master of the Offices, persuaded the emperor that
clemency would bring about the ruin of the empire. The emperor
sent an imperial legate with an order to massacre the people of Salonica. The people were invited to attend the circus, and when they had
taken their seats the doors were locked and the soldiers rushed in and
slaughtered men, women, and children at their leisure. Altogether
some ten thousand people of Salonica were put to the sword.

Ambrose, overwhelmed with grief by the senseless massacre,
wrote a letter to the emperor describing him as a murderer. The letter
survives, and shows Ambrose at his uncompromising best. He demands from the emperor a complete change of heart; intolerable
outrages must end; there must be a public act of contrition and repentance; henceforth the emperor will be excluded from the sacra-
ments. Not until the end of the year, six months after the massacre at
Salonica, was the ban of excommunication lifted. Theodosius, wearing a shroud, kneeling, praying for pardon, and shedding tears of
repentance, was permitted to return to the Church. The bishop had
triumphed over the Roman emperor.

Meanwhile Valentinian II was making his capital in Vienne, the
former capital of Gaul. He had grown into a handsome and sensitive
youth, and like Gratian he loved and revered Ambrose. Theodosius,
however, had no love for Ambrose and despised the young emperor,
who was forced to accept the services of the barbarian Arbogast, who
acted as chief minister, spy, informer, and local hangman. When
Valentinian issued an imperial rescript dismissing Arbogast from his
post, the barbarian read the document, tore it to pieces and flung it on
the ground. "You did not appoint me and you cannot dismiss me!" he
shouted, and turned his back on the young emperor, who had only a
few more days to live. Knowing that he was doomed, Valentinian

tried to kill himself, but failed. He sent an urgent message to Ambrose, urging him to come immediately to Vienne. Ambrose could not come, and even if it had been possible, he would not have been able to prevent the final act in the tragedy, for Arbogast had already decided to assume the purple. Two days after the letter was despatched to Ambrose, Valentinian was murdered. Arbogast set out to conquer Italy.

The armies of Arbogast and Theodosius met in the Julian Alps. At the height of the battle, which took place in a narrow defile, the *bora*, the northeast wind, rose suddenly in fury. The violent storm drove against the army of Arbogast, hurling some of his soldiers to the ground and blinding others. His army fell back, and panicked in the narrow defile, giving Theodosius the chance to cut it to pieces. Arbogast escaped from the battlefield in disguise, wandered over the mountains for two days, and then fell on his sword. Ambrose chose to believe that with this victory the murder of Valentinian had been avenged.

It was the last battle fought by Theodosius, who was already ill when he returned to Milan. The battle took place in September. Now, as winter came in, a strange thick fog gathered over the city, earthquakes were felt, and mysterious portents announced the approaching death of the emperor. Theodosius weakened rapidly. He died at the beginning of the following year, leaving his two young sons, Arcadius and Honorius, to be co-rulers of the empire when they came of age. The regent was Stilicho, a Christian general who had served Theodosius well. Ambrose, worn out by his exertions on behalf of the Church, fell ill two years later. Stilicho issued an imperial rescript: "Ambrose must recover." "When Ambrose dies," he said, "we shall see the ruin of Italy." When Ambrose heard of this, he said: "I have not lived among you shamefully, and would willingly live on, but I am not afraid to die, for our Lord is good." A few days before his death, he said he saw Christ standing by his bedside. He died on the dawn of Easter Eve, being fifty-eight years old and having been Bishop of Milan for twenty-three years and four months.

He left behind him no great body of doctrine. "The will of God is the measure of all things," he wrote once, and he was content with simple things. He married Roman austerity to Christian charity, and this was perhaps his greatest accomplishment. He was rigorous in his charity, saying that the Church amounted to little if it could not protect the poor; and he was continually ordering church vessels to be sold for their benefit. When the Arians charged him with sacrilege for selling the property of the Church, he answered: "Which do you consider more valuable, church vessels or living souls?" He had no sympathy for the rich and powerful, and hated them for the harm they did. The ostentation of the rich was a scandal crying out to heaven; the savagery of the powerful showed hell taking up its residence on earth. "Nature knows no rich," he once thundered. "She creates us all alike, and alike she encloses us in a sepulcher. What more resembles one dead man than another dead man?" The vanity of human ambitions was rarely so powerfully expressed.

Ambrose the patrician cared little for the patricians of this earth. He had known wealth and power, and thought little of them. Grief tempered him, and gave him a deep sympathy for the suffering of others. So he became a public servant, one of the few who have come out of the Church, and fought strenuously for the poor and the oppressed.

Jerome was made of softer metal: he was the dedicated scholar, the hermit who avoids the miseries of the world by turning his back on them. "He is always buried in books," wrote his friend Sulpicius Severus. "Day and night, he is always reading or writing." There was something inhuman about his careful avoidance of the world's agonies. He pursued a private sanctity, while Ambrose took the more heroic path of pursuing a public sanctity.

We know him by the name of Jerome, but he was born Eusebius Sophronius Hieronymus, the son of a small landowner somewhere in the region of the Julian Alps in what is now Yugoslavia. No one knows the date of his birth, and the town of Strido, which he mentions as his birthplace, has disappeared from the map, destroyed in Jerome's lifetime during the endless wars of the Illyrian frontiers. Though he wrote voluminous letters, which are now collected in an edition of 1700 pages, he nowhere makes more than passing references to his parents. His father seems to have been a freedman. He had a sister who committed some terrible sin in her youth, and there was a younger brother born twenty years after Jerome's birth. There were slaves on the estate, and Jerome remembered running in and out of their cells when he should have been working. Of his childhood this is all we know. Years later, when he was in Bethlehem and needed money for the hospice he had founded there, he described how he sold "some half-ruined cottages which had escaped the hands of the barbarians," and perhaps—though no one can be certain—those half-ruined cottages were all that remained of the ancient town of Strido.

From the beginning he was surrounded with an air of wealth, and there seems never to have been a time when he was in great penury. He became a student in Rome, where he studied hard and delighted in leading a carefree life of debauchery. He accused himself later of being a great sinner, who committed grave crimes "with unclean lips and with the eyes and with the foot and with the hand and with all his members," but he appears to have exaggerated the extent of his sinfulness. He studied grammar, rhetoric, and philosophy, and like many students of his time he learned his Virgil by heart. Quite suddenly he vanished from Rome with his friend Bonosus and wandered through Gaul. At Treves he showed signs of wanting to pursue a priestly vocation and copied some manuscripts, including Hilary's *Commentary on the Psalms,* and so began the vast study and compilation of manuscripts which was to become his life's work. But the habits of scholarship were not yet engrained in him. He was still wandering among the foothills of Christianity, still uncertain of his aims. When his friend Bonosus decided to live a life of meditation on one of the bare islands off the Dalmatian coast, Jerome marveled, but did not follow him. Instead he settled in Aquileia, then a great seaport, and gave himself up to more casual meditations than Bonosus had demanded of him. Among these casual products of his youth was a short story called *The Woman Struck Seven Times with an Ax,* which describes how a saintly woman suffered at the hands of an executioner: six times the ax was mysteriously turned away, but on the seventh she was left for dead, yet being protected by God's mercy she survived and went into hiding, "wearing a man's clothes until the scars formed on her wounds." The story is told vividly, and seems to reflect some deep-seated wounds in Jerome. There are hints of grave psychological disturbances, but we are never permitted to plumb their depths. Quite suddenly, some months after writing the story, he left Aquileia with a few friends, intending to make his way to the holy places of the East. He never revealed the reasons for his departure. All he says is that a sudden whirlwind—*subitus turbo*—descended upon him and he could no longer breathe the poisonous air of the seaport. He joined a community of hermits living on the edge of the desert of Calchis in Syria. There he slept in a bare cell, clothed himself in sackcloth, and for five years lived the life of an ascetic.

Lying at night on the bare ground, drinking only water and living on uncooked food, his shriveled skin turning as black as an Ethiopian's, Jerome pursued the vocation of saintliness with singular self-consciousness. He was continually writing letters to his friends, telling them what it was like. "The loneliness of the desert is Paradise," he wrote, but sometimes it was merely loneliness. He complained of the scorpions and wild beasts who were his only companions, and in the next breath celebrated the perfect contentment of the desert dweller. Once he wrote: "I have damned myself to this prison against the fear of Hell," and certainly his austerities derived from a lively knowledge that he needed to perform penances. To a friend called Heliodorus he wrote an urgent letter begging him to abandon his family and take up a life of austerity in Calchis, and suddenly he breaks out in a strange and wonderful hymn in honor of the desert:

O desert enameled with the flowers of Christ!
O solitude issuing forth the stones of the city of a mighty King!
O desert rejoicing in God's familiar presence!
O brother, whose soul is geater than the universe, what doest thou in
*   the world?*
How long shalt thou remain beneath the shelter of thy roof?
How long shalt thou repose within the smoky prison of the city?
Have faith in me, I see a wider light!
How sweet to cast away the burdens of the flesh and soar in purest
*   air!*
Art afraid of poverty? Christ calls poor men blessed.
Art afraid of labor? No athlete but is crowned with sweat.
Dost think of food? Faith feels no hunger.
Dost dread the touch of worn bruised fasting limbs upon the ground?
I say Christ lies by thy side.
Dost dread a wild beard and dishevelled hair?
I say thy head is Christ.
Dost fear the eternal vastness of the desert?
I say the spirit takes a gentle walk through Paradise.
Dost dread rough skin and unclean scurvy limbs?
I say those bathed in Christ need never bathe again.

(*Epistolae*, XIV, 10)

Jerome never again quite reached those ecstatic heights, and such moments of pure contentment seem to have been rare. Like all the anchorites and desert dwellers before him, he was compelled to confront the demons of the imagination and of noon. Sometimes he could not prevent his mind from contemplating the remembered dancing girls of Rome. He was not, and never became, a man satisfied with contemplations. He had little feeling for the desert and little understanding of it. He was more at home with books and began to learn Hebrew, which helped him to preserve his sanity. He went on to make a careful study of the Scriptures, and finally abandoned the desert altogether. In A.D. 379 he made his way to Antioch, where he was ordained a priest, and soon returned to Rome to collate the manuscripts in the papal library. He had a passion for mingling with rich and saintly women of the city, and sometimes employed them in the work of collation. He met Marcellina, the sister of Ambrose, and was especially close to the rich widow Albina, who lived with her daughter Marcella in a splendid palace on the Aventine. Marcella was beautiful. She had lost her husband a few months after marriage, and was dedicated to good works and sanctity. Jerome, with his brilliant tongue and his reputation for asceticism, his good manners and his excessive delight in virginity, his learning and his fierce temper, found consolation in the company of these women, who worshiped him and very nearly brought about his downfall, for soon after his arrival in Rome it was rumored that his purposes were not entirely innocent. He was lionized, but he was also calumniated. Gossip pursued the tall, striking figure with the pale ascetic face and the large dark eyes, who was already being regarded as a future pope. He had a viperish tongue, and he would answer the gossips in their own coin. Accused of cultivating widows, he wrote wonderfully satirical letters accusing the accusers, and he evidently rejoiced in his talent for satire. He would describe a high ecclesiastical figure with the same forthright impudence as he would describe the elegant women of Rome. At last, wearying of Rome, he returned to the East, staying briefly in Egypt, where he thought of founding a monastery in the Thebaid. Later he decided to settle in Jerusalem, but the city was full of "creeping heresies," even worse than the "purple-clad harlot" of Rome, and so he abandoned Jerusalem and came to Bethlehem. There he stayed for the remaining thirty-four years of his life.

Bethlehem in the autumn of A.D. 386 was everything Jerome thought desirable. The Roman Empire seemed to be at peace, and as he set about building a monastery not far from the Cave of the Nativity, he could look forward to long years of quiet study, with no temptations to trouble him except the temptations of scholarship. It was not to happen quite like that; but in those early years when he was building a hospice and a nunnery, his letters breathe a charming piety:

Here we find humble and wholesome food: bread and milk, the herbs we grow with our own hands, and all the delicacies of the countryside. Living thus, sleep does not overtake us in prayer, satiety does not interfere with out studies. In summer the trees afford us shade, in the autumn the air is cool and the fallen leaves give us a quiet resting place. In spring the field is clothed with flowers, and our songs are all the sweeter among the songs of birds. When snow and winter come, we have no lack of fuel: I am warm enough when I sleep or keep my vigil. Let the Romans have their turbulent crowds, let the arena be filled with cruelty, let the circus riot, and—since it is unpardonable to forget the ladies—let the female senate attend to their salons. Our happiness is to cleave unto the Lord and to put our trust in Him.

(Epistolae, LVII, 2)

What he found was a comfortable desert, where he could write without too many distractions, attended by the noble virgins who had followed him from Rome, and where he could be assured that every pathway and every hill had been trodden by Jesus. He was a little self-righteous about his selection of Bethlehem as the place of his labors, and the "holy pride," of which he once spoke, was perhaps more dangerous than he thought. He was especially pleased with the hospice he was building, noting that "if Mary and Joseph should pass this way again, they would not go unprotected." It would not have surprised him in the least if they had knocked on his doors, for everything was prepared for them. The quiet virgins read their psalters, and slept peacefully at night in the same shapeless brown robes they had worn during the day. These highborn patrician ladies became his devoted slaves, lighting fires, trimming lamps, shelling peas, boiling the vegetables, and laying the tables. No one was ever so well served. "In this little villa of Christ everything is rustic," he said, but it was the rusticity of the little country cottages built by Marie Antoinette at Versailles.

Here he wrote those voluminous and endless books, which poured out of him like breath. He wrote treatises, commentaries, letters which read like encyclicals, pamphlets which read like vitriol, dissertations which are as dry-as-dust as anything from a German theological school, and other dissertations which are as light and heady as new wine. He wrote a book on *The Sites and Names of Hebrew Places,* which he completed, and contemplated a huge history of Christianity, which he never started. He wrote epitaphs of famous Christians, and the book of epitaphs finally became a series of short biographies which he called *Concerning Famous Men,* beginning with Simon Peter and quite properly including Jerome himself who was placed at the end of the volume "as one born out of due time and the least of the followers of Christ." His greatest achievement and most Herculean task was his *Edition of Holy Scriptures in General Use,* his translation of the Bible into Latin, which became the classical text, the ultimate recension of the Bible in the West. Fourteen years were spent in the preparation of the text, and an even greater period in reading and checking innumerable existing texts in Latin, Greek, and Hebrew, a language that Jerome began to learn at the age of forty. His rhythms, his cadences, his interpretations and occasional mistakes, his feeling for language, and the very colors of his mind, were implanted in his translation; throughout it is stamped with his name. The Vulgate version of the Bible is one of the few books of which it can be said that they changed the course of a language. The Vulgate gave birth to Ecclesiastical Latin, the international language of the medieval world.

Jerome wrote at length on the subject of translation; it was a subject close to his heart, and he grappled with translations of one kind or another for most of his working life. In translating the Bible he attempted to render word for word, but when translating lesser works he was content to make a free version, not word for word, but sense for sense, following the example of Cicero who, when translating the speeches of Aeschines and Demosthenes into Latin, wrote: "I have not felt myself obliged to pay out each and every word to the reader; instead I have paid out an equivalent in value."

In this way, continually at his studies, living for God and for books, Jerome passed his days. He accumulated a large library, collected manuscripts from all over the empire, trained secretaries to take down his dictation, and wrote hundreds of letters, many of them of the length of treatises, on subjects as various as the proper conduct of virgins and the punishment to be meted out to profligate monks. He wrote with vigor and venom, like an exasperated angel, never happy unless he had slaughtered some heresy or corrected the ignorance of an adversary. He had a gift for savage irony, and used it well, perhaps too well, for irony was a murderous weapon in his hands. Once he wrote to the monk Rusticus: *"Christum nudus nudum sequere"*— Follow, naked, the naked Christ. It was the most brilliant sentence he ever wrote, but he never followed his own advice. To the end Jerome wore his garment of words.

In the summer of 410 Alaric, the king of a marauding nation of Goths, surrounded Rome with his army and quietly waited while the city slowly starved to death. Then, when there was no longer any prospect of resistance, his armies entered through the Salarian Gate and for three days and nights they plundered the treasures accumulated during a thousand years of history. Jerome heard the news in Bethlehem, and grieved like a man who has lost his home. It was no comfort to him that the attack was comparatively bloodless, for he recognized that Rome had suffered a psychological shock from which it was unlikely to recover. "Who could believe that Rome, who had spread over the earth the mantle of her victories, could crumble to dust?" he wrote. "The womb of the nations has become their tomb."

He grieved again when the refugees poured into Jerusalem and Bethlehem, with their tales of Gothic savagery and stupidity. Now for the first time in his life he felt abandoned by God, at a loss to understand what was demanded of him. He busied himself with good works, abandoned his commentaries, grieved helplessly, and wrote his letters furtively in the dead of night, when everyone else was sleeping. He was about sixty-three years of age, but already he felt like an old man. He survived for ten more years, working to the end, a thin, tall, almost transparent man with a feeble quavering voice, his body so weak that he had to be lifted up with the aid of pulleys. His last words were a complaint against the ravages of time and illness which no longer permitted him to write. "I am exhausted by grief and old age and torn by perpetual illness," he said, "and I can scarcely express myself at all."

That was what he had always wanted: the power to speak, to elucidate, to inform, to express himself. He loved words passionately, to such an effect that all the languages of Europe, their structure, their vocabulary, and their rhythms, were subtly influenced by him. Out of Bethlehem came the new speech.

Mosaics of Saphni

The Pantocrator in the Dome

The Nativity

The Baptism. (*Meletzis Spyros*)

The Entry into Jerusalem

The Crucifixion

The Incredulity of St. Thomas. (*Alinari*)

The Descent into Hell

The Transfiguration. (*Mansell Collection*)

II ✣ ST. JOHN CHRYSOSTOM

J UST as among the Fathers of the western Church there was one who was particularly beloved because he was passionate and suffered from human frailties, so too in the eastern Church there was a Father who was peculiarly human and passionate, at once gentle and commanding, given to sweetness and great rages, and seemingly determined on his own downfall. St. Augustine of Hippo and St. John of Antioch were contempories, though they were scarcely aware of one another's existence. They lived in different worlds, fought different battles, and followed different aims. Both were the sons of officials, and grew up in comparative wealth; their mothers were devout Christians; they formed deep attachments to youths when they were students; they earned reputations as great orators and reformers and exegetes; and there the resemblance ends. What they had supremely in common was the passion of their faith.

By one of those strange accidents that are always to be found among the early Fathers, we do not know and can scarcely guess at the appearance of Augustine. We know the appearance of John well, for the Byzantine artists faithfully recorded it. On ivories, miniatures, frescoes, and mosaics he appears always in the same form: an ascetic with a pale face, sunken cheeks, and emaciated frame. He was a small man, thin as a needle, with an enormous high forehead, a long nose, pursed lips, a pointed chin. Yet there was a certain nonchalance about him, a sweetness of expression, which derived perhaps from his continual sickness. He was always represented beardless, and therefore looks younger than the heavily bearded Fathers who are often shown standing beside him.

He was born about A.D. 347, his father being the descendant of an illustrious Greek family. The father bore the title *Magister militum orientis*, which would suggest that he had the rank of a general. Of the father we know virtually nothing more except that he died shortly after the child's birth. Of the mother we know only that her name was Anthusa, which means "flowering," and that her piety was unexcelled among the women of Antioch. She was only twenty when her husband died. Of John's early years we know little. He seems to have lived quietly and happily, surrounded by private tutors, on a large estate. He was fourteen when the Emperor Julian removed his capital from Constantinople to Antioch, which now became the center of the world.

John studied oratory under Libanius, a Neoplatonist with a great following. It was considered a mark of honor to have one's works read by so distinguished a philosopher. Libanius not only read but highly commended John's youthful writings, and when he was asked on his deathbed who was most worthy to succeed him, he answered: "John, if only the Christians had not stolen him from us."

At the age of twenty-three John was baptized, and was only dissuaded from living the life of an anchorite by his mother's pleading. He had already made the resolution to devote himself to the Christian life, and while living at home he practiced the austerities common among communities of monks. Soon Anthusa died, and then, feeling free of all attachments to the earthly life, John surrendered to the ascetic discipline which had been the delight and torment of his youthful imagination. Libanius had promised him a great future as a scholar, a lawyer, and an orator. John wanted only to lie at the feet of God, abject and triumphant. He retired to a cave, denied himself sleep, read the Bible continually, and spent two years without once lying down, in obedience to the injunction, "Be ye watchful." The inevitable result of these austerities was the ruin of his health. He returned to Antioch and was given, perhaps as punishment, the lowly position of altar attendant. He had to wait until he was thirty-five before he was made a deacon. This, too, was a lowly post, scarcely more than that of servant to a bishop in managing the affairs of the church, but it also involved much scurrying about the city while visiting and relieving the poor, and from this time dates John's extraordinary popularity with the common people of Antioch.

In that crowded, lawless city where, according to the Emperor

Julian, all the vices were practiced with impunity, and great poverty and suffering were widespread, John came like a ministering angel to heal the wounds of the sick and to give comfort to the dying. The small, thin, spidery man with the enormous forehead and the pallor of Lazarus understood them, sorrowed with them, and rejoiced with them. But when a few years later, at the age of forty, he was elevated to the priesthood, they observed a change in him. The ministering angel became a prophet threatening fire and brimstone. No longer gentle, he summoned and commanded them to repentance. The day of judgment was at hand, the torments of the damned awaited them unless they appealed to God's mercy. There came a long series of brilliant, excoriating sermons. From being the beloved deacon he became the feared presbyter.

The day of judgment, which he had promised so often, came in February 387. An imperial edict announced a forced levy on behalf of the army. The army claimed a donative of five gold pieces for every soldier, and the Emperor Theodosius, who feared the army and knew he could only rely on its support by bowing to its wishes, ordered that the wealthiest cities of his empire, especially Alexandria and Antioch, should raise the money. At Alexandria there was no revolt. At Antioch a mob formed, stormed the public baths, wrecked them, and then surged across the city to attack the praetorium, the governor's palace. The governor escaped and the mob vented its fury on the statues of the imperial family. The statue of Theodosius was thrown down, mutilated, and led in triumph through the streets. They were about to fire the city when the governor returned with a company of archers and dispersed the mob. That night the citizens of Antioch shivered in their beds. They knew that in the eyes of the emperor the whole city had committed the crime of *laesae maiestatis*. The punishment was death.

That day, or perhaps on the next day, the punishments began. Men arrested by the archers and the praetorian guards were summarily executed; even boys were burned or flung to the wild beasts. The governor sent a messenger to Constantinople to report the crime. Fortunately the messenger was detained by a fall of snow in the Taurus Mountains, and the full weight of punishment was not yet felt. John became the spokesman of the city's conscience, appealing to the governor for mercy, appealing to the people to await their fate calmly. In a long series of sermons which came to be known as *On the Statues,* he spoke as prophet and comforter, in one breath warning the people that they had brought their misfortunes on themselves and urging them to repent, in the next breath calling down God's mercy upon them. What if they were killed? It was nothing—they would enter Paradise all the sooner. Why had they rebelled? For the sake of a few gold coins? But had they not been spending money lavishly on the theaters, on horse races, on dancing girls, on building sumptuous houses for themselves? Sodom and Jerusalem had been destroyed, and now it was the turn of Antioch, and should God stay his hand? So he goes on, exhorting, threatening, consoling, conjuring up visions of Paradise for the martyrs, and offering his own firm faith to those who desired to live in Christ.

Day after day he delivered these staggering sermons which catch the quick panic and terror of those days in words that were meant simultaneously to hurt and to please, to console and to blame. The tortures went on. Day after day there were arrests and executions, and day after day they awaited word from Constantinople. "There is silence huge with terror, and utter loneliness everywhere," John said. It was a silence noisy with his own sermons, and there could have been little loneliness in the city where everyone was joined in the companionship of fear.

At last two imperial commissioners arrived with orders to make a complete report on the rebellion. The emperor relented. There would be no decimation of the populace, the city would not be razed to the ground, the prisoners who survived the execution squads would be pardoned. He ordered that Antioch should be degraded. Henceforward not Antioch but the neighboring city of Laodicea would receive the honor of being the metropolis of Syria.

On the day when the news of the pardon finally reached Antioch, John gave the last of his sermons *On the Statues.* "Today," he said, "I shall begin with the same words I spoke in the time of danger. So say with me: May God be praised, who enables us this day to celebrate our festival with so light and joyful a heart. May God be praised, who is able to do exceeding abundantly above all that we ask or think!"

The strain of those long weeks when the survival of the city hung in the balance weighed heavily on John, who fell dangerously ill. When he recovered, he continued to deliver his sermons as before, but with greater urgency and brilliance. The task he gave himself was the reform of the people of Antioch who had reverted to their evil ways. Theaters and horse races had been abolished, as part of their punishment for rebelling against the emperor, but in other ways they continued along the paths of sin. John's sermons are exhortations against the evil in men's hearts, but if this were all it is unlikely that anyone nowadays would read them. Together with exhortations went brilliant improvisations on the priesthood, on the nature of God's grace, on the incommensurability of God, and on a hundred other matters close to his heart. He came to be called "John Chrysostom," meaning John of the golden tongue, and the title was well-deserved. He never attempted to take heaven by storm, but was content to remain a sermonizer. He could put a sermon in a paragraph, and a paragraph into a single sentence. He drew strength from speaking to people, and because he loved them and was immediately concerned with their problems, he was able to speak to them as no one had ever spoken to them before, with a fiery wit and poetic excitement. He had a horror of luxury, the dominant vice of the Antiochenes, and some of his best pages are reserved for his denunciations against those who liked fine wines and seasoned food. Then as now women painted themselves, and he had no patience with them. "Her mouth is like a bear's mouth dyed with blood, her eyebrows are blackened with kitchen soot, her cheeks are whitened with dust like the walls of a sepulcher," he said, and went on to portray the shining cheeks and clear eyes of the woman who refused to adorn herself with cosmetics. Once he interrupted a sermon to inveigh against those who come noisily to Mass. "The table," he thundered, "is not for chattering jays, but for eagles who fly thither where the dead body lyeth." It was a typical statement, for all his life he regarded the Mass as a heroic offering to be attended by heroes.

John charged his sermons with poetry as well as invective; his rich and fertile mind was forever concerned with the poetry of Christ. He would take a text however uninteresting, and compose a poem around it. On a magnificent text he would embroider magnificently. Here he expounds a text from Isaiah in a sermon on the theme of the incomprehensibility of God:

Look at the sky, how beautiful it is, and how vast, all crowned with a blazing diadem of stars! For how many ages has it existed? Already it has been there for five thousand years, and shows no signs of aging. Like some young creature full of sap it preserves all the shining and the freshness of an earlier age, and manifests the beauty it possessed in the beginning, and time has not wearied it. And this vast, beautiful, ageless sky, unchangeable and gleaming, with all its stars, having existed through so many ages—this same God, whom some profess to be able to see with mortal eyes and comprehend with their own pitiable intelligences—this same God created it as easily as a man, throwing a handful of sticks together, creates a hut. And this is what Isaiah meant when he said, "He stretches out the heavens as a curtain, and spreadeth them out as a tent to dwell in."

(De Incomprehensibili, II, 6)

So John spoke, rejoicing in God's mystery and the certainty of His incommensurability. What distinguishes him from his contemporaries are soaring eloquence and daring imagery. In a famous passage he declared that God in coming to earth came like a man to a harlot:

God desired a harlot, and how doth He act? He doth not send to her any of His servants, He doth not send her angels or archangels, cherubim or seraphim. No, He Himself draws near to the one He loves, and He does not take her to Heaven, for He could not bring a harlot to Heaven, and therefore He Himself comes down to earth, to the harlot, and is not ashamed. He comes to her secret dwelling place and beholds her in her drunkenness. And how doth He come? Not in the bare essence of His original nature, but in the guise of one whom the harlot is seeking, in order that she might not be afraid when she sees Him and will not run away and escape from Him. He comes to the harlot as a man. And how doth He become a man? He is a conceived in the womb, He groweth little by little, and has intercourse with human nature. And He finds this harlot covered with sores and oppressed by devils. How doth He act? He draws nigh to her. She sees him and flees away. He calleth the wise men, saying: "Why are ye afraid? I am not a judge but a physician. I come not to judge the world, but to save the world." Straightway He calleth the wise men, for are not the wise men the immediate first fruits of His coming? They come and worship Him, and then the harlot herself comes and is transformed into a maiden. The Canaanite woman comes and partakes of His love. And how doth He act? He taketh the sinner and espouseth her to Himself, and giveth her the signet ring of the Holy Ghost as a seal between them.

(Eutropius II, 11)

In this world of images John was at home, his fine-spun mind finding analogies where ordinary men would never expect to find them, but he could speak when it suited him without this complex binding of many strands. He could speak very simply about matters that lay close to his heart, as when he described the benefits of the night and the comforts of the dark:

The night was not meant to be spent entirely in sleep. Why did Jesus pass so many nights amid the mountains, if not to instruct us by His example? It is during the night that all the plants respire, and it is then also that the soul of man is more penetrated with the dews falling from Heaven; and everything that has been scorched and burned during the day by the sun's fierce heat is refreshed and renewed during the night; and the tears we shed at night extinguish the fires of passion and quieten our guilty desires. Night heals the wounds of our soul and calms our griefs.

(Hom. in Psalm. VI)

So he spoke during those long years at Antioch, acquiring a reputation of eloquence and solemnity of utterance. To the Antiochenes he was simply "John" or "our bishop," a man who moved among them with a grave and terrible passion, waging a ferocious war on the wicked and exerting all his strength to protect the good. He had become a civic institution, and it was scarcely possible to believe they would permit him to leave Antioch. He had brought fame to the city, and even those who detested him were proud of him.

In September 379 there died in his palace at Constantinople the loose-living Archbishop Nectarius, who had ruled his see for sixteen disastrous years. The eunuch Eutropius, who bore the title Consul of the East, was then the highest civilian officer of state, with power to appoint archbishops. For some unknown reason it occurred to him to appoint John to the vacant see. Asterius, the Governor of Syria, was ordered to kidnap John and bring him under escort to Constantinople. On February 26, 398, John was enthroned as Patriarch of Constantinople, much against his will. He who hated power was now in the seat of power. He who fought against luxury and despised the kings of the world now lived in a luxurious palace close to the palace of the emperor. Only a few years remained to him, but all of them were filled with bitter fighting. Of these years six were spent in revolt and three in exile.

There were two Johns: one was the priest of Antioch, the other the Patriarch of Constantinople. The first held his temper in check, calm and fitful and brilliant, a man who demonstrated in the highest degree the spiritual excitement characteristic of the Antiochenes. The second assumed the fiercer colors of Constantinople. We see the small, thin, spidery archbishop growing leaner as the years pass, while the voice grows more raucous, and the face takes on the color of parchment. He stands before ornate altars, with thousands of candles gleaming, surrounded by servitors, wearing the heavy silken vestments of a prince of the Church, a man given over to loneliness and a ferocious impatience.

He had none of the acceptable virtues of a priest fulfilling a high executive position. He had no tact. He was always saying the first thing that came into his mind. He insulted the bishops by calling for their expense accounts, and then minutely examined them. He castigated them for their luxurious living, and made enemies among the people by his sermons against horse-racing. He ridiculed the wealth of Constantinople: the marble floors dusted with gold, the rich carpets, the silver couches, the gold spittoons. He injected strong doses of vinegar into the sweet wine of Constantinople. "Come to repentance," he said, addressing himself to rich and poor alike; and neither the rich nor the poor found any comfort in this stern patriarch who lived alone and deliberately set himself against ostentation. Because he lived so quietly and was often invisible, it was rumored that he spent his days in cyclopean orgies.

The Empress Eudoxia, the fair-haired daughter of a Frankish chieftain, was one of the few who were on friendly terms with the patriarch. Once when some relics were being translated to a chapel outside the walls, she followed the procession barefoot and unveiled, walking humbly like a handmaid of the Lord. John was overjoyed by this imperial tribute to the Church and a few days later he exulted in a sermon over the presence of the empress. "I exult, I am mad, and my madness is greater than wisdom," he declared. "Flying and dancing, I am borne on high! I am drunk with spiritual delights!"

The empress was a tall, slender, beautiful woman with a fiery temper. Like John, she owed her high position to the eunuch Eutropius, who permitted her to enjoy her high rank as the consort of the Emperor Arcadius, although he refused her the supreme title of Augusta. A defeat on the frontier and an ultimatum from the Goths led to the downfall of Eutropius, who had brought John to Constantinople and now worked actively against him. Eutropius was ordered to appear in the private apartments of the emperor and there he was stripped of all his honors, his estates, and his wealth. He made his way from the palace to the cathedral and took refuge in the sacristy. John was summoned just in time to prevent Eutropius from being arrested by soldiers who had forced their way into the cathedral, and although he had every reason to rejoice in the fate of the aging eunuch, he shouted: "You shall not slay Eutropius unless you first slay me! Take me to the emperor!" John was marched off to the palace between two rows of spearmen.

The interview in the palace was grotesque. The patriarch defended the eunuch, a weeping emperor demanded the eunuch's death. John was more resourceful than the emperor, for he claimed that since Eutropius had taken refuge in the cathedral he was henceforth God's prisoner and his punishment must come from God. The emperor was a man of great patience. He was prepared to humor John, knowing that in God's good time Eutropius would fall into his hands.

John celebrated his triumph over the emperor the next day by publicly assuming responsibility for Eutropius. Dressed in his pontifical robes John pointed to the eunuch who crouched beside the altar, weeping and shivering with fear, a symbol of the vanity of power. He declared:

Where now is the pomp and circumstance of his Consulship? Where are the gleaming torches? Where are the dancers, and the music of the dancers' feet, and the festivals? Where are the garlands and the curtains of the theater? Where is the applause which greeted him in the city? . . . They have all gone like visions of the night, dreams which vanish with the dawn of day, spring flowers withering on their stems with the coming of summer, no more than fleeting shadows or bubbles which have burst, or the torn threads of spider webs. Therefore let us sing this spiritual song: Vanity of vanities, all is vanity!

(*Eutropius* I, i)

Again and again in that sermon John returned to the theme of vanity as he pointed to the small crouching man who resembled "a hare or a frog chained to the altar-rail with ropes of fear." It was a brilliant sermon and the occasion was one to hearten the humble and mortify the proud. A few days later Eutropius slipped out of the cathedral, was arrested, and banished to Cyprus. Some weeks later he was arrested on what must have seemed to him the trivial charge of having mingled the imperial insignia with those of the consulate. He was brought back to Chalcedon for trial, and beheaded. The people danced in his blood, his wealth was confiscated by the imperial treasury, his name erased from his edicts, his statues were thrown down and smashed to pieces. With the death of Eutropius the long martyrdom of Chrysostom began.

No one knows how it began. At the beginning of the year 400 he was aware of a mounting tension in the air. Eudoxia, finally crowned Augusta, was turning against him, jealous of his influence with the Emperor Arcadius. Every day his enemies were increasing in numbers and looking for an excuse to depose him. A certain Acacius, Bishop of Beroea, once a warm admirer, was overheard saying: "I'll cook his goose for him!" The wealthy women of the court remembered his diatribes against luxury, the poor remembered his protests against the simple amusements which alone made their lives tolerable. In the early months of the following year he journeyed through Asia Minor in an effort to root out the corruption in the bishoprics, and made more enemies. At Ephesus he held a synod and deposed six bishops convicted of simony. When he returned to Constantinople, he may have known that he had sown the dragon's teeth.

For month after month he continued to fulfill the functions of a patriarch, aware of the winter in men's eyes, the frosty silence. He would say later that he was disliked because he lived in unrepentant humility and refused to flatter the effeminacy and sensuality of the rich, but these were not the only, or even the chief, reasons. He was hated as foreign bodies are hated; he was a foreigner in Constantinople who had never learned the ways of the great capital, the second Rome, and never thought they were worth learning. So they spewed him out.

A patriarch, however, could only be dethroned by another patriarch acting in concert with a synod of bishops and with the approval of the emperor. Theophilus, patriarch of Alexandria, once the secretary of Athanasius, became the agent of John's destruction. He was a rapacious intriguer with a vast hunger for power and a long history of arbitrary rule. In August 403 he sailed to Constantinople accompanied by twenty-eight bishops, determined to sit in judgment over the patriarch of Constantinople. Palladius, who wrote the life of

John, says he came like a beetle laden with dung. What is certain is that he came for no other purpose than to dethrone John, and for some months and perhaps years he had been in secret correspondence with John's enemies, who welcomed him as a heaven-sent accomplice in their intrigues. In the Palace of the Oak at Chalcedon the synod of bishops met under the protection of the Empress Eudoxia and formally condemned John to be deposed for crimes of treason and immorality. A few days later the emperor ratified the decree, and John was banished to Hieron in Bithynia. Officers of the court placed him under arrest and escorted him to the ship. John called them "spiders sent by a spider." He was like a man enmeshed in spiderwebs, concealed in their gluey darkness, a lost soul on his way to banishment in a distant frontier of the empire, while his enemies rejoiced. He must have prayed that the lightning would strike.

The lightning struck the next day. It took the form of an earthquake that shook the palace. Eudoxia, terrified because the earthquake was clearly God's judgment upon the imperial city, suffered a change of heart, and immediately sent a high officer of state to recall the exiled patriarch. John returned in triumph. At first he refused to enter the cathedral on the grounds that he could only be restored to power by the synod that had deposed him. But the synod was in full flight. Theophilus, together with his Egyptian, Persian, Armenian, and Mesopotamian bishops sailed away the same day, in fear of being hurled into the Bosphorus by the mob. A new synod of sixty bishops was convened, and the proceedings at the Palace of the Oak were annulled. Eudoxia and John exchanged friendly greetings.

These were the last friendly greetings they exchanged, for two months later the spiders were at work again. Eudoxia was a woman of fierce ambitions, and it occurred to her that there should be a silver statue of herself mounted on a high and slender porphyry pillar near the entrance of the cathedral. She was the empress, and could do as she pleased. John was the patriarch, and could do as he pleased. He was incensed. He is supposed to have said: "Again Herodias dances, again she rages, again she demands the head of John." His words were communicated to the empress, who had recovered from her superstitious fear of earthquakes and was determined to bring about his downfall. Once again the emperor issued an imperial decree, stripping John of his powers. He refused to obey. The Church had been entrusted to him by God, and he would not surrender it. Arcadius de-

cided on stern measures. He sent Thracian archers to plunder the
church treasure and to break up the crowds thronging outside the
cathedral, and when the priests took refuge in the public baths the
archers came and drove them out. All Constantinople was in an uproar as the emperor with his armed cutthroats fought against the
patriarch armed only with his spiritual power. John bowed to the inevitable. To prevent further bloodshed he surrendered himself to the
imperial officials charged with taking him into exile. Once more there
was a visitation from heaven. That night, after he had slipped out of
the city under escort, a mysterious fire broke out in the cathedral
built by the Emperor Constantius only forty-four years before. The
flames, driven by a violent wind, formed a fiery arch over the heads
of the panic-stricken people below, and by morning the cathedral was
a heap of ashes. Strangely, there was no loss of life.

Throughout his occupation of the patriarch's throne, the elements had worked for John. From the moment he left the city the
elements worked against him. For the rest of his life he was forced to
contend with storms and tempests, bitter cold nights and blazing hot
days, snowdrifts, barren mountains, and the raging of the winds.

At first no one told him where he would be sent. It was rumored
that his destination was Scythia, or perhaps Sebaste in Pontus, or perhaps Cucusus, a village in the Taurus Mountains on the edge of Cilicia
and Lesser Armenia. In high summer he wandered through Asia
Minor under guard, suffering from fever, headaches, general debility,
and there was a strange feeling of being adrift on high seas. At
Caesarea people came flocking to greet him; he was treated with kindness; a house was placed at his disposal and he recovered his health.
Then, just as he was beginning to hope that he would remain in
Caesarea, some fanatical monks armed with clubs plotted to do away
with him, and it was decided to continue the journey across the rocky
trails to Cucusus. It was a dangerous journey, for the Isaurian tribesmen were in a state of rebellion and attacked anyone who passed
through their territory. Finally, after hair-raising adventures, he
reached Cucusus. In that Armenian village on the edge of nowhere he
spent the greater part of the three remaining years of his life.

In Constantinople the police had orders to destroy his followers.
Thirty of his friends were flogged and tortured unmercifully; they
were roasted over oil lamps, their rib cages were opened, their flesh
was torn off with pincers. Those who survived the torture were

exiled to Arabia, Africa, Crete, and even to Gaul. At the height of the pogrom Eudoxia died. She had been among the closest of John's followers and his deadliest enemy; the Byzantines noted that her death occurred at an evil time, and for a while the pogrom was called off. In his distant village John still wielded a vestige of his power.

His influence was still being felt throughout the empire and even beyond, for he was still permitted to write letters. He wrote to the bishops of Thessalonica, Corinth, Laodicea, Jerusalem, Carthage, Milan, Brescia, and Aquileia. He wrote to Pope Innocent in Rome, who was sheltering some of his followers, and demanded the intervention of the Holy See. So many visitors came to Cucusus from Antioch that one of his enemies claimed that the entire population of Antioch was journeying to the obscure village in Armenia. "This formidable dead man," wrote Palladius, "is terrifying the living." Alarmed by his growing power, the Court ordered him to leave Cucusus under two praetorian guards and make his way to Pityus, a small village on the shores of the Black Sea, the farthest, the most miserable place in the whole empire. He never reached Pityus, for he died on the way. His last words were: "Glory to God for all things." He was sixty years old, and had spent forty months in exile.

In the year A.D. 438, thirty-one years after his death, the Emperor Theodosius II ordered his remains to be translated to Constantinople. Theodoret tells how the people gathered in close-packed boats on the Bosphorus to welcome him home in a blaze of torchlight. His relics were deposited near the altar of the Church of the Apostles, and the new emperor implored forgiveness for the wrongs committed by his father and mother. His bones remained in the Church of the Apostles until the tomb was rifled by the Crusaders in A.D. 1204. Then they were scattered all over Christendom.

In the Eastern Church St. John Chrysostom occupies the same position as St. Francis in the West. He is the saint who suffered humbly for the sins of the world, who possessed vast and terrible powers, and who sang angelically in his sermons. There was a brightness about this small, slender man who was so vulnerable and so urgent, and somehow remote from the world. One could not say of St. Basil that he was Christlike, but it is very easy to say it of St. John Chrysostom, for he alone among the saints of the Eastern Church seemed to move in a quiet glory, belonging more to heaven than to earth. So he appears in the mosaics, with that curious hesitancy, frail and wraith-like, as though at any moment he might disappear into the wall and leave only a shining light.

His people saw in him a man who behaved as Christ would have behaved if He had appeared in the Byzantine court: a man of wrath, physically insignificant, determined upon justice, summoning the people to repentance, announcing the new law in a golden voice, never at a loss for the perfect word. They saw strength in his frailty, and justice in his strength. Of the many things that were said of him after his death, the best was spoken by his pupil, Cassian of Marseilles: "It would be a great thing to attain to his stature, but it would be hard. Nevertheless even the following of him is lovely and magnificent."

12 ✠ THE CAPPADOCIAN FATHERS

T HE SEEDS of the Church flower in unlikely places. They flourished in obscure islands off the coast of Greece, in the deserts of Egypt, in the bare uplands of Asia Minor as well as in the great cities of Antioch, Salonica, and Rome. No one could predict where a seed might suddenly produce a tree. "The seed bloweth where it listeth, and thou hearest the sound thereof, but canst not tell whence it cometh, and whither it goeth: so is every one that is born of the Spirit."

No one would have guessed that the uplands of Cappadocia, in what is now central Turkey, would have produced in a single generation three great Fathers of the Church who profoundly influenced the course of Christianity. It is a harsh and unlovely land, dotted with strange nightmarish pillars of volcanic rock which on moonlit nights give the appearance of wandering ghosts. Wind and water have eroded them into tormented shapes; volcanic fire has painted them in savage colors. In winter it is bitterly cold, in spring feverishly hot on the days when there are no floods, or rain, or hailstorms, or biting winds. In summer it becomes so hot that men pray for the cold north winds to cool the burning earth.

In those days Cappadocia was not famous for theologians, although there were many converts during the apostolic age. It was famous for its horses and the wry good humor of its people. Cappadocia, Caria, and Crete were called "the three worst K's (*tria kappa kakista*)." Men who lived in more favored regions liked to tell how a viper bit a Cappadocian, and the viper died. They were a sturdy people, like most who live in the highlands, and under the Romans they

175

had the reputation of being good chair-bearers and bad fighters. They were uncouth and sweet-tempered, and their accents were barbarous. "They smell of fish-fry and stew," said the great scholar Libanius, "and they say to everyone, 'I adore you.'"

About 329, four years after the Council of Nicaea, Basil was born in Caesarea, the modern Kayseri. The town lay in the foothills of Mount Argaeus, once volcanic, now shrouded in everlasting snow, and was of some considerable importance, for it lay on the trade route from Babylon on the Euphrates to Sinope on the Black Sea, on the Persian royal road that linked Sardis to Susa, and on the Roman road joining Ephesus to the East. It was the capital of the Cappadocian kings, and in A.D. 260 was said to have a population of four hundred thousand. Today it is still a town of some importance, with its airplane factory and Russian-built cotton mills, though it has the ramshackle appearance of a provincial town. In the days of Basil, when it was the civil and ecclesiastical capital of Cappadocia, there were marble colonnades, hanging gardens, and palaces. The highways brought great wealth, and Persian, Syrian, and Greek culture contended for the minds of the Cappadocians.

Basil's father was a man of wealth, a lawyer with large estates in Pontus, Cappadocia, and Lesser Armenia. Of his nine children four became saints: his three sons Basil, Gregory, and Peter, and his daughter Macrina. His wife, the beautiful Emmelia, also became a saint. There is no other recorded instance of so much sanctity in a single generation in a single family.

At first there was no indication that Basil would become a saint. He was intended for the law, studied in Antioch under Libanius, and at the University of Athens, where one of his contemporaries was the future Emperor Julian. Basil reveled in the Greek classics, and to the end of his life, unlike most Christian theologians, he was inclined to defend them; and his writings are saturated with knowledge of classical authors. Returning from Athens to Caesarea he became a lawyer, but only briefly. When his younger brother Naucratius died suddenly while living as a hermit on the family estate at Pontus, Basil decided to follow in the path of his dead brother and set about founding a monastery on the family estate; his greatest claim to fame arises from the monasteries he founded, and the cautious rules he announced for their maintenance. He was ideally suited to be a superintendent of monasteries, for he was a patrician with an eagle-eyed devotion to principles, with no nonsense about him. A tall, heavy-set man with high cheekbones and a thick bristling beard, he was in all respects unlike his gentle, retiring brother Gregory. Basil made the laws. Gregory was a mystic who broke the laws whenever it pleased him.

The idea for setting up the monastery on the family estate seems to have come originally from Basil's sister Macrina. For her the world scarcely existed, and the word most often on her lips was "renunciation." All the wealth, power, and prestige that had descended to the family must be renounced for the glory of God. Without property, wearing a single garment, sleeping on the ground, eating only enough to enable the body to survive, one must live for God alone, and there must be no other thoughts except the thought of God. Basil, fired by her enthusiasm for the monastic life, set out on a prolonged tour of Egypt, Palestine, Syria, and Mesopotamia to study the anchorites in their caves and the little reed huts they built in the desert. The death of Naucratius and the desire of Macrina were the spurs to action; and when he returned, he built his own monastery at Ibora, a small hamlet on the river Iris, sheltered by high and thickly wooded mountains. For Basil this was his fortress, his kingdom, his highwayman's lair. He spoke of the estate in the authentic terms of a chieftain who has carved out a small principality for himself and intends to defend it to the death. "I am the master of the pass," he wrote, and he remained the master of it until his death.

The iron rules of the monastic community were compiled by Basil over many years. They amount to two hundred closely printed pages and resemble nothing so much as a corpus of laws regulating a community of Spartan warriors. Nothing has been left out; there is no moment of the day that is not provided for. The hours of prayer, of eating, and sleeping are exactly determined; so too is the exact punishment to be meted out to those who have infringed the law. The way the monks walk, and what they wear, and how they address one another and their superiors, all these matters are worked out with grave care. The monastic laws were concerned with safeguards and precautions against sin. Boys at puberty were not allowed to sleep in beds beside one another; there was always an older monk in a bed between them. Under no conditions must monks give way to laughter, for many sins have their origin in frivolity and lightheadedness. "All must remain at their appointed posts," Basil wrote. "No one must enter where he is not commanded to go, unless he has the permission of responsible authorities."

Basil believed that this formidable discipline could be made tolerable by a Superior of meek and charitable character. The stern laws were to be enforced, but humbly. If the Superior himself committed a fault, then he was to be judged by his peers, the Superiors of other monasteries. The Superior must be grave, earnest, gentle, lowly, and kind, the image of Christ, and therefore entitled to demand obedience unto death. The stakes were high, for it was the task of the Superior to carry his entire community of monks to heaven. Basil was quite sure that nothing was to be gained by living in isolation, like the monks of Egypt. "If you always live alone, whose feet will you wash?" he asked, thus damning the pretensions of the solitary hermits.

Basil hungered for power, and when he chose he could thunder like any tyrant. When a woman called Simplicia, a heretic who possessed immense wealth and innumerable eunuchs, attacked Basil for consecrating one of her runaway slaves, he answered:

Be mindful of the last day, and if you please, do not think of teaching me! We know more than you, and we are not so choked up by thorns, nor do we have the advantage of being able to mingle a few virtues with ten times as many vices. You have roused against us your lizards and toads, which are indeed animals of the springtime, though unclean. But there will come a bird from above to feed on them. It doesn't matter to me in the least what you think: I am concerned only with God's judgments. Should there be need of witnesses, then slaves will not step forward, nor any of those hapless and accursed eunuchs—I mean what I say—a race neither male nor female, women-mad, envious, of evil knowledge, quick to anger, effeminate, the slaves of their bellies, money-hunters, coarse oafs who grumble about their dinners.

(*Epistolae*, 95)

In this way Basil liked to rid himself of the interminable complaints of women and indeed of all those who crossed his path, and the violence of his temper was not notably improved when he became Bishop of Caesarea with authority extending over eleven provinces of Asia Minor. He raged against the court in Constantinople and its Arian emperor, and against worldly clerics and presbyters. He realized that the world was full of evil, and that it was beyond belief that a community of Christians would consist only of the virtuous. He discovered that a presbyter was living with his housekeeper; worse still, a deacon had trained a band of boys and girls in dancing and singing, and was leading them triumphantly through the countryside in a perpetual bacchanalia. Sometimes Basil threw up his hands in weariness and horror. Two years after becoming bishop, he wrote:

The teachings of the true faith have been overthrown. . . . Gone is the dignity of the priesthood. None tend the flock of the Lord with wisdom. Proud men squander the money intended for the poor on their own pleasures and in the giving of gifts. No longer is there the strict observance of the canons. Licence to commit sin has spread through the land; and those who have entered office by favor reward their masters with the gift that pleases them most—licence to commit any sin they please. Just judgment is dead. Everyone follows the whims of his own heart, and wickedness has no bounds at all.

(Epistolae, 91)

Basil was inclined to believe that the world was drowning in an evil flood. His enemies were legion. In particular, the Emperor Valens detested him and sent his lieutenant, the prefect Modestus, to Caesarea to conduct a court of inquiry into the actions of the bishop. The inquiry became a contest of wills, with Modestus growing increasingly angry and confused as Basil became increasingly calm. Once Modestus threatened to take out Basil's liver. Basil, who suffered from a disease of the liver, answered with a smile: "How charming of you. It hurts me intolerably, and if you remove it, you will relieve my suffering!"

Modestus reported to Valens that Basil showed an unholy obstinacy. "He is too strong for persuasion, and will yield to nothing but force," Modestus reported, having misjudged his adversary.

Valens was determined to bring Basil to heel, and sent one of his best generals, Count Terrentius, to try the effects of flattery. When these failed, he sent Demosthenes, the chamberlain who acted as *chef de cuisine* to the court. Basil refused to listen to Demosthenes, who was a eunuch and therefore scarcely human. Finally, in the following year, the emperor himself decided to interrogate Basil during a tour of inspection. On the Feast of the Epiphany the emperor presented himself in the basilica where Basil was officiating. After the service the emperor and the bishop met in private. Demosthenes was present, and began to argue theology. Basil smiled and said, "Demosthenes would be better served if he attended to his sauces," and the emperor was amused. The meeting was cordial, but the Arian emperor was unable to convert the orthodox bishop. At last Basil reminded the emperor that there was a great need for a hospital at Caesarea, with a chapel, dispensaries, dormitories, workshops for the artisans, and special buildings reserved for lepers. Valens offered a large contribution to the hospital and they parted on friendly terms.

When the emperor had gone, Basil returned to his sickbed. He was only forty-three, but looked like an old man, toothless, frail, in incessant pain. Some years before, in a rare moment of wry humor, he wrote: "My body is so wasted with fever that it appears to be even thinner than I." He was almost transparent, living on his nervous energy, and like many old men he was liable to be flustered if anyone entered his room unexpectedly. He was tormented by headaches and the slightest movement could cause him pain.

His greatest surviving work is not the *Longer and Shorter Rules* with their stern commands and careful provisions for the moral health of monks, but a short work called the *Hexaemeron,* or *The Six Days of Creation.* This book, ostensibly a commentary on *Genesis,* provides a wonderful hodgepodge of ideas on all kinds of subjects that attracted Basil's devout attention. Gregory of Nyssa, his younger brother, noted a curious omission. There is nothing in the *Hexaemeron* about the creation of man, which seems in Basil's eyes to have been of considerably less importance than the creation of the earth. In affectionate rebuttal of his brother's theology Gregory of Nyssa wrote an important work on the creation of man, without mentioning the creation of the earth. Basil possessed the characteristic Greek love of light, and he celebrated its creation in one of the best passages of the book:

For the heavens were enveloped in darkness, and now quite suddenly they appeared in the beauty they still wear in our eyes; and all the air was lighted up, light and air commingling together, and splendidly and quickly did they disperse in all directions, as far as they could go. Light sprang up to the very ether and the heavens, and the width and breadth of the world were bathed in light, north, south, east, and west. And the waters shone, glittering, shooting forth quivering flashes of reflected light from their clear surfaces.

(Hexaemeron II, 7)

Such moments of joy were rare in the life of Basil whose mood was more often that of a man weighed down with grief, stern and irascible by turns, only too aware of his own frailties and the frailties of mankind. His ruthless and inflexible mind dwelt lovingly on matters of discipline, the ordered arrangement of monkish communities, but dwelt less lovingly on ordinary humanity. Once he wrote: "Terrible among us is the famine of love," and he seemed to be speaking of himself. The difference between Basil and Gregory was clearly expressed by Rufinus when he wrote: "Basil is humble before God, but Gregory is humble before men also."

Basil died at the age of fifty, worn out by his labors. His greatest claim to fame was that he was the inventor of monastic discipline. Jerome, who cordially disliked him as he disliked most of the Fathers of the Church, said that "he ruined many gifts of continence and intelligence by the sin of pride." It was true, but he was a saint nevertheless. In a time of peril he commanded the fortress of God.

Gregory of Nyssa

THERE was a harsh, unyielding quality in Basil, and he possessed a curious contempt for humanity. His brother Gregory had no harshness in him, he yielded only too easily, and there was never a moment when he despised his fellowmen. On the contrary he saw them as angels walking through a divine landscape, and for him the earth was like a foretaste of heaven.

Four or five years younger than Basil, Gregory spent his youth under his brother's shadow, and he seems to have resented his own dependence and inferiority. His health was weak, he was often ill, and his schooling was irregular. He read widely in his father's library, reading all the Greek classics, and he seems to have had no particular attachment to the devotional life practiced by his mother Emmelia. When his father died, he lived on his share of the paternal estate and refused to adopt a profession.

He was about twenty when there occurred the first of the quiet revelations that came to him at intervals, reminding him that he had other duties to perform than the enjoyment of a library. One day, quite unexpectedly, his mother announced that the relics of forty martyrs which had come into the possession of the family, were to be solemnly translated to a chapel especially prepared for them on the family estate at Annesi. Gregory was ordered to attend the requiem Mass and the night-long vigils. He arrived at Annesi in a furious temper. Like many others in his time he was dubious about the merits of relic-worship, and he was annoyed both by the long journey and by the prospect of interminable psalm singing. The Emperor Julian had characterized the Christians as "mere bone-worshipers," and the sophist Eunapios had spoken of "those martyrs, before whose salted and pickled bones the monks and bishops grovel in the dust." When the rites for the forty martyrs began, Gregory quietly slipped away from the garden and fell asleep in another garden nearby. He felt he was well rid of those interminable ceremonies.

While asleep, he saw forty armed martyrs standing over him with menacing gestures, demanding why he was not present at the celebration. They threatened him and would have put him to death for impiety if one, more tolerant than the rest, had not shown him mercy. The dream was so vivid and harrowing that Gregory woke up weeping, and made his way remorsefully to the garden where the pickled bones of the martyrs, gathered together in an immense urn, were being worshiped by the faithful. A contrite Gregory watched the proceedings to the end. He became a practicing Christian.

Literature and rhetoric were his greatest loves, and though for a while he became a lector, reading to the congregation from the pulpit, he soon abandoned any thought of entering the Church. The vision faded. He married, and settled down to a comfortable living as a teacher of rhetoric. We know little about his wife except that her name was Theosobeia. When she died some twenty years later Gregory of Nazianzen called her "the glory of the Church, the adornment of Christ, the helper of our generation, the hope of womankind, the most beautiful and glorious among the brethren." She seems to have been a quiet and unassuming woman, a good wife to her husband, and a generous supporter of the Church.

Because he had married, the priestly life was closed to Gregory even if he had wanted to assume it. The marriage seems not to have been particularly happy; he had no vocation for marriage as he had no vocation for religion. In the treatise *On Virginity*, which he wrote after his wife's death, he showed a distaste for the physical side of marriage amounting to terror; he was tormented by the agonies of childbearing, and by the despair of a wife who loses her child and the despair of a husband who loses his wife. Mortality and marriage were bed-fellows; death brooded over the marriage bed; only the man who gave himself up to quiet contemplation with no human entanglements could hope for blessedness. As he pondered the impermanence of beauty and fame, his restless temper grew gradually quiet, for he had found peace in the Church. He became one of the monks living in Basil's monastic community in Ibora.

He was an awkward monk, never quite at ease unless he was alone. He had none of Basil's deliberate asceticism and fierce self-control. Basil liked to speak of his brother's "utter simplicity of mind," meaning that Gregory solved problems in childish and sometimes dangerous ways. He would have preferred more dignity, a more strenuous mind. Gregory, on his part, would have preferred a less resolute brother, one who was not so palpably in love with high office, and he was enraged when, as a result of an episcopal dispute over boundaries, Basil decided to appoint a whole flock of bishops in the region around Caesarea to prevent Bishop Anthimus of Tyana from encroaching on his territory. Among the appointed bishops was Gregory, who was given the see of Nyssa, a small town ten miles from Caesarea which survives today as an obscure village and horse station. Gregory had no administrative ability, detested giving orders, and especially disliked ecclesiastical panoply. He therefore refused the appointment. Basil, who could be as stern as God, simply ordered him to obey. Gregory said afterward that the day of his consecration was the most miserable in his life.

In time he came to love Nyssa, though he never succeeded in deriving any pleasure from being a bishop. He loved his small house, his humble furniture, his rows of books. He liked sitting by the fire on winter nights. He lived simply, slept on sackcloth, and drank only water. Suddenly, when he had been bishop for three years, he was accused of embezzling church funds. He was suffering from pleurisy when the unlikely charge was read to him. The provincial synod meeting in Ancyra, the modern Ankara, ordered his arrest. The Bishop of Nyssa was bound in chains and led off to meet his accusers, and at some time during the journey he managed to escape. He went into hiding. He enjoyed his period of eclipse, and said he was happier in hiding than when he wore the robes of a bishop. Many months later, when the charge against him was forgotten, he returned to Nyssa in triumph. His letter describing his return, written in a peculiarly modern style, has survived:

There was a chill wind blowing through the clouds, bringing a drizzle, which hit us with its dampness. The sky threatened such rain as no one had ever known, and to our left came the thunder— unending thunder—and quick flashes of lightning, thunder and lightning in rapid succession. . . . Later the rain fell. It was not unpleasant, just enough to moisten the air. We were close to home when the clouds bellying above us suddenly emptied, and because of the storm our entrance was very quiet, no one being aware of our coming.

And then as we reached the covered porch [of the bishop's palace], the sound of the carriage wheels was heard and the people poured out to meet us, as though they had been mechanically propelled from nowhere, I know not how or why it came about, but they were all there, flocking round us so closely it was not easy to descend from the carriage, for there was not a foot of clear space anywhere. So we persuaded them, but with some difficulty, to allow us to alight and let the mules pass, but the crowd surrounded us and would have crushed us with excessive kindness, and I was near fainting. When we were well within the covered porch, we saw a river of fire pouring into the church, and this came from the choirs of virgins carrying wax candles in their hands as they marched in procession, kindling a blaze of splendor. Then I went into the church and rejoiced and wept with my people—for I wept and rejoiced as they did —and after I had said prayers I hastened to write this letter to Your Holiness, being myself exceedingly thirsty, but determined to write to you before surrendering to my physical wants.

(Epistolae, 3)

A good deal of Gregory—his naïveté, his humility, his eloquence, even his playfulness—is in this letter. Almost alone among the Fathers he could convey a very human delight in physical things, and he had an eye for detail. He did not always write like this. His vast tract against the Eunomians is a masterpiece of turgidity, an unrelenting examination of dull theories by a mind dulled by contact with them. He had no skill in theological debate; his genius lay in his power to contemplate first and last things. He writes about the dawn of creation, the vision of God, and the Last Judgment with equal felicity. Like Origen he has the forgiving temper, and it is impossible for him to imagine that God would banish sinners to eternal torment. He held firmly to the belief in the final *restoratio*, when all, sinners and saints alike, enter the blessedness promised by the resurrection of Christ, for the dignity of man demands a fate worthy of his dignity. For Gregory all life is sacramental, and Christ is everywhere, even among the dead and most certainly among the damned.

In this way, with a kind of leaping joy and without any hesitations, Gregory celebrates the divinity of man. In his treatise *On the Making of Man* he wrote of Adam at the dawn of Creation:

> *By its likeness to God human nature was made as it were a living image partaking with the Godhead both in rank and in name, clothed in virtue, reposing in the blessedness of immortality, garlanded with the crown of righteousness, and so a perfect likeness to the beauty of the Godhead in all that pertains to the dignity of majesty.*
>
> (De hominis Opificio IV, 136)

The theme of Gregory is the majesty of man and man's perfect freedom under God—that God who is unknowable and yet known, seen and unseen, very close and infinitely far away. The saints and the prophets had spoken often about the vision of God, reaching many different conclusions. At Sinai God said to Moses: "There shall no man see me and live." In the *Gospel according to St. John* it is written: "No man hath seen God at any time." St. Paul said: "Whom no man hath seen, nor can see." But there was Old Testament authority that God had been seen in visons, for how else could one read the words of Habakkuk: "His brightness was as the light; he had horns coming out of his hands; and there was the hiding of his power." Was this the vision?

Gregory wrestled with the vision of God in many of his writings, notably in his great mystical works *The Life of Moses* and his *Commentary on the Song of Songs*. For him the culminating moment in the life of Moses occurs in the visionary darkness of Sinai. He describes the ascent in short, quick sentences that glow like flickering flames:

> *He sees the flame springing up, and lightly climbs toward it, removing his sandals. He claims the same liberty for his family and for his people. He has seen the enemy sink and drown beneath the waves. He has lived under the Cloud. He has quenched his thirst on the Rock. He has harvested bread from Heaven. And stretching out his hands, he has triumphed over the enemy. He has heard the trumpet blasts. He has entered into the dark place. He has entered into the secret recesses of the tabernacle not made by human hands. He has*

learned the secrets of the divine priesthood. He has brought down the idols. He has begged God's mercy. He has restored the law, which has been broken by the Jews. He has shone in glory. And having reached this summit, he burns even now with insatiable desire, and he still thirsts for that which already fills him, and as though he had received nothing, he begs God to give him more; he demands that God should appear to him, not as analogy, but as He is. . . .

So he desires, not the reflection or the mirrored image of God, but God seen face to face. And the divine voice by refusing offers him what he desires: a few words which open out into an immense abyss of thought, the magnificence of God fulfilling his desires, but never promising either peace or satiety. For this is the true vision of God: that those who lift their eyes toward Him never cease to desire Him. And that is why God said: "Thou canst not see my face, for there shall no man see me and live."

(De Vita Moysis, 401)

For Gregory the voice of God speaking in the darkness was itself the vision, and the ascent was not an ascent so much as "a motionless movement," a progress which is all the more resolute because the worshiper is motionless, absorbed in the sweetness of contemplation. With these paradoxes Gregory is at home, as he describes the ascent which is a falling away, and a stumbling which is a rising into grace.

To the end Gregory saw men shining in angelic raiment; they were husbandmen reaping immortal wheat. When his sister Macrina lay dying, Gregory engaged in a long conversation with her; over many nights and days they talked about the purpose of life and the inevitability of the resurrection and of how in the end all things will be gathered into blessedness. Once Macrina said words that sound strangely like the words of Gregory. She said: "Because beauty is boundless, love shall never cease."

No one knows when Gregory died, though it must have been about the year A.D. 395. Four hundred years after his death, at the Seventh General Council held in A.D. 787, the assembled princes of the Church granted him a title which exceeded in their eyes all the other titles granted to the Fathers of the Church; they called him "Father of Fathers." It was an odd yet singularly appropriate honor to bestow on an obscure, retiring man who went through life as though it were a dream, scarcely touching the earth. He was one of those who drank at the wellspring.

13 ✠ GREGORY THE GREAT

TODAY Gregory the Great is best remembered because he saw the Archangel Michael sheathing a bloody sword above the mausoleum of the Emperor Hadrian in Rome. We are told that in the year A.D. 590 he was marching at the head of a penitential procession to St. Peter's, praying for deliverance from the plague, when he saw the vision. He looked up, and suddenly he saw a towering angel in gleaming armor attended by a choir of angels singing the anthem, "Queen of Heaven, rejoice!" It was a fleeting vision, but at that moment Gregory knew that the plague would be stayed. In the reign of his successor, Pope Boniface IV, a shrine was built on the mausoleum and dedicated to the Archangel, and some time later a statue replaced the shrine. So it came about that the tomb of a contemplative emperor became Castel Sant'Angelo, the fortress of the holy angel.

Gregory was a man who lived in visions while remaining hard-headed and practical. He wrote magnificently in a prose that bears the stamp of authority whether he is describing the miraculous events he had seen with his own eyes or relating the fables he had learned from some Roman wiseacre. He had the ablest mind in Rome, and yet no one could be more credulous. He was pope, prefect, lawyer, fabulist, author of innumerable homilies and commentaries, and worker of miracles. He was responsible for the conversion of the English, and he wrote one of the enduring masterpieces of the Middle Ages.

He was born to wealth and high position, his father a senator who possessed large estates in Sicily and a palace on the Caelian hill. The names of many senators were to be found among his ancestors.

One of his ancestors was a pope, while his mother Silvia and two of his aunts are remembered in the calendar of saints. His family name was Gordianus, and it is possible that he was descended from the emperor of the same name. The portraits of his mother and father survived into the ninth century when they were seen by his biographer John the Deacon. Gregory was made in the image of his father, with small brown eyes, long arched eyebrows, a full nose with wide nostrils, and a prominent chin with a scant tawny beard.

His father died when he was still young, and he seems never to have completely recovered from his grief. It is one of the characteristics of the Fathers of the Church that nearly all of them lost their fathers at an early age. At the death of Gordianus, his wife retired to a monastic cell, and Gregory was left alone in the palace with his tutors, who taught him grammar, dialectics, and rhetoric; to the end of his life his grammar remained defective, and his knowledge of dialectics never went beyond the stage reached by schoolboys. Yet he was a master of rhetoric and became a proficient lawyer. Grave in speech and prematurely old, bearing one of the greatest names in Rome, he began to climb the *ordo honorum*, being remarked for the clarity of his mind and his determination to get things done. Suddenly, at the age of thirty-three, he found himself appointed prefect, or mayor, of Rome.

No one knows why he was given this high office. Like Ambrose, who became governor of a province at a comparatively early age, Gregory must have owed his appointment as much to his high connections as to his own brilliance. The prefect of Rome wore the purple cloak of the ancient emperors and rode in a chariot drawn by four snow-white horses. The whole economy of Rome depended upon his will: the grain supplies, the free doles for the poor, the construction of new buildings, baths, sewers, and riverbanks—all these had to be decided by the prefect, whose rule extended far beyond the confines of Rome, for it included the adjacent territory of Latium, Naples, Calabria, and Sicily. His appointment, which occurred in the year A.D. 573, coincided with the invasion of Rome by the Lombards, the death of a pope, and the death of Narses, the imperial viceroy who ruled in the name of the Byzantine emperor. On Gregory's shoulders there fell some of the burdens of the dead pope and the dead viceroy.

It was a time of troubles, with the invaders marching across Italy, and Rome very nearly defenseless against the marauding Lombards. Although he was a talented administrator, Gregory had no taste for governing a city, and soon he was busy dividing up his inheritance. One portion was given to the poor, another went to the endowment of six monasteries in Sicily, another went to the conversion of the palace on the Caelian hill into a monastic retreat for his family. From being a prefect he became a simple monk in his own house.

In later years Gregory looked back on the three years he spent in monkish seclusion as the happiest of his life. He gave himself up to fasting and prayers: fasting ruined his digestion, and night-long prayers played havoc with his heart. He lived on raw vegetables sent to him by his mother on a silver dish, the one remaining heirloom in the possession of the family. One day he gave the dish away to a shipwrecked sailor begging alms in the street, and saw a vision: the shipwrecked sailor suddenly appeared as an angel, and the dish was given back to him. That was the first vision. There were many others.

At the end of his three years' retreat Gregory was summoned by Pope Benedict I to be the ecclesiastical administrator of one of the seven districts of Rome. That year there was a plague followed by a tremendous rainfall, and there were some who thought the end of the world had come. Famine was rampant; the Lombards were at the gates; the pope died; and the Romans were in despair. The new pope, Pelagius II, placed his trust on the Emperor Tiberius in Byzantium and decided to put Gregory in charge of a papal mission to the imperial court, where it was hoped that funds would become available to succor the Romans. Gregory became the *apocrisarius* or papal legate, with all the powers of a minister plenipotentiary.

For nearly seven years Gregory, who never learned Greek, ate out his heart in the eastern capital. He admired Tiberius, a tall, deeply religious man whose gray eyes peer down from many mosaics, but he was unable to convince him of the need to defend distant parts of the empire. Gregory sent a stream of petitions to the court, with no success. Tiberius died, leaving to his successor Maurice an empty treasury and his own daughter. The Byzantine court changed character, for Maurice was a short, bandy-legged general who made no claim to elegance or religious emotion, and indeed he had been raised to the purple for no other reason than his reputation for honesty. Gregory regarded his years in Byzantium as a trial to be endured, and he was overjoyed when the time came for his recall to Rome.

During his last years in Byzantium Gregory began writing the extraordinary daybook which has come down to us under the title of *Moralia*. Theoretically the book is an extended commentary on *Job*, but the scriptural texts are only the springboard for his daydreams, his hopes, his passions, and his most intimate thoughts. He wrestles with interpretation of the texts, forces them to bear recondite Christian meanings, and it soon becomes evident that this wrestling is merely the muscular exercise needed before coming to grips with his own thoughts. He is a modern Job, questioning the universe, yet sure of himself. With his deep-seated belief in the miraculous there goes a cautious understanding of the world as it is. The administrator, the ascetic, the papal legate, and the enchanted visionary are all present in the *Moralia*.

He was never an accurate or even a very grammatical writer, but he could write with wonderful power when he chose. He could say: "In this golden cup of Babylon, Eve was the first who became drunk of her own accord," and in this single sentence he composed a poem to Eve. He would describe a proud man as one who "walks with himself along the broad spaces of his thought and silently utters his own praises," and it is evident that he knew pride well, and was revolted by it, and ultimately came to terms with it. "What is man but a leaf which fell from a tree in Paradise?" he asked once. Here and there in the *Moralia* we come upon astonishing passages in which we see him wrestling with his own thoughts and writing with angelic patience and sudden lyrical improvisations. Here he is describing the deathly cold of the enemies of God:

Abraham was heaven, Isaac was heaven, Jacob was heaven. But because the persecutors of the Lord, the high priests of the Jews, who were frozen with the torpor of unbelief, sprang from the race of those ancestors, the frost came, as it were, from heaven, because the frozen herd of unbelievers came forth from the lofty offspring of the saints. For when Caiaphas was born from Abraham, what else was it, but that ice came forth from heaven? Satan also came forth like ice from the womb of God; in this way the teacher of iniquities came forth, frozen with the torpor of sin, from the warmth of His mysteries.

(*Moralia*, XXIX, 55)

Such statements defy logic and belong to poetry, a world in which he was perfectly at home. He was fond of strange analogies, violent turns of phrase, arguments which were entirely lacking in logical cohesion, and he especially enjoyed long and learned discussions on the resurrection of the flesh, maintaining that if a man could grow from a small seed, emerging from nothing, he could after his death emerge just as easily into life again. "Look at the acorn, and then at the oak," he said; and from long pondering he came to the conclusion that the resurrection of the flesh was as certain as sunrise.

He was still writing the *Moralia* when another pestilence and another flood were visited on Rome, and in the general excitement there rose a popular clamor to make him pope. It was an office he felt too burdensome for his narrow shoulders. Like Ambrose, he was terrified by the prospect of high position, and wrote to the Emperor Maurice a letter begging him to refuse his consent—in this way he hoped to be spared the heavy weight of a duty which threatened to destroy him. He said he was a recluse, not a public person; he was unfitted to be pope; he demanded only to be left in peace. The letter was intercepted by Germanus, the prefect of Rome, and another letter declaring the desire of the city that Gregory should be pope was substituted. Gregory fled from Rome. His first biographer, a monk of Whitby, described how he was carried out of the city in a basket and lay concealed for three days while the Romans sought him with prayers and penitential fasting. Finally, on the third night, a brilliant light shone from heaven and revealed his hiding place. Captured, he was brought to Rome in triumph and consecrated in St. Peter's. He was about fifty years old.

Gregory ruled like a king, surrounded by monkish courtiers. He extended the political power of the papacy, and lived according to the strict *Pastoral Rule* he had composed in order to convince his bishops that presumption and pride were their chief enemies, and only a holy humility gave them power to rule their flock. The *Pastoral Rule* is a very human document, stern and yet yielding, warning the pastors against the foibles of the human heart—do not be too severe with sinners for they will then find contentment in greater sins—and extolling the virtue of affection above all others. A bishop should love his flock; without love, all things are vain; loving them, they may be led along the path of salvation. He makes a point of asking bishops to speak the language of common men. Gregory's own sermons to the laity testify to his skill in speaking the language of the people, but the twenty sermons on Ezekiel are more carefully contrived, being intended for a more exalted audience. Ezekiel entranced him with its mysterious intimations of the divine presence: the thunder rolls, the stars wheel across the skies, and the air is filled with the sound of wings. Even as Gregory was speaking in the last years of the century, the Lombards were causing havoc on the outskirts of Rome; and sometimes he took comfort from the thought of the imminent destruction of the world:

Everywhere we see sorrows, everywhere we hear lamentation. Cities lie destroyed, fortresses overthrown, harvests ravaged; the land is brought to desolation. No peasant in the fields, scarcely a dweller in the cities is left; yet even these little remnants of the human race are still smitten today unceasingly. The scourges of Heaven's justice have no end; for not even through these scourges are guilty actions turned to right. Some of our people we see led away prisoners, some mutilated, some slain. What, then, is there to please us in this world, my brethren? If even thus we still love it, we love now not its joys, but its wounds. Rome herself, once mistress of the world, how do we see her now? Worn out with mighty griefs, bereft of her citizens, trodden down by enemies, full of ruins. Where now is her Senate? Where her people? Their bones lie rotting, their flesh consumed, all the pride of her worldy glories is dead and gone.

(*Hom. in Ezek.* II, 6:22)

Like another Jerome, but with even more urgency, he celebrated the defeats of Rome because they brought men closer to heaven. He had no thought of salvation for himself alone, but cared deeply for the salvation of men. John the Deacon tells the story that when Gregory heard that a poor man had died of hunger, he chastised himself and refused to say Mass for several days, saying he was himself his brother's murderer. He was always giving money to the poor, carefully inscribing their names, addresses, and professions in a notebook. He liked facts, figures, and balanced accounts, and woe betide anyone who failed to give the pope a proper reckoning. Out of the papal patrimony—that vast collection of estates bequeathed to the Church—he paid ransoms, built hospitals, fed the poor, and shored up the ruins of Rome.

Yet always he was aware of the Day of Judgment, the flames already licking the world, the taste of ashes already in the air. No one could be more practical, but no one could be more visionary. For him the world was like a fairground, where marvelous and strange events were continually taking place. How credulous he was we know from his famous *Dialogues*, those holy fairy stories full of ghosts and goblins with the moral pointed always to the rewards of the godly and the disasters that fall inevitably on those who belong to the devil's party. He told the story of a certain Bishop Datius who chose a beautiful house in Corinth even though it was known to be haunted by the devil. In the dead of night he heard the roar of lions, the braying of asses, the hissing of serpents, the grunting of pigs, and the squealing of rats; and this torrent of noise, far from disturbing him, merely amused him, for he recognized the weapons employed by the devil to prevent good bishops from sleeping. When the devil appeared, the bishop taunted him with the question: "Why, since you wish to be like God, do you succeed only in imitating the beasts?" The devil, says Gregory, slunk away in terror.

Some of the stories told by Gregory are gay, others are brutal, still others read like the dreams of an old pontiff as he stirs restlessly in bed in the half-light of the coming dawn. Gregory said he liked to listen to old men's tales, and found them sufficiently rewarding to record them in the intervals of attending to the duties of the pontificate, but it is possible that he invented many of the stories, for sometimes they suggest the strange flame-lit corners of his own mind. There is the story of a certain Boniface, bishop of Ferenti, who was invited to dinner by a nobleman after celebrating Mass. The bishop was about to chant a pontifical grace when, to his complete astonishment, a strolling player with a monkey appeared at the door. Worse still, the man was clashing his cymbals together. The bishop was furious at the noise and cursed the poor player: "Alas, alas, the wretch is dead, the wretch is dead!" He went on in increasing wrath: "Not a word have I yet uttered for the praise of the Lord, and that fellow comes with his monkey and clashes his cymbals! Go of your charity and give him to eat and drink; but know that he is a dead man!" Then the bishop said grace at the table, while the strolling player was entertained with food elsewhere. The next day a great boulder fell on the strolling player as he was leaving the house, and the bishop's prophecy came true. The same bishop was once plagued with a swarm of caterpillars in his garden, but he said a prayer over them, gently requested them to depart, and watched them trooping out in formation through the gates.

As Gregory tells these stories, running breathlessly to a conclusion, all the measured terror of the voice which thundered through the *Moralia* dissolves into a soft holy laughter. In the evenings, sitting beside a fire, such stories warmed the cockles of his heart and gave him a much-needed recreation. There is no doubt that he believed them, or at least suspended his disbelief. He had the same uncritical respect for relics, wherever they came from, and he was continually sending presents of small pieces of bone and hair and splinters of wood to the potentates who ruled Europe. To King Recared of Spain, who succeeded in uprooting the Arian heresy within his kingdom, a grateful pope sent "a little key made of iron from the chains of blessed Peter the Apostle, to bring you the blessing of that which has touched his most holy person; a cross containing wood from the Lord's Cross; and some hairs of John the Baptist."

Yet it would be wrong to suggest that Gregory was merely a credulous believer with a gift for sermonizing. He was one of those men who possess an effortless authority. He was a striking figure with a lofty forehead, dark eyes, strong mouth, finely cut jaw, and expressive hands with delicate fingers. When he wore his pontifical robes he looked more like a king than a pope. He was imperious by nature, stern and uncompromising toward heresies, with no nonsense about him. "Please do not keep on writing 'your handmaiden,'" he wrote in a letter to the aristocratic Lady Rusticiana in Constantinople. "Once would be quite enough. As pope I am the servant of all." He called himself *servus servorum Dei*—the servant of the servants of God— and no doubt there were times when he truly felt he was the servant of all mankind. "Your servant in his poverty," he wrote at the end of a letter to the Emperor Maurice.

Many of the things that Gregory is said to have done he did not do. He did not compose the Missal; the Gregorian chant probably derives from another Gregory. He was no great innovator. His task was to command the Church in a time of peril, always watchful. The Lombards were coming closer, the Church was in decay, sin was triumphant, ruin lay all around him; and all the time he acted as though the Lombards would fall back, and the energies of the Church would be restored. When he died in A.D. 604, having reigned for thirteen years, his epitaph proclaimed him to be "God's Consul." It was a singularly appropriate epitaph for a man who exerted himself to the uttermost, a Roman to the end, and the last of his line.

14 ✢ JUSTINIAN

T HERE were great emperors and
kings who left their own stamp upon Christianity, changing it according to their own character, their own preoccupations and dreams; and
there were other emperors and kings who seemed to be no more than
conductors, permitting the flow of Christian thought while leaving no
deep impress upon it. Constantine changed the course of Christianity
for all time, for he stood at the gates and ushered Christianity into the
imperial city. Justinian stood at the heart of the city and admiringly
watched his own absorption in a cult which he little understood,
though he celebrated it as no one had ever celebrated it before in the
church he erected in honor of the Holy Wisdom.

The portrait that gazes down from the mosaic in San Vitale in
Ravenna is that of a convinced voluptuary, sleek and ornate beneath
his triple tiara of pearls, emeralds, and rubies. He has the heavy features, the plump cheeks, the rounded chin, the cultivated half-smile of
a voluptuary who has never known a passion that is not immediately
fulfilled, a desire that is not immediately transformed into satiety. He
looks like a maharajah, and one could easily imagine him riding on a
painted and caparisoned elephant through the streets of an oriental
city. In fact he came neither from the East nor the West, but from
the Slavic North. His original name was Upravda, from the Slavonic
pravda, meaning justice. He was of middle height, with reddish
cheeks, large soft brown eyes, brown hair which he wore in the pre-
vailing windswept manner, and a heavy petulant mouth. The historian Procopius, who intensely disliked him, described him as a man
who never consciously permitted himself to speak the truth and com-

bined in his own person all the concentrated wickedness of mankind —faithless to his friends, implacable to his foes, possessed of an insatiable greed and an illimitable capacity for murder. Procopius tells us that he was often close to tears, "not because he was manifesting pleasure or suffering, but because his tears served to make others acquiesce to his demands." Procopius, however, is not an altogether reliable witness; no doubt the emperor was murderous and treacherous on occasion, but neither murder nor treachery gave him his greatest satisfaction. What pleased him most was his own glory.

When Justinian set about building the Church of the Holy Wisdom in Constantinople, he was in fact celebrating his own glory. Himself a practicing architect of great daring and originality, he knew exactly what he wanted to build. The Church of the Holy Wisdom was to be the living expression of exquisite magnificence, a temple worthy of God and Justinian. He employed the brilliant mathematician Anthemius of Tralles as his architect and continued to supervise design and construction to the end. No expense was spared; all the resources of the empire were dedicated to this building, the largest, the most daring, the most sumptuous of all. Even today, plastered with the great circular medallions announcing the greatness of Allah, the once glittering columns covered with the dust of ages, and only a few of the mosaics surviving, it can take the breath away. The dome, originally painted gold, floats eerily in the distance, seeming not to rest upon solid foundations but to have been let down from the heavens. "Glory to God, who has judged me worthy of accomplishing such a work as this!" Justinian cried on the day when the church was dedicated. "O Solomon, I have outdone thee!"

So he had, but at a price which crippled an empire. The Church of the Holy Wisdom was a magnificent engineering feat demanding mathematical ability of a high order and the use of unprecedented technological resources, but it was also a wasteful extravagance. The monograms of Justinian and Theodora, the brilliant courtesan who became his empress, are carved all over the church, and no doubt there were towering portraits of the emperor and empress rendered in mosaics at strategic places. Outside, a colossal equestrian statue of the emperor once more emphasized his triumph. There is a sense in which this vast building was no more than the private chapel of the reigning family.

Procopius has left us a formidable account of the many buildings erected by Justinian, but his account of the Church of the Holy Wisdom is surprisingly meager. He resorts to dithyrambs, as though overwhelmed by the spectacle of a church which hovers a little menacingly between heaven and earth. He notes that the walls rise like sheer cliffs, that the semidomes seem to hang dangerously over the worshipers, and everyone who enters is struck with awe amounting almost to vertigo. Visitors go about "with knitted brows," too perplexed by the unfathomable beauties of the place to understand what they are seeing. "They cannot rest their eyes on anything," he says, "and you see them continually turning about as they seek to find some part more admirable than the one they have just seen." Bewildered and stupefied, the worshipers were caught in a net of enchantment.

The present-day visitor sees a vast cavern-like building almost completely devoid of color. The great pillars have lost their early glint, and only a few mosaics gleam dimly in the half-darkness. In the days when the church was still fresh from the hands of the builders, the shining of the columns, which had come from the four ends of the empire, was a feast for the eyes. The empire was ransacked for precious stones. Eight porphyry columns, the gift of a rich widow, were despatched from the Temple of the Sun at Baalbek; eight more came from the Temple of Diana at Ephesus; there was verd antique from Carystus; and from the mountains of Phrygia came scintillating marbles, rose-colored or veined with scarlet and silver. More porphyry "powdered with bright stars" came from the banks of the Nile, while Sparta sent emerald-green marble and from Numidia there came marble the color of crocuses. Paulus Silentarius, a poet and high official of the court, contrived a poetic inventory of all the marbles used in the church, describing them as though they were landscapes or fruit. There was a marble which had the colors of the sea or of cornflowers in grass, with here and there a drift of fallen snow. Most charming of all was the marble from the Celtic mountains which shone "like a wealth of crystals, like milk poured here and there on a flesh of glittering black."

Sensuality entered into it, for these columns, as Paulus Silentarius describes them, resembled exotic many-colored limbs with the glow of freshness, thrusting to support the dome, leaping up as though they were alive, while at their feet the rivers ran and the meadows and groves were a riot of color. "Whoever shall raise his eyes to the lovely heaven of this dome," he wrote, "dares scarcely gaze upon it. All the stars are there, and from the green marble there springs, so it seems, the flower-bordered streams of Thessaly, and budding corn, and groves of trees, and skipping flocks, and twisted olive trees, and vines with green tendrils, and the deep blue peace of summer seas."

In this way Paulus Silentarius attempts to describe the indescribable opulence of the church that above all others represented the cultivated refinements of the artists attached to the Byzantine court. If there was any failure, it was in being too refined, too exquisite altogether: a jewel box nearly two hundred feet high. The modern visitor can scarcely envision how jewel-like it was when a thousand candles gleamed on the sheets of mosaics and silver lamps, shaped like ships and budding trees, hung down from the mysterious dome. On the high feast days of the Church, when the priests appeared in their brilliant vestments, the dazed spectator might be pardoned if he thought he had entered one of the antechambers of heaven.

Nevertheless it was a worldly church attended by a worldly people who sometimes amused themselves by carving on the columns and balustrades of the galleries satirical drawings of the bishops in their ceremonial clothes, or the portraits of their friends. These scratchings and doodlings are to be found chiefly in the galleries, where the women sat. They had time on their hands and were separated from the main worshipers below, where piety was the rule and crude doodlings were rare. Beside the columns there can be seen the hollows worn in the pavement where the worshipers knelt before the holy icons, and in the column of St. Gregory there can still be seen the hole where dampness once exuded from the marble, and the faithful would put their hands in the hole and then touch their eyes, for the damp had the miraculous property of safeguarding the eyesight and curing diseases of the eyes. The deeply spiritual, the fervent, the credulous, and the gossips who came to church to pass the time away all had their place under the vast golden dome. Here the ceremonials of Christian worship were performed with stupendous pomp.

The setting of the Church of the Holy Wisdom, directly facing the palace and looking out on the broad square of the Augusteum, with the Church of Hagia Eirene, the Holy Peace, nearby, was magnificently conceived. There was an air of spaciousness, of immense distances opening out, of gardens and orchards and avenues of trees, and the sea nearby. In the days of Justinian this part of Constantinople was not built-up, and a man could wander pleasantly through the gardens to the palaces and churches. As in Venice, the sea gave to Constantinople a continual shimmering.

Justinian was determined to build Constantinople in his own image, and was continually pulling down buildings and re-erecting them in a manner more suitable to his taste. The cost was dangerously high. The Church of the Holy Wisdom alone cost 320,000 pounds of gold, and this was only one of the many churches he built. Procopius, in his *Aedificia*, recounts all the great buildings erected by Justinian throughout the course of his reign, and it is significant that most of them were built far from the capital. No other emperor in ancient times built so many roads, fortresses, palaces, churches, and monasteries.

What is surprising is that he had the time to build so many monuments, to carry out such a vast design, when his throne was never secure, and for a good part of his reign he was at war. He was not brave, and he was never popular. He was affable, kindly, treacherous, and very largely indifferent to the fate of his subjects, who were taxed on a scale never known before. Yet Procopius tells us that "even the most humble and obscure were allowed not merely to have audience of this tyrant, but they were permitted to discuss things with him and to have private interviews."

While Justinian was affable and sometimes disposed to listen to the complaints of the humble, the Empress Theodora remained a mysterious remote figure living in imperial seclusion. She was a small woman with a sallow skin, not unprepossessing, but not particularly beautiful. She had fierce eyes, a sharp chin, and a nervous manner, but all the commentators agree on her extraordinary charm, which was deliberately cultivated. She was the daughter of a bear tamer who died when she was young. In her early years she was an actress, a prostitute, a camp-follower. As an actress she played in low comedies, and to the end of her life she was renowned for her ready wit and gift for mockery. Justinian, who admired her wit and daring, married her before he ascended the throne, and he seems to have been amused by her strict adherence to imperial protocol once she became empress. She became more imperial than the emperor.

As she appears on the Ravenna mosaics, with her lean features and her air of determined spirituality, she seems to be the archetype of a Byzantine empress. She wears her royal dignity as though she were born to it. To the end she remained a daring adventuress, happy in her intrigues, consumed with a rage for power, never satisfied until she had humbled her adversaries.

She had many adversaries, the most powerful being John the Cappadocian, the praetorian prefect of the city, whose origins were as humble as her own. She had her agents throughout the city, and with their help hoped to destroy him, even though Justinian had a high regard for him. There is some evidence that she instigated the Nika riots which broke out in January A.D. 532. The riots began with a commonplace factional fight between the Blues and the Greens, the two parties which vied with one another for success at the games. Soon there was heard the cry: "Down with John the Cappadocian." Some rioters, led off to execution, were rescued, and the mob became ugly. The prisons were opened, houses were looted, palaces were fired. Respectable citizens fled to the Asiatic mainland. Receiving no reply to their demands, the rioters began to set fire to the city, and at this point Justinian accepted their demand and ordered John the Cappadocian removed from office.

The emperor acted too late; the riot was becoming a revolution. Hypatius, the nephew of the late Emperor Anastasius, was proclaimed emperor. Justinian lost his throne, and overnight became a fugitive in his own palace. But when he spoke of escaping in disguise, the Empress Theodora, who had known the misery of wandering in poverty in foreign lands, refused. "We must all die," she said, "but it is unendurable that a man who has been emperor should become an exile." He spoke of crossing the Bosphorus and taking refuge in Chalcedon; there were secret tunnels leading from the palace to the sea. She said mockingly: "The ships are ready, and so is the sea! But first think whether it is better to suffer a glorious death than to live in ignominious safety. I love the old saying: 'How brave a sepulcher a kingdom is!'" And while the emperor wavered, she prepared her plans for a counter-rebellion that would put an end to the uprising.

The mobs had victory in their grasp when it was suddenly snatched from them by the veteran soldier Belisarius who forced his way into the crowded hippodrome at nightfall at the head of the household troops and set about methodically killing everyone he found there. The revolution ended in a bloodbath, and a victorious emperor, restored to the throne, had the pleasure of announcing the execution of the usurper. In six days eighty thousand people perished.

Most of them died on that last terrible night in the hippodrome.

With Constantinople at peace and in ruins, Justinian decided on a massive program of rebuilding. He rebuilt so many churches, palaces, baths, aqueducts, cisterns, hospitals, convents, barracks, and princely houses for the nobility that in effect the old city of Constantine perished and in its place there was the city of Justinian. If the new Church of the Holy Wisdom was the greatest of his achievements, this was only because it was the largest and the most daring of many vast buildings; and the chroniclers of his reign, grown weary of his wars and of the political dissensions in the capital, weigh down their pages with measurements and designs and tabulations, with inventories of the jewels and precious metals employed in embellishing the buildings.

Meanwhile there were wars to be fought, and Belisarius, the most talented general of his time, was called upon to defend the frontiers of the empire. With 15,000 mercenaries he invaded the Vandal kingdom of Africa, seized Cathage, and returned to Constantinople in triumph with Gelimer, the Vandal king, in chains. Justinian sent his tax gatherers to Africa: Carthage must pay for the damage caused by the Nika riots. Then it was the turn of Italy, and soon, with Africa as a supply base, Belisarius was invading Sicily, storming Naples, and marching on Rome, which he defended for a year against the massed armies of the Ostrogoths. Justinian knew the Roman Empire could scarcely endure without the reconquest of Italy, and at the same time he hesitated to give aid to his general. Belisarius lacked the confidence of the emperor, who regarded his most brilliant commander as a potential rival. Suddenly, in the middle of the Italian wars, Belisarius was recalled to Constantinople and ordered to mount an invasion against Persia; the invasion came to nothing. Once more Belisarius was sent to Italy, only to be recalled by Justinian who decided to give the command to one of his imperial relatives. Belisarius vanished into retirement. Then the Bulgars invaded the area north of Constantinople, and once more Belisarius was commanded to defend the empire. He swept the Bulgars back into their impenetrable forests, and the savior of the country was rewarded with obscurity. Legends accumulated around his last days, and it is said that he became a blind beggar, wandering the streets of Constantinople in search of alms.

The tall, handsome Belisarius, with the quiet manner and the forgiving nature, was no match for a harsh and intolerant emperor. It appears that in an unguarded moment the general gave his opinion about the incompetence of the emperor. Justinian despised, feared, and admired Belisarius, and never trusted him; and Belisarius respected and distrusted the emperor, and never showed any fear of him. In that unequal contest Belisarius was bound to go down to defeat.

Yet it was Belisarius who recreated the empire, and his conquests established Constantinople once more as a great metropolitan city. Justinian took full advantage of these conquests, and we are told that his tax gatherers succeeded in ruining Africa and Italy in the space of ten years. The emperor styled himself according to the fashion of the finest days of the empire. He was "the most happy, most illustrious emperor, victorious and triumphant," and he bore the titles Africanus, Vandalicus, Alemannicus, Germanicus, Gothicus, and Franciscus. He made no appearance in any of these campaigns.

But it was not for his empty titles that Justinian still commands the attentions of men. His greatest achievements lay in architecture, but his achievements as a lawgiver and codifier of laws were to be remembered long afterward, and indeed they form the basis of Roman law as it is known today. The *Code* in twelve books, the *Digest* in fifty, the *Institutes* in four, and the 160 new laws called the *Novels* form the *Corpus Juris Civilis*, a monument of industrious research and massive expropriation, for the greater part of these laws are merely borrowed from compilations made at intervals during the past. The *Corpus* covers four hundred years of Roman law, beginning with Antoninus Pius. It is not so much a codification as an inventory of the accumulated experience and wisdom of centuries. It proclaimed the rule of law as a fundamental conception of the Christian Roman Empire, and was designed to serve imperial ends. Although in theory all these laws had their origin in the commandments of God seen under the aspect of the Most Holy Trinity, the greater number of them derived from pagan Rome and were first promulgated under pagan emperors. Justinian was therefore merely insisting upon traditional concepts of law reinforced by the enlightened presence of the Trinity. Tradition, not Christ, was the cement binding the empire together.

The *Novels*, which form the fourth section of the *Corpus*, are largely devoted to ecclesiastical law and the needs of property owners. There are generous provisions against official bribery and salutory warnings against arresting the innocent. Judges are warned against fining a district in which a crime has been perpetrated; their business is to arrest and punish the criminals. Blackmailing governors are automatically deprived of their right to govern, but there is no indication of any machinery by which they can be impeached. Monks who frequent taverns must be handed over to the *defensores* of the city, chastened, and reported to the abbot, who will then undertake to expel them from the monastery "for having abandoned the angelic state for the life of shame." The *Novels* furnish lengthy ordinances on the disposition of estates, on the methods of tax gatherers and the payment of debts, on the behavior of notaries and the proper way to draw up a will. Implicit in the continuing argument is the knowledge that the bureaucracy and the notaries weigh heavily on the people, who are entitled to redress. So many cases of malfeasance are cited that the reader comes in the end to regard the *Novels*, not as a set of laws to be obeyed, but as an indictment of the imperial system.

Sometimes, too, we come upon traces of beliefs going back to the most ancient times. Many of the *Novels* are concerned with immorality. Swearing and blasphemy are forbidden "because it is owing to offenses of this kind that famines, earthquakes, and pestilences occur." There must have been a good deal of swearing and blasphemy in Justinian's empire, for the last years of his reign were darkened by a pestilence which carried off 300,000 of his subjects.

At the end of his life he could look back on a reign of unexampled splendor. His empire was very nearly as large as the empire of Trajan. He had recovered North Africa, Italy, and the islands of Sicily, Sardinia, and Corsica. He had lost Britain and Gaul, retained a foothold in Spain, kept the Persians at bay, and rebuilt the city of Constantine. The seven deadly sins, especially pride, anger, and luxury, were his constant companions in life, but to the end he continued to regard himself as one of those who are specially protected by Christ.

Dante, too, regarded him with high favor, and in the *Paradiso* he is portrayed as a figure of the utmost sanctity, robed in the raiments of the sun, and granted the supreme grace in his own lifetime of gazing upon the Thrones of the eternal triumph—*li Troni del trionfo eternal*. The emperor emerges from the bright light of the Heaven of Mercury with the superb words: *Cesare fui e son Giustiniano*— I who was Caesar am now Justinian. A special virtue accrued to him for having brought into existence with divine aid the *Corpus Juris Civilis*. Only Beatrice, St. Bernard, and St. Francis receive higher praise. For Dante, Justinian represented the perfection of imperial grace, the incarnation of the Roman spirit, the sun whose rays bent an entire empire to his will; and to Justinian in heaven was given the pleasant task of reciting the vast accomplishments of Rome, which had brought peace to the world.

There was very little truth in Dante's portrait of Justinian, the great and the just. The Slavonic peasant who married a Greek dancing girl had taken care to cultivate his own legend.

15 ✠ THE EMPIRE OF MUHAMMAD

THOSE who believe that the chief forces that move civilizations are social and economic must find it hard to come to terms with Muhammad ibn-Abdullah, the visionary who stirred the desert to revolt. That heavy-set, handsome man with broad shoulders and thick curling beard did not have the appearance of a conqueror; he looked indeed like a shopkeeper or a merchant, and in fact these were his trades during the greater part of his life. There was something feminine about his movement and his gestures, and people remembered his laughter, the sweetness of his smile, and the sudden opening of his enormous eyes. He was gentle and eager to please, with an aristocratic courtliness of manner; sometimes he was as savage as a hurricane.

Of all the great founders of religions Muhammad is the one we know most about. After his death the disciples wrote out or dictated all they could remember about him, with the result that we know his appearance well, and what he thought on every conceivable subject. There was no reticence in him. We know his likes and dislikes, and his very human eccentricities. The events of his life, except the early beginnings, are so well established that it is almost possible to construct a day by day itinerary of his movements. He stands against the desert, clearcut and luminous, and the only mystery is the mystery of his genius. He never learned to read or write. He never wandered far from Mecca, except during a period when he led camel trains to Syria. He was a Meccan to the core, and something of that harsh, violent, beautiful landscape entered into him. On Mecca the rain rarely falls; when it does, the flash floods roar like thunder.

Like Jesus and like Buddha, he grew up in an enchanted flowering landscape, for at the age of two he was entrusted to a foster mother living in Taif, a small hilltown southeast of Mecca, and there he remained for the next four years. To the end of his life he was to remember vividly that wonderful green oasis on the edge of the desert, full of apple trees, peach trees, and vineyards; and the shock of luxuriance was to color his prophecies. Then he returned to live with his mother in Mecca. She died a year later, leaving him nearly destitute, his sole possession being an Abyssinian slave girl. He was taken in by his grandfather Abd al-Muttalib, and when his grandfather died he was given into the care of his uncle Abu Talib, a kindly man who dealt in cloths and perfumes and owned some sheepfolds in the hills. Abu Talib was not rich and he was concerned that the boy should earn his keep. Muhammad became a shepherd boy tending sheep on the edge of the desert.

Already the pattern of his life was being determined—long days of peaceful contemplation, the sense of being abandoned, his wits sharpened by adversity. He had lost his father before his birth, and he had scarcely known his mother. The search for the lost father provides a clue to many of his prophetic utterances.

His restless childhood was followed by a restless youth. It was a time of unrest among the tribesmen. Abd al-Muttalib had been the leader of the powerful Quraysh tribe; after his death there were many contenders for the leadership. There was trouble, too, with the Bani Hawazin, a Bedouin tribe owning great areas of land in the Najd. A war, known as the "impious war," broke out when the Bani Hawazin violated the oath against fighting during the sacred months. The Quraysh took to arms, and Muhammad took part in these obscure skirmishes between the tribes. When the skirmishes were over he returned to Mecca to tend his uncle's sheep and goats and to sell small quantities of merchandise. Deeply religious, he took part in the pagan ceremonies of the city made holy by the presence of the mysterious Black Stone embedded in the Kaaba on the main square. In reality the Black Stone is a deep reddish-brown, very small, about twelve inches across. Men believed it had dropped from the moon and was therefore sacred to the moon-god Hubal, but of its origins no one could speak with certainty; and this mysterious stone, worn smooth by the kisses of the worshipers, still exercises its fascination on the Arabs.

Muhammad was twenty-five when there came the first great turn in his fortunes. A forty-year-old widow, Khadija, who had lost two husbands and acquired an impressive fortune, heard from one of her agents of Muhammad's skill as a camel-driver. She asked to see him and immediately fell in love with him. The marriage was an entirely happy one. Khadija entrusted her business affairs to him and gave him six children, four girls and two boys. The boys died in childhood; to his grief there was no surviving male issue. But this was his only grief. Rich, improvident, charming, handsome above the average, happy in his home life, he was remarkable only for being unremarkable. His friends were the merchants of Mecca, and he had no enemies. He had no need to fortify himself with ambitions, for he had acquired effortlessly the wealth and security that others dreamed of.

There was nothing in this contented young husband to suggest that within a few short years of his death armies proclaiming his beliefs would storm out of Arabia, conquer Egypt, destroy the centuries-old Persian empire, and sweep across North Africa to take possession of Spain, or that an Islamic civilization of astonishing richness and delicacy would spring fully formed from these conquests.

He was about forty when he took to meditating alone in a cave outside Mecca, perhaps influenced by the wandering hermits called *hanifs* who turned their back on idol worship and proclaimed the virtues of solitude and the worship of the one God. One night, while lying in a cave on Mount Hira, he heard a voice saying, "Recite!" He answered, "I cannot recite!" Again and again, with terrible force, the voice said, "Recite!" until at last he answered, "What shall I recite?" The voice thundered:

> *Recite in the name of the Lord, the Creator,*
> *Who created man from clots of blood!*
> *Recite! The Lord is most merciful,*
> *For He has taught men by the pen*
> *And revealed the mysteries to them.*

With these strange words ringing in his ears, he stumbled out of the cave, and heard a voice saying: "Muhammad, thou art the Messenger of Allah, and I am Gabriel!" Wherever he looked the Archangel was gazing at him. When he turned to the east the Angel was there, and when he turned to the west the Angel was still there. Trembling, he watched the vision fade.

It was the first of many visions, many visitations by the Angel, who spoke always in verses of extraordinary authority. He would tell these verses to members of his family, but at first only Khadija and her cousin, the old Christian Waraqa, believed in them. Waraqa knew Hebrew and had written down the Gospels from the Hebrew version; from him Muhammad derived his extensive knowledge of Christianity. The verses were written on palm leaves and given to friends. Soon he was making converts; within a year there were forty people in Mecca who believed he was the Messenger of Allah. Official Mecca disapproved of the strange visionary who would hide beneath a blanket and emerge with still another intensely wrought verse from the lips of the Angel.

The movement grew slowly. Muhammad proclaimed his revelations, and incurred the anger of the Meccans. Hunted, he took to the hills, while his followers scattered. Salvation came from an unexpected source—the Jews. The city of Yathrib, due north of Mecca, was composed of Jewish and Arab tribesmen in uneasy alliance, and in the hope of bringing peace to the city the elders approached Muhammad and offered to make him the mayor, believing him to be the Messiah. Muhammad arranged that his followers should make their way secretly to Yathrib. In September 622 he entered the city, becoming its earthly ruler and spiritual leader. He was about fifty years old, and had ten more years to live.

Those last ten years were years of war, of many skirmishes and sudden raids. Yathrib straddled the northern trade route; to break through, Mecca was forced to attack repeatedly. The chroniclers have left precise and detailed accounts of these battles, with their surprisingly small casualties. At the battle of Badr, fought some ten miles to the southwest of Yathrib, fourteen of Muhammad's army fell, forty-nine of the enemy. At the battle of Uhud, fought in the following year among the black basalt hills to the north of the city, the casualties were greater: the followers of Muhammad lost seventy-four dead, and Muhammad himself was seriously wounded. Shaken by defeat, he took refuge within his walled city. Not many days later there came a message from the Angel: "Endure! Endure to the end! Stand firm in the faith and fear God, so that you may triumph!"

For eight years the war continued; then quite suddenly and unexpectedly the Meccans opened their gates and surrendered. At dawn he entered the city on camelback robed in the white garments of a pilgrim. His first task was to destroy the idols kept within the sacred enclosure of the Kaaba. Then, having destroyed them, he came to the door of the Kaaba and pronounced the coming of a new dispensation.

"There is no God but God," he said. "There is none with Him. He has made good his promise and helped his servant. From this day every claim of privilege or blood or property is abolished by me, except the custody of the Kaaba and the watering of the pilgrims. Know that man springs from Adam, and Adam from dust. Know that God created you male and female, and made you peoples and tribes so that you may know one another; and most noble are you who worship God most."

In these words he stated his ultimate beliefs. It remained only to consolidate his small kingdom, which reached from Mecca to Yathrib, and to hear the concluding words of the Angel. He died two years later in the arms of his young wife—Khadija had died long before. His last words were: "No, the friend, the highest in Paradise . . ." He was buried where he died, in the city of Yathrib, which had been renamed Madina Nabi Allah, the Place of the Prophet of Allah, in his honor.

Immediately after his death the verses heard from the lips of the Angel were assembled, and gradually over the years they were placed in the order believed to correspond to the intentions of Muhammad or the designs of the Angel. These verses vary in mood, for some are composed with extraordinary violence, while others are calm and prayerful, and still others merely instruct the faithful on the problems of everyday life. Some recount the life of Jesus, others are clearly intended as revelations of the prophetic soul of Muhammad on the purpose of man's life on earth and in heaven. In the revelatory passages there breathes the sense of God's majesty, His honor, His awful dignity. This God is stupendous in His power and in His terrible beauty, and therefore men must submit (*islam, muslim*) wholly to Him. Man is not created in the image of God; he is a mere clot of blood, which owes its existence to God's overwhelming mercy. But if God's mercy is overwhelming, it is not absolute. He is not the all-loving Father who cares for his children, but a stark, elemental power beyond human comprehension. He rides the whirlwinds, fixes the stars in their courses, penetrates into the dark recesses of the human heart, and all things are known to him.

To devout Muslims the Koran is the infallible, unchangeable

word of God, a fathomless well in which all truth is contained. To nonbelievers these verses seem strangely uneven, and curiously chaotic. The stories of Abraham, Moses, and Jesus are retold in abundant detail, but with inexplicable variations from the Old and New Testaments. Concerning Jesus the Koran speaks with grave reverence, and indeed the Prophet speaks more often of Jesus than of any other religious figure of the past. He is the Messiah with power to heal the sick and raise the dead, a sign, a mercy, a parable, an Angel of formidable powers whose Second Coming will usher in the world's end. Allah, Jesus, and Mary form a trinity: Father, Son, and Holy Ghost. Mary, too, is regarded with reverence, and the annunciation and birth of Jesus are described in detail. Yet the Koran refuses to accept that he died on the Cross, insisting that a mere replica of him ascended the Cross, for he was altogether too godlike to permit himself to suffer. And while the Crucifixion is denied, the Ascension is described as a fact which took place according to the will of Allah.

So that men should live orderly lives, the Koran prescribes a strict regimen of duties. Men must pray five times daily, observe the fasts, pay tithes, give alms to the poor and to destitute relatives. It is God's will that men should be kind to one another. "The servants of the Merciful are those who walk upon the earth softly, and when the ignorant address them they reply, 'Peace.'" At the heart of the angelic vision there is the Oneness of God and the Oneness of Man. Again and again the Koran maintains: "All people are a single nation." Negro slaves, tribal princes, great theologians are all equal in the sight of God. When it occurred to Muhammad to institute the ceremony of summoning the faithful from the roof of the mosque, he chose as his first summoner the Negro slave Bilal.

While Christianity quickly produced its local hierarchies of rulers, with bishops, deacons, and presbyters standing in the place of power, Islam remained relatively democratic. If all were equal in the sight of God, all must be heard; and the voice of the poor Negro was as important as the voice of the sheikh. The Christian hierarchies adopted the forms of government already worked out under the Roman Empire; the Muslims adopted the form of government common in the desert, with a single tribal leader, the caliph, who was Muhammad's earthly representative. In war they were therefore more resilient and resourceful, untroubled by those quarrels between emperor and pope that plagued Europe for centuries.

The strength of Islam rested on its simplicity, its monolithic power. Sects emerged, but they never seriously threatened the power at the center. It blended easily with the pagan underlayer in Arabia, and later in Persia and Syria, but the visionary power of Muhammad remained dominant, riding above the local folklore. Muhammad, the Kaaba, and the Koran proved to be singularly coherent, and they forged a pattern of life that remains virtually unchanged to this day.

Perhaps the chief source of strength lay in the poetry and language of the Koran. It was a language possessing extraordinary resources of music and enchantment; the most complex and tenuous ideas could be expressed in it. Like Italian, Arabic is a language that sings. Muhammad gave it color and weight and precision, reshaping the language for his own purposes. Even in English his powerful imagination can be seen at work in the most beautiful of all the verses in the Koran:

God is the light of the Heavens and the earth.
The similitude of His Light is as a niche wherein is a lamp,
And the lamp is within a glass,
And the glass as it were a pearly star.
The lamp is lit from a blessed tree,
An olive neither of the East nor of the West:
Almost this oil would shine, though no fire touched it.
Light upon Light, God guideth whom He will to His light,
And He speaketh in parables to men, for He knoweth all things.
This Light is revealed in the temples
Which God hath permitted to be raised in His name:
Therefore men praise Him in the morning and in the evening,
Whom neither trade nor traffic divert from the remembrance of His
    name,
And they offer prayers and make payment of alms
Through fear of the day when hearts and eyeballs shall roll,
In hope of reward for their most excellent deeds.
                                                    (Sura xxiv)

In this way, like another David, Muhammad sang psalms to God, while employing an image derived from the altar lamp on a Christian altar. His attitude to the Christians was one of mingled reverence and contempt. Believing himself to be the last of a line of prophets stretching from Abraham to Jesus, he regarded Islam as the summary of all that had gone before, and therefore it superseded Christianity, as it superseded Judaism and the paganism of the Arabs before his time.

The character of Muhammad dominates the Koran. There was a strange sweetness in him combined with a terrifying harshness. He watched the massacre of the Jews at Yathrib with delight, and yet on occasion he could be kind and generous to them. He preached the most violent sermons against the worshipers of idols, but when he conquered Mecca he could not bring himself to destroy the Black Stone. In love with the desert, he dreamed, like all desert dwellers, of a Paradise where the streams flow abundantly, the earth is green, and every delight of the senses is granted to the faithful who have died in his service. He was at once sensualist and ascetic, mystic and practical man of affairs, lover and hater; and he hated as abundantly as he loved. To the end he remains an enigma. No one like him had appeared in Arabia, and no one like him ever appeared again.

When Muhammad died quietly in Madina, no one could have guessed that his followers would set about conquering the known world. Arabia was a land feared by no one, as remote and inhospitable as it had been in the days of the Romans. The palaces of Byzantium and the bazaars of Damascus knew nothing of him; in Egypt his name was unknown. Within ten years of his death Arab armies conquered the Sasanian Empire of Persia, captured Syria and Egypt, the two fairest provinces of the Byzantine Empire, and threatened Byzantium itself. Within a hundred years the ever-widening circle of Islam embraced all of north Africa and much of Spain. All Europe was threatened by the Arab conquerors.

Out of the desert there came a mysterious power that obeyed none of the laws generally thought to be appropriate to power. They were provided with simple weapons: horses, camels, and swords. They possessed no engines of destruction, and they were strangers to Byzantine fire. They seemed to have emerged only recently from the Stone Age, and possessed no clearly defined aims, no culture except the hallucinatory verses of the Koran, no philosophy, no arts. There was no grand design. They raided wherever the enemy was weak, and since the enemy was especially weak in the Near East, they discovered to their astonishment that their small raiding parties were more powerful than the enemy's massed armies. Their horses, camels, and swords were not their chief weapons: their chief weapons were their faith in Allah and the quality that the Arab philosopher ibn-Kaldun was later to call *assabiya*, the freshness and resourcefulness of the untamed.

Justinian proclaimed that the Byzantine Empire rested on foundations so strong that it would endure for eternity. The Arabs proved that the foundations were temporal. Damascus fell in 635, Jerusalem in 638, and then it was the turn of Caesarea. For 900 years these cities had been outposts of Hellenic culture; in a decade they were lost to the Greeks forever.

Two men dominated the Arab revolt. One was the tall and slender Khalid ibn-al-Walid, a fiery cavalry general who was eventually to be relieved of his command for insubordination and die in obscurity; the other was the small thickset Amr ibn-al-As who was over ninety years old when he died, retaining to the end of his life the honors and titles which came to him as Governor of Egypt. They were among the greatest generals who have ever lived. They were the hammers who broke the mold and shaped it anew.

Eight years after the death of the Prophet, in the hot summer of 640, Amr ibn-al-As led his troops to the walls of Heliopolis, the ancient On, most sacred of Egyptian cities, where the priests still worshiped the sun under the protection of their Byzantine masters. Amr ibn-al-As was in no hurry. He waited for reinforcements, sent his spies through Egypt, wrote lengthy reports for the caliph, and prepared to do battle with the viceroy Cyrus, who was also patriarch of Alexandria. Cyrus was timid and deceitful, and no match for the Arab commander, who destroyed the Byzantine army and permitted the survivors to fall back on Alexandria, then the most powerful naval base in the world, capable of summoning ships and supplies from all the Byzantine cities on the Mediterranean. In Alexandria there were siege works, catapults, heavily fortified battlements. Here Alexander lay in an ornate crystal tomb, here Cleopatra had died, here St. Mark had been martyred.

The Arabs camped outside the walls of the white city and waited. The scholarly and ambitious Cyrus, dogmatic, complicated, accustomed to the intrigues of the court, confronted the simple Arab chieftain with his rabble army. There was a long siege, secret negotiations were opened, the Byzantine Empress Martina, the widow of Heraclius, taking a hand in the deceptions and broken promises intended to weaken the Arab invaders. The Alexandrians continued to receive supplies by sea. They were still powerful, and they went about their daily affairs as though there were no enemy at the gates. Cyrus, weak-willed and easily swayed, seems to have thought he could retain the position of viceroy under the Arabs, paying tribute to Mecca instead of to Constantinople. For nearly two years the battle of wills continued. At last, on the orders of the empress, on September 12, 642, the Byzantines abandoned Egypt and set sail for Rhodes. Amr ibn-al-As entered the second richest city in Christendom. He wrote to the caliph: "I have taken a city of which I can only say that it contains 4,000 mansions, 4,000 baths, 40,000 poll-tax-paying Jews, and 400 theaters." The caliph was not particularly impressed. When the messenger arrived with the news, the successor of Muhammad listened attentively and then rewarded him with a meal of bread and a few dates.

When Amr ibn-al-As rode on horseback through the Gate of the Sun, and along the Canopic Way, past the great Pharos and the glittering tomb of Alexander and the palaces of the caesars, the history of the world took a sudden turning. The ancient civilization of Egypt, which had endured for nearly five thousand years, surviving the Ptolemies and the Roman and Byzantine officers who ruled in the name of distant emperors, came finally to a halt. An obscure Byzantine empress and an elderly Arab decided the fate of Egypt.

With the coming of the Arabs the power of Egypt as a civilizing force vanished from the earth as though it had never been. The Arabs were to produce an intricate and impressive civilization of their own, and soon enough they were to learn the benefits of great cities. But except on very rare occasions, and at long intervals, Egypt herself produced no works of art, showed no interest or excitement in her past, and remained in a state of torpor. The Arab victory was complete. In the words of E. M. Forster: "Though they had no intention of destroying her, they destroyed her, as a child might a watch. She never functioned again for over a thousand years."

The ignominious defeats, accomplished in so short a time, deprived the emperor at Constantinople of more than half his empire. The fall of Jerusalem, where only a few years before Heraclius had reinstated the True Cross, had the effect of reducing his spiritual authority; he could no longer claim to be the deliverer of Christendom and restorer of the eastern empire. In ostentatious humility, accompanied only by a few servants, his clothes dust-stained, the Caliph Umar

entered Jerusalem in triumph, to be met by the Patriarch Sophronius
in his glittering robes. Sophronius submitted to the inevitable, merely
contenting himself with the remark that the caliph was "the abomina-
tion of desolation" which Daniel had prophecied. The caliph professed to treat the Christian churches with veneration, and scrupulously avoided entering the Holy Sepulcher. But these occasional acts
of toleration only emphasized his power.

In time the Arabs were to display an extraordinary mastery of
the arts, and in the darkest ages of Europe they produced a civilization far more richly endowed than the civilization of the West. Great
philosophers, mathematicians, geographers, and encyclopedists arose
to confound the Europeans and to restore the primacy of reason in a
continent given over to faith. From Islamic civilization came the redis-
covery of Aristotle, and the first works of scientific medicine since
the time of the Greeks. Where Byzantium stood still, Islam unswerv-
ingly maintained its onward march. The restless marauders from the
desert became restless seekers after truth.

At first they were copyists imitating the Byzantine and Persian
arts. Byzantine architects and mosaicists were employed to build and
decorate the great mosque at Damascus; the minarets were derived
from the Syrian bell towers; even their coinage was based on
Byzantine coins. Their political advisers were Christians, their ships
were built by Christian naval architects. Within a generation they
were enjoying the civilized luxuries they had formerly despised.
Gradually they exchanged the freshness and resourcefulness of their
untamed youth for the more convenient and comfortable resourcefulness of middle age. Islamic civilization abandoned the desert and
took up its abode in the cities.

Yet always the vision of the desert remained to haunt the followers of Muhammad. Where the harsh laws of the desert rule, they are
at home. There is nothing in the Koran which is not sternly mascu-
line; there is no gentleness, no compassion. Man is a speck, a clot of
blood, seen against the vastness of the desert, at the mercy of a cruel
God. It was a religion for a race of warriors.

16 ✠ CHARLEMAGNE

The GREATEST service the papacy could render to itself and to Europe was the preservation of peace after so many centuries of strife. The *pax Dei* might be a dream, never to be completely accomplished on this earth, but the dream represented the unfulfilled longings of millions of people who saw themselves deprived of any reason for existence as long as the armies marched endlessly across Europe. Over large areas of Europe, especially in France and Italy, men yearned to be one Christian people, all of whose members were equal in the sight of God, with one language for worship and government, obeying a single emperor and a single God.

Scholars might argue, as they did, about the exact interpretation to be given to the *civitas terrena* and the *civitas Dei,* and the tribute to be paid to Caesar and to God, but since the time of St. Augustine the belief that God needed and demanded peace on earth was nearly universal. "The heavenly city during its peregrinations in this world makes use of the earthly peace," wrote St. Augustine, implying that it could make no use of war. Almost he was saying that peace on earth was very close to the peace of heaven.

But the peace which men yearned for seemed far in the distance in the age of the Merovingian kings, who regarded their people as property to be taxed and pressed into military service according to their needs. The dismal wars described by Gregory of Tours were nearly always civil wars. The lands ruled by the Franks were continually disintegrating, as rival kings fought against each other, murdered one another, and then set about murdering their rivals' followers until it seemed that there was scarcely anyone left to murder. These primitive kings committed continual acts of treacherous brutality; they were brutal by instinct, treacherous by design. Childebert invited one of his counts to his palace in Metz and showed him some dogs worrying a poor animal to death. The count knew what was expected of him: he laughed pleasantly. "Then," says Gregory of Tours, "a man who had received the order, seeing the count intent on his sport, swung his ax and cleft his skull, and afterward his body was thrown out of the window." It was not enough that the count should have his head broken like a cracked egg; he must be hurled from the window as well. The Merovingians rejoiced in their own decadence, and thought the world well lost as long as they could enjoy their ferocious wars and commit causeless acts of brutality. They did these things because they were frightened, and because the sense of order had vanished from the West. Well might the pope despair. With the Franks at the mercy of their civil wars, and Italy at the mercy of the Lombards, Gregory the Great opened out his heart to the emperor in Constantinople. "All Europe," he declared, "is given over to the barbarians. The cities are destroyed, the camps overthrown, the provinces depopulated, the husbandmen no longer till the soil." It was a cry that had been heard many times before, notably from the lips of St. Jerome, but Gregory the Great was not a man who despaired easily. In A.D. 603 he wrote to the Emperor Phocas, praising him for ruling over free men while the kings of the West ruled only over slaves. He called upon the emperor to assume once more the rule of the universal Roman state for the sake of liberty and peace. He wrote:

> *Let the liberty of all men be now restored to them under the yoke of the pious empire. For there is this difference between the kings of other nations and the emperors of the Roman state: that the kings are the lords over slaves, while the emperors of the Roman state are lords over free men.*
>
> (*Epistolae*, XIII)

Such an appeal delivered by one autocrat to another may sound hypocritical to modern ears, while the final words—*imperatores vero reipublicae domini liberorum*—seem to contain altogether too many contradictions. For us, republics are not ruled by emperors, and lords no longer rule over free men. But for Gregory, as for the men of his age, the *respublica* was the Roman state, the machinery by which the *pax romana* was brought about and prolonged through the ages, and he would have seen no contradiction between lords and free men, for all men, even those who are free, must be ruled for the sake of peace. In "the pious empire," according to Gregory, pope and emperor would rule together, stamping out the quarrels of the princelings and acknowledging the authority of the God who rules over all.

As the years passed, the dream faded, to revive at intervals with sudden flares of brightness. It was not an insubstantial dream, for in the time of Augustus the *respublica* stretched from Spain to Persia and from Britain to Africa; and what had been accomplished once could be accomplished again. Pope Gregory, who possessed the sharpest intellect in Christendom, was imploring the help of the most empty-headed of all the Byzantine emperors; and nothing came of it. Yet hope still ran high. Five years later, when Gregory was dead and the world was in greater turmoil than ever, a marble column forty feet high surmounted by the golden statue of the Emperor Phocas was erected in the Roman Forum to testify to the vigor of a dream. The statue has gone, but the column remains to this day.

The event for which Gregory prayed was long in coming to pass. Two hundred years went by before another emperor was crowned in Rome.

When Charlemagne, the grandson of Charles Martel, received from the hands of Pope Leo III the golden crown of the Holy Roman Empire in acknowledgement that he was the long-awaited emperor destined to fill the place once occupied by Augustus, he was greeted by the acclamations of the people. These acclamations were well rehearsed, with every word carefully weighed in advance. Charlemagne was greeted as the personification of the revived *pax romana*. "To Charles, the most pious Augustus, crowned of God, the great and peace-giving Emperor of the Romans, be life and victory!" He had brought into existence an empire which had very little in common with the ancient *imperium romanum*, and he had bought peace at the price of terrible massacres. Nevertheless, he had established his rule over a vast area of western Europe, and from his capital at Aachen he could look out on an empire where none dared to oppose him. His greatest claim to the affections of the pope and of the people was a very simple one: in those war-weary countries over which he ruled he was a giver of peace.

Charlemagne himself was perfectly aware that he personified the imperial tradition of Rome. Like the eastern Roman Emperors he wore on occasion the purple *chlamys;* the books written for him were penned in purple ink; his palace at Aachen was modeled on the imperial palace at Constantinople. On great feast days he presented himself to his courtiers in imperial panoply, his clothes and shoes adorned with precious stones, wearing a gold diadem studded with jewels. At other times he wore ostentatiously simple clothes; only a blue cloak and a jeweled sword distinguished him from the courtiers.

There was some irony in the fact that he became the Holy Roman Emperor, for he was always behaving like a barbarian chieftain. Eginhard gilds the lily, and will have us believe that no more gentle and Christian emperor ever lived. In fact Charlemagne was a man of unexampled ferocity, quick-tempered and sometimes treacherous. He stood nearly seven feet tall, bull-necked and powerful, with a full paunch, and like many powerful men he had a weak voice. He liked roast meat, and was something of a trencherman. He could not read, but to the end of his life he was taking his tablets to bed with him in the hope of making up for lost time. Eginhard tells us that he spoke Latin as well as his own tongue, and had a useful command of Greek, speaking it badly but understanding the language well enough when it was spoken to him. He encouraged learning and had a passion for astronomy, for we are told that "he investigated the motions of the heavenly bodies most curiously, with an intelligent scrutiny." But what he liked most of all was carousing with his numerous wives and mistresses, hunting, and waging war.

As a war-leader, he was absolutely ruthless to the chosen enemy and nearly as ruthless toward his own people. Scarcely a year passed when he was not engaged in war. He was continually pushing against the borders of his kingdom, north, south, east, and west. He fought in turn against the Lombards, the Saxons, the Moslems of Spain, the Basques, the Serbs, the Avars, the Byzantine provinces in south Italy, the Bretons, Bavarians, Frisians, Danes, Slavs, and Huns. There was scarcely a race in Europe which he did not attack and slaughter. Peace—such peace as there was—was won by blood and fire.

Charlemagne did not always win his battles. In A.D. 778 he marched into Spain at the invitation of the Abbasid governor of Barcelona who was making war against the Omayyad Emir of Cordova. The circumstances are obscure, and Charlemagne seems to have believed that in return for his aid he would be granted sovereignty over all the regions north of the river Ebro. He took Pamplona by storm and was laying siege to Saragossa when he heard that the Saxons had revolted; then he lifted the siege to put down the Saxon uprising. As his army was marching through the Basque province of Gascony in the lower Pyrenees, his entire rearguard was annihilated. The Basques were in the wooded heights; they drove down on the unsuspecting rearguard at dusk and spent the night cutting it to pieces. They were lightly armored; they knew the forest pathways; and they were determined to capture the baggage train. "In this battle," says the chronicler Eginhard, "there were killed among many others Eggihard, the surveyor of the royal table, Anselm, the Count of the Palace, and Roland, Prefect of the Breton marches."

In later years Roland acquired the dimensions of a towering legend, the paladin of paladins. In *The Song of Roland* the defeat at Roncesvaux becomes a spiritual triumph; the Basques become Saracens; the young Charlemagne is presented as an aged monarch; the obscure Roland becomes the chief officer of the Carolingian court. History is massacred to provide an epic.

The *Song of Roland* was the work of a Norman cleric living shortly before or after the First Crusade, some four hundred years after the defeat of Charlemagne's rearguard, when all the details of the ambuscade were forgotten or colored with legendary feats which occurred elsewhere. The purpose of the epic was to celebrate the chivalry of French knighthood. Roland is the knight of the faith in a war to the death against the infidels, who are depicted in grotesque caricature. The story is told in short and vivid scenes as though on a stage; and indeed there can be detected beneath the jerky movement of the epic the shape of a dramatic performance, with the stage perhaps set up before the gate of a church, with Gabriel and Michael descending on ropes to lift the dead Roland to Paradise, and with Charlemagne wearing the same robes and beard that he wore the week before when he assumed the role of God. The *Song of Roland* is intensely theatrical.

The *Iliad* flows in powerful waves, one scene flowing into another. The *Song of Roland*, like the Bayeux tapestry, is neatly enclosed in a series of set pieces, each provided with a moral. Virtue is painted in brilliant colors; the vices of the Moslems are painted uniformly black, so that we are not surprised when we learn that their ruler is a twisted black gnome, half-brother to Satan, commander of an army a hundred thousand strong. Roland fights valiantly; so too does his beloved Oliver who is killed in the battle, to be followed in death by Archbishop Turpin, the heroic representative of the embattled Church. In his dying moments Roland is disturbed at the thought that his sword Durandel will fall into the hands of his enemies. It is a holy sword, containing in the golden hilt a tooth of St. Peter, a drop of the blood of St. Basil, some hairs of St. Denis, and a portion of the hem of the Virgin's dress. These relics describe the hero: faithful to the Church, to monastic discipline, to France, and to the Virgin. Roland tries unsuccessfully to destroy the holy sword by bringing it down with all his force against a rock. The sword, being holy, remains whole. While the sword is still ringing in his hands, he laments his fate:

> *Ah, Durandel! How fair and bright you are,*
> *Reflecting the brightness of the sun's rays.*
> *Once at Moriane King Charles was bidden*
> *By an angelic messenger to grant that this sword*
> *Be girt about one of his great captains:*
> *So was this sword given to me.*
> *With it I conquered Anjou and Brittany,*
> *With it I conquered Poitou and Maine,*
> *With it I conquered Normandy the free,*
> *With it I conquered Provence and Aquitaine,*
> *And Normandy and all Rumania. I won*
> *Bavaria, and all of Flanders fell to my sword,*
> *Burgundy, too; Poland, and Constantinople,*
> *Which swore to serve my master always,*
> *And he commands the realm of Saxony.*
> *With it I conquered Scotland, Ireland, Wales,*
> *And England too, where he holds dominion.*
> *With it I conquered all the many countries*
> *Held by Charles whose beard is white with age.*
> *For this sword's sake a heavy grief weighs on me,*
> *Lest it should fall into the hands of pagans.*
> *God, Father, never let France be shamed!*
>
> (*Song of Roland* 2312–35)

The dream of the sword has very little relation to reality; neither Poland nor the British Isles fell to the sword, and Constantinople remained unconquered by Charlemagne. The dying Roland portrays the Holy Roman Empire as a cleric living four hundred years later would like it to have been. Indeed, the whole epic breathes of the Crusades and the atmosphere of religious exaltation that accompanied them; the call is to the holy sword, and the work it will do; no quarter was to be given to the enemies of Durandel, "the enduring blade." It is as though the sword had a life of its own and spoke through the lips of Roland, announcing mysterious conquests which had come about independently of human aid.

The Song of Roland, though written so many years after the event, reflects the barbaric splendor of the times. Those ghostly Saracens confronting the Christian knights belong to a continuing tradition. In the time of Charlemagne there were men still alive who could remember when Charles Martel defeated the Saracens at Poitiers and drove them back to the foothills of the Pyrenees. But in one respect *The Song of Roland* was singularly misleading. The poem describes a defeat, and in the long reign of Charlemagne the victories far overshadowed the defeats.

The king was well-served by his generals. His Frankish marshals were men of extraordinary capability and daring. Eric of Friuli, William of Toulouse, and Gerold of Bavaria were men with great organizational power, capable of massing, arming, and feeding vast armies, and leading them against any enemy. The Avars, a Mongoloid people from Central Asia, had established an empire from the mouth of the Danube to the mouth of the Oder. For two and a half centuries they had been preying on all the neighboring tribes. They received enormous tributes from the emperors of Constantinople, who paid them to keep the peace. In some years the tribute amounted to 120,000 gold *solidi* in addition to innumerable gifts of silk, spices, and jewels. They were a small, broad, yellow-skinned, pig-tailed people who lived in walled encampments known as "rings"; the largest of these rings was said to be thirty-eight miles in circumference. Charlemagne made war on them continually, played one Avar lord against another, captured one ring after another, and finally siezed the Avar capital. Fifteen wagonloads of treasure, each wagon drawn by four oxen, were conveyed to Aachen. It was more than a king's ransom; Eric of Friuli had captured enough treasure to finance an empire. Eginhard was present in Aachen when the huge wagons rumbled into the city. "In no war since the memory of man have the Franks won such riches," he declared. "Up to this time you might have said they had no wealth."

The wealth of the Avar hoard—fantastic heaps of Byzantine gold coins, rings, clasps, arm bands, jeweled swords, silver cups, and silken robes—was to provide Charlemagne with more financial security than he needed, for the immediate effect was a precipitous rise in prices. The hoard, consisting of the accumulated treasure of nearly three centuries of predatory wars, deserves to be remembered with gratitude, for it enabled Charlemagne to endow more and more monasteries, and it was by grace of these monasteries with their *scriptoria* filled with clerks busily copying ancient manuscripts that Greek and Roman literature has come down to us. Nine out of every ten surviving manuscripts derive from Carolingian copies.

While Charlemagne bent the greater part of his energy on conquest, there remained enough energy left over for pursuing the arts. He had a talent for assembling scholars at his court. Alcuin of York, a humanist before the age of humanism, whom Charlemagne met by chance in Parma and appointed head of the Palace School, accomplished his work well. He knew his Roman classics, read Cicero, Virgil, Ovid, Horace, and Pliny, and had no illusions about the nature of the task he had been called upon to perform. He was minister in charge of culture, and his task was nothing less than to bring about the revival of the ideals of classical antiquity. He was not performing the last rites over the dead; instead, he was presiding over the resurrection of the ancient arts.

There are knights of culture, as there are knights of faith: men who heroically stand over the treasures of the past and preserve them in the face of all the disasters which time and improvidence work on them. They are the men who find the lost manuscripts, the lost works of art, the lost breath of life. They mend the books and pour their own spirit on the broken pages. Of these men Alcuin was among the greatest.

He was not an original thinker, and his fluent verses are rarely more than pleasant exercises. He was a man of deep faith and much kindness and gaiety; on his thin shoulders rested a burden of immeasurable weight, as he sought to confront the past with the present, to give direction to the tumultous energies which Charlemagne's victories had released. He collected manuscripts, saw that they were properly copied, inveighed against carelessness and slovenliness, sent his *negotiatores* throughout Europe to purchase rare *objets d'art* for his king, and with extraordinary single-mindedness guided his armies

Christ the Light of the World. Mosaic in the apse of the Cathedral at Cefalu. (*Alinari*)

Cathedral at Monreale

Mosaic of Christ in the apse of the Cathedral at Monreale

The Virgin. Mosaic in the apse of the Basilica of Santa Maria and Donatus at Murano. (*Osvaldo Böhm*)

The young Christ. Mosaic in the Cathedral of St. Mark, Venice. (*Anderson*)

The Nativity. Mosaic in the Cappella Palatina, Palermo.

The Coronation of the Virgin. Mosaic in the Basilica of St. Maria Maggiore, Rome. (*Alinari*)

The Coronation of King Roger II. Mosaic in the Church of the Martorana, Palermo.

MARIA VIRGO ASSVPTAE AD ETHEREV TBALAMV INQVO REX REGV STELLATO SEDET SOLIO

ΡΟΓΕΡΙΟC ΡΗξ · IC̄

of clerks in the performance of their duties. He was the Great Pre-
server, but he was also the Great Innovator, for on everything he
touched he left something of himself. He has left an indelible mark on
calligraphy, for the Carolingian script which he devised has been the
model for fine calligraphy ever since, and when the humanists of the
Renaissance ransacked the monasteries of Europe for the manuscripts
of the classics which they later printed, they found that the great
majority of them were written in Carolingian script, and they
adapted this script on their printing presses. For some reason they believed they were copying the script of the ancient Romans, and they
called it *scriptura romana*, but in this they were mistaken. What they
found was a beautiful and cunningly wrought variant of the Roman
letters. Alcuin gave grace and dignity to the stern outlines of ancient
Roman handwriting. Here, for example, is part of a famous inscription at the base of the Trajan Column showing Roman lettering at its
best, followed by examples of Carolingian script:

Trajan (114 A.D.)

BERGE

Carolingian (850 A.D.)

BERGE

RATIONISIHV

Alcuin called himself "an old piping shepherd" in one of his
poems, but there was a gay youthfulness and even impudence in his
manner. He had a weakness for giving nicknames to his friends, and
so Charlemagne became David, his eldest son Pepin became Julius,
Angilbert who seduced one of Charlemagne's daughters before becoming Abbot of St. Riquier became Homer, and Eginhard became
Beseleel after the man "filled with the spirit of God, in wisdom and in
understanding and in knowledge and in all manner of workmanship."
Alcuin gave himself the name of Flaccus, by which he meant that he
was a deserving disciple of the poet Horace.

In this way, by forming a small and powerful literary society close to the throne, Alcuin was able to exert his influence. In one of his letters he complained that no one showed any interest in the study of the classics, but he meant only that not enough interest was being shown. Charlemagne threw his weight into the battle. The Monk of St. Gall tells a story of Charlemagne visiting a school where poor boys and the sons of the nobility were taught by the same masters. The poor scholars worked more diligently than the rich. "You have done well," Charlemagne said, "and now study to attain perfection and I shall give you bishoprics and splendid monasteries and hold you in honor." Then he turned in outrage toward the sons of the nobility. "You have done badly," he said, "and given yourself up to luxury and sport and unprofitable pastimes. By the King of Heaven, I take no account of your looks or your noble birth, though others may admire you for them. Know that unless you improve upon your laziness by vigorous study you will never receive any favors from Charles."

A few years later Charlemagne was busily planning a program of free universal education for all the subjects of his empire. It was the first time that such a program had ever been planned.

Under Charlemagne the arts flourished with a vivid and sometimes barbaric magnificence. Like all conquerors, the emperor paid special attention to architecture. His palace at Aachen stood on top of a hill, connected by a long covered gallery with the royal chapel at the bottom of the hill. This royal chapel was modeled on San Vitale at Ravenna, the central space forming an octagon, the dome gleaming with mosaics showing Christ in a purple mantle, blessing the world, while at his feet the twenty-four Elders of the Apocalypse rise from their seats to offer him their jewel-encrusted crowns. The background of the mosaic was the eternal blue of the heavens studded with stars. Charlemagne's marble throne stood on the gallery, so that "he could see all and was seen by all," and just as his own vast palace stood high above the chapel, so he himself, when enthroned, looked down upon his priests. Yet he was a devout churchman, lavished great treasure of gold and silver on the chapel, and attended services three times a day with the regularity of clockwork. He took especial care that the chapel should be spotlessly clean, and Eginhard tells us that "he constantly warned the sextons not to bring anything dirty or improper into the building or to permit anything of the sort to remain there."

The palace could be seen from many miles away, the bright red walls glinting under the huge bronze eagle with outstretched wings on the palace roof. The palace was half parliament building, half royal residence. There were private apartments for Charlemagne and his family, baths, wardrobes, libraries, a treasury, an armory, an archive room. The reception hall was a hundred and fifty feet long, and there was the inevitable throne which looked down on the assembled courtiers. Aachen, previously a small village, became a thriving town bustling with the affairs of the empire. A vast bureaucracy was housed in buildings around the palace, and there was a constant stream of ambassadors and prelates, merchants and cutthroats. Thieves congregated in the capital, finding in the city the opportunities they rarely found in the provinces, and safety in the crowds. Every day the mule trains brought visitors from Spain, France, and Italy; and the almond-eyed Avars worked in their chains.

Aachen indeed was the center of the earth, more powerful than Byzantium, and nearly as magnificent. At that time there existed only one other power to rival it. The empire of the Caliph Harun al-Rashid, ruling from Baghdad, extended from the frontiers of India to western outposts beyond Libya on the littoral of North Africa, while Morocco and Spain were ruled by the Umayyad dynasty of princes who regarded the caliph as a heretic. Between the two empires lay the shrinking Byzantine Empire, permanently at war with itself. It was to Harun al-Rashid's advantage to make peace with Charlemagne, and accordingly embassies were exchanged. Fabulous gifts from the workshops of the Orient reached Aachen. We hear of caravans of costly silks and perfumes running the Byzantine blockade. An elephant, gaily caparisoned, was one of the more notable presents. We hear, too, of a waterclock with an intricate mechanism of brass balls which fell one by one with the passing hours, while twelve knights emerged one by one from gilded windows. To the Carolingians the most amazing present was a massive many-colored tent having so many compartments that it resembled a palace.

The Orient poured into Aachen and left its traces on Carolingian art. It was an art which absorbed and fused together so many artistic idioms that it seemed always in danger of losing its own character. The spirals and interlaces of the Northmen, the patterns of Sasanian silks, the brilliant mosaics of Byzantium, and the robust sculpture of the Romans were all called into service, subtly modified, and then hammered into a recognizable Carolingian pattern. Even long-forgotten Hellenistic forms were taken over, as we learned recently when the frescoes on the walls of Santa Maria Antiqua at Castelseprio in Lombardy were rediscovered. The Golden Altar in the church of Sant'Ambrogio in Milan testifies to the vigor of Carolingian craftsmen working in hammered gold, filling panel after panel with scenes from the Gospels and with angels in wild flight. The altar quivers with furious life; the gold sea is turbulent with God's creatures; the rims of the panels are encrusted with barbaric processions of jewels.

Among the few and precious survivors from the Carolingian age, the most astonishing is the Psalter that has been preserved for the last two hundred and fifty years in the University of Utrecht. The Psalms, the Pater Noster, the Apostles' Creed, and the Canticles are written in Carolingian miniscule on 108 vellum leaves, always accompanied by drawings interpreting the verses. Those quick, happy, oddly impudent drawings tell us more about the habits and customs of the Carolingians than about the Psalms. Christ wields a twelve-foot spear, and is attended by Charlemagne's cavalry. Mountains melt like wax, prophets gesticulate, lovers embrace, angels descend in whirlwinds, castles go up in flames. The artist employs a rapid, swirling, scratchy pen, and when it pleases him he becomes ruthlessly literal, so that he sketches God in bed while an angel roughly awakens him with

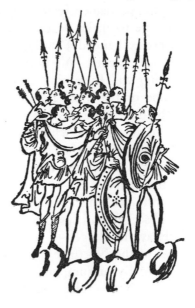

the admonition, "Sleeper, awake." Those charming and tumultuous drawings suggest the character of Charlemagne himself: restless, rough-edged, completely sure of himself.

To the end Charlemagne remained the barbaric chieftain, his graces of mind subordinated to his general ruthlessness. His coronation at St. Peter's basilica on Christmas Day, 800, was merely a recapitulation on a higher plane of the ceremonial adorations he had permitted the people to offer him at Aachen. He regarded Pope Leo III with majestic indifference. He had not come to receive the crown from him; he had come to claim it as the acknowledged emperor, converter of the pagans, tamer of the barbarians, and defender of the Church.

The ceremony took place very quietly. Once Charlemagne decided to be crowned in Rome, the machinery of Christian panoply and ceremonial went quickly into action. Eginhard relates that he had no particular affection for the title of emperor; and according to the Royal Annals it pleased him that the coronation should assume a more or less accidental character. The official Frankish version describes how the king was praying before the tomb of St. Peter and was just rising from his prayers when the pope placed the crown on his head, and immediately there came the ringing cries of acclamation, and afterward the pope prostrated himself before the new emperor. The *Liber Pontificalis* describes the coronation as an extraordinary event, while the Royal Annals describe it as a perfectly normal event. For the pope and for the Romans it was extraordinary, while for Charlemagne and his retinue, accustomed to triumphs, there was nothing extraordinary at all.

Nevertheless that coronation, which could not have taken more than three or four minutes to perform, was to have extraordinary consequences. Symbolically, if not in actuality, the Roman Empire was reborn at the precise moment when the crown touched the head of Charlemagne. He had become by his bloodless conquest of Rome the inheritor of Augustus and of Constantine. In the East the Byzantine emperors ruled and called themselves Roman; in the West Charlemagne ruled as Roman Emperor in fact and in name.

Though his empire did not long survive him, the idea of a Christian Roman Empire in the West was to dominate men's minds for centuries to come. The idea took the form of a dream of Europe united at peace under the earthly rule of a single emperor and the spiritual rule of a single pope. It was a dream which haunted men until the Renaissance, and still haunts them.

Charlemagne himself seems never to have understood the implications of his coronation. He returned to Aachen, fought more wars, set up watchtowers against the Northmen and the Saracens, and gave himself up more and more to religious meditation. Once, while he was on the march, a meteor blazed across the sky and his horse shied, throwing him to the ground, so that, as Eginhard tells us, "the girdle of his cloak snapped and his sword belt slipped away, and when the attendants came up to him they found him disrobed and disarmed." In an age of portents such things were taken seriously, and Charlemagne never completely recovered from the unspoken prophecy. He grew old and lame, and became querulous. The problems of his empire tormented him, fevers kept him awake at night, and gout troubled him. He died at last on January 28, 814, in great pain but conscious to the end, and was buried in a tomb of white marble in the palace chapel at Aachen. On one side of the tomb there is an inscription describing him as "the great and orthodox emperor who nobly increased the kingdom of the Franks and reigned prosperously for forty-seven years"; on the other side there is a carving showing the Rape of Proserpine.

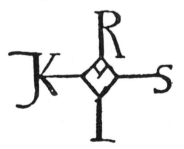

17 ✠ THE COMING OF THE NORTHMEN

EUROPE, which had suffered in the seventh and eighth centuries from the depredations of Arabs emerging from the deserts of Arabia, was to suffer in the ninth and tenth centuries from depredations from a totally unexpected quarter —the icy wastes of Scandinavia. Like the Arabs, the tall flaxen-haired Northmen despised the traditions built up over so many centuries in western Europe. They had no use for the Church, for law, or for the culture which arose from Greece and Rome. They came like a whirlwind, looting and plundering at will.

We may never know what obscure change of diet or alteration in their habits led to the sudden increase in population which brought about the desire to escape overseas. At first a few ships crossed the sea, then there came a spate of them; the rivers of Russia and the entire coast of Europe saw these marauders. Soon they were sailing down the great Russian waterways to the Caspian and the Black Sea, and setting up beachheads on the coasts of England, France, and Italy. Their roads were rivers, burned towns, the wide sea. They encircled Europe with the flames of burning towns. A new prayer was spoken in the churches: "Deliver us, O Lord, from the fury of the Northmen!"

The pantheon of their gods was dominated by Odin and Thor, who were both war gods. Thor was Odin's son, and the voice that spoke in the thunder. Odin was the father of all (*Allfadir*), creator of man and of poetry, leader of the savage hunt, a wild intractable god who never comes completely into focus, for he is continually changing his shape and assuming strange forms. He becomes at will a fish, a snake, a bird, a bull, or a monster. In his more human shape he grasps the spear Gungnir, which has been forged by the dwarfs, and rides faster than the wind on the eight-legged horse Sleipnir, while two crows perch on his shoulders and whisper into his ears all they have seen and heard about the world. Two wolves attend him, and he rejoices in bloody sacrifices. His name comes from a root meaning "fury."

Thor, the Thunderer, with his long red beard and his haunting voice, was scarcely more than a mirror-image of his father, being also a god who presided over the fortunes of war. His emblem was the swastika. His mother, Frigg, occupies the rather obscure place always occupied by the wives of the great gods; it was said of her that she knew men's fate, but never revealed it. She had greater affection for the race of men than her husband, and she would sometimes protect warriors whom Odin had decided to kill. The one-armed Tyr, invoked by warriors going into battle and by men drawing up contracts, was also the son of Odin. Tyr, Odin, Thor, and Frigg have given their names to four days of the week. It is strange that they should be so well remembered, for only one of them was superbly powerful.

The Northmen with their three war gods were amply provided with excuses for battle. They were skilled and courageous seamen, who were not afraid to voyage out into the far Atlantic in their small rowing vessels with ferocious dragon prows, steering by the long oar in the stern. They used sails only with a fair wind, and for the most part the machinery which drove their vessels was brute human force. Poorly armed at first, they came to have the best weapons of their time, acquiring helmets and shirts of mail from the spoils of the conquered towns, and then improving on them. Their swords were light, rarely more than three pounds, seldom more than thirty-two inches long, very supple. They were designed for hand to hand combat. So too was the great double-headed ax with a five foot shaft and a single broad blade, which was capable of splitting a man in two, as though he were cordwood.

The earliest raids of the Vikings [1] are lost to history. We do not know the names of the first towns they sacked and put to the flames.

[1] From the old Norse word *wic*, meaning a camp or group of warriors.

They emerge for the first time in history about A.D. 789 when "three ships from Herethaland" burnt Wareham on the Dorsetshire coast of England and made off with some small booty after killing the local sheriff. Four years later the rich abbey on the holy island of Lindisfarne, off the Northumbrian coast, was plundered by Danish raiders. They gutted the church and bishopric, devoured the cattle, killed many monks, and carried off the church plate, a rich booty of jewels and vestments, and a few young monks who might fetch a good price in the European slave markets. The raid took place in the depth of winter and was carefully planned. News of the atrocity spread like wildfire through England, and soon reached the continent. Alcuin, writing from the court of Charlemagne, wept at the news, for he was himself from Northumberland. "For three hundred and fifty years," he wrote, "we and our forefathers have dwelt in this fair land, and never before have we witnessed in Britain such terrible things as we have now suffered from the heathen. No one would have thought they could have made such a voyage . . ." It was a feeling he shared with many others. The daring, the recklessness, even the absurdity of the adventure shocked him almost as much as the loss of his friends.

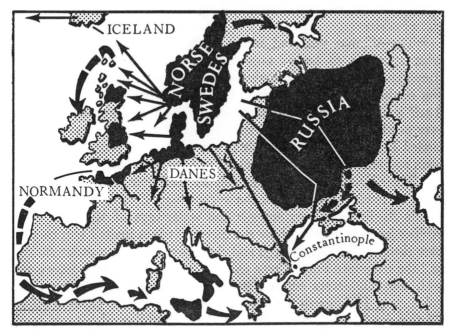

About 900 A.D. the raids of the Vikings circled Europe.

Was there no stability in life? Was every coast to be at the mercy of marauders? The following year the raiders returned, landing near Jarrow, but this time they had less success. There was a pitched battle, the Viking chieftain was seized and tortured to death, and only a few survivors succeeded in reaching the longboats. For a while they left the English coast alone. Iona was pillaged in 802. Thirty years later the storm broke in fury. They began to sail out in large formations, with well-equipped and highly trained armies. They struck at England, Ireland, the Lowlands, Germany, and the three coasts of France. They reached Spain and North Africa, landing wherever there were coastal towns, and ascending the rivers to attack the cities. They colonized the Shetlands and the Faroes, reached across the seas to Iceland, Greenland, and the inhospitable coasts of Labrador. They discovered America and conquered the land we know as Russia, which derives its name from one of their tribes, the Ruotsi. Alcuin had prayed that they would be like nightmares that vanish with the morning. Instead, they came to stay.

The Viking incursions were not all plunder and violence; the former pirates sometimes became merchants. The tomb of a Viking chieftain in the Hebrides revealed alongside his sword and battle-ax a pair of scales.

The Vikings swarmed across all the waterways of Europe in what appeared to be an unpremeditated debauch of rapine and slaughter, of burning and looting without plan or purpose, but there was method in their madness. They knew what they were doing. Their aim was nothing less than the conquest of Europe, and they very nearly succeeded in their aim. By the year A.D. 900 they had encircled Europe, settled deep within the lands they proposed to conquer, and sent expeditions to Iceland and the Far East.

Their legendary exploits, as sung by their epic poets, were sometimes curiously remote from the events they described. When the Swede Rurik set out to conquer the waterways of Russia, a convenient legend described how the Slavonic tribes invited him to rule over them. "Our land is large and rich, but there is no order among us," the tribesmen said. "Come and rule over us." In this way, we are told, the conquerors entered Russia by invitation, founding their colonies at Holmgarth (Novgorod) and Newgarth (Kiev). After Rurik's death, Oleg, his kinsman and the guardian of his son Igor, overcame the independent princes of Kiev, which henceforth became the capital of Russia.

In the tenth century they established commercial relations with Constantinople and Baghdad. In the markets of Constantinople they exchanged the commodities of the north—furs, hides, and slaves—for the corn, wine, oil, and precious cloths of the south. The river Dnieper opened the way to the Euxine and the Hellespont; the Volga opened the way to Baghdad. They became settled merchants, sending embassies to foreign courts, acting outwardly as though they loved stability, though they were never able to disguise their thirst for conquest.

The riches of Constantinople excited their cupidity; they dreamed of themselves as the inheritors of the Roman Empire, ruling the earth from the second Rome. Four times (A.D. 860, 880, 907, and 914) they flung their powerful fleets against the eastern empire, and four times they were repulsed. We are told that on each occasion they were very close to conquering it. The chronicler describes how they dragged their ships ashore, mounted them on wheels, and sailed them on dry land right up to the city walls.

Europe suffered staggering losses during the Viking invasions. In the first half of the tenth century they nearly succeeded in destroying the whole fabric of European civilization. Ireland never recovered from their depredations, and to this day there are large areas of England that bear the marks of the Viking invasions. What saved Europe was the Viking habit of taking service as mercenaries under foreign kings. The most resourceful defenders of Constantinople were the Varangian guards, recruited from among the Vikings. In the same way Charles the Bald was able to hire a Viking chieftain to dislodge the Vikings entrenched in the region of Jeufosse northwest of Paris for a fee of 5,000 pounds of silver and sufficient rations for the expedition. Viking fought against Viking. It was as though some deadly disease moved them to fight against their own kin.

Christianity came to the Vikings by obscure ways, often for reasons of accommodation. Vladimir, Grand Prince of Russia, led an embassy which visited many countries in search of a religion. The official chronicler reported:

When we journeyed among the Bulgarians, we beheld how they worship in their temple called a mosque, while they stand upright. The Bulgarian bows, sits down, looks hither and thither like one pos-

sessed, and there is no happiness among them, but instead only sorrow and a dreadful stench. Then we went to the Germans and saw them performing many ceremonies in their temples; but we beheld no glory there. Then we went on to Greece, and the Greeks led us to the edifices where they worship their God, and we knew not whether we were in heaven or on earth. For on earth there is no such splendor or such beauty, and we are at a loss how to describe it. We know only that God dwells there among men, and the service is fairer than the ceremonies of other nations. For we cannot forget that beauty.[1]

Vladimir discussed religion with the Jews, the Roman Christians, and whatever other sects passed through Kiev. He found the Roman Christians wanting because they declared that "whatever one eats and drinks is for the glory of God," which he dismissed as a monstrous perversion of the truth, since it was obvious that one ate and drank for one's own pleasure, and he had no confidence in the Jews because they had been forced to abandon their own home. "If God loved you and your fathers, you would not find yourselves dispersed in foreign lands," he declared. "Do you expect us to accept the same fate?" He was impressed by reports of the superhuman beauty of the ceremonies at Hagia Sophia, and he had already decided to embrace Christianity when he led an expedition against Cherson, the jewel of the Byzantine crown. He captured Cherson, and then sent a message to Constantinople offering to marry the sister of the Greek emperors Basil II and Constantine VIII. If refused, he threatened to kill the entire population of Cherson and to march on Constantinople.

The blackmail proved successful, and the Greek emperors consented to the marriage on condition that the ceremony was performed in Constantinople and that Vladimir would be baptized. Accordingly the Princess Anne became the wife of the Grand Prince Vladimir, and the alliance between the rulers of the Byzantine Empire and of Russia was firmly established. Russia inherited the Byzantine Church, a script based on Greek script, and an attitude toward government that was thoroughly impregnated with Byzantine concepts.

With all the fervor of a convert Vladimir returned to the pagan city of Kiev and ordered the ancient Slavonic gods to bow to Christ. The entire population was ordered to plunge naked into the conse-

---

[1] S. H. Cross, *The Russian Primary Chronicle* (Cambridge, Mass., Harvard University Press, 1930), p. 199.

crated waters of an old stream, while a priest read the service of baptism. Vladimir became a saint, the Slavonic Church regarding him with the approval reserved for princes who open up their country to the faith. It was conveniently forgotten that he had murdered his own brother and maintained a harem of 3,500 women.

In much the same way a certain Rollo, the son of Rognwald Jarl of Norway, embraced Christianity. He had led his Vikings against England and France, and after forty years as a freebooter and pirate captain he was able to establish himself on the Seine at Rouen. In A.D. 888, the fatal year that saw the final dismemberment of the empire of Charlemagne, he felt himself sufficiently strong to besiege Paris, which was defended by Count Eudes. He failed to capture Paris, but the Frankish King Charles the Simple granted him by treaty the large area of northern France which he already regarded as his own on condition that he embraced Christianity, swore an oath of allegiance, and protected Normandy against further Viking raids. In A.D. 911 at St. Clair-sur-Epte the treaty was signed, and Rollo married Gisela, the daughter of Charles the Simple. When Rollo was commanded to pay homage to his sovereign by prostrating himself and kissing the king's toe, he refused, saying indignantly: "Ne si, by Got!" (Not so, by God!) And when later it was arranged that the act of homage he performed by proxy, it was said that Charles was thrown backward by the young Danish soldier who raised the king's foot in order to kiss it. The Norman chieftain kept his word, and became a faithful vassal. He went to the defense of the Frankish king, kept order in Normandy, and formed an alliance with the Vikings of the Loire.

The Vikings fared less well in England, where they were confronted with the son and grandson of Alfred the Great, both redoubtable warriors. In the middle years of the tenth century most of what is now England, from Cornwall and Wessex in the south to Northumbria in the north, was under the control of Athelstan, the grandson of Alfred. The Anglo-Saxons were defending themselves well, and gradually the terror of the Vikings was being forgotten.

The Vikings had not, however, given up all hopes of conquering England. In A.D. 1066 Harald Hardrada, King of Norway, led a fleet of three hundred vessels up the estuary of the Humber, marched on York, and established his camp at Stamford Bridge a few miles to the east. He thought he had England in his grasp. He had never lost a battle, and he had probably more military experience than any other man of his time, for he had served when young in the Varangian guard in Constantinople, led his guardsmen against the Saracens in Egypt and Syria, and fought in Greece and Italy. Returning to Norway through Russia, he married Elizabeth, the daughter of the Grand Prince Yaroslav. He had accumulated a vast treasure, and he appears to have offered half the treasure to his nephew, King Magnus of Norway, in exchange for half the kingdom. When Magnus died, he became sole King of Norway.

The English cherished no love for Harald Hardrada, "the hard-minded," and were determined to put an end to him. The English King Harold drove north by forced marches, surprised him in his camp at Stamford Bridge, and routed the Viking army. Harald Hardrada was slain in the battle. Three days later, on September 28, William, Duke of Normandy, landed his forces at Pevensey, and King Harold was compelled to lead his battle-weary troops by forced marches to the South of England to meet the new invader. William was supplied with cavalry; Harold had none. William's troops were fresh and eager for combat, while Harold's were exhausted by their long march to the north and then to the south. The battle was fought on October 14. Within three weeks Harold had won a great victory and lost his kingdom.

The Bayeux tapestry describes in simple detail the Norman legend of the battle and the events that led up to it. That extraordinary tapestry, 230 feet long and twenty inches wide, has something of the effect of a relief carved in stone, to be set around the walls of a cathedral; and indeed it appears to have been made at the orders of Odo, half-brother of King William, shortly after the conquest in order to decorate his cathedral at Bayeux, in memory of his own accomplishments during the conquest. Odo appears as bishop and war leader, a figure of decisive importance during the campaign. Almost he overshadows William.

The tapestry, which is really an embroidery picked out in woolen thread, shows some sympathy for the English, who were poorly armed with spears and clubs. Among them were farmhands armed only with pitchforks and stones. The Normans were armed with maces, lances, bows and arrows, and they rode on heavy horses, the ancestors of the farm-horses seen in England today. It was an unequal contest, for the English were no match for the Norman cavalry and archers. Both sides prayed to God for victory. "Dex aie!" cried the Normans. "God help us!" We are told that the English went into battle calling upon the Holy Cross and Almighty God, and when they were in sight of the enemy they roared: "Out! Out!" at the Normans. Toward evening, as the sun was going down, the Normans rushed the English camp, shooting their arrows high in the air because they had been unable to penetrate the English shields, and among those who were killed by this rain of arrows was the English king. William, who was crowned in Westminster on Christmas Day, spent the next five years subduing a country which did not take easily to conquest.

A tall and corpulent man with ruddy cheeks and small mustaches, he was one of those who change the course of history with scarcely any thought of the consequences. He lived for the moment, irascible and capricious, at the mercy of his hot temper and his lusts. The bastard son of a Duke and a tanner's daughter, he could behave at one moment with ducal dignity, at the next moment he would be carousing like a village drunkard. He left a trail of disaster wherever he went. When he finally succeeded in conquering England, he looted all its wealth and reduced the inhabitants to a common poverty. Only the Norman knights lived in ostentatious luxury.

He was lying ill in Rouen when news came that King Philip of France was jesting about the candles he would light to celebrate the recovery of his enemy. William swore the strongest oath he knew— *Per resurrectionem et splendorem Dei!*—"By the Resurrection and the splendor of God, I shall have a hundred thousand candles burning, and all of them at Philip's expense!" When he was well again, he set out to capture Mantes, determined to put the city to the flames. He was riding over the hot embers of the burning city when his horse stumbled and he was wounded by the high iron pommel of his saddle. Carried back to Rouen, he died in agony a few weeks later, and his body was floated down the Seine for burial in Caen. As the funeral procession made its way through Caen, the streets, according to the ancient chronicler, burst into flame. It was a fitting ending for a conqueror.

About the same time that William was invading England, two other Normans, Robert and Roger de Hauteville, were contemplating a daring plan for the conquest of Sicily, then ruled by Arab princes who owed allegiance to the Sultan of Tunis. In May 1061 the brothers crossed the straits of Messina and invested the city; for the next thirty years they were engaged in a prolonged campaign to reduce the island to subjection. They conquered Sicily inch by inch. They set the Arab princes against one another, employed whatever mercenaries they could find, and demonstrated a magnificent indifference to the pope. For centuries Greek Christians had been living on the island. The brothers appointed Greek bishops in order to please the Greeks, and Latin bishops to please their own followers, and they confirmed the Muslim religious leaders in their powers. Tolerant toward Arabs and Greeks, they set about forming a society that was Norman, Latin, Greek, and Arab, all the nations held in equal honor. Surprisingly, a vivid and powerful civilization emerged from so many conflicting strains.

The succession passed to Roger II, the son of Roger de Hauteville. More than William the Conqueror, the new king resembled a Viking chieftain with his long fair hair, full beard, and powerful frame. While William employed only Normans in positions of authority, Roger employed the best minds available, and gave the highest offices to brilliant foreigners. The Arabs retained their mosques, their kadis, and their freedom to trade. The Jews, too, had their trading depots. As Roger's ships patrolled the seas under the command of captains called "admirals," Sicily became the leading maritime power of the Mediterranean and wealth flowed into her cities.

Roger's palace chapel, the *capella palatina*, is only seventy feet long and forty feet wide. "Come close, kiss the stones of this sacred place, and embrace its beauty," reads the Arabic inscription on its doors, which are now in the museum at Palermo. Although eighteenth century restorers have worked over the crowded mosaics in the chapel, and reduced perhaps a tenth of them to roccoco caricatures of Byzantine forms, enough remains to convey a sense of exquisite magnificence. Seen during a wedding, when all the candles are lit, the royal chapel has the effect of blinding the spectator with the jewellike colors gleaming from the walls.

Not far from the *capella palatina* is a single room of Roger's palace, the only one to survive. This, too, is crowded with mosaics, with long-tailed peacocks and heraldic animals in stately calm, all seen in the twilight haze of blue and gold.

Roger's son, known to history as William the Bad, was more Moslem than Christian. His Norman barons revolted, killed all his eunuchs and imprisoned him in the council chamber, deliberating whether to kill him or send him into exile. He escaped, and with the help of the Muslims, revenged himself against the nobles. When he died at the age of forty-six, he was mourned by Saracen women who rushed about in sackcloth and rent the air with their shrill funeral odes sung in his honor.

His son, William the Good, attempted to hold the balance even, but he too was deeply influenced by his Arab companions. He spoke Arabic, surrounded himself with Moslem eunuchs and dancing girls, and was guarded by Moslem slaves. His vizier and chamberlain, both eunuchs, were Moslems, and the signet ring with which he sealed all official documents was inscribed in Arabic with the words: "Praised be the Lord as is His due." His father's signet ring bore the inscription, also in Arabic: "Praised be the Lord for all His benefits." He kept the Arab merchants at arm's length, and saw that they lived in a ghetto far from his palace and taxed them beyond endurance. He hoped to capture Constantinople and did in fact capture Salonica, where he may have found the great masters of mosaic who embellished his cathedral at Monreale. He was the last of the Norman kings to reign in Sicily, and he left a prodigious legacy.

William the Good was only about thirteen when he came to the throne, and he died childless at the age of thirty-six. His mother was Margaret of Navarre, his wife was Joanna, daughter of Henry II of England, and there was Norman, French, and Spanish blood in his veins. Such a man, living in the oriental luxury of a Norman court, could be expected to spend his wealth without any thought of the consequences, but in fact he spent it wisely. A large portion of his fortune went in completing Monreale.

In that vast church which stands in the hills above Palermo there are two portraits of the king. In one he receives his crown from Christ, in the other he offers the church to the Virgin. The mosaicists portrayed him with commendable honesty: an unathletic man with sloping shoulders, a round face, enormous dark eyes, a thin yellow beard, a drooping mustache. Though he wears a heavy jewel-studded dalmatic in conscious imitation of the Byzantine emperors, he looks less like an emperor than a young poet. His head droops under the heavy crown, and he has the air of a man who is weary of luxury.

They said of him that he was "that magnificent king whose life pleased men and God":

> *Rex ille magnificus*
> *Cuius vita placuit*
> *Deo et hominibus.*

But his brooding gaze suggests an infinite distaste for giving pleasure. He had a few simple pastimes—he liked to take his Saracenic dancing-girls on boating expeditions in the bay of Palermo, he had a passion for the sweet wines which grow on the slopes of Monte Pellegrino, and he enjoyed listening to discussions on the nature of God. Above all, he enjoyed building palaces, but all his palaces have vanished, including the one he built at Messina, which was "white as a dove," and dominated the whole shore. There remains Monreale, the great cathedral he built on the slopes of Monte Caputo on the edge of a hunting park and overlooking the Conca d'Oro.

The Sicilians told the story that when he was out hunting he came to the village of Belhara and fell asleep beneath a fig tree. While he was sleeping, the Virgin appeared to him, saying that a great treasure had been buried beneath the tree. When he awoke, he dug up the treasure and solemnly dedicated it to the building of a cathedral to honor the Virgin. It is more likely that he issued a decree increasing the taxes of the Arab and Jewish merchants.

The cathedral was begun in A.D. 1172, when he came of age, and was completed eleven years later, as we know from a letter from Pope Lucius III, dated February 1183, praising him for having built the church in so short a time, and adding that in all of Christendom there was none to equal it. No church in Sicily ever received so rich an endowment, so many rights and privileges, so many estates in perpetuity. The foundation included a town in Apulia, a street in Palermo, all the proceeds of tunny fishing off the island of Fimi, the entire village of Bulchar, a mill for grinding sugar cane, several castles, and many vineyards; these donations were solemnly inscribed in an elaborate deed, with a gold seal, which the king offered on the altar on the festival of the Assumption of the Virgin. If any man can obtain a place in heaven by building magnificently, William succeeded.

Monreale is the largest of all Byzantine churches with the mosaics still in place. The floor is a marble lake, the grey granite columns have been stolen from a Roman temple, and there is a sense of grave spaciousness. The great walls are hung with acre upon acre of mosaics, like sheets of flame. The creation of the world, and the Old Testament prophecies, and the story of Christ's life are told in intricate detail by a master who was able to sustain a single mood. The saints of Monreale are more robust, more earthy, than the saints of Daphni, and the designs from the model-books have been subtly changed to suggest the existence of muscles beneath the clothes. There is vigor in the Christ who peers out from the apse; he is full-fleshed, and he commands by his physical presence, unlike the Christ at Cefalu, who commands by his nobility and grace. Monreale could only have been built by a king certain that his dynasty would endure, for everything about it proclaims assurance and stability. Six years after Monreale was completed, the dynasty came to an end.

From the time when Roger invaded Sicily to the death of his great-grandson there was only a little more than a hundred years. During that time Sicily presented the spectacle of a country where all the races lived together tolerantly. The king wore a dalmatic embroidered with Kufic characters in gold, and rode in state with an Arab bodyguard. There were Greek cities, Muhammadan villages, Norman castles, Lombard colonies, and there were streets of Pisans, Genoese, Amalfitans, and Jews. From all over Europe came scholars, doctors, and officials, all willing to take the bounty of a Norman king. The chanting of monks mingled with the voice of the muezzin from the minaret, and the roads were filled with knights in chain-mail, Arabs in long cloaks, Greeks in long gowns, and Italians in short doublets. It was as though the peace of God had descended on the island. Then, abruptly, the reign of the Norman kings was over. Cefalu, Monreale, the *cappella palatina*, and the Martorana remain to testify that for a brief period they ruled magnificently. The descendants of Vikings had become civilized at last.

And therefore I have sailed the seas and come
To the holy city of Byzantium . . .

I THINK," wrote the poet W. B. Yeats, "that in early Byzantium, maybe never before or since in recorded history, religious, esthetic and practical life were one, that architect and artificers . . . spoke to the multitude and the few alike." To the Byzantines themselves, conscious of their imperial dignity, the claim would have seemed perfectly natural. They were a rough, turbulent, and deeply pious people who seem to have found no particularly acute disadvantages in living simultaneously the life of the spirit and the life of the world. They believed, almost as an article of faith, that the spirit and the world met in the frontiers of art.

The arts of Byzantium, lavishly displayed in the churches, were cultivated with a peculiar abandon by the emperors, who saw no impropriety in building churches and creating works of art to their own glory. When Justinian rebuilt the church of Hagia Sophia, he squandered the treasure of the empire on its adornments. With secular pride, he set ten thousand workmen to labor on it, and thought his munificence worthy of the enterprise—the enterprise of building more sumptuously than anyone had ever built before. When at last on the day when the church was consecrated he stood beneath the blazing lights and gleaming mosaics, and declared that he was greater than Solomon, he was saying no more than the truth. Hagia Sophia remains the supreme achievement of Byzantine art.

It was not only in their churches that the Byzantine artists demonstrated a superb mastery. In ivories, enamels, marbles, wall paintings, illuminated manuscripts, wrought gold and silver, and in all their handicrafts they showed a prodigious sense of what Yeats called "the artifice of eternity." Their arts never failed them. To the very end of the Byzantine Empire, which endured for 1,123 years, they continued to produce an art which possessed unparalleled vigor, rarely declining into vulgarity. It was an art which centered very largely on Constantinople and the neighboring Byzantine cities, dominated by the power of the imperial court. Power, refinement, self-assurance, a deep and pervading faith were the characteristics of Byzantine art from the beginning to the end.

The triumph of Byzantine art arose from the absorption of the artists in their spiritual tasks. They were not journeymen hammering out beautiful objects for the pleasure of a secular lord; and indeed they did not regard the emperor as a secular lord, for he combined in himself secular and spiritual powers, calling himself God's arch-priest, appointing and dismissing the patriarch at will. The artists performed a priestly function, for they depicted the splendors of the celestial city. The churches were not simply places of worship, but portions of heaven. They were built with a majestic unconcern for temporal problems, on a scale of breath-taking immensity, so that they seemed to be prolonged to infinity; and though they were built by human hands, they were designed to give the impression that they were spiritual works of the Creator, as insubstantial as light.

This effect was achieved by the use of brilliantly colored mosaics. The churches were lined with glass, with millions upon millions of small glass tessellae, some as small as a pinhead, others as large as a fingernail. About 52,000 tessellae were used in every square yard. The worshiper was enclosed in a subtly illuminated glass shell.

Light does not fall on a mosaic surface as it does on a mirror. The broken surface refracts the light strangely, so that in sunlight, and even more in candlelight, the shapes painted in mosaic colors seem to hover in the air, to be detached from the church wall. Because the surface is not smoothed out and every tessella is inclined at a different angle, the observer has only to alter his position a little to see subtle changes in the light flowing over the mosaics. Even if he were completely motionless, the motions of the sun or of a candleflame, or of the moon and starlight, would produce a sense of movement in the mosaics. Vast stretches of the interior of the churches were painted in mosaics made of gold fused with glass. These sheets of gold shine with a shattering brilliance. The light fumes and breathes, pulsing with movement, and possessing a life of its own. The walls become cascades of jewels reflecting the heavenly light.

Gradually there emerged a deliberate and comprehensive design for the mosaics in churches. The figure of Christ occupies the center of the dome, the four Evangelists are set in the pendentives of the dome, the Virgin stands in the conch of the apse, and the story of Christ's life on earth is told in a series of running friezes along the walls. The saints, the martyrs, and the Fathers of the Church usually occupy the space closest to the ground. That Christ and the Virgin should be depicted on the curved surfaces may be explained by their overwhelming importance, but it is precisely on these curved surfaces that the mysterious interplay of light produces its most dazzling effects, the colors acquiring depth and resonance from the ceaseless reflections from one side of the curved surface to the other, from the flickering ground-fire caused by refraction, and from the peculiar properties of light enclosed in a glass nest. Such figures seem more substantial than the others, more palpable, though they shimmer and glow and change their expressions with every breath of the observer and every shift of light.

There are only a few places left on earth where churches filled with mosaics can be seen. Fire has melted the tessellae, earthquakes have shaken them loose, Turkish conquerors have defaced them or hidden them under whitewash. There remains only one church entirely covered with mosaics, and one small chapel. Both are in Palermo, built by Byzantine craftsmen in the service of Norman kings.

While it is rare to come across even a whole wall filled with mosaics, there are some twenty churches in Greece and Italy which retain superb relics of the mosaicist's art. The labors of archaeologists have succeeded in uncovering the fragmentary mosaics of Hagia Sophia, but these fragments can only suggest the immense glittering tapestry of colors which once clothed the church. Surviving fragments uncovered in the southern gallery include a *Deësis* of the twelfth century which is perhaps the most ravishing single work of the Byzantine artists. The panel, first brought to light by Professor Whittemore in 1933, represents the Virgin and John the Baptist interceding with Christ for the sinners of the world. Only the head and a shoulder of the Virgin remain; nothing is left of Christ and the Baptist below the waist. Nevertheless, the effect is of a finished work of art, for time has removed only the inessential. The Virgin bows her head in entreaty, but there is in her look so much sweetness and gentleness, and so much imperious power, that it would be inconceivable for Christ to refuse her request. He stands there in supreme majesty, yet with a look of one about to yield, and there is a humanity and candor in his expression rare in Byzantine art, while the yearning gaze of the Baptist is expressed with a delicacy and controlled violence which is even rarer. The Baptist's bronze-colored hair sweeps backward in waves of power, the dark beard is tangled with a despair which mirrors the urgency of his burning thoughts, the eyes are earnest and beseeching. It is a portrait overflowing with human warmth, with an intensity and realism far removed from the stiff, hieratic portraits of an earlier age. In the brilliance of its coloring, in the refinement of its composition, and in the depths of compassion conveyed in the three faces, the *Deësis* panel is to be counted among the supreme achievements of the world's art.

Six miles west of Athens, behind a screen of cypresses, there stands the ancient monastery of the Virgin of the Golden Laurels on a site where there once stood a temple to laurel-crowned Apollo. The small domed church, known as the monastery of Daphni, has a violent history. It was seized and partially rebuilt by Frankish barons in 1205; until the fourteenth century it remained in the possession of Cistercian monks; then it became the private chapel of a Florentine banking family, and here the last Duchess of Athens was strangled by a nephew who had entered the service of the Turks. Later the Turks pillaged it and converted it into a mosque. Later still it came into the possession of orthodox monks, who abandoned it after repeated raids by Saracen and Christian pirates. In the nineteenth century it was at different times a powder magazine, a police station, a lunatic asylum, a sheep pen.

The wonder is that any mosaics survived. In fact some nineteen panels, together with some separate figures of saints and angels, have survived for nearly eight centuries with extraordinary tenacity. The church was probably built about the year 1020 during the reign of the Emperor Basil II, under whom the empire reached its greatest extent. Most of the surviving mosaics are fragmentary, but as with the *Deësis* in Hagia Sophia, enough remains to convey the brilliance of the whole design.

In the Baptism we see Christ standing naked in the Jordan, his youthful body in the familiar posture of an ancient Greek kouros. John the Baptist, with long hair and wild beard, stands on the rocky bank with one hand reaching out across the river to touch the head of Christ with his fingertips, while the hand of God points down and a dove descends. Two graceful angels stand on the farther bank, holding up the garments of Christ. Beside John the Baptist stand two onlookers, an old and venerable sage and a more youthful man who peers out of the gold heavens with that curiously intent look which we associate with the self-portraits of artists introduced into renaissance paintings. It is almost certainly the portrait of the artist. The slender Christ dominates the design by the whiteness of his flesh and the perfect balance of the composition. He stands there in unworldly glory and transcendental beauty, not yet of the world, surprised and a little fearful of the blessedness which has been granted to him, just as the classical Greek kouros always seemed surprised and a little fearful of the energy flowing through his youthful body.

Elsewhere on the wall there is a Crucifixion which for its simplicity and beauty must be among the greatest Crucifixions ever conceived. We see the same lithe dreaming Christ, still youthful, unaltered by the passage of years, his body bending slightly at the hips, no longer naked but wearing a loin cloth which falls in intricate folds, hanging on the Cross as though hovering in the air. To his right stands the Virgin enclosed in her blue gown, to his left St. John in the voluminous folds of a gown almost too heavy and too sumptuous for him. Once again, in the St. John, we recognize the familiar features of the artist, a self-portrait of grave dignity and sweetness.

But it is not only for the superb delicacy of the composition that this Crucifixion acquires its fame. There is one astonishing detail which is to be found in no other Crucifixion. From the wound below the right breast there spurts a curving jet of blood, vanishing before it reaches the ground. The jet forms an arch, curving upward before it falls. In most Crucifixions the blood simply spurts out: at Daphni it rises and falls in a graceful parabolic curve, as from a fountain. The intention is clear: suffering has been stylized; the anguish has melted away, leaving in its place a kind of sacramental dance. As St. Bernard was to say later, the death of Jesus was no more than a falling asleep, while to dwell on the anguish of the dying Christ is to forget his divinity.

Such elegance derives from court art, for it is only in the royal courts that elegance and strength can combine to produce a great work of art. The refinements of court life demand this stylization, and since the court stands at the center of power the court artists are less inclined to represent power as urgent or vigorous. They know that real power on earth is exerted by a whisper, and inclination of the head, the pointing of a finger. So the Virgin points to the dancing blood, and Christ inclines his head, and the fountain rises and falls.

The Baptism and Crucifixion at Daphni are supremely beautiful figures, but they do not compare in authority or design with the great Pantocrator on the dome, the most successful rendering of a powerful and august divinity ever fashioned by human hands. There is nothing comparable with it in Constantinople, in Salonica, at Hosios Loukas, or at Nea Moni on the Island of Chios, the four other centers where Byzantine mosaics have survived on Greek soil. Here the whole firmament has been rolled back and we come face to face with the *Rex tremendae majestatis*. It is not the face of power only, for it goes beyond power; nor of majesty only, for it goes beyond any imaginable kingship. Here is God in his starkness and plainness, in his terror and beauty, in his ultimate solicitude for all created things. Here the unsayable has been said.

Many things have gone into the making of the Pantocrator at Daphni, and not the least of them is the memory of the great chryselephantine statue of Zeus carved by Phidias at Olympia, which had been removed to Constantinople and may have been still standing when these mosaics were created. We know what Olympian Zeus looked like from the surviving coins, and there is not the least doubt that these mosaicists were steeped in knowledge of classical Greek art. Olympian Zeus with his heavy curls and thick tangled beard, his deepset eyes and ponderous lips, is present at Daphni, providing the groundwork from which the mosaicist constructed these features, but it was only the groundwork. Phidias depicted the august monarch of heaven, serene and imperturbable. The Daphni mosaicist depicted a spiritual being of unimaginable power, monarch of all universes, the judge of the quick and the dead. He is not still, nor silent, nor gentle, nor kind. He is the God who demands that those who have received from him the gift of life shall be obedient to his purposes. He has no pity, and offers no hope to the evil-doer. He speaks out of the whirlwind: "Be still, and know that I am God."

What is so astonishing is that an artist armed with a few thousand colored stones could make a portrait of God so vivid, so comprehensive, and so terrible that it gives an impression of finality.

The mosaicist had at his disposal only six colors for making the portrait—white, black, brown, pink, blue, gold—the gold being streaked into the brown hair. White face, eyes outlined in black, blue gown. There is a calculated simplicity of means, so that under certain conditions, as when the light is fading in the church, the portrait seems to be no more than a sketch in charcoal, so heavy are the lines, so harsh the design. Seen in the full light coming from the windows it acquires plasticity and depth, fully modeled, sculptural. The gold background, the deep blue gown, the silvery blue arms of the cross set in the aureole have the effect of softening the features, or at least giving them a more human quality. It is the face one remembers; the rest is decoration.

Every device known to the Byzantine artists has been employed to suggest the power and the fierce solicitude of God. They are conscious devices used with conscious effect. There are lines deeply etched on the forehead, but they are not the troubled lines of a man deep in thought: they consist of two arches above the eyebrows and a loop like a shoe tongue over the bridge of the nose. There appears to be no explanation for the surprising loop except that it has the effect of making the features more powerful, more expressive of the strangeness of divinity. The eyes, too, are strange, for they do not gaze directly at the worshiper but are directed to one side, and that sidelong glance also has the effect of strangeness. The hands are contraries, for one delicate hand is raised in blessing, while the other resembles the tangled roots of a gnarled tree as it clutches a jewel-studded Gospel bound in gold. Everything about this mosaic suggests divine authority, the power of the living God. In his loneliness and eminence God looks down on the troubled world, commanding it to silence and perfection.

In Cefalu on the northern coast of Sicily there is another mosaic of the Pantocrator in an even better state of preservation. The figure is vastly larger than the Daphni Pantocrator, for it fills the apse and dominates the Cathedral, seeming to stand there in an attitude of majestic benediction, all gold and blue and russet, with the glow of life on his face, urgent and commanding. His right hand blesses, his left holds an open book with the words in Latin and Greek: "I am the light of the world: he that followeth me shall not walk in darkness, but shall have the light of life." High up, reaching to the roof of the Cathedral, attended by the Virgin and the Archangels, whose long wings are swept apart in the utmost reverence, this stern and youthful Christ stands in his solitary grandeur beckoning all into his presence, and there is about him nothing of the Judge, and he does not belong to the heavens only. He is the Christ of the Norman king who built the Cathedral, half-brother to Thor and Odin.

The cathedral at Cefalu was founded by Roger, Count of Sicily, apparently as a thank offering after being miraculously saved from shipwreck. Five years later, in 1130, he became King of Sicily and was able to devote large sums of money to the building of the cathedral. He was a freebooter and adventurer, who thirsted to establish the rule of the Hautevilles over all of Italy and succeeded in carving out for himself a small empire which included part of southern Italy and North Africa from Tripoli to Cape Bona. He even hoped to capture Constantinople, and the army of his great admiral George of Antioch stood close enough to the walls of Constantinople to fire arrows through the windows of the emperor's palace. Roger was a tall man, well-built, with powerful shoulders, thick flowing hair, and a full beard; and the Christ at Cefalu clearly portrays some of the physical characteristics of the king.

The refinement and beauty of this Christ comes as a shock to the beholder, who is not accustomed to seeing so aristocratic a figure dominating a cathedral. The mosaicists have obviously been imported from Constantinople, and the general design is wholly Byzantine, but the spirit is Norman-French, clearcut, vigorous, deeply poetic. The Pantocrator at Daphni is very God, the gaunt and all-powerful sovereign of universes. The Pantocrator at Cefalu is Christ in his royal beauty and the light of this world.

Roger II, "the half heathen king," had a passion for mosaics and built the *capella palatina* in Palermo as his private chapel, covering the entire wall space with mosaic panels representing the Fathers of the Church, the saints, and narratives from the life of Christ. The effect is one of bewildering opulence, as though one had entered into a jewel casket, but the mosaics of the Pantocrator are curiously diffuse, without the urgency of the Pantocrator at Cefalu, and although some of the narratives from the life of Christ are brilliantly presented, too many have been restored and reshaped to permit the observor to see it as it was when Roger II worshiped there. George of Antioch also built in Palermo a small church, shaped like a Greek cross, which was covered with mosaics. Most of them have perished, but enough remain to show that the Greek mosaicists were perfectly capable of adapting their techniques to suit their patrons. There is an imperial grandeur at Cefalu and in the *capella palatina*, while in the church built by George of Antioch, known as the Martorana, there is a delicacy and gentleness more appropriate to a high minister of state than to a king. On one of the pillars we see Roger II receiving his crown from Christ, while George of Antioch falls at the feet of the Virgin. The man who bore the title of "admiral of admirals" is represented in old age, frail and white-haired, his body so shapeless that it might be the carapace of a tortoise, in total submission to the Mother of God.

But it was in the great cathedral of Monreale, built by William II, the grandson of Roger II, that the mosaicists were given their most challenging opportunity. Only the apse of the Cathedral at Cefalu is decorated with mosaics, and the *capella palatina* and the Martorana are small; but at Monreale the entire wall space is covered with mosaics. Those great sheets of color have a dazzling splendor as they ripple across the walls of the vast cathedral, but already the sense of vivid movement is absent. There is no single panel that can be compared with the Crucifixion at Daphni, and the great figure of Christ in the apse cannot compare in authority with the Christ of Cefalu. The mosaicists have lost their cunning, and the vigor of the Hauteville dynasty was being drained away. Roger II had not bequeathed his vitality to his grandson William, *Christissimus rex*, the most Christian of Kings. William II went down in history as William the Good, and Monreale was a testament to his goodness and deep religious feeling, but not to his artistry. The rot had already set in.

Here and there in Greece and Italy we come upon the ruined remnants of those great mosaicists who made the walls of churches gleam with the artifices of eternity. The best are to be found at Constantinople, Salonica, Hosios Loukas, Daphni, the island of Chios, Cefalu, Palermo, Rome, Ravenna, and Venice. In these ten places there are preserved the greater part of the legacy. Until recently there was still another great complex of mosaics in the Church of the Assumption at Nicaea in Asia Minor, but the church was wantonly destroyed in 1920 and none of the mosaics survived. When the Church of St. Demetrius in Salonica was accidently burned in 1917, a few mosaics perished, but by an odd chance the fire revealed the presence of hitherto unknown mosaics on the piers of the nave. No doubt more mosaics will be found in time, as the archaeologists carefully cut away the whitewash from churches taken over by the Turks. For a little while longer the balance may be kept even: then gradually over the years we must expect them to disintegrate, as the little tessellae fall away from the plaster and form dusty mounds at the foot of church walls.

The process of disintegration is already at work. One can see it, for example, in the superb fourth century mosaics in the Rotunda of St. George at Salonica, where the saints in ceremonial vestments pray with uplifted arms beside ornate palaces representing the heavenly city. Earthquakes have struck the high dome, leaving cracks and fissures like tongues of flame; birds brush their wings against the tessellae; the city traffic jars them from the plaster; and the observer finds himself gazing with fascination and despair at the bright little cubes of green and gold and cerulean blue lying where they have fallen.

Salonica, indeed, has the largest collection of mosaics in the world. Nowhere else are there so many surviving mosaics from so many periods by artists working within the imperial tradition. A man can spend a day in Salonica and see a thousand years of mosaic-making, beginning with the fourth century saints and peacocks of the Rotunda of St. George and then going on to the fifth century Christ, unbearded and feminine, of Hosios David, and the seventh century Basilica of St. Demetrius with its shimmering panels showing the boyish saint as the protector of bishops and children. In the dome of the vast church of Hagia Sophia a magnificent Ascension is depicted, showing the Apostles twisting their heads as they gaze upward, and these mosaics belong to the ninth century. Finally in the Church of the Holy Apostles he can see the ruined remnants of mosaics of the fourteenth century describing the life of Christ. As one might suspect, the best are the earliest, but there is no gradual decay. The style changes, there are subtle modulations of tone and alterations of emphasis as the centuries pass, but the essential artistry remains unaltered. A new boldness appears in the ninth century, there is a greater sense of humanity in the fourteenth century shortly before the fall of the Byzantine Empire, but these changes come gradually and there is no lack of vigor in the last mosaics. The art changes and remains the same.

Roman mosaics tend to be parochial and provincial, and even in Ravenna and Venice there are few mosaics which can compare with the work of the court artists employed in Constantinople and Salonica. The Renaissance restorers ruined half the mosaics of St. Mark's in Venice; the Virgin of Torcello and the rarely seen but even more magnificent Virgin of Murano are closer to the imperial tradition than anything to be found in St. Mark's. If power, opulence, and refinement are the characteristics of imperial art, then the mosaics of Ravenna are notably deficient in power, the mosaics of St. Mark's are deficient in opulence, and the mosaics of Rome are deficient in refinement. Some of the most unimaginative mosaics ever executed are to be found in Santa Maria Maggiore in Rome. Here and there in Rome we come upon echoes of the great tradition. The golden cross covered with the snow white doves of San Clemente has a vivid tenderness and a disturbing power; the Christ in the tribune of Santa Pudenziana possesses an authentic refinement; and there is at least one mosaic in Santa Maria Maggiore—the Coronation of the Virgin—which could have been designed by Byzantine artists. Nevertheless it was an art rooted in Constantinople, losing its vitality the farther it traveled from the source.

For nearly five hundred years there have been no mosaic-makers working in the great tradition. It is a dead art which may never be revived, and it is no longer fashionable to pay tribute to those unknown masters. Yet in its time it was an art of prodigious accomplishment, profoundly affecting the lives of the worshipers, who saw before their eyes the shimmering immaterial presence of Christ and the saints, and were comforted.

19 ✝ THE ROMANESQUE POWER

SHORTLY after A.D. 1000 Raoul
Glaber, whose name means Raoul the Bald, wrote in crabbed Latin an
account of the strange flowering of churches which had appeared in
his time. He wrote with charm and dignity, and with a curious way-
wardness which is one of the characteristics of the churches he described. He wrote:

*Therefore it happened that after the above-mentioned year 1000,
which is now about three years past, all over the world but especially
in Italy and Gaul there was a rebuilding of churches, even though the
greater number were already well built and needed no such care.
Nevertheless every nation in Christendom rivalled the others in building nobler ones. It was as if the whole earth had shaken herself and
cast off her rags and was now apparelled everywhere in a white robe
of churches.*

The Cluniac monk who wrote these lines was a man with a
penchant for recording the most unlikely miracles, but this miraculous flowering of the churches had in fact taken place before his eyes.
Quite suddenly, without any preliminary gestation such as usually
accompanies the emergence of new forms of art, the Romanesque
churches arose. The old basilicas took on a new shape. A new and
strongly fortified imagination went to work. It is almost as though a
single mind had dictated the new forms the churches were to take.

That single mind embraced many minds, and many causes went
into the building of "a white robe of churches." Two or three of
these causes may be singled out. The most important was the state of

255

Christ, from the tympanum of the Church of St. Pierre, Moissac. (*Yan*)

The Church of St. Pierre, Moissac, west portal. (*Roger Viollet*)

The Church of St. Pierre, Moissac. The tympanum.

The Church of St. Pierre, Moissac. Jeremiah. (*Roger Viollet*)

Cathedral of St. Lazare, Autun. Christ in glory, from the tympanum by Gislebertus. (*Hurault-Viollet*)

Cathedral of St. Lazare, Autun. Angel awakening the three wise men, by Gislebertus. (*Hurault-Viollet*)

Cathedral of St. Lazare, Autun. Journey to Egypt, by Gislebertus. (*Trianon*)

Virgin and Child, from a church in Montmorillon (Vienne). (*Hurault-Viollet*)

peace which fell upon Italy and France in the later years of the tenth century. There had been widespread prophecies that the earth would be given over to judgment and devastation in the year 1000, but these prophecies had been proved groundless; spring, summer, autumn, and winter still came; and with a great sigh of relief the people realized they had been delivered from millenarian terrors. Danger no longer threatened from the Magyars, who had been converted and had set up an apostolic monarchy in the same year that the prophets were proclaiming the end of the world. The Northmen, too, no longer menaced the Church and scarcely menaced the state. They had been converted in the regions where the Church was powerful, and with the eagerness of converts they knelt before the priests they had previously massacred. On the Romanesque churches they left the imprint of their refined barbaric art, so that we find on the walls of churches in the Languedoc and in Provence and in Lombardy the peculiar interlaces and interweavings which appear on Scandinavian buckles, dragonheads and the tortuous convolutions of medieval manuscripts. They had been conquerors; now they were tamed; and their art was laid at the service of the Church. Meanwhile they lost nothing of their high spirits and they continued to be marauders and raiders along the coasts of Italy and Sicily and ever farther afield.

Islam, too, was receding, and in the process of recession, like a wave which leaves strange rocks on the seashore, it left fragments of Islamic imagination, so that we sometimes find striped horseshoe arches in Romanesque churches as in the cathedral of Le Puy, where Kufic inscriptions have been found. Through Islam and through Byzantium there came the taut and curiously stretched forms of Sasanian Persia, the swinging folds in garments, the double eagles, the majestic imperial presences. Remnants of Persia can still be found in those obscure villages where Romanesque churches remain intact.

One other cause needs to be mentioned, and this derives from the centuries of wars which preceded the coming of the white robe of churches. The new churches were more than houses of God; they had become reliquaries of the holy martyrs killed by the marauding enemies, Northmen, Arabs, and Hungarians alike. The passion for acquiring relics was not a recent one: we hear of relics being gathered and carefully hidden away during the persecutions under the Roman emperors, but it was not felt that any divinity attached to the relics in the early years of martyrdom. Now, however, the relics worked miracles, they protected whole communities and even whole nations, and they were regarded as sacred in themselves. The martyrs had defended the Church during the centuries of trial: now they came into their reward. In order to welcome them, the churches were enlarged. Ambulatories were provided in the choir so that the faithful could worship the relics, and sometimes there were two ambulatories with chapels containing more relics radiating from them. The churches were now rarely named after Christ, the Virgin, or the Apostles, but bore the names of the martyred saints. Death was given a place of honor. The bones beside the altar of the living God proclaimed a new and hitherto unexpressed belief in the regenerative power of martyrdom.

The chronicler Raoul Glaber spoke of a sudden spate of rebuilding, not of building. The churches were being altered and renovated on sites long hallowed. The choirs were rebuilt to house the martyrs; the façades were rebuilt to proclaim the greater majesty of God. The faithful were not led gradually into the mysteries of the faith: the Romanesque sculptors rarely depicted the Birth, the Baptism, the Miracles, or the Passion. Suddenly, dramatically, over the entrance of the church we find Christ in majesty attended by the four beasts of Ezekiel's vision. He is the Christ of the Second Coming, of the Apocalypse, of the final moment when time will be no more.

The dramatic fervor, the sense of a tremendous spiritual drama is present throughout the Romanesque church. It is not a place where a man rests only in prayer, but one where he charges himself with spiritual energy. The Romanesque sculptors portrayed a world in ceaseless movement. Gestures are abrupt, unrestrained energy pours from the sculptured figures, the symbolic and allegorical worlds are held in a continual dance. God is the *tremendum*, unreachable, unapproachable, but He is also merciful. Supporting the tympanum with its majestic depiction of Christ in Glory there may be a column showing lions open-mouthed and ready to spring. They are designed to remind the faithful of the imminence of death. *Libera eas de ore leonis*, says the offertory of the Mass for the Dead—"Deliver them from the lion's mouth, that Hell swallow them not up, that they fall not into darkness . . ." The Prophets guard the entrance, for have they not prophecied His Coming? Below the tympanum they dance like David before the Ark of the Covenant, rejoicing because Christ has shown himself in his glory.

In the Romanesque church, joy—spiritual joy—is mingled with an earthly grief. We are reminded of the tribulations of mortality, but also of the vast promise of the Kingdom. On the capitals we may see the sufferings of the martyr, whose ghostly presence hovers over a jewel-studded reliquary. Candles gleam, for only a little light comes through narrow windows. Within the church there is the sense of a welling darkness and an unfathomable mystery. Not for many years was God's sunlight to come streaming through the windows.

The little village of Moissac near Montauban in the southwest corner of France has a church founded in the seventh century, rebuilt many times, but containing today the cloisters, the royal gate, and an abundance of statues that have remained intact since they were completed in the year 1115. At first there is little to distinguish the church of St. Pierre at Moissac from hundreds of other village churches. For eight hundred years history dealt kindly with this forgotten town. The Arabs and the Hungarians, and later the armies of Richard the Lion-Heart and Simon de Montfort, sacked it. During the French Revolution it was sacked again, then it was left in peace. What remains is the supreme achievement of Romanesque art.

The royal gate, protected by a deep archway, portrays Christ in majesty with an authority equaled only by the great design in the dome of the Church of the Golden Laurels near Athens. One would have thought it beyond any sculptor's power to depict the moment of the Second Coming credibly. Such things might be accomplished with the unearthly light glittering from mosaics, but not with recalcitrant and compact stone. Nevertheless at Moissac the impossible was accomplished.

The unknown sculptor, who worked with stone from the local quarries, took as his text the stupendous passage from the Revelations of St. John:

Behold, a throne was set in heaven, and one sat on the throne. And he that sat was to look upon like a jasper and a sardine stone: and there was a rainbow round about the throne, in sight like unto an emerald. And round about the throne were four and twenty seats: and upon the seats I saw four and twenty elders sitting, clothed in white raiment; and they had on their heads crowns of gold. And out of the throne proceeded lightnings and thunderings and voices: and there were seven lamps of fire burning before the throne, which are the seven Spirits of God. And before the throne there was a sea of glass like unto crystal: and in the midst of the throne, and round about the throne, were four beasts, full of eyes before and behind. And the first beast was like a lion, and the second beast like a calf, and the third beast had a face as a man, and the fourth beast was like a flying eagle. And the four beasts had each of them six wings about him; and they were full of eyes within: and they rest not day and night, saying, Holy, holy, holy, Lord God Almighty, which was, and is, and is to come. And when those beasts give glory and honour and thanks to him that sat on the throne, who liveth for ever and ever, the four and twenty elders fall down before him that sat on the throne, and worship him that liveth for ever and ever, and cast their crowns before the throne, saying, Thou art worthy, O Lord, to receive glory and honour and power: for thou hast created all things, and for thy pleasure they are and were created.

(Revelations 4:2–11)

Such was the vision which Abbot Ansquitil commanded for the entrance to his church, but never saw, for he died before the great tympanum was completed. Today we see it as Abbot Roger, his successor, saw it, and perhaps even better, for when it was first erected it was richly painted. Here and there we can still see traces of scarlet paint on Christ's gown. Originally all the crowns were painted in gold leaf, and the gowns of the twenty-four elders were white and the background was midnight blue.

The tympanum is in an astonishing state of repair: there is some small surface damage, here and there the stone has worn away, but no heads have fallen and there is no indication of any restoration. The sculpture might have been carved two or three years ago.

The sculptor has used extraordinary means to depict an extraordinary scene. He has arranged his figures as they have never been known to have been arranged before, with great daring. The enormous elongated Christ sits on his throne, one hand holding the Scriptures, the other raised in blessing, his feet resting on the wavy "sea of glass like unto crystal." The eagle, the calf, the lion, and the beast that has the face of a man form a kind of ring around him, and all are dancing, while Michael and Gabriel stand like worshipful sentinels beyond the ring of the heraldic Gospel-writers. The twenty-four elders, each holding a viol and a cup in his hand, gaze longingly and expectantly at Christ, the rippling folds of their brocaded gowns and jewel-studded crowns forming a kind of cup supporting the central scene.

These elders are depicted in three registers, and no doubt they are intended to represent the kings of the world. They are grave and dignified men, thickly bearded, some sitting cross-legged on their thrones, others with their knees apart, their bodies at ease, their faces watchful. Each head has a peculiar awareness, a stance of its own. They are squat figures, and their squatness, characteristic of Romanesque art, where many scenes had to be represented in narrow bands, contrasts vividly with the elongated Christ and his attendant archangels, and though they demand to be observed and admired, they become in the end no more than the foam or mist rising from the glassy sea. Below them are eight rosettes magnificently and delicately carved, spewed out of the mouths of demons, and these no doubt represent the many worlds which have come into being and are now passing away.

But it is the figure of Christ, with his austere authority, which shows the sculptor's power in its most masterful form. In the folds of his garments and in the portrait of the majestic King there can be detected Persian influences. Sasanian art serves to provide the core of the design. Islamic and Spanish influence can be detected in the lion and the calf. A commentary on the Apocalypse written by Beatus, Abbot of Labiena in Spain, which is provided with crude and powerful illustrations all thoroughly imbued with Islamic feeling, shows the lion and the calf in the same positions, the heads flung backward in adoration, the bodies smoothed down until they seem to have no bones, but resemble dolphins. The commentary of Beatus is in fact fundamental to the whole design, for it shows sketchily the entire scene, which is here rendered with wonderful completeness. A sketch made in the second half of the tenth century profoundly influenced a gateway carved in the early years of the twelfth century.

While the mind and the eye are immediately attracted to the commanding figure of Christ attended by the triumphant and turbulent evangelists, it is the orderly composition of the whole which finally demands our awed admiration. It is a symphony in honor of the Second Coming in many movements, with many contrasting themes, composed by a single composer of prodigious brilliance, who was not afraid to employ deliberate dissonances and sudden violent alterations of mood, selecting elements from widely different cultures and fusing them into a whole by the pressure of his powerful imagination. The delicate scroll patterns were first designed by Sasanian silversmiths, the elongated angels can be seen on Byzantine ivories, and the squat elders might have been the work of Gallo-Roman artists. But it is not important that there are derivative elements. What is important is the single flame which pours through all of them.

The rare visitors who come to Moissac are usually not content to see the tympanum, for there are other carvings in and around the church which betray the presence of an authentic master. Beside the ferocious lions on the pillar supporting the tympanum stands Jeremiah with many-braided beard, legs crossed, hands gripping a stone ribbon which once bore his name or a prophecy visiting destruction on all those who forsook the covenant of the Lord. His head is bent sorrowfully as he turns away from the lions. The figure is elongated almost to breaking point, taut, nervous, hieratic. Sanctity attends him: one could not imagine any ordinary man being represented in this way. At first, surprised by this tall, gaunt, and slender saint, one thinks of him merely as emblematic of sanctity and the powers of prophecy. Then it occurs to us that he is dancing his holy dance, rapt in adoration before the presence of Christ whose Coming he had foretold. This is not the Jeremiah of the thundering imprecations or the fearful visions; it is the other, quieter Jeremiah who worships Christ and turns appealingly to God, saying: "I know that the way of man is not in himself: it is not in man that walketh to direct his steps." So long-legged Jeremiah dances beside the open mouths of the lions, and on the cusped side-columns we see Paul and Isaiah dancing the same dance. They are smaller and executed in a more cursory fashion, as though the sculptor was careful not to detract attention from the great tympanum.

This dance, this curious weaving of the body characteristic of Romanesque art, derives from the contorted and swirling shapes of the ancient Scythians and the furious interlaces with which they decorated their scabbards and swords. Their artists contained the utmost movement in the smallest space, and to do this they were compelled to twist natural forms into hitherto unknown shapes. Within a few square inches they would hammer out of bronze or gold a flight of deer pursued by lions with a breathtaking violence and naturalism, for even when they were deliberately contorting the shapes of animals, the breath of life seems to flow through them. They are never abstractions. They leap, they dance, they hurl themselves with passionate ardor on their adversaries. This art was carried from the borders of China across the steppes of Russia and subtly influenced the European artists of the Middle Ages, with the result that the same forms can be seen in the figureheads of Scandinavian ships, in the brilliant illuminations of the Book of Kells, and in the paintings and sculptures of Romanesque churches. It was an art very alien to Byzantium, but even the Byzantine artists would sometimes surrender themselves to those swirling designs and sinuous interlaces.

There was still another element which Scythian art contributed to Romanesque art. Among the Scythians there appears to have been a belief in the unity of the animal kingdom, as though they were all born from one Mother Goddess and could change their shapes at will. A single life flowed through them; a stag, a lion, a horse, a cockerel, a snake were all one, interchangeable. Out of the stag's horns there might emerge a cockerel, and out of the mouth of the cockerel a snake, and the stag might have the hindquarters of a lion, and the lion might have the long flowing tail of a horse. So they painted on hides, tattooed on their bodies, and carved on metal the strange forms of animals compounded of many animals. They were nomads of the steppes, at home in the animal kingdom, and they seem to have possessed some faculty of seeing this kingdom from within, with a savage joy and authority. Yet they were not savages and possessed highly developed technical skills.

These strange animals pleased the Romanesque artists, who delighted to include them in their designs. These gargoyles and grotesques came to inhabit Romanesque churches; in the cloisters they appear suddenly on columns, and they appear again in the somber portraits of monsters tormenting the sinners in Hell. In Romanesque churches grotesqueries abounded. Scythian savagery was tamed, for the Romanesque artists were usually incapable of the ultimate violence and daring of those craftsmen of the steppe.

Scythian art was only one of the many influences which fed into the mainstream of Romanesque art. On that same tympanum at Moissac we can recognize the influence of Sasanian goldsmiths' work from Persia, the carved lintel displays *rosaces* which derive from

Greece although they have been modeled on the shapes of local this-
tles, while the columns and their capitals recall Cordova. Moorish and
Catalan influence is visible in most of the Romanesque churches in
southwestern France, but becomes notably less prominent in the
churches of central France and Italy. The fusion of so many elements
from foreign sources appears to have been undertaken deliberately
to convey a sense of spiritual drama acted out with unrestrained
energy.

So, too, in Romanesque painting we discover an urgent vital
energy, the rawness which comes from deep feeling. The paintings
may sometimes seem crude, but it is the crudity of life. Often it is
provincial art, unencumbered by any classical traditions and deriving
from local craftsmanship, so that we find great differences of treatment in frescoes painted within a few miles of one another at about
the same time. Christ, blue-robed, with enormous eyes, his body stiff
as a tree trunk, arms like sticks, surveys his Church with the air of a
thickset farmer surveying his ripening fields, yet there is no doubting
his energy, his authority, his commanding presence. Always the Romanesque possessed a keen sense and intimate knowledge of the
native soil. The church at Moissac rises out of the earth with natural
grace: it is not imposed on the site. Humility, sorrow, fear haunt the
Romanesque churches, but there is that feeling of natural grace, and
the smell of humanity. And where the Gothic cathedrals give the impression of being palaces fit only for God, the Virgin, and the angels,
Romanesque churches are the habitations of worshipful men.

Henri Focillon, the great authority on Romanesque art, was the
first to observe the predominance of abstract designs and the fact that
the sculptures are subordinated to the frame. This is true, but too
much can be made of it. All arts involve abstract design, and all architectural sculptures must employ the available space, the frame of reference. The Romanesque artist in his humility merely obeys the demands of the frame more scrupulously; and if the figures do not fill the
space easily, he will bend and batten them until they do, and in the
process he achieves a proper strangeness.

For him the pathways of God were strange, untraveled, infinitely remote, almost beyond conceptual thought. No human eyes
ever saw the angels, and therefore he represents them as beings on the
edge of vision: visionary creatures beyond our knowing, glimpsed in

dreams and flashes of lightning. He does not represent the Virgin as a human mother holding a human child. Like the Byzantine artist he represents her as a divinity. Where the Byzantine with his shimmering mosaics suggests a majestic being who is both present and absent, the Romanesque artist who has no mosaics at his disposal must suggest her otherness in other ways, and he does this by employing all the artifices of abstraction. Look at the Virgin and Child in the vault of the Romanesque church at Montmorillon. The Virgin lifts the Child's hands to her lips, and her face is a human face but her raiment is such as no human has ever worn: vortices, cascades, cataracts, swirling fold upon swirling fold, the wheeling blue gown melts into the white waterfall of the undergarment. The calm face is real, but the gown becomes an abstraction of tumultuous power. In this prodigious abstraction, based at an immense distance on the characteristic whorls of Byzantine artists, the Romanesque artist has demonstrated his extraordinary capacity to imagine the unimaginable—the infinite grandeur of the Virgin combined with a human tenderness.

Wherever the Romanesque artists traveled, they carried with them a singular resourcefulness. Where the Scythians saw the unity of the animal kingdom, every beast linked and interwoven with other beasts, so the Romanesque artists saw all creation linked and interwoven, of a common texture, possessing a common faith, a common blood, a common flesh, springing out of the person of Christ. All that exists flows from God, and is a part of God. So Anselm had said at the end of the eleventh century: "All that exists exists only thanks to a single cause, and this cause which is the only power which exists through itself is God."

To demonstrate this thesis and to make it convincing, the Romanesque sculptors needed all their resourcefulness, as they covered the walls and capitals of cathedrals with their extraordinary visions. The most resourceful and most inventive of these sculptors was Gislebert of Autun, who had no qualms in writing his own name beneath the feet of Christ in the great tympanum he carved in the Cathedral of St. Lazarus. With this tympanum and the vast series of sculptures decorating doorways and capitals, he showed himself to be a master of space. If he lacks the superb calm of the Moissac sculptor, that sense of the overwhelming dignity of God, he makes up for it by his controlled energy, his passion to infuse the living stone with living forms. A capital offers only a small space for an artist to work in, but Gislebertus uses even these small spaces with a flawless sense of the abundance that can be extracted from them. Isaac awaits the knife, the Virgin awaits the birth of Christ, the three wise men from the East lie asleep under a single coverlet waiting for the angel to announce the star of Bethlehem. All things are waiting for the coming of God, and so he depicts them in their eagerness and joy, tense and quivering, stretched out by the tension of the mystery, and even the damned in Hell struggling against the open-mouthed lions of death are unrestrained in their misery and seem in their desolate way to be enjoying themselves.

These capitals were once painted in vivid colors, and even today we can find traces of the original red, blue, green, and gold paint. The Romanesque churches, now so colorless, once glowed with paint, as later the Gothic churches glowed with the sunlight streaming through stained glass. Paint is earthy, coming from the earth, but the light of heaven shines through glass. And when that peculiar form of art which we know as Gothic arose, there came into existence an entirely new aspect of Christianity. The Romanesque churches were warmed with the humble aspirations of common men who knew themselves to be the creatures of earth, weighed down with sin, aware of their imperfections. The Gothic churches had their roots in the royal court and the aristocracy, who were rarely aware of their imperfections and regarded themselves as immune from sin. And where the Romanesque churches were houses for men to live in, rough-hewn and urgent, Gothic churches were built like palaces on the foot-hills of heaven. They were clean and spacious, with immensely tall columns and cold intricate designs, very formal, almost inhuman in the perfection of their stonework bathed in a jeweled light. They were churches for kings in their regalia, for archbishops in their ornate vestments, for courtiers and priests in their finery. They were not for ordinary people.

The Romanesque churches sought to express the mystery of Christ, his unattainable perfection, the calm of his peace. They were shelters against the storms of the world, places where men could rest during their earthly pilgrimage. They spoke directly to the mysteries and tribulations of the human heart. To enter a Romanesque church is to be aware of a warm human energy coursing through the stone, to know man in his nakedness and in his human dignity, which is not the dignity of the royal courts. The Romanesque churches answered to his human needs; the Gothic churches answered to his dreams.

Something very precious to Christianity died when the Gothic church was born.

IN THE first years of the twelfth century there appeared in France—in the Midi, in Anjou, and in the Isle de France, the domain of the Capetian kings—a new architectural instrument, the ribbed vault, which effectively solved many problems which had been tormenting architects for centuries. The ribbed vault permitted churches to be built higher than ever before and to throw open vast areas of wall space which had hitherto been occupied by masonry. The discovery of the ribbed vault was to change the shape of churches and to affect the course of Christianity. On the outskirts of Paris the new architecture was first adapted by an architect of genius singularly conversant with the properties of stone, and possessing advantages denied to most architects. Abbot Suger of the royal abbey of St. Denis designed the first Gothic church about the year 1130. He was in a position to see that his designs were carried out, for he was on terms of close familiarity with the king and the treasure of the kingdom was placed at his service.

Abbot Suger, the great innovator, was born in poverty in St. Denis. His parents sent him to the local monastery school, where his schoolmates included the young prince who later came to the throne as Louis VI. Suger was introduced to the royal household, and King Philip I encouraged the friendship between his son and the brilliant youth, whose abilities were carefully noted. He was quite young when he was sent to Rome on a diplomatic mission to the Curia. There came a time when he was appointed prime minister of France, and for his laborious cultivation of the royal interests he received the title *pater patriae*—the father of his country. He was a man who spent a good deal of his life in intimate contact with great political events, and when he consulted the king or when he asked a favor, he was listened to. He was a small, heavy-set, powerful man with a low brow, enormous eyes, and an oxlike face, for so he presents himself in a stained-glass window in his own church.

When Suger became abbot of St. Denis in 1130, he was fifty-one years old, at the height of his power and influence. He decided to tear down the Carolingian church which had stood on the site for more than three centuries and to replace it with a church of sumptuous magnificence worthy of the patron saint of France whose bones were in the crypt. He planned to dispense with the crypt. Instead the bones would lie within the altar, the altar itself being on a high platform. In this way all the faithful would be permitted to view the holy relics. He saw the new church as a jewel-studded, brilliantly lit reliquary, the chancel flooded with light from stained-glass windows.

Suger wrote three books which survived. They were written in a rather crude but highly wrought Latin which reflects a tempestuous and ambitious character. One book describes the regulations of the abbey, another deals with administrative problems and the reconstruction of the church, and the third offers an account of the consecration. He makes no attempt to conceal his delight in building a church unlike any that had existed up to his time, and he hints that the Abbey of St. Denis, as transformed by him, was at least the equal of Hagia Sophia in Constantinople.

He was not a man who permitted any obstacles to his plans. He organized the work in minute detail, saw that the king and the nobility paid handsomely for the privilege of possessing a noble church, "for its adornment cannot be costly enough to match the value of the relics," and searched avidly for precious jewels and precious metals. He was consumed with the problem of finding the right wood and the right stone. When he heard that there were no more giant trees in the abbey forests, for they had all been used in defensive works, he simply walked into the forest and found the trees which the foresters had failed to see. In this way he found the great beams he needed for the narthex. He thought of hauling columns from the Baths of Diocletian in Rome to Paris, for he needed them in his great plan of widening the nave, but another miracle occurred when he discovered the right kind of stone in a quarry at Pontoise. He was inclined to interpret everything that happened in the building of the church as miraculous. The columns, dressed at Pontoise, had to be brought up a steep slope near St. Denis in carts. There occurred for the first time that strange phenomenon which was to be repeated in the building of other churches all over France, when the rich and the poor became draft animals, tying ropes round their arms, shoulders, and chests, and so dragging the columns uphill. The cult of the cart, usually thought to have begun with the rebuilding of Chartres cathedral, began about 1138 at St. Denis.

Suger was determined that the altar and the casket of relics and the crucifix should shine with thick encrustations of precious stones, and that the windows of the ambulatory should be of colored glass, thus making the jewels and the gold shine in a melting oriental light. He did not invent stained-glass windows; what was new was his decision to bathe the choir in a continuous light. He spoke of a *lux continua*, and with those two words he announced the beginning of the style we know as Gothic. Henceforward the walls would be shattered to let the light in; the solemn darkness of Romanesque would give place to a continuous radiance.

Many accidents and improvisations, and many discoveries, went into Gothic architecture. From Persia by way of Armenia came the ribbed vaults, known as *claves*, or keys, which permitted the large windows to come into existence. From Byzantium perhaps came the insistence on the jeweled light. Suger was continually cross-examining travelers who had seen "the treasures of Byzantium and the ornaments of Hagia Sophia." From Syria perhaps came the mysterious works of Dionysius the Areopagite, who believed that "every creature, visible or invisible, is a light brought into being by the Father of Lights," and who celebrated God's holy fire pervading the entire universe. By an extraordinary series of accidents St. Denis of France, whose relics were in the abbey of St. Denis, was confused with Dionysius the Areopagite, whose works were in the abbey library, the gift of the Byzantine Emperor Michael the Stammerer to King Louis the Pious, the son of Charlemagne.

In Suger's three books describing the building of the church there are no less than thirteen separate inscriptions in which he celebrates the holy light in which the church was bathed. He wrote:

> *Portarum quisquis attollere quaeris honorem,*
> *Aurum nec sumptus, operis mirare laborem,*

Nobile claret opus, sed opus quod nobile claret
Clarificet mentes ut eant per lumina vera
Ad verum lumen, ubi Christus janua vera.

Whoever seeks to exalt the honor of these gates,
Let him not marvel at the golden treasure but at the workmanship.
Bright is the noble work: this work shining nobly
Enlightens the mind so that it may travel through the true lights
To the True Light where Christ is the true door.

The verse was written to celebrate a gate of bronze sheeted with gold, and inevitably Suger found himself describing the heavenly light which the mind travels through in order to reach the True Light of Christ. *Splendor, claritas, nobilitas* are words he uses constantly to conjure up the special qualities of the light he loved.

Nobile claret opus . . . Bright is the noble work . . . Such is his continuing theme, and it is not one he ever permits himself to forget. The church was blazing with color from the jeweled windows of the choir and along the whole length of the nave, and especially brilliant was the retable of gold encrusted with precious stones and the majestic gold cross inset with jewels and cabuchons, which dominated the church. A king's ransom adorned the relics of St. Denis and his two followers, St. Rusticus and St. Eleutherius. From the king came gifts of emeralds, from the powerful Count Thibault of Champagne came hyacinths and rubies, and every nobleman at court was compelled to pay his tribute of jewels. It was a time of civil war and general misery, but Suger was impervious to the claims of the poor. His aim was to glorify God and to build a church so beautiful that the worshiper would be compelled by beauty to reach out to God. Beauty was the snare which captured men to divinity.

Bernard of Clairvaux thundered against the abbot who was desecrating the church with gold. "What has gold to do with the sanctuary?" he roared. "Look how the church inlays the stones of her cathedrals with gold, while leaving her sons naked!" Nevertheless Bernard of Clairvaux attended the solemn dedication of the abbey, which took place on June 11, 1144, the day of the feast of St. Barnabas. The king and his queen, who was Eleanor of Aquitaine, and the bishops of Bordeaux, Rouen, and Canterbury, and many others watched the translation of the relics from the crypt to the great

gilded reliquary. Abbot Suger describes the huge concourse of people
who took part in the processions with unconcealed pride. He was a
very small man—he described himself once as "an idiotic little body"
—*imbecille corpusculum*—but on that day he towered over everyone.

He had reason to be proud, for he had set in motion a form of
architecture which would endure for four hundred years. He was the
father of Gothic, its sole founder. His influence can be felt in all the
Gothic churches which rose in northern France, and it can be felt especially at Chartres, which was designed and built by workmen
trained at St. Denis. He had invented a new landscape of worship;
and if it derived partly from Byzantium, where a love of jeweled
panoply was encouraged by the emperors, it was shaped and con-
toured according to the dictates of the western imagination. He knew
exactly what he was doing: he was bringing heaven down to earth
and setting the worshiper in the heavenly light. It was something that
no one had ever thought of doing.

This mysterious pilgrimage to the light was accomplished by a
man with an exquisite sense of the power of jewels to affect the mind.
He spoke quite simply of the trance state which arises from the contemplation of glowing colors. "When the house of God with its
many colors shining with the radiance of precious stones called me
from the cares of the world," he wrote, "I seemed to find myself, as it
were, in some strange part of the universe which was neither wholly
of the baseness of the earth nor wholly of the serenity of heaven; but
by the grace of God I seemed lifted up in a mystic manner from this
lower world toward that upper sphere." And so like a jeweler lost
among his jewels, in the glint and flash of precious stones, he stepped
out of this world altogether into another world which was a simula-
crum of heaven.

The vision, once announced, was to lead to unsuspected ends. St.
Denis is a comparatively small church with a long narrow nave aris-
tocratically proportioned. What would happen if the space were
opened out, if spaciousness were to become the rule, and the colored
lights were permitted to pour in waves across acres and acres of stone
and polished marble? What would happen if the walls were almost
completely made of glass? What would happen when the church became so vast that the ceiling was lost in distant shadows? Finally,
what would happen to God when his habitation became a house of

glass?

Gothic architecture subtly influenced the character of worship. The Gothic God is far more remote, more intangible, and more spiritual than the Romanesque God, who was always represented as the possessor of infinite power and rigor. To the Gothic imagination God is presented as a divine glory, the Light of Lights, ethereally present. In the Gothic church the flesh of Christ, the holy face, are lacking. Romanesque proclaims the sense of human effort to overcome evil, the raw vigor of the human heart as it strives to acquire holiness, while Gothic with its springing arches and delicate spires and almost transparent walls suggests that no effort is needed, for holiness is in the very air. The sinfulness of man is washed away in dancing light.

Chartres is a palace dedicated to the Virgin, who now begins to play an increasing role in the Church. The Gothic cathedral, vibrant and delicate, is essentially feminine. Here the quiet, contemplative Virgin, holding her Child and lost in her dreams, is perfectly at home as she gazes out of colored glass or stands alone in a rainbow of jeweled colors. She is all light and mystery, grace and courtesy. She is the silent presence, the gaze enfolding her own palace.

That the Virgin had taken up her abode at Chartres became an article of faith, and it was appropriate that the cathedral should possess two relics associated with her. One was the veil she wore at the Annunciation, now preserved in a reliquary near the high altar. The veil was sent by the Byzantine Emperor Constantine V to Charlemagne in A.D. 792, and was first offered to the cathedral eighty-four years later by Charles the Bald. In the Middle Ages it was the custom of kings and princes to heap jewels on the golden casket enclosing the veil, and the honor of kissing the crystal window and walking beneath it was reserved only for the highest potentates. So much wealth accumulated around the casket that it was said to equal the entire revenue of France for a single year.

The other relic was the mummified head of St. Anne, the mother of the Virgin, found by the conquering Crusaders in Constantinople, and sent to Chartres in 1205 by Louis, Count of Chartres, "in order that the head of the Mother might rest in the house of the daughter." The legends of St. Anne are accordingly given great prominence in the cathedral, which was now doubly feminine because the mother was present with her daughter. If the veil appears to be a Byzantine work of the sixth or seventh century, and the mummified head is only one more of the countless improvisations of Syrian relic-hunters, nevertheless the acquisition of the two relics shaped the purposes of the cathedral and colored the forms of worship. The Virgin was represented as the daughter, young and sweet-tempered, possessing the generosity of youth, a princess rather than a queen, all the more appealing because she is so human. She walks in gaiety, and one can imagine her dancing on those colored floors.

So she appears in the stained-glass windows of the west façade: very young, very French, with a certain elegance about her. In the window depicting the Annunciation she wears a rainbow-colored dress and an enormous yellow halo, which might be a bonnet of straw; she is girlish, not majestic, and when she raises her hand in protest to the green-winged angel, she does so gently, as though making a gesture of greeting. In *la belle Verrière*, the most wonderful of all the stained-glass windows at Chartres, the features were repainted in the nineteenth century, and we can only guess at the original expression, but as she sits enthroned with her child on her knees, with the censing angels all round, there is no doubt of her majesty and of her tenderness toward all living things.

The makers of stained-glass windows were men of extraordinary accomplishment, possessors of a secret skills, adepts in a mysterious art, learned in the properties of glass and precious metals. They regarded themselves as jewelers and knew the many ways of fusing color into glass. Those ruby-reds, ox-blood reds, flame-reds, and purple-reds were not produced by accident. They calculated to a hairbreadth the precise tones and textures of the glass. The making of stained-glass windows is the least accidental of arts, for it involves a rigorous constraint within the webbing and an exact understanding of the luminous qualities of colored glass and the interaction of the separate colors. They knew that blue was recessive, and they used this knowledge to the full. Everything is seen in brilliant fragmentation. There is the sense of a world which is simultaneously fragmentary and whole, divided and unified. And while they can claim kinship with the Byzantine mosaicists who also studied the shatterings of light, they have an abiding kinship with the Impressionists.

"The juxtaposition of red and blue is perilous," wrote Viollet-le-Duc in his *Dictionnaire raisonné de l'architecture française*, after studying the stained-glass windows at Chartres. He formed various theories about how the glaziers avoided this peril by employing strips of beading between the two colors, or by a heavy hatching of the blue where the colors met. But in fact red and blue were permitted to meet without beading or hatching of any kind wherever it pleased the glaziers. They gloried in the perilous meeting of colors. The effect is to produce a light never seen before: the blue of summer seas fused with the colors of a winter dawn. An imperial opulence bathes this palace of the Virgin, but no emperor ever walked with such streaming banners before him. In Chartres time and space are formed out of pure color.

These artists were not so much painters of light as choreographers of living color. Everything points to heaven, and the dance of the angels. The pointed arches, the immense height of the columns, the deliberate attempt to create fragility and lightness in heavy stone, the sense of spaciousness and of space divinely lived in, create an overwhelming impression of a world which is not of this world, or even a foretaste of the world to come; it is a world *divinely other*, not susceptible to known laws, calculated to produce a state of exaltation and adoration.

The Romanesque church was designed as a place of prayer; the Gothic church was designed as a place where divinity could be adored. The need for prayer gave way to the need for adoration. Sorrow gave way to joy.

All over Europe the white spires rose and the blue and ruby windows shone on the worshipers. The bent and tormented figures of Romanesque sculpture were replaced by figures springing up to their full height, with ease of movement and a gentle grace of gesture. The smiling angel at Reims tilts her head with an inviting gesture; "the beautiful God" of Amiens raises his hand in blessing, vividly aware of his own beauty. The bodies move at ease beneath their vestments, and there is often a classical purity in the designs. St. Theodore at Chartres might have sat at Plato's feet and been carved by a Greek sculptor transported to France. The sap had risen; life was flowing again.

With that new awareness of the value of human life, no longer bent in prayer, there came the discovery of nature: the colors of flowers, the shapes of trees, the small animals of the hedgerows, the sleek shapes of domestic animals. The capitals and spring-courses were covered with fruit and flowers. At first, in the twelfth century, they were content to render the buds and half-opened flowers of early spring. In the thirteenth century the small spiky leaves are full-grown, the flowers have opened wide their petals, the seed pods have burst, almost there is opulence. Then in the fourteenth century the fruit hangs heavy on the boughs, the flowers are arranged in massed bouquets, and garlands weigh down the pillars as in Hellenistic Greece. It is full summer moving toward a frosty autumn. And indeed in the fifteenth century the flowers wither, the leaves become ragged, a blight sets in. The artists play with the delicate convolutions of leaves and petals, painting every blemish, sacrificing art to artistry and a strained realism. By this time the impetus of Gothic has come to an end; and the jeweled light fades from the massive windows.

Gothic art traveled well, taking the protective coloring of the countries it visited. Canterbury, being close to France, preserved the sense of imperial grandeur and spaciousness. The entire chancel was designed by Guillaume de Sens, the builder of Sens cathedral, and the French influence is predominant. At Lincoln, Durham, and Ely the English architects have infused their own sense of form into Gothic. At Ely the great lantern, with its sudden explosion of welling light, runs counter to the Gothic tradition that the light should be diffused over the whole church, and in its assertiveness and inventiveness it stands alone. In England, Romanesque influence survived, haunting the imaginations of men long after the introduction of Gothic, with the result that most of the English cathedrals retain elements of Romanesque sturdiness and harshness. In the clouded skies of England the adoration of the heavenly light is not easily come by; nor is the knowledge of sin so easily wiped away.

Out of the great experiments at St. Denis and Chartres there came a new dignity and a triumphant vindication of the human spirit. When the churches became palaces, all men became noblemen free to saunter in the royal courts. The splendor and the glory came down to earth; lucidity was seen to be a desirable quality in Christian worship; and reason, too, was permitted to enter the hallowed places. Suger had intended to build a sumptuous adornment for God, but he set in train a series of brilliant improvisations which led to the sumptuous adornment of man. The beauty of the Gothic church, quivering with color, testified as much to the grandeur of man as to the grandeur of God.

Like the ripples on a pool when a stone is flung into it, the influence of Gothic extended over Europe. It was one of the most prodigious of the inventions associated with Christianity, for it still has power to move our hearts and to affect our styles of architecture. Dante had spoken in the *Paradiso* of the divine light penetrating the universe according to its dignity—*la luce divina e penetrante per l'universo secondo ch'e degno*—and the Gothic church celebrated this light as it had never been celebrated before. Suger brought the colors of the rainbow into the church, and there they have remained, nor is it likely that they will ever be removed.

Yet Gothic art by its very nature suffers from limitations. The tragic spirit vanishes, as joy walks in stupendous coverings. In its gentleness and courtesy the Gothic cathedral is closer to Galilee than to Jerusalem, closer to the blue lake than to the bare rocks, closer to the early years of Christ's ministry than to the agony on the Cross. For tears, for consolation, for the vision of the blood-soaked Son of Man on the Cross, we must go to the Romanesque churches, dark and urgent with prayer and the knowledge of suffering. It is there that the heartbeats can be heard.

Gothic shouts and exults in its freedom, and lets the light of heaven wash sin away. Romanesque prays, and knows that only Christ can wash sin away.

21 ✠ THE MYSTICAL EMPIRE

OVER the years there had come into being a great body of Christian doctrine. The ecumenical councils met and decided issues, the theologians discussed the intricacies of the faith, and the supreme pontiff from time to time interrupted the daily operation and government of the church with pronouncements designed to add or subtract from the beliefs of the faithful. The church was a shepherd herding the flock into narrow sheepfolds of remarkable complexity. Here and there we find a few sheep slipping out of the fold.

These stray sheep were not heretical; they did not except on rare occasions set themselves up against the church; they seemed to be indifferent to the church, and most of all indifferent to the power and dominion wielded by the pope. Their purpose was the celebration of God's glory, the continuing dialogue between the soul and God. The world with all its vanities had no meaning for them, and the church itself sometimes seemed to them to be no more than a vain thing. In obscure monasteries and in great abbeys these men lived out their quiet lives of contemplation, remote from the world's tumult, dedicated to mystery and the movements of the soul.

From the very beginning the mystical element had been prominent in Christianity, deriving strength from the visionary learning of Christ and St. Paul. Yet the established church found little comfort in its visionaries, who rarely subordinated their visions to ecclesiastical laws. They formed an anarchic enclave, which could not be assimilated but only tolerated. Chaucer speaks of "the dark light that shall come out of the fire that ever shall burn." The visionaries warmed themselves in the dark light of the ever-burning fire, and the church, with enough mysteries at hand to keep the theologians busy, preferred to warm itself in the light of revealed truth, where there were shadows but where there was no darkness.

There were popes who were mystics: Gregory the Great pursued the contemplative life, and in magnificent Latin prose he described the struggle of the soul rising to contemplate celestial things. There were brief moments when, as he says, he thought he glimpsed the face of God, the uncircumscribed light of lights, only to be beaten back upon himself, retreating into the darkness of his own blindness. He tells us, too, that the grace of contemplation cannot be long-lasting, because the weight of the corruptible flesh drags the soul into the flesh. For him, as for Pascal, there is always *Deus absconditus*.

Gregory the Great lived in the sixth century; for some four hundred years afterward the contemplative life in the West appears to have suffered from the barbarity of the times. Not until the eleventh century do we hear the authentic voice of the visionary again. Gregory the Great was a Roman, and his mysterious voyagings are recounted with a stern Roman gravity. Jean de Fécamp, a Lombard who settled in northern France, sings in a more gentle voice. We know very little about him. He died on February 22, 1078, but we do not know when he was born and all we know of his appearance is derived from his nickname Johannelinus, "little John." He became prior and then abbot of the monastery of Fécamp, a small town in Normandy lying in a valley between high chalk cliffs overlooking the English Channel. It was a place of gulls and sea-mists beside the sea and a small river, and Jean de Fécamp seems never to have left the place. He had no desire for earthly fame and his writings are nearly forgotten now; no doubt he would have argued that there was a special grace in being forgotten. But for centuries his writings were well-known. He wrote a short work on the contemplative life, and not long after his death it began to be widely circulated under the title, "The Meditations of St. Augustine." The style was not characteristically Augustinian, and at this late date it is impossible to explain how they came to be attributed to St. Augustine. In time these meditations were translated into all the languages of Europe. They appeared in German, Italian, Dutch, Spanish, Polish, Swedish, Greek, and English. No devotional work was ever more popular. Jean de Fécamp kept firmly to the vision of the Heavenly Jerusalem. This world would pass, the earth with all its glories would melt away, and at last man would enter into his appointed heaven, where there was no time, no sickness, no despair, and no death. He wrote in a simple, charming Latin which conveyed the fervor of his belief, and something of that fervor survives in Thomas Rogers' translation published in 1581:

O thou most happy lyfe, oh kyngdome which art blessed in deede, whiche lacketh death, whiche art without ende, no tyme doth successively passe at any tyme to thee. Whereas continuall day without night knoweth no tyme, whereas that captaine and conquerour is accompanyed with those queres of aungells, singyng of Hymnes and Songes, they sing unto God without ceassing the balet of Balets of Sion. Oh most noble head which art compassed about with a perpetuall crown, oh that pardon and forgevernesse of my sinnes were graunted unto me, and then immediatly, this burden of my flesh layd away, that I might enter into thy ioyes to have true rest, and that I might get within the goodly and beautifull walles of thy Citie to receive a crowne of lyfe at the hand of our Lorde, that I might be amongest those most holy queres, that I might stand with the most blessed spirites of the creator of glory, that I might see presently the countenaunce of Christ, that I might behold alwayes that most hye and unspeakeable light, incomprehensible whiche can not be conteined as in a place. And so I should not onely be out of all feare of death: but also I might rejoyse alwayes at the gift of everlastyng incorruption.

The meditations of Jean de Fécamp gave comfort to the old, the sick, the afflicted, for he was able to turn men's minds toward "that most hye and unspeakable light." The great and the powerful read these meditations, and so did the poor and the outcast. Queen Elizabeth of England, when young, wrote a passage from these meditations in the fly-leaf of her New Testament. The meditations were the solace of generations who had never heard the name of Jean de Fécamp.

For the little abbot the Heavenly Jerusalem was as real as the cliffs of France and the winding river below the monastery wall, and he described it with tenderness and yearning. His mysticism was colored by the French landscape. Already there was emerging a characteristically French character—gay, lyrical, and improvident—and this character too was to impose itself on the twelfth century mystics.

The visions of the new Jerusalem sometimes resemble France seen with the naked eye.

Bernard of Clairvaux was born twelve years after the death of Jean de Fécamp. They were both aristocrats by birth, and both wrote meditations on the Heavenly Jerusalem with grace and passion. Bernard was born near Châtillon-sur-Seine, the son of Tescelin, soldier and landowner, a former officer in the court of the Duke of Burgundy, into whose family he married, and Aletta de Montbard, a severe and deeply religious woman. He was a sickly child, small and slender, with pale yellow hair and enormous soft blue eyes. William de St. Thierry, who became one of Bernard's closest friends, says he was brought up under a strict discipline which allowed no evil thoughts to penetrate his mind. It is at least possible that the stern discipline at home accounts for the extraordinary qualities of Bernard's mind.

He grew up into a devout and ardent youth, determined to devote his life to God. He was twenty-one when he finally decided to cut himself off from the world and join the poor monastery at Citeaux some fifteen miles from Dijon. Citeaux was one of the most wretched and poverty-stricken monasteries imaginable. It was surrounded by an unwholesome swamp and had a reputation for being a place where men came to grief. His father gave his approval, but warned him against excesses. "I know," he said, "how difficult it is for you to restrain your high ardor, but do try to observe some moderation and avoid dangerous extremes." Bernard was to be ardent to the end of his life, and he was rarely able to avoid dangerous extremes.

It was the year 1113—the same year which saw the great carvings on the west portal of Chartres—and all over France men were flocking to the monasteries. Religious fervor was spreading like wildfire; the life of complete dedication to God was valued more than the life of earthly pleasures. Bernard threw himself into his devotions with such relentless austerity than within a year he was ill, and he seems to have spent his second year at Citeaux on a sickbed.

When Robert de Molesme founded the Cistercian order, he deliberately encouraged a severe asceticism. Too many monasteries were wealthy; too many monks were fat and lazy. At Citeaux there were no ornaments, no embroidered vestments, no lace, no cloth of gold: only the plain wood altar, the brass crucifix, the iron chandelier, and a single silver-gilt chalice for the wine of the Eucharist. He pampered no one. The monks worked hard, and ate only one meal a day between September and Easter. Once again there were to be athletes of God.

Robert de Molesme was one of those dedicated men who soon fall into disfavor with the Church. He carried everything to extremes, and even more disturbing was his lighthearted aversion to the papal inspectors. The papal legate, Hugh de Die, refers to his "habitual levity"—*solita levitas*. It was a vice which Franciscans were later to proclaim a virtue, but the legate found it to be inappropriate, and encouraged Robert de Molesme to move elsewhere. The legate's successor imposed an even sterner discipline. Happily he died, and his place was taken by Stephen Harding, an Englishman and a native of Dorset, who relaxed the discipline and even permitted the monastery to accept endowments.

A hundred miles beyond Citeaux, in a valley along the river Aube, there was a plot of waste land known as Vallis Absinthialis, meaning "the valley of wormwood." Here, at the age of twenty-five, Bernard set out to found a new monastery, following in the path of Robert de Molesme, who was accustomed to seek out his monasteries in horrible places. It was a lair of robbers and a haunt of wolves, and Bernard with his small company of monks rejoiced in its dangers, the insalubrious air, and the dismal comforts. They cut the wormwood away and settled down to the task of producing an agreeable farmland, which they called Clairvaux, meaning "the valley of light." The first years were terrible. They lived on coarse bread and water, wild carrots, and whatever berries they could find. Bernard had seen in a vision the abundance which would later flow to the monastery: the orchards, the tilled land, the streams of pilgrims. There would be an immense stone monastery, vineyards on the slopes, flowering meadows, fishponds, a spring of sparkling water. All this came to pass, but for the present there were only the small wattle huts of the monks, and many months passed before they were able to build the house which comprised at one and the same time a chapel, a refectory, a dormitory, and a workshop. Once Bernard said: "What I know of the divine sciences and holy scriptures I learned in woods and fields, I have no other master than the beeches and the oaks." It was, of course, the purest exaggeration, but there is in his prose a peculiar rhythm which suggests the waving of branches and the trembling of leaves, and when he shouts—he shouts surprisingly often—you hear the whipping of the trees in a high wind and the crackling of boughs. Like St. Francis, he was determined to throw open the Church to the open air.

Two years passed before the stone building went up and the desert began to flower. Bernard was delighted with his flowering valley, but took care not to be tempted by its wealth; and he continued to live in a wattle hut, and rejoiced in the menial occupations he gave himself. He helped to prepare the meals, washed dishes, numbered the pigs, counted the poultry, and greased his own sandals. Yet he was indisputably the head of the monastery, its guiding force, and the creator of the daughter-monasteries which almost immediately began to flourish. He was forever planning these new monasteries, and by the end of his life there were no less than one hundred and sixty of them, including Fountains Abbey in Yorkshire, which was named after his own birthplace, Fontaines les Dijon, the small hamlet near Châtillon-sur-Seine dominated by his father's castle. All over Germany, Italy, France, and England there were these monasteries which owed their existence to him. His power was prodigious. Popes and kings began to fear him, and since he maintained a vast correspondence and was cheerfully interfering in matters which scarcely concerned him, he was sometimes regarded as a man who loved power for its own sake. Yet he had little love of power. It was forced on him by his commanding position as the head of the Cistercian order, and sometimes he would throw up his hands in despair at the thought of all the letters he had to write or dictate to his secretary Nicholas, who proved to be a usurper, for many letters signed with Bernard's seal proved to have been written by the secretary for his own pleasure and advancement.

Throughout those years of trial his temper remained mystical. He had the mystic's preoccupation with governing the affairs of this world, and like St. Catherine of Siena he would send off sharp letters to those he thought to be in league with the devil, prelates or kings or emperors who had incurred his wrath. Then, abruptly, he would remove himself from the world, vanishing into his wattle hut to commune with God and to write those prayers and sermons which were to remain long after his earthly pursuits were forgotten. He wrote angelically about the nature of God, saying: "He alone is God who can never by sought in vain, not even when He cannot be found." In the eighty-four sermons on *The Song of Songs* he discoursed on the

Mystical Body of Christ at astonishing length and with an extraordinary wealth of poetic feeling, a verse from the ancient Jewish bridal hymn providing the springboard for pages of lyrical commentary.

As a contemplative writing upon contemplation, Bernard is always captivating. He writes with a strange gentleness concerning the mystical union with God, and with such verisimilitude and conviction that it is impossible not to believe that he had, in his own words, "kissed God's mouth and known the joy of entering within." He uses sexual imagery freely, as did many of the mystics; he even speaks of "a carnal love for Christ." He honored the flesh, as he honored the austerities practiced on the flesh. He wrote once: "I believe the chief reason which prompted the invisible God to become visible in the flesh and to hold converse with men was to lead carnal men, who are only able to love carnally, to the healthful love of the flesh, and afterwards, little by little, to spiritual love." He was one of the very few mystics who had anything good to say about human love.

"How is God to be adored?" Bernard asks, and answers that He must be adored with kisses. There are three kinds of kisses. There is a kiss of the feet of God, meaning that the soul embraces God's mercy and truth in an act of adoration. There is the kiss of the hands, from which the lover derives divine strength. There is the kiss of the mouth, from which the lover derives an ecstatic union with God. Sometimes he speaks of this union in a strange vocabulary of his own, half sexual, half intellectual, as though he were describing a landscape on the borderline between the flesh and the spirit. Of his own union with God he wrote:

I confess in my foolishness that the Word has visited me, springing up in me, and this has happened more than once. But although He has frequently entered my soul, He has come in such a way that I have never been sensible of the precise moment of His coming. I have felt Him in me, I remember He has been within me, I have sometimes known a presentiment of His coming into me. By what means He made entrance or departure, I confess I know not to this day. He did not enter through my eyes, for He is not a color, nor through my ears, for He is not a sound, nor through my nostrils, for He mingles not with the air but with the spirit of man, nor again does He appear to enter through the mouth, for He cannot be eaten or sipped on the tongue, nor may He be touched, for He is not tangible.

By what way, then, did He enter? Perhaps He did not enter, for He does not come from without like an exterior thing. Nor does He come from within, since sanctity, I know, is not in me. How did I know He was present, since there is no way to describe His coming? I knew He was there, because He was living and full of energy, and as soon as He entered within me He quickened my sleeping soul, He aroused and softened and pricked my heart, until then in a state of stupor, as hard as a stone. Thereupon He began to pluck and destroy, to plant and to build, to water the dry places and illuminate the dark corners, opening all that was closed, warming all that was cold, straightening the crooked paths and making the rough places smooth, so that my soul blessed the Lord and all that was within me praised His Holy Name.

So I mounted to the higher part of my soul, and higher still reigned the Word. Strange exploration. I entered into the depths of my soul, and perceived Him in still lower depths. I looked outside. I saw He was beyond all. I looked within, and He was more close to me than my soul. So I have been filled in some degree with the loveliness of His beauty, and I have marvelled on the immensity of His power.

(Sermo LXXIV in Cantica)

There is no doubting the authenticity of the mystical experience, so similar and yet so remote from the vision of Gregory of Nyssa. Bernard speaks softly, never raising his voice, while Gregory quivers with excitement and wonder at his own blessedness. Bernard speaks with a curiously matter-of-fact tone, discussing God's presence with good sense and discretion. One suspects that the knowledge of God was habitual with him, and he was never particularly surprised when God entered into him.

So it is throughout his commentary on *The Song of Songs*, the calm endeavor, the sweetness, and the gentleness interrupted at times by characteristic bursts of Gallic temper, as when he finds himself under the need to belabor the monks who were lazy, or fond of their food, or their drink, or their comforts. He hated fussiness as much as he hated intemperance; the monk who complained about his food was as absurd as the monk who drank secretly, and Bernard rebukes them both gently. His sermons are full of ironical warnings against fuss-pots, yawners, scratchers, solipsists, swaggerers. He knows the monk-ish vices well, and is prepared to pardon them. Here he rebukes the fuss-pots with unexpected tenderness:

What does it profit a monk to restrain himself from pleasure if he is always bothering about the appearance of his food and how it is served? Vegetables, he says, give me wind, cheese weighs down my stomach, milk is bad for my head, my chest suffers if I drink water, beans make me melancholy, leeks heat my blood, fish from ponds and muddy water spoil my complexion. Oh, I beg you to have pity on your own peace of mind and on those who wait on you. Try not to be a burden on the house and consider a little the good of your soul.

(Sermo XXX in Cantica)

But while Bernard could coo like a dove, he could roar like a lion when he was enraged. Learning that German Christians were massacring the Jews, on the grounds that they were more impious than the Saracens, and therefore more deserving of death, he wrote:

Do you not understand that the Church triumphs more abundantly over the Jews in converting them than in putting them to the sword? Wherefore we utter our universal prayer for the unbelieving Jews, uttered incessantly in the Church from the rising to the setting of the sun, that God shall take away the veil from their hearts and lead them out of darkness that they may be led into the glorious light of the truth. Unless therefore the Church believes they will enter the fold, though now they are unbelieving, how vain and superfluous it were to offer prayers to them. But to kill them—that is a monstrous doctrine, a foul council, contrary to the prophets, hostile to the apostles, destructive of piety and grace—a damned harlot of a doctrine impregnated with the very spirit of falsehood, conceiving anguish and bringing forth iniquity!

(Epistolae, XIX)

In this way Bernard would sometimes emerge from his wattle hut to take part in the affairs of the world. He called upon the Christians to become Crusaders, wrote out the rules of the Knights Templar, and bitterly attacked the pope for not invigorating the Church, which seemed to be dying before his eyes. He was offered the greatest offices the Church could bestow on him. Archbishoprics and bishoprics were his for the asking, but he refused them all. He was invited to lead the Crusaders to the Holy Land, and this invitation he rejected as being too dangerous a burden on the soul, for how could a simple monk lead two kings and a vast army to Palestine and still retain his humility and peace of mind? "I beseech you," he wrote to the pope, who had offered the invitation, "that by the love you owe me you do not deliver me over to these human desires." So he returned to Citeaux, to the unshaven monks, the kitchen gardens, the long brooding afternoons spent with the *Psalms* or *The Song of Songs* on his knees, and sometimes a servant would come from the monastery hoping to tempt him to eat or drink, but he drank little except water, which he loved, and ate sparsely. Long before he died, he had left the world.

He died shortly after sunrise on August 20, 1153, at the age of sixty-two. On the day before he was carried protesting into the monastery, where he might have a better chance of healing his infirmities. He looked haggard and very old, with bloodshot eyes and swollen limbs. The monks urged him to take food, but he felt no hunger. "Why do you try to detain me?" he asked, and when they said they wanted him to live for their own comfort, he smiled and said: "I do not know whether to stay with you or to go to Christ, and therefore I leave it to the will of God." He had long ago prepared himself for death, and he slipped away very quietly.

During the last twenty years of his life he had wielded more power than the pope. His monasteries with their harsh and simple rules were in every land; his letters were read everywhere; his orders were obeyed. He gave himself the task of invigorating the Church, and in this he largely succeeded.

His followers were legion. Many were young aristocrats hot for certainties after the long weariness of wealth, hoping to escape from the frivolities of life and the absurdities of the Church. They made their homes in his monasteries, which were growing up like wild flowers. Among the most charming of his followers was the Northumbrian Aelred, who became one of the few authentic saints of the English Church.

Aelred was born in 1110 and grew up in the court of King David of Scotland, becoming steward of the royal household when he was about twenty. He had the gift of meditation, and would sometimes fall into a fit of abstraction while superintending the royal table. He was twenty-four when he was sent on an official visit to the archbishopric of York, and just outside York he met for the first time a community of Cistercian monks. They were established at Rievaulx in the valley of the River Rye, and once he had seen them in their plain white gowns, he simply abandoned his service in the houschold

The Gothic Splendor

Christ Instructing, from the south portal of Chartres Cathedral.

Stained-glass window at the Basilica of St. Denis, Paris, showing the Abbot Suger kneeling before the Virgin. (*Roger Viollet*)

Porphyry and gold vase from the treasury of St. Denis, now in the Louvre. (*Caisse Nationale des Monuments Historiques*)

Chartres Cathedral. (*French Cultural Services, New York*)

Chartres Cathedral. Tympanum over the central portal of the west front.

Chartres Cathedral. Old Testament figures, central portal of the west front.

Chartres Cathedral. John the Baptist, from the north portal. (*Robert Laillet*)

The Sainte Chapelle, Paris. (*French Government Tourist Office, New York*)

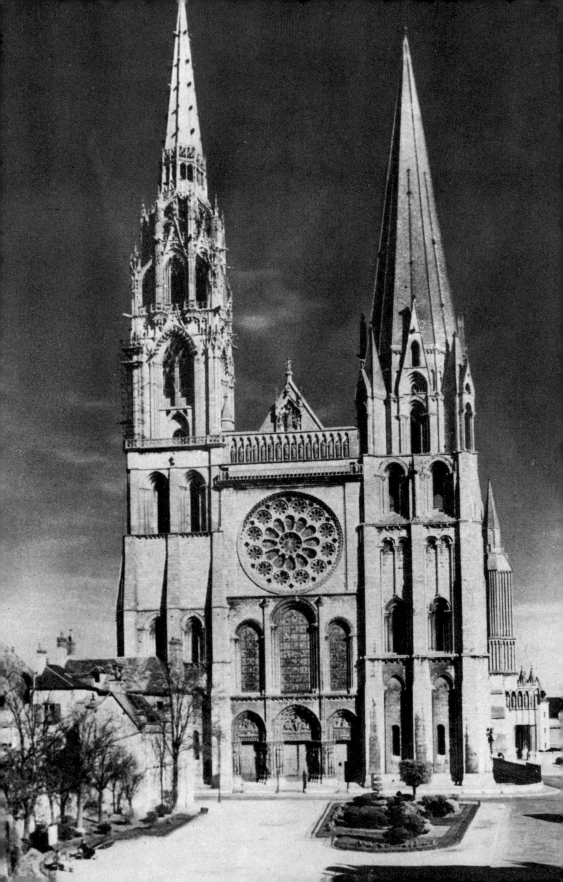

of King David and without another word entered the monastery as a novice. There he remained, except for one visit to Rome and occasional visits to neighboring monasteries, for the remaining thirty-three years of his life.

Aelred was English to the core: a gentle, tempestuous man, half in love with physical beauty, delighting in companionship, in good talk, in his wanderings over the farmlands. Physically frail and small, he was uncommonly handsome, and he liked to have handsome novices around him. He especially admired the devotional writings of Jean de Fécamp and St. Augustine's *The City of God*, and he corresponded with Bernard. Sex tormented him, and accordingly he built a kind of bathroom under the novice-house where he was able to immerse his body in icy cold water from the neighboring rills and so quench the heat of his vices, with the predictable result that he suffered atrociously from bronchitis and arthritis in his middle age. But it is not for his self-inflicted torments that he is remembered today. He is remembered for his writings in which he was never able to quench his lust for beauty: the sensuous beauty of the earth, of flowers and trees and skies, and the physical beauty of the young men who gathered around him when he became the abbot of the monastery. His rule was lax, for he could forbid them nothing. While he was novice-master he wrote for his charges a manual of devotion called *The Mirror of Charity* in which he celebrated friendship as an essential element of the divine economy, and sometimes he will break away from the contemplation of the scriptural meaning of friendship to praise God for the friendships he has enjoyed in the monastery:

The other day while I was going round the cloister garth of the monastery, the brethren were seated together like a crown that is most dear to me: it was as though I were amid the liveliness of Paradise and I kept admiring the flowers and fruit of each of the trees, and I found no one in that multitude whom I did not love and by whom I was not confident that I was loved. I was suffused with a joy so great that it surpassed all the delights of the world. For I felt my spirit transfused into all and that the affection of all had passed over into me, so that I said with the prophet: "Behold how good and how pleasant it is for brethren to dwell together in unity."

For Aelred charity is love, but this love has a twofold aspect: no less important than the love of God is the love of one's fellow men.

"Bind all this world together in your heart with a bond of pity and love," he wrote in a long meditation addressed to his sister, and it is clear that he regarded loving the world as a necessary prelude to the love of God. For him Christ is the companion, the friend who is the model of all friendship, the loyal confidant who treasures our trust in him. In his meditation *On Jesus at twelve years old*, which he wrote for Ivo, a monk of Wardon, toward the end of his life, he speaks of Christ's three days in Jerusalem as a boy, and immediately finds himself asking those questions that were most characteristic of him. "Where did Christ lodge?" he asks. "What food did he eat? What company did he enjoy?" And when he comes to meditate upon the days when Mary and Joseph searched for him in vain, he sees the boy in all his beauty while assuming the form of a young acolyte with a begging bowl, sharing the importunity and lowliness of the world:

> *Where wast thou during those three days, O good Jesus? Who gavest Thee food and drink, or a bed to sleep on? To whom was given the great privilege of untying the latchets of Thy sandals, for even John the Baptist thought himself unworthy of doing so? Or who was allowed to prepare baths and oils for Thy youthful limbs? Sweetest Lord, I do not know, but I know that Thou wert able to assume our weakness and uselessness just as Thou wert able to assume almighty power. So it seems to me that Thou didst go about begging from door to door, thus sharing in our poverty and assuming all the lowliness of our human nature.*

In this way Aelred meditated on the texts, and like Bernard he casts over them the sensuous light of his own sensual imagination. He has no use for a Christianity that deprives the world of its graces. He was continually attempting to depict the beauty of Christ, and he was curiously evasive, and nearly always incomprehensible, when he attempted to depict Hell-fire, the Last Judgment, and the reign of Satan. For him there were the rolling woodlands of Yorkshire, the rills and the sea and the white-robed boys who looked for all the world like angels, and he was content that they were portions of God's grace. He was content even when he was very ill, crippled by arthritis and lying in a kind of grave sunk into the floor. Then he would spend his days in prayers and vigils, weeping sometimes because the world was so beautiful and heaven was even more beautiful. The light of angelic visitation would shine upon his head, and he would converse with angels. The sick would be brought to him; he would bless them and they would be cured. When he lay dying, a hundred monks gathered round him to receive his last blessing and to hear his last words: *"Festinate, for crist luve."* (Make haste, for Christ's love.) It was typical of him that he should speak in mingled Latin and English. Long before he had said that it was a special virtue of the English language that, unlike Latin, it reserved a single resounding syllable for the name of Christ.

The tenderness of Aelred was characteristic of his age, when the harsh, dogmatic laws of the Church were giving place to a decent lawlessness. The mystical imagination was free and untrammeled by dogma, for every mystic saw God in his own way. Joy and color were entering the Church, and soon the brilliantly lit Gothic cathedrals would rise in the place of the dark and mysterious Romanesque churches; and for a while the worship of Christ was subordinated to the worship of the Virgin. Not the agony on the Cross, but the calm beauty of the Virgin holding the Child in her arms dominated the imaginations of men. Almost the agony was forgotten in the contemplation of the joy incarnate in the Virgin.

Bernard, writing his grave meditations on *The Song of Songs* opened the way. Others went further. In the Abbey of St. Victor a great congregation of scholars, poets, mystics, and theologians gathered together to contemplate God in a new way. The abbey was on the left bank of the Seine in the open meadows just outside of Paris, in the grounds now occupied by the Jardin des Plantes. It began with the small chapel built by William of Champaux under the protection of the king, who helped him to build a magnificent library. Soon scholars from all over Europe were flocking to the abbey in the knowledge that the king's protection gave them a relative freedom. Frenchmen, Bretons, Normans, English, Scots, Norwegians, Germans, and Italians were to be counted among the canons. The Victorine renaissance had begun.

The special characteristic of the Victorines was a subtle clarity, a lively style, the sense of life as a beautiful and majestic sacrament. Freedom gave them wings. They wrote as they pleased, often on the edge of heresy, with a superb delicacy that derived perhaps from Bernard but was colored by the bright and misty landscape of the Seine. Hugo of St. Victor came to the abbey in 1118 at the age of twenty-four, and there he spent the rest of his days. A German, he wrote with French lucidity, and he was especially concerned to describe the movements of the soul as it reaches out to God. Like St. Bernard, but with even more gentleness, he employs the images of the bride and the bridegroom. In *De Arrha Animae* (The Perfume of the Soul) he relates a dialogue between the soul and man, between the uncomprehending spirit and the human intelligence:

THE SOUL says:

Tell me, what is this thing of delight that merely by its memory touches and moves me with such sweetness and violence that I am drawn out of myself and carried away, I know not how? I am suddenly renewed, I am changed, I am plunged in ineffable peace. My mind is full of joy, all misery and pain forgotten. My soul exults. My mind is made clear. My heart is on fire. My desires are truly gentle and kind. I know not where I am, because my beloved has embraced me, I am possessed of something and know not what it is, but I try to hold fast to it for fear of losing it. My soul in joy strives never to be separated from that which she desires to hold forever. Exulting in sovereign gladness, seeking nought, desiring nothing, but to rest in this. Is this, then, my beloved? Tell me, that I may know him, and if ever he comes again I may entreat him to leave me not, but to stay with me always.

MAN says:

It is indeed thy beloved who visits thee, but he comes in invisible shape, he comes disguised, he comes incomprehensibly, he comes to touch thee, not to be seen of thee. He comes not to give himself wholly, but to be tasted by thee: not to fulfil thy desire, but to lead upward thy affections. He offers a foretaste of his delights, and the earnest of thy betrothal consists chiefly in this, that he who shall afterwards give himself to be seen and possessed by thee perpetually, now permits himself to be sometimes tasted, that thou mayest learn how sweet he is. This shall console thee for his absence, and the perfume of his gift shall keep thee from despair.

(*Patrologia Latina*, CLXXVI, 970)

How admirable is the conversation between the man and the soul at the moment of awakening consciousness, for it is hardly permissible to believe that the dialogue touches only on the immanence of God. The beloved is not Christ alone. That sense of quickening life comes as much from God as from the world around; the landscape of

France is also implicated. So, too, is the realization that the world is being newly recreated in the dawn of a new age. The old theologies have been swept away; freshness enters as the naked soul reaches out to God, like a leaf uncurling and reaching out to the sun. "Exulting in sovereign gladness, seeking nought, desiring nothing, but to rest in this."

Richard of St. Victor was born in Scotland in 1123. Like Hugo he wrote with an angelic lucidity. Dante said of him that "in contemplation he was more than man." His mystical theology derived from the visions of Ezekiel and the biblical description of the building of Solomon's temple, which he annotated with extraordinary passion, finding a relevant mystical interpretation of every cubit and every carved stone. The jaded reader may find himself disapproving of those interpretations by which walls, curtains, and chambers assume the role of the virtues, but they should be regarded as experiments in analogy or perhaps as poetic improvisations on the theme of virtue. In much the same way Hugo of St. Victor in his short treatise *De Amore Sponsi ad Sponsum* (The Bridegroom's Love for the Bride) discovers the virtues and the vices lurking in *The Song of Songs. I will get me to the mountains of myrrh and to the hills of Lebanon, and I will speak to my bride:* he has no difficulty in extracting recondite meanings from the text. He notes that myrrh serves to preserve the dead from corruption and therefore denotes the mortification of the flesh, while Lebanon means whitening and cleansing, and therefore denotes the purification of the flesh. Why then do we hear of mountains of myrrh and only hills of Lebanon? He answers that the mountains of myrrh signify the eminence of spiritual courage and the lowly hills of Lebanon signify the depths of humility. On this level the Victorines wrote with deliberate and happy obscurity, rejoicing in their power to transmute all things into virtues and vices, at ease among symbols. In the end they played the game too easily to be able to extract any profit from it.

The greatest triumphs of Richard of St. Victor lie elsewhere. It is when he writes of the movements of the soul and of the degrees of love that he is most convincing, for he seems in some mysterious way to have penetrated into the soul's machinery. For him the soul's love of God is as complex as the bride's love for her husband. The soul, too, has its modesty, its pride, its resentments, its furious rages. The lover of God suffers banishment whenever he feels that God is absent; hurt, he recoils upon himself, hides, withdraws into obscurity, and in the process makes his presence abundantly known to God. In his treatise *De quatuor gradibus violentae caritatis* (The Four Degrees of Passionate Love) Richard of St. Victor describes the subtleties of the lover's progress from the burning pain of separation to the embrace, the perfect ecstasy, and the final withdrawal into humility.

He gives names to the degrees of love. The first degree is "the wounding," the second is "the embrace." At first the soul is quickened by God's presence, then the pain of quickening gives way to an awareness of the divine compassion. With the third and fourth degrees it ascends into regions where pain and compassion no longer have any meaning, into that ultimate Heaven where God is Glory and Christ is Humility; and having reached God, the soul can only "descend below itself" in order to reach others in compassion and charity. To have known God, to have seen Him face to face, is to know that one must re-enter the world of men with absolute humility.

So in the most brilliant passage of the work he declares that while the third stage brings the mystic into "the likeness of God," the fourth stage leads him into "the form of a servant." He is not playing with the mysteries, but simply relating what he knows of the divine ambiguities. So he says:

In the third degree the soul is glorified, in the fourth it is humbled for God's sake. In the third it is conformed to the divine light, in the fourth it is conformed in the humility of Christ. And although in the third it assumes almost the likeness of God, nevertheless in the fourth it begins to empty itself, taking the form of a servant and finding itself according to its own way in humanity. In the third degree it is as it were put to death in God, in the fourth it is raised in Christ.

In this way he appears to be playing with the stages of love when he is most serious, most determined to describe what he knows. He follows the wayward path to God, permitting himself the luxury of pausing at the stages of love, as though they were rungs on a ladder, yet never for a moment does he lose sight of the fact that there is no ladder: there is only the movement of the soul in the presence of God, and this movement takes the form of a parabolic arc, an entering into God and a coming away. In the end the soul hurtles like an angel or like molten metal into the ordinary human world we live in. "Like molten metal running downhill, so does the soul humble itself in the service of the divine providence."

In the most delicate way Richard of St. Victor describes the divine economy, relating the soul to God and the world. We are no longer beside the lake: twelve centuries of commentary and thought have fed the stream of the Victorines. The original music is now richly orchestrated, and the songs once sung by Christ are drowned in the sound of the new instruments. Christianity paused when it came to the Victorines, and to this day it bears some of the delicate colors they wove into the fabric.

"Charity is everything," Hugo of St. Victor wrote in his *De Laude Caritatis* (In Praise of Charity). "It is the choice, the journey, and the arrival. It is the dwelling-place and the blessedness. Love God, therefore, choose God; run, seize, possess, enjoy."

In their meadows beside the Seine, in sight of Paris, the Victorines showed that it was not necessary to obey; it was only necessary to rejoice.

Nᴏᴛ ᴇᴠᴇɴ in its beginnings was Christianity simple, for many different ideas went into its making. Out of the life and sayings of Jesus as recorded in the Gospels, out of the letters of St. Paul and the fiery visions of the unknown John of Patmos the faith grew until it resembled a great oak tree turning its innumerable leaves to the sun. Innumerable roots fed the tree; the branches were concealed in the dense foliage. A branch might be torn away, but it would grow again; and though lightning might strike the tree, it lived on. Its seeds would be carried into countries unknown when the first seed was planted, and strangers would rest in the tree's shade. There came a time when the tree seemed to reach up to the heavens, throwing its bright shadow over all men's lives. It was indestructible.

But even at the beginning there were men who wondered what Jesus said. The words spoken beside a dreaming lake were not easy to interpret or to understand. Who was to say whether Mark erred, or Luke forgot? Did Paul write all the letters attributed to him? Were the revelations of John of Patmos to be accorded the same authority as the words spoken in Capernaum and Jerusalem? What of the apocryphal Gospels surviving in fragments widely dispersed throughout Europe? Was the Church a depository of divine wisdom, or merely a political power using scriptural weapons to preserve its aims? In the tenth, eleventh, and twelfth centuries many sects arose independently, all seeking a faith outside the sanctions of the Church, obedient to the Gospels rather than the bishops, who acted as though they were earthly lords. Tours, Milan, and Turin became centers of

revolt. Though the revolts were soon crushed, there were always a
few who escaped from the net. Peter Waldo, a rich merchant of
Lyons, sold his goods and gave them to the poor, preaching voluntary
poverty eleven years before St. Francis was born. He made a translation of the New Testament into *Provençal,* and his followers became
the priests of his newly founded church, explaining the texts as they
wandered through the villages of southern France. In the eyes of the
pope Waldo was a heretic, and accordingly he was excommunicated,
but the Waldensian movement survived in secret, becoming absorbed
in the general movement of Protestantism in the sixteenth century. In
time his heresies were to become the doctrines of the Protestant
Church.

For many Christians the Church had become the enemy of the
faith, and the pope was Antichrist. The rigidity, absolutism, and organization of the Church seemed contrary to the freedom they associated with Christ. The revolt was widespread, and sometimes it was to
be found within the Church itself.

The most formidable opposition to the Church was offered by
the sect known as the Cathars, from the Greek word meaning "the
pure." We hear of them first in 1028 when a group of peasants,
clerics, and nobles established themselves at the castle of Monteforte
between Turin and Genoa under the protection of the countess.
They were a quiet, friendly people, dedicated to purity, teaching that
there was only one God and that Christ, who was not God, was the
soul of mankind in whom God delighted. They regarded God, not
the pope, as head of the Church. It was observed that these people
possessed an enviable serenity and gaiety, even when they were
offered the choice between obedience to the Church and the stake;
and they went eagerly to the flames.

It was a time when Europe was swarming with hermits, wandering preachers, and goliards who were accustomed to pursuing their
own thoughts and dreams. Discontent with the Church was growing.
From the East, especially from Bulgaria and Dalmatia, came the new
prophets of a simpler dispensation, in which there would be no rich
bishops, no ostentatious displays of wealth by priests and monks, no
complicated ceremonies of worship. Animism, Manichaeism, and
Gnosticism colored the thoughts of these people who resembled the
early Christians; and the early heresies, never completely obliterated,
revived in the minds of these missionaries who regarded the Church

as spurious, and faith as simple. The reformation of the Church did not begin with Luther. It began in the early years of the eleventh century in the valleys of northern Italy and southern France.

Catharism spread like wildfire. In 1045 it was found in Châlons, in 1052 Cathars were hanged by the Emperor Henry the Black at Goslar in Germany. It took root, so that there seemed to be two Churches, the one ruled by the pope, the other by the perfect, the black-robed leaders of the sect who dedicated themselves to poverty, abstinence, and devotion to their flocks. They were always in danger of arrest, and many were arrested, put on trial, and burned. The blood of the martyrs was the seed of the new Church.

The Cathars cut through the vast ornamentation which had grown over the Church. In their view the Church was doing the devil's work. They read the Scriptures literally, believing like the early Christians that the Second Coming was at hand, and therefore the life of the spirit was of infinitely greater value than the earthly life, and nothing was to be gained by loving the flesh. They rejected the ornaments of religion, as they rejected the Mass, the Virgin Birth, Baptism, Absolution, and Purgatory. They even rejected the sacrament of marriage. They believed in penance, the life of the spirit, the divinity of God. It was a religion which kept to the core of faith and had no patience with the bright garments willingly worn by her. They lived for God and for God alone.

There was of course nothing new in Catharism. All over Europe, at all times, there have been sects determined to cut through theological complexities and to live lives of perfect dedication. In the eyes of the Cathars the world was evil: into this world had come the pure Word of Christ, who was very God, and therefore it was inconceivable that he suffered on the Cross or was resurrected in the flesh. Christ was God's ghostly presence, a phantom, almost pure spirit, to be worshiped and imitated but never adored. The priests wore no vestments; there were no candles, no incense, no altars. When the worshipers met together the eldest present broke the bread and gave it to the assembled men and women with the words: "Thanks be to the God of our Jesus Christ. May the spirit be with us all." They practiced penance for their sins, but they were simple penances. "Penance, true, chaste, and virginal, is alone capable of bringing forth Sons of God," wrote one of the Cathars. They read the Gospels, especially the Gospel of St. John, but they also possessed their own books, including *The Book of the Two Principles*, which were the principles of good and evil, and *The Secret Supper*, which consists of a colloquy between John and Christ and includes passages of quite extraordinary poetic feeling. "The sun is the Prince of this world and the throne, and the moon is the law of Moses, and the stars are the spirits that minister unto the Prince. There will be no place for the Apostles to reign, but Christ, the Son of God, is the seven-fold Sun, and He shall reign." When John asked Christ how he came to wear the shape of the human Jesus, he was told: "When it occurred to my Father to send me down to earth, then He sent before me in order to receive me an angel called Mary. When I came, I descended into her ear and left from her ear." In Byzantine mosaics and early Italian paintings of the Annunciation a spear of light can be seen descending from the heavens to the ear of Mary. The tradition that a ray of divine light entered Mary's ear was older than Catharism and had the authority of some Fathers of the Church. The Cathars preferred that Christ should be born from Mary's ear and saw no reason why the womb should give birth to a spirit, for they despised the flesh as a satanic shroud.

Inevitably the Cathars produced their own rituals. These were of astonishing simplicity, and were performed very much as one performs a simple ceremony among friends. At the *consolamentum* those who desired to be included among the perfect received the laying on of hands, the New Testament was placed on their heads as they swore an oath, and then the attendant perfects bowed to the new perfect, who bowed to them in return. The taking of the oath was the most important part of the ceremony. The candidate for perfection promised to dedicate his life to God and the Gospels, never to lie or swear or touch a woman, never to eat meat, cheese, or eggs (since they came into being as the result of acts of reproduction), but only fish and vegetables cooked in oil. There was nothing overtly heretical in the *consolamentum*. They employed only one formula that might have appeared strange to a Catholic: in the Lord's Prayer "supersubstantial bread" was substituted for "daily bread." St. Gregory of Nyssa had made the same substitution, scarcely believing that Jesus would ask men to pray for something as palpable and finite as bread. Since flesh was to be despised, or at least held within its narrow limits, the Cathars prayed: "Have no mercy on the flesh born in corruption, but have mercy on the spirit held in prison." The perfect yearned not so much to be free of the body as to be immune from its contagions.

The *consolamentum*, perhaps in a slightly different form, was performed for those about to die. This, too, was a very simple service, with the dying man being asked to sit up in bed and to recite the Lord's Prayer and the other responses. A perfect who saw death coming would sometimes give himself up to fasting, and such fastings assumed the aspect of a ritual, with the faithful in attendance rejoicing as they watched the dying man doffing the garment of the body and putting on the garment of the spirit.

All Cathar ceremonies ended with the "Peace," the solemn kiss of brotherhood, a ritual they shared with the early Christian communities. The perfects kissed one another, then kissed the brethren, who afterward kissed one another. A woman perfect would never kiss a male perfect. Instead she would kiss the Gospels and then give it to the man who would kiss it in his turn. They held the Gospels in such veneration that the holy book took the place of the Cross of the Catholic Church.

By 1200 Catharism was a force to be reckoned with. All northern Italy and southern France were honeycombed with the sect. The common people were intoxicated with the simple faith of the Cathars. So, too, were the nobility, who protected and encouraged the perfect, and remained their protectors to the end. Among these protectors was Roger II Trencavel, Viscount of Béziers and Carcassonne. Ordered by the Church authorities to end his protection of the Cathars, he refused. In 1178 he was excommunicated, and three years later the cardinal-legate Henry, Abbot of Clairvaux, led a crusade against him, which failed ignominiously. Great nobles like Raymond, Count of Toulouse, and Raymond-Roger, Count of Foix, continued to protect the Cathars; almost the entire aristocracy of southern France was devoted to the sect. The Church was in danger. At the Fourth Lateran Council in 1215 a solemn reaffirmation of faith was announced; it took the form of a sentence by sentence refutation of Cathar doctrine. Pope Innocent III pronounced against the heretics, saying they were worse than the Saracens. On March 10, 1208, Innocent III had already delivered sentence of death on the heretics. He called upon the northern nobility to crush the south, offering both indulgences and land to the crusaders in the army dedicated to the destruction and final obliteration of the heresy. The army found its leader in Simon de Montfort, a young French nobleman from the Ile de France who by his marriage to an English heiress also bore the title of Earl of Leicester.

The crusade opened at Béziers, where Simon de Montfort demanded that the city fathers hand over the 222 Cathars known to be in the city. The city fathers refused, and the crusaders thereupon massacred the entire population. Every man, woman, and child in this city of 20,000 inhabitants perished. Not even the priests were spared. When Abbé Arnaud-Amalric, the head of the Cistercian order, was asked how to distinguish the heretics from the faithful, he answered: "Kill them all! God will recognize His own!" The massacre of July 1209 was a foretaste of massacres to come. After Béziers it was the turn of Carcassonne, which fared better, for the inhabitants fled in time. Then all the villages and castles in the neighborhood were taken, and the conquered lands fell into the possession of Simon de Montfort. Catharism flourished. It flourished all the more because the Church and the northern knights were pitiless.

For thirty-five terrible years the crusaders brought fire and sword to the south of France. The treachery of the crusaders was as remarkable as their cruelty. In the summer of 1210 the citizens of Minerve offered to surrender on condition that their lives were spared; the instrument of surrender was drawn up and solemnly signed; and de Montfort's troops went on to butcher some hundreds of heretics who had thought that the promises of the crusaders would be kept, while the pope's legate looked on.

As the crusade continued, it became more complex, more desperate, and more absurd. King Peter II of Aragon, loyal Catholic who had led a crusade against the Arabs in Spain and won a famous victory at La Navas de Tolosa, joined forces with Raymond, Count of Toulouse, protector of the heretics, against Simon de Montfort. When King Peter II was killed in an obscure battle, the tide turned. Simon de Montfort entered Toulouse in triumph, only to be killed by a woman who threw a stone at him from the city walls; it must have been a very large stone, for according to the chronicler it crushed his helmet and shattered his skull so that "he fell down of a sudden and instantly turned black." He was succeeded by his son Amaury, who was equally vengeful and equally avaricious, but a bad general. In his eagerness to imitate his father he lost nearly all the battles he fought, and to this day in those regions of southern France where he led his armies, an *amori* is an imbecile. In 1224, worn out by incessant defeats, he retired from the war.

The task of crushing the Cathars now fell on King Louis VIII of France, known as "the Lion." He had been very briefly King of England, and was a redoubtable warrior, capable of waging if necessary a long war against the independent principalities in the south of France. In a series of quick campaigns he destroyed the armies of the Count of Toulouse, but died at the age of thirty-seven before he could enjoy the fruits of victory. In his place there was the eleven-year-old Louis IX, who was to become a saint, and his mother, Blanche of Castile. During the reign of the saintly Louis IX, Catharism in southern France was destroyed.

The war went on. The Inquisition was set up in Toulouse and wherever else it was thought to be necessary. All women over the age of twelve were ordered to abjure heresy; boys, who were thought to be less prone to heresy, had to commit themselves to the true faith by the age of fourteen. The faith of the heretics rested on the Gospels, and therefore it was ordered that no one except the priests should have the Gospels in their possession, whether in Latin or in the vernacular. The only books allowed were the Psalter, the Breviary, and the Virgin's Book of Hours. Under the Dominicans the Inquisition became a permanent institution. The remaining Cathars were hunted down like wild animals.

Catharism, which had previously had its home in the towns and the princely courts, took to the woods, the forests, and the hills. In small towns people sometimes retained their faith while outwardly obeying the instructions of the Church, but the force of Catharism now rested among the groups of villagers in the foothills of the Pyrenees. Their chief refuge was the holy mountain of Montségur, known as the Mountain of the Holy Grail. On top of the mountain an old castle had been transformed into a Cathar church.

The church was very nearly impregnable because all the approaches could be easily defended. On one side of the mountain there was a sheer drop of four hundred feet, on the other sides there were narrow valleys where a handful of men could hold up advancing armies. The holy mountain became a refuge, a source of supplies, a hiding place for their treasure and their holy books. Here men came when they believed they were dying, or when their communities were destroyed. It was the headquarters of the saintly Guilhabert de Castres, who kept the flames of Catharism alive. He was a very old man, but he possessed remarkable powers of endurance and would march the whole night to reach some wretched villagers whose faith was trembling in the balance, and he had great influence among the nobility.

By 1242 the pope and the King of France had lost all patience. The "most unholy and most damnable heresy" of Catharism was still gaining converts. The young, half-English Raymond, Count of Toulouse, was forced to submit to the Church, being led down the aisle of Notre Dame "naked except for his shift" to beg absolution for the sin of having sustained the heretics. As further punishment he was ordered to raise ten thousand troops and to lead them against Montségur. He told the king that no force on earth could capture such an impregnable fortress, but was reminded that spiritual forces would work in his favor. Half-heartedly the man who had given most aid to the heretics led his army against the holy mountain.

The siege of Montségur lasted ten months. There were never more than three hundred armed men in the fortress-church, and never less than ten thousand in the tents below. The army arrived during the first days of May 1243. At first they hoped to starve the defenders into submission. There were sporadic attacks that were beaten back. By the end of October none of the attackers had come within hailing distance of the church. The defenders were constantly receiving supplies from men who passed secretly through the lines at night along footpaths unknown to the enemy, or they climbed the cliffs with the aid of ropes.

Within the church the ordinary life of the Cathars went on quietly. Guilhabert de Castres had died, and his place was taken by Bertran d'en Marti, who presided over the Cathar ceremonies and continued to bring new converts into the fold. Among the converts was one of the daughters of Raymond de Perella, lord of Montségur. Her name was Esclarmonde, and she had been ill from birth. Her mother, Corba de Perella, and her grandmother, the Marquesia de Lantar, also became Cathars, and so did Philippa, the wife of Pierre-Roger de Mirepoix, who was in command of the armed men inside the church. Most of these soldiers and sergeants-at-arms were sympathizers, not believers. They fought because they had seen too many of their friends burned at the stake.

In November the tide began to turn, for in that month some mercenaries from the Basque country were able to capture a shoulder of the mountain only five hundred feet from the wall of the church, and here Durant, Bishop of Albi, a man with a great experience of military strategy, was able to install a stone throwing machine. Stones weighing from sixty to eighty pounds were hurled against the church, in a cannonade that rarely ceased, and sometimes went on all night. This advantage was somewhat offset by the arrival of new troops led by the engineer Bertran de la Beccalaria, who set up stone-throwing machines inside the church. He had forced his way through the lines. By this time Pierre-Roger de Mirepoix was already accepting the possibility of defeat, and he gave orders that the gold and silver treasure should be taken to a safer place. Late in December the Basques succeeded in climbing the sheer cliffs on a moonless night and took the church tower by surprise, massacring everyone in it. Jean Bernat, a traitor, had shown them the way up the precipitous cliffs.

The Basques remained in the tower, but the fighting went on. The Bishop of Albi brought up more stone throwers, which tore great holes in the roof but had little effect on the rugged walls. A few more soldiers came to help the defenders, but the end was not far off. All through February, all day and all night, the fire arrows were falling into the church and boulders were crashing against the walls. "The dragon's head, Montségur, must be cut off," Blanche de Castile had decreed, and the time for the blood-letting had come.

On March 1, 1244, Pierre-Roger de Mirepoix went out under a flag of truce to make the best terms he could. They were unusual terms, for the lives of all the soldiers were spared, and so too were the lives of all those who abjured the heresy. The fortress-church was to become the possession of the pope and the King of France. Finally, permission was granted for the defenders to remain on Montségur for a further two weeks. It was hoped that the Cathars would, in those two weeks of respite, see the error of their ways.

They did not see the error of their ways. As the days passed, more and more of the defenders embraced Catharism, receiving the *consolamentum* from the hands of Bertran d'en Marti, who moved among them like a spirit sent from God. It was remarked that the defenders were strangely quiet during those last days. Those who were to die distributed their possessions among those who would remain alive. Bertran d'en Marti gave his supplies of oil, salt, pepper, and wax to Pierre-Roger de Mirepoix. On the night of March 15, Pierre Authier, the treasurer, was lowered by rope over the cliff wall with

instructions to make his way to the Château d'Ussat in the High Pyrenees, where several of the faithful had already taken refuge and were
guarding the treasure. A beacon light on the peak of Mont Barthé-
lemy would signify that they had arrived safely in territory where the
king's men would never follow them.

Just before dawn on March 16, 1244, the watchers in Montségur
saw the beacon light burning on the mountaintop, and this signal of
their deliverance came only just in time, for later in the day the faithful walked down to the sloping meadow at the foot of the mountain
and quietly lay down on the fagots already prepared for them within
a wooden palisade. Two hundred and sixteen of the Cathars came
down the mountain to die, while another two hundred or so, including all those who were prepared to abjure the Cathar faith, were permitted to leave the fortress under arms. The procession marching to
the stake was lead by Bertran d'en Marti, and not far from the head
of the procession walked Corba de Perella, her mother the Marquesia
de Lantar, and her sick daughter Esclarmonde, whose name means
"to bring light to the world." Then the field of fagots was set alight,
and the soldiers withdrew to a safe distance while the flames leaped
and a great cloud of smoke rose over the meadow. By noon there was
only a smouldering white field of wood ash on the slope of the mountain.

The holy church of the Cathars, which they called Mount
Tabor, still stands, white and glittering on the summit of the mountain. It is roofless, but the walls give an impression of extraordinary
strength and they still show the marks of fire. On the *Pré de Cremats*,
"the meadow of the burning," a small altar of stones gathered from
within the church has been erected. On the altar someone has carved
words written in the ancient French spoken by the Cathars:

ALS CATARS
ALS MARTIRS
DEL PUR AMOR
CRESTIAN
16 Mars 1244

Below this inscription to "the martyrs of the pure love of Christ"
the same hand has carved the badge of the Cathars, a five-pointed star
above three crosses, an eye, and a hand holding the Gospel.

Catharism did not perish with the destruction of Montségur.

The secret life of the sect continued in defiance of the king and the Church. A papal bull *ad extirpanda* was promulgated by Pope Innocent IV in 1252, commanding the Dominicans to employ torture to root out the heretics, but torture was not a weapon the Cathars feared. They became sterner, harder, lived in smaller groups, practiced the rites of *endura*, and sometimes fought back against the Dominicans. In 1300 some thirty-nine Cathars were placed on trial in Albi for heresy: they were not sentenced to death, but some nineteen were imprisoned in perpetuity in order "to drink the waters of agony and the bread of sorrow."

Catharism lived on. Like the Waldenses they fed into the mainstream of Protestantism. They could not be obliterated, because they represented an aspect of the truth.

23 ✣ ST. FRANCIS

As we see him in the magnificent portrait by Cimabue, sorrowful and silent, standing alone and a little apart from the Virgin, as though he dared not draw near to her, a small, dark-skinned man with a brown habit folded loosely, with a low forehead, eyes like black olives, a long nose, a puckered mouth, a scrubby beard, with a wound at his side and one hand bearing the red stain of the stigmata, he comes to us across the centuries with a disturbing immediacy. We know him well, and would recognize him if he entered the room. He seems to belong not to any particular age, but to all ages. At first sight he has the look of a beggar pleading for mercy, but what he begged for was something which no power except God could give him, and what he hoped for was nothing less than the rebirth of the divine spirit in man, a new charity, a new love. He tore down the veils of the Church and demonstrated in his own life the starkness and nakedness of Christ.

After his death when the legends began to accumulate, he was sometimes depicted as a gay and sweet-tempered saint who performed charming miracles and delivered sermons to birds. He was given the affectionate name of *il poverillo*, the little pauper, and the anecdotes about him were collected together under the title of *fioretti*, the little flowers; but there were thorns in the flowers and the pauper on occasion could give orders that sent tremors through Christendom. On occasion there was gaiety in him, but it was rare. There was iron in his soul, and there was very little that was comforting in him. "He called men to weeping and mourning," wrote St. Bonaventura. There were harsh and strident notes in his simple songs.

Francesco de Bernardone was born at Assisi in September 1182, the son of a rich cloth merchant from Lucca, and of a mother born in Provence. At his baptism he was given the name of Giovanni, but the name was changed to Francesco on his father's return from a business trip in France, apparently to honor the land of his mother's birth; and indeed his character was more French than Italian. He spoke and sang in French all his life, though imperfectly, and devoured the *Chansons de Geste* of Provence during his youth. Born to wealth, he grew up into a carefree young man. He was skillful in earning money, says his first biographer, Thomas of Celano, but very frivolous in giving it away. Thomas of Celano describes him as a short man with a round head and a low forehead, a thin nose, small ears, and dark hair. His lips were thin, and he had short arms with unusually long and slender hands. "What am I?" Francis once asked, and went on to describe a dream in which he saw himself as a little black hen. "Look at me well," he laughed. "I am that hen, small of stature and dark."

He was a man who dreamed often, and he liked to relate his dreams. As a youth he dreamed of some great position in life, and his parents, half proud, half alarmed, said: "He is not like the son of a merchant but of a great prince." When he was captured during one of the interminable wars fought between Assisi and Perugia, his bearing and appearance caused him to be imprisoned in the noblemen's quarters, and some time later, when he became squire to a count, he equipped himself with such splendor that he threw the count in the shade. He enjoyed the gleam of armor, silken clothes, and fine horses; and when he dreamed that his father's shop was filled from floor to ceiling, not with rolls of cloth, but with suits of armor, bright spears, and shining shields, and heard a voice saying, "All this shall belong to you and to your warriors," he imagined that he was destined to become a great soldier and that he would spend his life in the field. One day, while suffering from a fever in Spoleto, he had another dream in which he heard a voice saying: "Who can benefit you most: the Lord or the servant?" Those words had the same effect on him as the words heard by St. Augustine. Instantly his mind was made up. Instead of journeying to Apulia to become a knight, he returned quietly to Assisi to contemplate the new way of life which had suddenly opened to him, still uncertain of himself, certain only that he would never become a knight.

In the summer of 1205, when he was twenty-two, there came to him the final long-awaited revelation which took place while he was presiding as Master of the Revels over some festivities at Assisi. Suddenly the world seemed to vanish before his eyes, he lost consciousness of himself, and as he related later, he would not have known if he had been cut to pieces limb from limb. He returned to consciousness only when a friend asked whether he was thinking about a bride. "Yes," he answered, "and you have never seen a nobler, wealthier, or more beautiful lady than the one I intend to take." From this moment there was no turning back. His bride was poverty.

From being the richest young man in Assisi, he became a beggar, haunting the hermit caves and piously shoring up the ruins of abandoned churches. He embraced lepers, lived on scraps of food, and wore the uniform of poverty—an old sack tied together with a rope, which was knotted three times in honor of the Trinity. He determined to live according to the rule which Christ had given to the apostles, with an absolutely literal observance. The three texts he chose to follow were:

If thou wilt be perfect, go and sell all thou hast, and give to the poor, and thou shalt have treasure in heaven. (Matthew 19:21)

Take nothing for your journey, neither staves, nor scrip, neither bread, neither money; neither have two coats apiece. (Luke 9:3)

If any man will come after me, let him deny himself, and take up his cross, and follow me. (Matthew 16:24)

For three years he lived in poverty, ministering to the outcasts and the lepers. His father disinherited him, but since he was married to poverty he regarded the lack of an inheritance as a blessing. He worshiped in the ruined little church of St. Mary of the Angels, known as the Portiuncula, down in the valley, far from the priests whom he half despised. His design was to found a religious order with the mission "to promote peace and patience, tend the wounded, relieve the distressed, and reclaim the erring." Disciples gathered round him, and when there were twelve they obtained the sanction of Pope Innocent III to organize in communities dedicated to apostolic preaching and work among the poor.

The medieval Church since the days of Constantine had been wedded to the pomp and power of the world. It had become a political hierarchy possessing great resources in land and property. Francis quietly assailed the earthly power of the Church by pointing to a higher purpose and a more demanding ritual: his purpose was nothing less than the imitation of Christ, and the ritual was poverty.

His preaching stimulated a great revival of religious feeling in Umbria. A second order, composed of nuns, was created under the rule of the saintly Clare, and later there came into existence a third order composed of laymen who were not asked to leave their families but to devote themselves to spiritual works. Francis was not an organizer, and he seems to have derived very little pleasure and to have suffered a good deal of inconvenience in his attempts to legislate for his flock. He was a man given to solitudes and sudden acts of daring, and he prized the soul's adventures above preaching to the crowds.

At the first opportunity he abandoned Umbria and set sail for the Holy Land. He was shipwrecked and returned to Italy. A few years later he sailed for Africa to convert the Moors, but once again he was unsuccessful. In 1219, he sailed for Egypt, where the Crusaders were besieging Damietta. Francis was taken prisoner, and brought before the Soldan, who listened to a sermon with good grace, and then sent him back to the Christian camp. He then visited the Holy Land, where he remained until September 1220. Nothing is known about his journeys through Palestine. He returned to Assisi to learn that dissensions had broken out among his flock, and he abruptly decided to abandon the order he had founded. In the short speech in which he announced his abdication he said: "Lord, I give Thee back this family which Thou didst entrust to me. Thou knowest, most sweet Jesus, that I have no longer the power and the qualities to continue to take care of it. I entrust it, therefore, to the ministers. Let them be responsible before Thee at the Day of Judgment, if any brother by their negligence, or their bad example, or by a too severe punishment, shall go astray."

In the late summer of 1224 Francis, accompanied by some of the brethren, went into retreat in the mountain of La Verna to prepare himself by a forty day's fast for the feast of St. Michael Archangel. He had a special devotion to St. Michael the Standard-bearer, *signifer sanctus Michaelis*, whose trumpet would wake the dead on the Day of Judgment, and he had no thought except to contemplate the dreadful angel and to remain in seclusion on the mountain. St. Bonaventura says that his contemplations were interrupted by a command to open the New Testament, and whenever he opened the book, his eyes fell on the account of the Passion. He opened the book three times, and each time he was confronted with the Passion; and it seems to have occurred to him that the time of his own Passion was about to come.

He had been in retreat on the mountain for more than a month when there took place in the early hours before dawn the supreme event of his earthly life. It happened, according to St. Bonaventura, "about the time of the Feast of the Exaltation of the Holy Cross," in the middle of September.

Francis was praying on the side of the mountain when a flaming six-winged seraph descended from heaven and hovered before him, and as his eyes grew accustomed to the angelic light he saw between the wings "the shape of a man crucified, having his hands and feet stretched out in the form of a Cross, and the man was fastened to the Cross." From contemplating St. Michael, he had turned to contemplating the Passion, and now he saw the Passion enclosed within an angel of fire. The vision faded, but not before he became aware that henceforward he would wear "the likeness of Christ Crucified," and would bear on his body the stigmata, those signs by which Christ was recognized after his death. On his hands and feet there appeared deep wounds, and the flesh formed itself into the shape of black, round-headed nails. On his side there formed a livid scar, as though a spear had pierced him and the wound had healed. Sometimes blood would trickle from these wounds.

Francis said nothing about the stigmata to the brethren that day, and for the few remaining months of his life he remained mysteriously reserved about them. Altogether, no more than fifty persons saw them. Probably Leo, his closest companion, was the first to see them, for he was called upon to bandage them every day, a difficult task because the points and heads of the nails projected; and it was said that Francis refused the bandages between Thursday afternoon and Saturday morning because he wished to suffer with Christ. Among those who saw the stigmata were Clare and the future Pope Alexander IV. Francis had no difficulty in hiding the wounds, for he now spent most of his life in seclusion.

Though he hid the stigmata as well as he could, he was shaken and exalted by the knowledge that he had received "the likeness." He had identified himself with Christ; now in a mysterious way he had become Christ, who had spoken to him in words which he never dared to reveal as long as he lived. When asked about his wounds, he would say evasively that he had no desire to talk about them, and sometimes he would use the words of Isaiah, "My secret to me," as though it were a secret he shared only with Christ. If he felt that the wound on his chest was about to bleed, he would lay his bandaged hand on the place to prevent the blood on his habit from being seen, and he took to wearing an under-garment that reached up to his shoulders. But the brethern who washed his clothes knew about the wound, and one brother actually measured it by laying his hand upon it: it was the length of three finger-widths.

How triumphantly Francis received the stigmata we know from a prayer and a benediction he wrote for Brother Leo, who asked for something in his hand against the time of his death. He wrote the prayer on one side of a sheet of parchment, the benediction on the other. Most of the prayer has faded away, but the benediction is still clearly visible in its reliquary in the sacristy at Assisi. Here is the benediction as Francis wrote it, adding as his signature the Cross rising from the rock of Golgotha:

The benediction reads, *Benedicat tibi Dominus et custodiat te, ostendat faciem suum tibi et misereatur tui, convertat vultum suum ad te et det tibi pacem* (The Lord bless thee and keep thee, show his face to thee and have mercy on thee, turn his countenance to thee and give thee peace.). Then he wrote,

Dominus bene
dicat
f Leo te

and though the words can be translated simply, "The Lord bless thee, Brother (*frater*) Leo," such a translation does injustice to the extraordinary delicacy and beauty of the inscription designed to show Francis' special affection for Leo. The Cross cuts through the name of Leo like a sword. Francis was writing when he was still shaking from the vision, but the handwriting is firm and controlled in spite of the wound in his hand and the fierce excitement in his heart. Only when he came to draw the rock of Golgotha does he seem to falter, the lines wandering off in all directions. According to Brother Leo, the rough sketch included the skull which can be found on many medieval paintings at the foot of the Cross; no doubt the skull is that strange object, like a fruit, from which the Cross emerges.

This benediction for Brother Leo, together with the faded prayer on the reverse side of the parchment, with its invocations to God's goodness, truth, and humility, is all that survives of the saint's handwriting.

For the last months of his life Francis was a desperately sick man. He had contracted a painful sickness of the eyes in Egypt; he suffered from strange trembling fits; and the wounds of the stigmata caused him fearful pain. Yet he treasured the agony, and if a brother attempted to comfort him, begging him to pray for some relief, saying that God would surely lay a lighter hand on him, Francis would groan and cry out: "Did I not know the purity of thy soul, I would have shunned thy company for daring to believe that the divine commandment has afflicted me." He called his agonies "his sisters," and to those who were closest to him he would speak mysteriously of an extraordinary grace which had been given him, a grace even greater than the stigmata. The strange words of Isaiah, "My secret in me," were never far from his lips.

He could not walk, because the nails protruded from his feet, and was carried in a kind of hammock around the countryside. "Emaciated as he was," wrote St. Bonaventura, "he was carried to the cities and the castled villages, that he might incite others to bear the Cross of Christ, and to the brethren he would say: 'Let us begin to serve God, for until now we have made little progress.' " Most of the last year of his life was spent at Assisi in the convent of San Damiano, which belonged to the order of the Poor Clares. On his sickbed he was continually singing.

He composed the *Canticle of the Sun* in the summer of 1225

while living in the garden immediately below Clare's window at San Damiano. His house was a small shed made up of wattles, and its chief purpose on those long hot summer days was to keep the sun away from his eyes, for any bright light caused excruciating pain. A surgeon, following a medieval prescription, had hoped to ease the pain in his eyes by cauterizing one side of his face from the eye to the chin with a red-hot poker; the wound had not healed. From time to time his hands, feet and chest bled from the wounds of the stigmata. That summer he was hardly more than a twitching nerve living a strange underground life in a wattle hut thickly buttressed to prevent the light from creeping in.

So he lived like a mole, very quietly, seeing no one, alone with himself and his God, slowly dying. Sometimes some of the brethren would gather silently around the hut to see whether he was alive and to push food through a flap. The food attracted the field mice, and he complained that they came out at night, running over him, making it impossible for him to pray or rest or sleep. They, too, were God's creatures, and surely they must be fed. So he endured them, and for nearly two months he remained there in the stifling heat of the little hut, and then one day, when he could endure the creaking of the mice in the straw no longer, he addressed a plea to God to free him from his sufferings, and he heard a voice saying: "Brother Francis, would you not rejoice if you received a treasure greater than any other?" Francis answered: "Such a treasure, O Lord, would be very precious." And on the following day, while meditating on the treasure, he heard a voice saying: "Rejoice in your sufferings." For another night he pondered these words, and the next day he summoned the brethren to come closer because he had something important to tell them. It was then, lying in the darkness of the shed, that he began to recite the *Canticle of the Sun*, the great song which stands at the beginning of Italian poetry:

Highest, almighty, good Lord,
  thine be the praise, the glory, the honor, and all benediction:
  to Thee alone do they belong,
  and no man is worthy to mention Thee.

Praised be my Lord with all Thy creatures,
  especially for master Brother Sun

who brings the day and illumines us through Thee,
and he is fair and radiant with great splendor,
and from Thee, O Highest, derives his significance.

Praised be my Lord for Sister Moon and the stars:
in Heaven Thou hast made them clear and precious and lovely.

Praised be my Lord for Brother Wind,
and for the air, cloudy and fair and every weather,
through which Thou dost give sustenance to all Thy creatures.

Praised be my Lord for Sister Water,
who is very useful and humble and rare and chaste.

Praised be my Lord for Brother Fire,
by whom Thou dost illumine the night,
and he is comely and jocund and vigorous and strong.

Praised be my Lord for Sister our Mother Earth,
who sustains and governs us
and puts forth different fruit and colored flowers and grass.

Then, following the invocation of all flowering things, he stopped as though in mid-sentence, unable to go on. He had omitted many things he had praised before; he had forgotten the birds and the gentle rocks that had so long upheld his wandering feet; he had forgotten food, which he had always blessed, though wondering a little why men should be plagued with the necessity of eating. Having praised the moon and the stars, he went on to praise the fire which illumines the night, thinking perhaps of the flickering bonfires on the hills which the shepherds tended at night in order to keep the wolves at bay. The fires that glowed at night were often in his mind, and of all created things he loved the sun and fire most. He said once:

In the morning when the sun rises, every man should praise God Who created it for our use, so that it might give light to our eyes in daytime. And in the evening, when night falls, then every man should praise God for Brother Fire, who gives light to our eyes at night: for we are all blind, and by these two brothers of ours God gives light to our eyes. Therefore, and especially for these two and for other created things which serve us by day, we must praise the Creator.

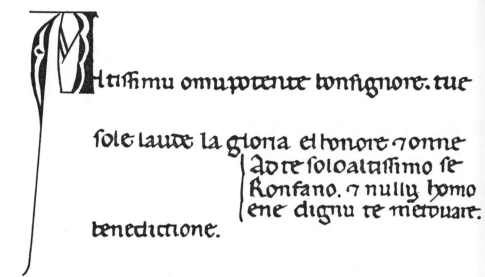

Earliest version of the *Canticle of the Sun,* from a manuscript in the Biblioteca Comunale di Assisi written shortly after the death of St. Francis.

Almost he had the ancient Persian reverence for fire. "He never wanted a flame to be extinguished, whether of a lamp or of a candle, so dearly did he cherish it," wrote one of the brethren. For him fire was a blessedness, unearthly, angelic, a thing to wonder at perpetually, so that when his habit caught fire his companions had to run and seek out his spiritual guardian before Francis would give them permission to put out the flames. When the doctor was about to cauterize his cheek and perforate his ears with the glowing iron, he spoke to the fire: "Brother Fire, noble and useful among all that is created, be courteous to me now, for I have always loved you and shall continue to do so for the sake of Him Who created you. I pray our Creator, who made you, to temper your heat now, so that I can endure it." He shuddered when the hissing iron came near, and made the sign of a Cross over it, but felt no pain. He was surprised at this, and asked the doctor to apply the iron again, thinking that the doctor had failed to cauterize him. But the doctor had succeeded only too well, and the burned face frightened the brethren. It was a strange face, utterly unlike the calm face that peers from Giotto's paintings. It was swollen with dropsy, one broken eye had sunk deep in its socket, and there was a livid purple wound down the length of his cheek.

When autumn came, his one remaining eye could bear the sight of the sun again, and he came out of his wicker shed. But the brethren knew he was dying. Fearing another winter in Assisi, they carried him on a stretcher to a small hermitage at Alberino near Siena, thinking the kinder climate would improve his health. He seemed to be getting better. He could eat a little food, and sometimes he fell asleep in the middle of the day, and he still sang his songs in a thin croaking voice. Just after the New Year he coughed up blood. The brethren thought it was the end and gathered round him, while he dictated his last testament: charity, poverty, submission to the Church. Brother Elias hurried to Alberino and gave orders that Francis should be brought back to Assisi. He seems to have been anxious that the body of Francis should not fall into foreign hands.

It was the worst thing that could have happened. All the trials he had experienced until this moment were nothing compared with the trials of that winter journey. It was a particularly stormy winter. Lying on a covered stretcher, still singing his songs, he grew feverish. The dropsy became worse: his whole body was swelling visibly before their eyes. All the time Brother Elias was planning how to outwit his enemies. Near Cortona he ordered a halt and drew up a plan of campaign. He decided to make the journey longer. Instead of going directly to Perugia, where there was some slight danger that Francis might be kidnaped, he ordered a long detour by way of Norcera to the west, where a troop of soldiers was waiting to escort him home. So Francis, who hated war and never praised spears or swords, returned to Assisi surrounded by armed soldiers.

He was taken to the Portiuncula at the foot of the mountain, to lie once more in a little straw shed just outside the diminutive church he had built with his own hands not so many years before. His life was ebbing away. Already there were quarrels among the brethren, and there were more quarrels in the town, where the bishop and the mayor were at daggers drawn. There was talk of a war breaking out between the followers of the bishop and the followers of the mayor. When the bishop excommunicated the mayor, the mayor decreed that no one should sell anything to the bishop, or buy anything from him, or do any business with him. Francis roused himself to song, and one day in the spring he was heard singing a little litany of pardon, which he asked the brethren to add to the *Canticle of the Sun:*

> *Praised be my Lord for those who grant pardon for love of Thee*
> *and suffer infirmity and tribulation.*

> *Blessed are those who persevere in peace,*
> *for they shall be crowned by Thee, O Highest.*

Thereupon he asked Brother Pacifico and one other brother to carry the message to Assisi. They sang the song through the streets, and they sang it again before the bishop and the mayor, who realized (though they must have realized it long before) that they were weaponless in the face of the commands of a dying saint; and put their swords away, and promised faithfully to keep the peace. Francis was pleased, but he did not ask to be carried into the town. He remained in the little shed through the summer. When winter came, he knew his death could not be long delayed.

In those last days he still called his sufferings his sisters, and spoke continually about the work that remained to be done. The terrible swelling continued. He sometimes gave the appearance of a man broken by his agony. Once toward the end he sprang from his bed and threw himself violently on the ground, jarring his bones, and then he kissed the earth, saying: "I give thanks, O Lord, for all my sufferings." He asked to be taken inside the Portiuncula when he felt death coming. It was Saturday, October 3, 1226. When he asked Brother Angelo and Brother Leo to sing about Sister Death, they sang instead the *Canticle of the Sun,* and when they had ended he sang the three remaining verses:

> *Praised be my Lord for sister our mortal death,*
> *from whom no living man can escape.*
> *Woe unto those who die in mortal sin.*

> *Blessed are they who are found in Thy most holy will:*
> *for the second death will do them no harm.*

> *Praise and bless my Lord and give thanks to Him,*
> *and serve Him with great humility.*

Now at last the song was over, and there remained only a few prayers, a few admonitions, a few farewells. He begged the brethren to place the Holy Gospel before all other ordinances, and stretched out his hands over them. He asked for bread, blessed it, and divided it among them, and the next day he asked them to read from the Gospel of St. John, beginning at the words: "Before the feast of the Passover . . ." but before they had finished reading he was singing the Psalm: "I cried unto the Lord . . ." He asked that his gown be removed and that he be laid naked on the earth with ashes sprinkled over him, and there he lay, very calm and quiet, staring up at the sky, his hands folded over his chest, while the last rites were performed. He died toward evening when the larks in multitudes were ascending the sky.

One day shortly before his death he summoned the brethren and whispered: "Be strong, all my sons, in the fear of the Lord, and abide in Him for ever." *Be strong, all my sons* . . . Almost the same words were spoken by Alexander the Great on his deathbed.

A S THE Church grew more powerful, and as Christianity made its way across the whole length and breadth of Europe, so the nature of Christian worship subtly changed to reflect the power and extent of the new ideas pouring into it. The simple words of Jesus by the lakeside were now burdened with endless commentaries; there were commentaries on commentaries; theologians wrestled as best they could with problems that Jesus had never raised. The edifice of the Church, grown rich and learned, seemed to sink under the weight of the past. By growing older, the Church had not grown more peaceful.

As the theological complexities increased, and as the scholars continued to fill the shelves with more and more books intended to clarify Christian doctrine while in fact making the doctrine more unintelligible and remote from ordinary human preoccupations, the songs and hymns also became more complex. The simple refrains were now orchestrated; new sounds, new voices, and new instruments were heard; and the new languages of Europe flowed into the common stream of song. Christianity had always expressed itself in song. Aramaic had given way to Greek, a language admirably suited to convey the subtleties of Christian thought, and then over large parts of the western world Greek gave way to Latin, an austere and sonorous language of extraordinary precision, especially suited to pronouncements on law and dogma. In the hands of the Church, Latin became more malleable than the language spoken by Cicero, but it remained the language of the clerks. It was bookish, a little remote from everyday life. The new Romance languages, which emerged from Latin, were closer to the people. With them a new leaven, a new virility, came to Christian song. From the Nordic languages of northern Europe there came an even greater virility.

The Venerable Bede, writing about 730, described how the first Anglo-Saxon hymns were composed in the monastery at Whitby some fifty years before his time. The composer was an ignorant stableman called Caedmon, already old, who had shown no talent for singing, and indeed he would steal away from the table when the harp was being played. One night he left the table early to avoid being called upon to sing, and went to the stable to sleep. Then there occurred the miracle by which, says the Venerable Bede, "he received the gift of poetry direct from God, without the intervention of a human teacher."

He lay down at the appointed time and composed himself for sleep, and in a dream he saw someone standing beside him, who saluted him, calling him by name and saying: "Caedmon, sing me a song." And he answered: "I do not know how to sing, and that is why I left the feast and came here." Then the man addressing him said: "Nevertheless you shall sing for me." "What shall I sing?" he asked. "Sing for me about the Creation of all things," the other answered. And having received this answer, he immediately began a song in praise of God the Creator that he had never heard before, and the burden of his song was:

> *Now let us praise the guardian of Heaven,*
> *The might of the Lord and His divine purpose,*
> *The work of the Father of Glory, the author of wonders,*
> *As he, the eternal Ruler, established them from the beginning.*
> *He first created the heavens for the children of men*
> *As a sheltering roof, O holy Creator.*
> *Then the eternal Ruler, the guardian of mankind,*
> *Gave to men the earth as a dwelling place.*
> *He is the Father Almighty . . .*

In this way Caedmon began his short and fruitful career of song. He became a monk and began to set whole books of the Bible, beginning with *Genesis*, to the music of the harp. The Venerable Bede says he sang the Exodus and the journey to the promised land, "and he sang too of the Lord's Incarnation, Passion, Resurrection, and Ascension into heaven, the coming of the Holy Spirit, and the teaching of the apostles." He even founded a literary school. He was the beginning; then came the flood.

Caedmon may not have written the surviving Anglo-Saxon religious epics known as the "Caedmonian cycle," but he clearly influenced them. In these epics Christ is "the bold leader," "the mighty warrior," the stern war-chief of the Christian *comitatus*, powerfully built, bending all nature to his divine will, half-brother to Beowulf. The sounds are harsh and urgent. *Nunc laudate Dominum coeli* becomes *Nu sculon herigean heofonrices Weard*. The new language has developed muscle and weight; it flows like the waves of stormy seas, while the Latin flows like molten metal. Christ is seen emerging from the winter mists, huge, powerful, and demanding, and we are far from Rome.

Just as the Florentine artists of the Renaissance painted Christ walking in the villages of Tuscany, so the Anglo-Saxon poets depicted him marching through England at the head of his war-host. When they uttered prayers to God, they described their own land, which God had blessed, and the recital of blessings included a natural English gift for portraying a landscape. Here Caedmon or one of his followers puts into the mouths of the holy men of Israel a prayer which is wholly English:

> *May the wonder of earthly skill and all labors,*
> *May the heavens and angels bless Thee, gracious Father!*
> *And the clear waters which by just decree*
> *Abide in glory above the heavens, they honor Thee;*
> *And all creatures, and the shining stars in the sky,*
> *Holding their courses, the sun and the moon,*
> *May all in their degrees praise Thee, Almighty!*
> *The stars of heaven, the dews and sweet rain,*
> *May they glorify Thee, and may the souls praise Thee.*
> *Almighty God, may burning fire and shining summer*
> *Praise the Saviour, all night and day,*
> *And may all lands in light and darkness, in heat and cold,*
> *Praise Thee in their degrees, and may frosts and snows*
> *And bitter winter storms and the coursing of the clouds,*
> *May they all praise Thee on high, Almighty Lord.*
> *And may the lightning flashes, swift and gleaming,*

Praise Thee, and all the faces of the earth,
The hills and plains and high mountains,
Salt waves, the flood and surge of the deep-sea waves,
And the rising of fountains, may they praise Thee,
Eternal Lord and righteous God.

(Daniel 362–85)

Again and again in these Christian epics we see the burned summer hills of England and the steaming forests, the sea all around. In
Exodus the passage of the Egyptian Army through the Red Sea becomes inextricably confused with memories of disasters nearer home.
A darkness menaces the Egyptian host; the mist rolls in; the huge
waves are red with blood; the screams of the dying can be heard on
the cliffs. "The war-shields flashed; the wall of water, the raging sea-
stream, rose over the heroes."

In the Christian epics angels wear the clothes of sailors and the
swans' road leads to Christ. "The green field stands in God's keeping," says the author of *Guthlac*, a visionary poem about an English
hermit who waged a relentless war against demons, but it is only
rarely that we see the green fields in the calm summer light; the
sounds of war and the crash of waves are constantly ringing in the
ears of the poets. When Guthlac dies, the mist comes in, thick and
palpable:

So did the holy one's breath mount up
The livelong day till evening,
Then the bright splendor sank away,
And the black northern sky lay dark under clouds.
The world lay wrapped in mist, darkness everywhere.
Night came rushing over the world,
Over the jewels of the earth.

(Guthlac 1276–82)

The mists and fevers of the North had entered English poetry,
never entirely to leave it. Doom and the torments of the damned are
contemplated with lingering awe; in the dark house of death, souls on
fire reel in their drunken dance. The Anglo-Saxon poets found comfort in the Day of Judgment attended by a full orchestra of battle
sounds:

A shout sounds through the great Creation; before the Lord
There sweeps the greatest of raging fires over the wide earth.

The hot flame hurtles; the heavens crash; the stars
Tumble from their places, the steadfast and shining ones.
The sun, which shone brightly over the ancient world,
Shedding its light on the sons of men, turns the color of blood,
And the moon also, which illumined mankind in the night,
Sinks away, and the stars are swept hither and thither
By the force of a hurricane in the storm-laden air . . .
Over the wide earth the peal of heaven's trumpet sounds,
And the winds howl on seven sides in an uproar,
And the world withers away in the blast of heaven.
All the creatures of earth are riddled with fear.
Then there is heard the heaviest of crashes,
Loud, immense, deafening, beyond all hearing,
Most terrible of all.

(*Christ III* 930–40, 947–55)

For page after page the poet exults in the Day of Judgment, taking courage from the very violence of his imagination. The mountains melt away, the cliffs fall into the sea, the walls of cities become rubble, the waters burn like wax. The poet notes that all the sea monsters die in agony, and he ponders with satisfaction the ultimate fate of "the adornments of gold, all the ancient treasure of earthly kings." But it is that loud crash of Doomsday which provides him with his keenest excitement.

The imagination of the Anglo-Saxon poets was colored by ancient Nordic myths. The gods of Scandinavia wear the borrowed robes of Christ, who "swings the victor-sword in his hand" as relentlessly as Thor wielded his hammer. They describe the disasters which are visited upon the earth with delirious enjoyment. Latin verse, with its precise metrics and monumental calm, never reaches these heights.

Of the poet Cynwulf, we know only what he has consented to tell us in his poems. He bore a common name, and seems to have been aware of his uncommon power, for he signed his name in runic letters to four of his poems, including *Christ*, which was his masterpiece. In *Elene* he tells us that he came late to Christian poetry, but in his youth achieved some fame as a singer, receiving apples of gold from his lord. He speaks of much wandering on horseback, and hints at battles in which he fought. He must have read widely, for his poems echo the homilies and sermons of the Fathers of the Church, especially Gregory and Ambrose. What he read was assimilated into his poetry, becoming wholly his own. He writes in words not to be engraved on marble but in letters of fire across the heavens.

While *Christ* remains the supreme achievement of Anglo-Saxon religious poetry, *The Dream of the Rood* with its vision of the Cross towering in the heavens and drenched in the Saviour's blood, illuminating the universe with its radiance, comes so close to perfection that it would be difficult to find any verses to equal them in visionary power. The vision of the tree gleaming with gold and jewels, and wet with blood, has no known source outside his own works; and in the telling of the vision there is an urgency and deliberation which suggests that he had no need to consult the works of others, for it was something he had seen with his own eyes.

> *At midnight on a dark night I lay dreaming*
> *With men around me, and then I saw*
> *The marvellous Tree high in the air,*
> *So bright was its shining, all clothed in light.*
> *Wonderful the sign all patterned in gold;*
> *Jewels were set in it, some at its feet,*
> *Five on the crossbeam blazed with strange splendor.*
> *Throughout all Creation the holy angels*
> *Gazed at the glory, the Cross without shame,*
> *And the holy spirits and all men everywhere*
> *And all of Creation gazed on its shining.*
> *O wonderful the Tree, the emblem of victory,*
> *And I, a transgressor stained with sin,*
> *I, too, looked upon the Tree gleaming so joyously,*
> *Arrayed in brightness and laced with gold,*
> *The Cross of the Saviour studded with jewels.*
> *Yet through the gold work there could be seen*
> *The ancient evil encompassed by sinful men:*
> *On the right of the Cross the wound of bleeding.*
> *So, troubled by sorrow and trembling with terror,*
> *I saw the Tree, the adorable vision,*
> *Now stained with wetness, the flowing of blood,*
> *Now glowing with treasure, now laced with gold.*
>
> (*The Dream of the Rood*, 1–23)

The Tree speaks to the poet and tells how Christ, the young hero, stripped before he mounted the Cross. Naked among warriors, in sudden darkness, Christ fought on behalf of God, and was at last taken down, "wounded of limb," and gathered into the grave, "where he rested alone," before he was translated to heaven.

The heroic vision of the Anglo-Saxon poet ran counter to the traditional pieties of southern Europe. Christ as hero had his roots in ancient Scandinavia, not in Galilee; the jewel-like gleaming of the Tree derives perhaps from the sunlight sparkling on the northern snows. The Anglo-Saxon poets showed no particular affection for the Christian virtues of humility, charity, and obedience, and presented Christ as a warrior armed with formidable power. In Italy and France the Christian poets, weary of war, celebrated the kindliness of God and the more civilized virtues.

About the time that *The Dream of the Rood* was being composed, Charlemagne is said to have composed a poem in honor of the young poet Paul the Deacon. It is unlikely that Charlemagne wrote the poem attributed to him, but he may have permitted his name to be attached to it. The poem, found among the manuscripts of Monte Cassino, describes a traveler hurrying to return to the peace of a Benedictine monastery:

> *Speedily, my script, we climb through all the valleys,*
> *Up hills, through woods, searching for the gentle roof*
> *Of Benedict, who is beloved of God.*
> *So the tired travelers come to their certain peace,*
> *Being welcomed home with fish and abundant bread,*
> *And pious peace and humbleness, delightful concord of brothers,*
> *Love, praise, and the worship of Christ through all the hours.*

The poem seems to have been written with a single breath, so effortlessly does it flow. Yet there is much art in it, and much learning. The poet had read his Horace, and was evidently steeped in Latin literature. If Charlemagne did not write it, it was at least worthy of the school of poets he collected around him.

Some fifty years later Sedulius Scottus, an Irishman who lived most of his life in France, wrote an Easter song in Latin which opens with a resounding organ note: *Surrexit Christus sol verus vespere noctis.* From that wonderful beginning he goes on to paint the risen Sun, who is Christ, with a passion which is evidently unfeigned and overflowing with joy:

> *Christ the true Sun rose from the dark last night*
> *Amid the mystic harvest of the fields of God,*
> *And now the joyous crowd of wandering bees*
> *Is murmuring merrily among the honeyed flowers.*

The heavens are steeped with birdsong, and all night long
The plaints of nightingales were heard beyond the church,
Where now we sing the canticles of Zion,
A hundred voices chanting Alleluias.
O Father of us all, thine be the glory
Of the holy joy of Easter. Behold the light!

It is, of course, a scholar's lyric written at a time when scholars were busy rewriting Virgil and Horace, substituting churchmen for shepherds and nymphs. Scottus could write impudent verses asking a bishop for a keg of ale as easily as he wrote verses celebrating Christ. Verse writing was in danger of becoming a monkish habit. By the eleventh century it had become almost too easy, and Sigebert of Liège, where Scottus appears to have founded a school of poets, could write about martyrs trippingly:

> *Hinc virginalis sancta frequentia,*
> *Gertrudis, Agnes, Prisca, Cecilia,*
> *Lucia, Petronilla, Tecla,*
> *Agatha, Barbara, Juliana, . . .*

> *The holy virgins come in flocks:*
> *Gertrude, Agnes, Prisca, Cecily,*
> *Lucy, Petronel, Thecla,*
> *Agatha, Barbara, Juliana,*
> *And many others whose names I have not read,*
> *Or having read, no longer can recall.*
> *Worthy of God they were indeed*
> *Who died in wholeness of their faith.*
> *Now wandering through fresh fields they go,*
> *Seeking in all the tender unknown places*
> *Roses for Christ's passion,*
> *Lilies and violets of love.*

This poem, *The Passion of Saint Lucy*, was written to celebrate the translation of the relics of St. Lucy to Metz, but there is no passion, no sense of the blessedness of relics, in these decorous verses where the rhymes fall in place with an effect of cloying prettiness.

Perhaps it was inevitable: one suspects that the habit of writing pretty verses goes back to the earliest Christian times. By the tenth century rhymed hymns and devotional verses were commonplace, and henceforward there was no escape from the prison of rhyme.

The great hymns of the following centuries were all in rhyme; and if rhyme sometimes ornamented the verses, and gave depth and resonance to the words so that they had the effect of reverberations, nevertheless rhyme had its disadvantages. Rhyme is easy in Latin, and a facile poet could spin out interminable measures of rhymed verse in impeccable taste with no more effort than it took him to breathe.

The greatest hymns survived their rhymes by the fierce purity of their passion. There are always one or two verses where the rhymes possess a perfection of their own, entering the poem not because they are ornamental, but by right of conquest. *Veni, Sancte Spiritus*, written perhaps by a French monk about the year A.D. 1000, begins splendidly with an invocation to the Holy Spirit:

> *Veni, Sancte Spiritus,*
> *Et emitte coelitus*
> *Lucis tuae radium.*
> *Veni, pater pauperum,*
> *Veni, dator munerum,*
> *Veni, lumen cordium . . .*

> *O Holy Spirit, come*
> *And send down from Heaven*
> *The radiance of Thy light,*
> *Come, father of the poor,*
> *Come, granter of blessings,*
> *Come, light of our hearts . . .*

But long before we have reached the last verse, the passion has become subservient to the rhyme. Such things are to be expected in hymns which take the form of invocations with lengthy enumeration of God's titles and attributes, but they are less pardonable in hymns concerning divine events. Too often the hymn-writer appears to be gazing at a religious painting, describing over and over again what he sees there. After the first magnificent lines of *Stabat Mater*,

> *Stabat Mater dolorosa,*
> *Juxta crucem lacrimosa,*
> *Dum pendebat Filius.*

> *The dolorous Mother stands*
> *Weeping beside the Cross,*
> *While her Son hangs. . . .*

the same theme is repeated with only minor variations through twenty verses. There is no movement, no sense of a purpose being accomplished. The Mother sorrows, the sword of grief drives through her, the devout observer offers to share her grief, and the rhymes follow one another for no discernible reason and in no discernible pattern. The glory is in the first verse; none of the remaining verses reach that height.

Stabat Mater was written by Jacopone da Todi, the greatest of the Franciscan poets. He belonged to the noble family of the Benedetti, studied law at the University of Bologna, and then returned to Todi to live the life of a landowner and a cultivated man about town. He was nearly forty when he married the beautiful Vanna di Guidone: not long after the marriage she was crushed to death when a platform fell during a dancing party. Grief-stricken, he turned furiously to religion. He would embrace anyone he met "for the love of Christ," and he would throw his arms round a tree and whisper blessings to it and kiss it passionately, as St. Francis kissed the stones that hurt his feet. He wanted to enter the Franciscan order, but at first the Franciscans would have none of him, thinking him a madman. At last he was permitted to enter the convent of San Fortunato at Todi. He became an exemplary friar, orderly and precise, the days of madness over, and soon he became the leader of the Spirituals who denounced the Church and sought to return to the original rule of St. Francis. A satire directed against Boniface VIII led to his imprisonment in a dungeon at Palestrina. He was not tortured, but nearly starved to death, and in later years he would complain against the sharpness of the stones in his cell. He remained in prison from 1298 to 1303, the year of the death of Boniface. Three years later, prematurely old, he died in the convent of the Poor Clares at Collazzone, a village near Todi, and a hundred years later he was buried in a magnificent tomb in the convent at San Fortunato. The inscription read: "Here lies a fool in Christ who cheated the world with the novelty of his art and took Heaven by storm."

Jacopone's Latin poems smell of the lamp; when he wrote in his native Umbrian dialect he was all fire and energy. *Stabat Mater* moves in a small circle round a single point, but he could write of Mary at the foot of the Cross with a wonderful directness, as though he stood beside her. In this poem he is no longer gazing at a painting on the wall, but at the Cross itself:

Son Thy soul has flown
Son of the loneliness
Son of the overthrown
Son bruised by sin of men.

Son so pure and white
Son who is peerless
Son I call unto Thee
Son I am dispossessed.

Son so white and red
Son with laughing face
Son why did all the world
Heap curses upon Thee?

Son so sweet and gay
Son O sorrowing one
Son why did all these men
Sentence Thee to death?

John is my new son.
Dead is your brother.
I feel the falling earth
And the earth cut down.

O Son and Mother slain
Dumb death has vanquished us
Mother and Son together
Are frozen on the Cross.

In such a simple way, the dead Mother and the dead Son brought into the sharpest focus, Jacopone described a scene incomparably richer and more tender than the scene described in *Stabat Mater*. In much the same way he would describe a Nativity, a Transfiguration, or simply an encounter with Jesus in a cornfield, or a man drunk with love. He could write single lines that have the power of echoing and reechoing down the centuries. *"Ordina quest' Amore, o tu che m'ami,"* he wrote in one of his *laudes*. "Set Love in order, thou that lovest Me." The poem was attributed for many years to St. Francis, for it seemed hardly possible that so angelic a poem could be written by anyone else.

Yet it was not Jacopone da Todi but another Franciscan, Thomas de Celano, the friend and biographer of St. Francis, who wrote the greatest of the hymns of the Middle Ages, a hymn so starkly heroic and so visionary, filled with such anguish and hope, that even today, when we are accustomed to the belief that the Last Days are very close to us, it can stir the blood and send the mind reeling. The hymn roars as though it came out of the mouth of the lion. Perhaps never before or since have the shuddering and the terror been expressed so poignantly, and so accurately:

> *Dies irae, dies illa*
> *Solvet saeclum in favilla,*
> *Teste David cum sibylla.*

The slow drumbeat is announced in the opening verse, and it gathers momentum and force through all the ensuing verses. There is no movement around a fixed point, but a steady, all-encompassing rush toward the flames. The hymn cannot be translated into English verse, and it is better to render it in prose:

> *The day of wrath, the very day that will dissolve the world in ashes, as David and the Sibyl prophesied.*

> *How great the trembling when the Judge shall come to draw up his strict accounts!*

> *The trumpet spreading a wondrous sound through the sepulchres of the whole world will gather everyone before the throne.*

> *Death and Nature will stand aghast when Creation rises again to confront the Judge.*

> *The written book will be brought forth, wherein is contained everything by which the world will be judged.*

> *When the Judge is seated, whatever is hidden will be revealed; none shall go unpunished.*

> *What then shall I say in my wretchedness? What protector shall I appeal to, when even the righteous will barely be saved?*

King of awful Majesty, who savest freely those who are to be saved, save me, O fount of mercy!

Remember, O loving Jesus, that for my sake Thou didst walk the earth. Let me not be lost on that day.

When seeking me, Thou didst sit down in weariness. Thou didst redeem me from the Cross. Let not that labor be in vain.

Righteous Judge of vengeance, grant the gift of pardon before the day of reckoning.

I groan like one condemned, my face reddens with shame. O God, spare the suppliant.

Thou who didst absolve Mary and didst pardon the thief, to me also thou hast given hope.

My prayers are not worthy, but do thou in Thy goodness graciously grant that I shall not burn in the everlasting fire.

Grant me a place among the sheep and separate me from the goats, placing me at Thy right hand.

When the wicked are in confusion, consigned to the bitter flames, call to me among the blessed.

Humble on my knees I pray, my contrite heart like ashes. Have compassion on me in my last hour.

This will be the day of tears, when the guilty rise from the ashes to be judged. Therefore spare them, O God.

O Lord, merciful Jesus, grant them rest.

In this hymn the King of awful Majesty, *Rex tremendae Majestatis*, hovers over the fading earth, power streaming from his five-bladed hands. He saves freely those who are to be saved, consigns to ultimate perdition those who are guilty, and stands in exalted majesty like one remote from human preoccupations. He alone bends the bow of the universe, and there is no hint of the Comforter.

The power of the hymn derives from the fact that it is at once an exaltation of divine omnipotence and a stately march toward the Last Day, a requiem and a prayer. It is a drama in which the whole human race is involved, although only Mary and the thief on the Cross are mentioned. The grave music speaks of peace and ultimate blessedness, but the words are concerned with the terror and anguish of the human heart, the sense of desolation which comes to men who believe they may be abandoned by God in their last hour. Mercy is very far away, almost beyond hope, yet it is there.

With the *Dies Irae* we are altogether beyond the range of the hymns and songs composed in previous centuries. Quite suddenly, like a flare illuminating all creation, the voice of God can be heard, and almost we see his face. The stark judgment is about to be received, the lips of God are about to open. The feeling is wholly Byzantine: and indeed Umbria preserved Byzantine traditions long after they were forgotten in Rome. Though *Dies Irae* was written a few years later than the *Canticle of the Sun*, it belongs to an earlier age, to the age of the dark Romanesque churches and the Byzantine basilicas with their mosaic portraits of the *Rex tremendae Majestatis* high in the dome. But there is a sense in which it is ageless, belonging to no time, being the ultimate hymn, the consummation of centuries of Christian song. Beyond this it is impossible to go.

25 ✠ THE CRUSADES

THE UNKNOWN knight who wrote the *Gesta Francorum*, which recounts the adventures of the pilgrims to Jerusalem during the First Crusade, never wondered how it all began. He had a direct and simple mind, singularly free of complexities. He begins his narrative with the calm statement that the time had come, of which Jesus spoke when He said:: "If any man will come after me, let him deny himself, and take up his cross, and follow me," and because the time had come, there was a great stirring among the Franks to take the road to the Holy Sepulchre as quickly as possible. Overnight the Franks were sewing the cross on their right shoulders and marching off to Palestine.

Why in the late autumn of 1095 there should have been this sudden desire to invade the East and to set in motion so many campaigns with so many unpredictable consequences was of no concern to him. For him it was a very simple matter: the time had come. Beyond this he made no inquiries, though he notes in passing that Pope Urban II offered the Crusaders no earthly rewards, only "misery, poverty, nakedness, persecution, need, sickness, hunger, thirst, and many other sufferings." The time had come for the Christians to suffer for the sake of Christ such agonies as they had never endured before.

The author of the *Gesta Francorum* was a knight without a fief, neither rich nor poor, a devout layman, conscientious and scrupulous. He did not thirst for glory: the Crusade was a job to be done, an agony to be endured. As he tells his story, describing the battles as he saw them and the decisions of the great princes as they were told to him around the camp fires—for he took only a minor part in the

334

war—he gives an impression of complete honesty and sincerity. He was often confused. He rarely knew the real reasons for the decisions made by his leaders, but being himself scrupulous he knew very well when they were being unscrupulous; and when it became evident to him that his feudal lord, Bohemond, Prince of Taranto, was more interested in establishing a principality for himself in Antioch than waging war against the infidel and capturing the Holy Sepulchre for Christians, he left the Prince's service. He was a man with very few illusions.

If we watch the unfolding of the Crusade through the eyes of this knight, who left by far the most vivid account to have survived, we are at once confronted with the fact that thousands and perhaps hundreds of thousands of Crusaders were men of good faith who asked nothing for themselves, lived reasonably virtuous lives, loved God, and felt a compelling need to safeguard the Holy Sepulchre. That the Holy Sepulchre was in the hands of the infidel was sufficient reason for making the arduous journey. Greed, ambition, lust, cruelty, and murder played their inevitable part, but the purpose of the campaign, as seen by the rank and file, was a simple and honorable one.

The great princes who commanded the Crusaders were not simple men, nor were they particularly honorable. Their desires and rivalries caused them to embark on wild and dangerous adventures, to break their vows with impunity, and to stop at nothing in their determination to carve out kingdoms for themselves. Godfrey of Bouillon, whom Gibbon regarded as a man of fierce probity, thought nothing of breaking a solemn oath to the Emperor Alexius, and Bohemond, who became the acknowledged commander-in-chief of the campaign, thought nothing of attacking cities already in the hands of his allies. National rivalries were continually threatening to break up the loose federation of the Crusaders; and sometimes the leaders hated one another more than they hated the enemy.

One man, and one alone, set the Crusades in motion. This was Urban II, a tall, heavy-set man of French descent, born in Châtillon-sur-Marne, near Rheims, of a family of the nobility. He entered a monastery of the Cluniac order, interested himself in delicate diplomatic negotiations, and was soon summoned to Rome. He was a man of a commanding presence with a gift for oratory; he was charming and indulgent, and famous for his thick golden beard. He had a sharp tongue for emperors and kings, and when in the summer of 1095 he left Rome and journeyed across the Alps into France, his main purpose seems to have been to excommunicate the French king for offenses committed against the Church. He had been elected pope in 1088 during the schismatic pontificate of the antipope Guilbert, who was acknowledged by the German Emperor Henry IV. Guilbert was in possession of the Holy See, and although Urban II was the lawful pope, he was without possessions or power, a wanderer on the face of the earth. Intelligent, fearless, and unscrupulous, he knew that in order to maintain his pontificate he must act with great boldness. Of earthly monarchs who might help him to advance his cause, there was only the Byzantine Emperor Alexius Comnenus, whose armies were then being torn to pieces by the Seljuk Turks. The power of Byzantium would come to the aid of the Roman Pontiff; the Roman Pontiff would come to the aid of Byzantium. In November 1095 Urban summoned a council at Clermont in the Auvergne and announced that it was the duty of all Christians to go to the aid of the beleagured emperor in Byzantium. Salvation lay in wresting back the lands lost to the Turks.

Urban spoke not in Latin, but in the romance language spoken by the French. He was speaking as a Frenchman to Frenchmen, but he was also speaking as the Supreme Pontiff to the emperor in Byzantium. His task was to defend Christendom, and to throw the weight of French knighthood against the Seljuks who were converting the churches of Asia Minor into mosques and committing unspeakable crimes on the Christians who fell into their hands. He commanded and threatened. He reminded his audience that he was not speaking for himself, but came to them as a messenger to whom the divine command had been revealed. He repeated over and over again that he spoke in God's name—"It is not I but God who beseeches and exhorts you as heralds of Christ," he declared. He went on to make a special appeal to the French knights, reminding them that they were spending their energy on private feuds, and it was time for them to stop killing the faithful: their task was to kill the infidels. "When the winter is over and the spring comes, let them set out with cheerful hearts to take the road under the guidance of the Lord."

Of the many chroniclers who reported his speech only one, Fulcher of Chartres, was present at Clermont. In Fulcher's account nothing was said about conquering Jerusalem and the Holy Sepulchre. The danger was nearer home. According to Fulcher, Urban spoke of the need to defend the Bosphorus, then known as the Arm of St. George. It was there that the armies of the faithful were commanded to gather in order to roll back the Seljuks from Asia Minor.

A pope without an army, without a throne, was summoning into existence the greatest European army known up to that time. At his bidding perhaps half a million people set out for Constantinople during the following year.

As Fulcher records Urban's speech at Clermont, it does not seem calculated to inflame the masses. He spoke with the authority of God's vice-regent on earth, wearer of the triple crown, and pontiff of the whole world, but these were merely titles which he claimed from his election. What gave his words strength and power was his claim that he spoke out of a direct revelation from God. As he stood on a platform erected in a field to the east of Clermont on that cold autumn day, he was less the pontiff than the newly revealed prophet of a new dispensation. He was another Isaiah calling the world to judgment.

The speech was not published; no written copies were prepared for the attending bishops and prelates; nor was it necessary for it to be put in writing in that age when men could memorize long epics. The bishops, returning to their sees, communicated it to their priests, the wandering preachers communicated it to the people in the market places and fairgrounds, and soon there was scarcely anyone in France who did not think he knew what Urban said. In the process Urban's words were embroidered. Obvious traces of embroidery appear in the chronicles of Guibert of Nogent, Balderic of Dol, and Robert the Monk, all of them writing many years later, all of them reciting the speech and offering widely different versions. The popular imagination has gone to work. The chroniclers put into his mouth curious catalogues of the tortures inflicted by the Seljuks on the Christians: how their bowels were cut open with a sword, and their intestines pulled out and slit, so that what was hidden there could be revealed. We hear of the Seljuks befouling the altars with excrement and forcibly circumcising Christians and pouring the blood of the circumcision on the altars. Such things may have happened, but it is unlikely that Urban would have addressed himself to them. The unknown knight of the *Gesta Francorum* says that he offered men the twelfth century equivalent of "blood, toil, tears, and sweat." These are sufficient rewards for the adventurous.

With his speech Urban set in motion the machinery of the Crusade, which was to continue for two hundred years before it finally ground to a halt. In those years Europe and the Near East witnessed a strange quickening, and there is a sense in which the confrontation between the Cross and the Crescent brought about an increase in the vital forces working on the two civilizations. Renewed direction and purpose were given to two civilizations which had little in common except the desire to possess a small strip of land between the Dead Sea and the Mediterranean, and especially the city of Jerusalem set in its barren wilderness. There was something curiously unreal in those scattered and episodic combats, as though dreams were marching among nightmares. Men became legends overnight. The pace was quickening. Europe, which had built a wall against the East, suddenly became aware of a vast treasure house hitherto hidden from sight.

The leaders of the First Crusade were Norman princes only a few generations removed from their ancestral homes in the fiords of Norway, while the Arabs in the Holy Land were only a few generations removed from the desert. Many wars were fought by the warriors who took part in the Crusades, but the least predictable of those wars was the one fought by Norway against Arabia. The arctic was making war against the tropics.

Bohemond, Prince of Taranto, was one of those adventurers who spring out of obscurity to take command of important events and bend history to their will. Anna Comnena, the daughter of the Byzantine Emperor Alexius I Comnenus, had ample opportunity to see him at court, and she described him as though he were a new kind of man possessed of incalculable gifts and devoid of many of the sentiments commonly held by men. He appeared to her as the living embodiment of ruthless power and heroic splendor. She might have been describing Achilles when she wrote:

Never before had any man like him, either barbarian or Greek, been seen in the land of the Byzantines, for the sight of him created admiration and his reputation invoked fear. Let me describe the appearance of the barbarian in detail. He was so tall that he overtopped the tallest by a cubit, and he was slender, not at all stout, with wide shoulders, a well-developed chest and strong arms. His person as a whole was neither gaunt nor corpulent, but in conformity, one might say, with the canon of Polycleitus. He had strong hands and a firm stance, with a robust neck and build. . . . Was his beard red or some other color? I could not say, for the razor had passed over it, leaving a surface as smooth as marble; yet it certainly seemed to be red. His blue eyes expressed both courage and dignity. He breathed freely through his nose and his nostrils, his chest was in keeping with his nostrils and his nostrils with his wide chest.

There was about this warrior a certain charm, though partly spoilt by something frightening that emanated from him. For the whole man, in every part of his person, alike in his stature and his glance, was hard and wild, and even his laugh made those about him shiver. Body and soul, he was so made that in him courage and love were barbed and both were turned toward war. His mind was supple, full of guile, and rich in subterfuge on all occasions.

What Anna Comnena had detected in Bohemond was the berserk fury of the Northmen, a fearful eagerness for violence, any violence. He had not the least interest in the Crusade as a Crusade; he scoffed at the minor miracles which attended the progress of the Crusaders; and he quarreled with everyone. What he wanted above all was to carve out a principality of his own, to fight champions worthy of his steel, and to scratch on the rock of history a mark so deep that it would not easily be erased. He acquired the principality of Antioch, saved the Crusaders by his daring engagements with the Seljuks, and took no part at all in the conquest of Jerusalem. Having poured his energy into leading the Crusade across Asia Minor, he abruptly abandoned the struggle and permitted lesser men to reap the glory.

Such things continually happened during the Crusaders' strange battles in the East. Leaders of great accomplishment, like Prince Bohemond and King Richard the Lion-Heart, arose, engaged the enemy, fought with astonishing skill, and abruptly departed from the battlefield, as though they could no longer reach out toward the promised land. There was a failure of nerve, a willful display of ill-temper, a sudden inadequacy. Such men quarreled with themselves and with each other. From the beginning to the end it was a war with too many leaders all vying for the place of honor. Those who became kings of Jerusalem were sometimes the weaklings who took possession of the throne unobserved while the great champions were fighting elsewhere.

While Bohemond represented to an extraordinary degree the energy of the West descending violently on the East, Godfrey of Bouillon, Duke of Lower Lorraine, represented the essential piety and reasonableness of the western mind. Bohemond was a thunder-cloud, larger than life, and Godfrey was merely a man attempting to perform his duty. He was not among the great princes who led the Crusade. He was a staff officer rather than a general, content to work out battle plans, and he liked to assume a subordinate place. He sold all his possessions in order to equip his knights and to take part in the expedition, and he was as devoted to the cause as Bohemond was devoted to nothing except his own power. Godfrey built one of the siege towers which led to the fall of Jerusalem, and showed himself to be an excellent tactician. He was not responsible for the terrible butchery which occurred when the Crusaders, nearly mad with thirst, finally broke into the holy city. Eight days later he was offered the crown, but refused it, saying that he would wear no crown of gold where Christ had worn a crown of thorns. Wearing only a white shift, barefoot, he entered the Holy Sepulchre and assumed the title of Advocate of the Holy Sepulchre, which in his eyes was the highest title that any man could aspire to.

Nevertheless he had founded a dynasty which was to endure for nearly a century. The grave, quiet, cautious man, who looked like a priest, took command while his knights quarreled, and the difficulties of maintaining a kingdom in a hostile land only made him more determined to make Jerusalem a Christian city

Shortly after the conquest of Jerusalem he launched a sudden attack on Askelon, then occupied by the Egyptians. The battle began at dawn and was soon over. The Egyptian emir fled, leaving behind his jeweled sword and silver standard surmounted by a golden apple. A vast booty fell into the hands of the Crusaders, who quarreled so violently among themselves over the treasure that they never penetrated into the heart of the city, which they lost as soon as it was won. For fifty more years Askelon remained in the possession of the Egyptians.

For the first time the Crusaders were presented with the problem which was to confront them throughout the history of their settlement in Outremer: to conquer a city, and to keep it, were two entirely different matters. They never had sufficient man-power and their leaders were often at odds with one another. They made sudden raids, acquired booty, commanded the highways between Egypt and Syria, made alliances with local emirs, and lived continually on the edge of catastrophe. They built prodigious fortresses, but could man them with only a handful of dependable knights. Treachery was in the air. It was something they lived with, as commonplace as silk raiment and the habits of chivalry, which they largely learned from the Arabs.

With Godfrey there began that strange and vivid flowering of the western mind, which was brought about by the sudden transplantation of priests, knights, and adventurers to a foreign land. The influence of these small communities on western thought was out of all proportion to their number. The very climate seemed to affect them with new modes of thought, new habits, new desires. New medicines, borrowed from the pharmacopoeia of the Moslems, were introduced into Europe, and Moslem skills in architecture, drainage, painting, and landscape gardening subtly influenced the West. The Crusaders took on the protective coloring of the country, and submitted all too eagerly to the refinements of Arab life. They wore flowing gowns, rested on divans, hung silk curtains on their walls, and covered their floors with Persian rugs, and their sideboards with intricate copper and silver dishes. They learned to speak Arabic, and sometimes they became more Arab than the Arabs. And they suffered from the strange processes of alienation which arise when a man lives in a country where he has no roots.

Gradually they were able to put down roots and evolve a genuine civilization of their own. The Kingdom of Jerusalem, although hemmed in by enemy tribes, proved to be enduring. The early kings were wise and cautious men who knew how to maintain the loyalty of their subjects. Godfrey died in 1100 and was succeeded by his brother Baldwin, the first to assume the kingly title. Baldwin I had once been a clerk in orders, and like his brother he was one of those grave and serious men who inspire confidence. He captured Caesarea, Acre, and Beirut, thus greatly extending the kingdom to the north, and he was the first to bring about an alliance with an Italian city. Just as the Venetians enjoyed a favored position in Byzantium, so now the Genoese enjoyed a favored position in the Kingdom of Jerusalem, receiving a share of the booty and exemption from tolls in exchange for their assistance. For thirty years, under Baldwin I and his nephew Baldwin II, the fortunes of the kingdom prospered. There were lucky accidents. Sigurd of Norway came to the Holy Land in

1107 with a fleet of fifty-five ships manned by Vikings who thirsted for battle, and thus the kingdom acquired a fleet. Sidon was captured; so was Aila, at the head of the eastern arm of the Dead Sea; and in the reign of King Fulk, who married Melisinda, the daughter of Baldwin II, the kingdom extended to the east of the Dead Sea, where the great fortress of Krak of the Desert controlled the trade route from Damascus to the Red Sea. In these three reigns the kingdom achieved its greatest extent. Thereafter it was to grow smaller, inchmeal, shrinking a little day by day, as the will grew weaker and the strength lessened.

There were ten kings of Jerusalem during the first hundred years of the Crusades. With two exceptions they were all men of grace and authority, scholarly and eloquent. One of the most successful was the handsome young boy king Baldwin IV, who came to the throne at the age of thirteen only to discover three years later that he was afflicted with leprosy. He died at the age of twenty-four, but his short reign demonstrated an astonishing resurgence of Christian power in the Holy Land. The sixteen-year-old king led one of the most daring and successful attacks against Saladin. With some 3,000 troops, including knights and footsoldiers, he broke out of encircled Askelon and attacked Saladin's army in the ravine at Montgisard and annihilated it. There were 30,000 in Saladin's army; only a handful succeeded in making their way to Egypt. Saladin himself was saved only by his bodyguard, which swept him away from the ravine to the Sinai desert where he survived thirst and the treachery of the Bedouins by a miracle. Saladin respected his adversaries, and three years later, in 1180, he signed a truce with the ailing king, who was already pleading to be relieved of a burden too heavy for him.

The victory at Montgisard was the last great victory won by the Crusaders. Thereafter the Crusaders suffered defeat after defeat.

Seven years later came defeat on the Horns of Hattin, overlooking the Sea of Galilee. Baldwin IV had died, and the succession had passed to his brother-in-law, Guy de Lusignan, the husband of his sister Sybilla. The new king was hot-headed, treacherous, and according to the chroniclers of the time, *simplex et insufficiens*, meaning perhaps that there were no depths in him and that he was ill-equipped to deal with the tasks imposed on a king of Jerusalem. Among his closest advisers was another adventurer, Raynald de Châtillon, Prince of Antioch, who had been granted the fortress of Krak of the Desert. The fortress, as we have seen, dominated the great trade and pilgrim routes from Damascus to Egypt, and Raynald de Châtillon, in defiance of the treaties between Christians and Muslims, exacted tribute from the pilgrims who crossed his territory and he plundered the caravans. He built a fleet, and even made an attempt to raid Mecca and Medina, thus attacking Islam at its source. In 1186 he attacked a caravan in which the sister of Saladin was traveling, and the Muslims, who had been prepared to accept the truce, saw no reason to keep it any longer when the Christians were breaking it at their pleasure. They had permitted infidels to live in the Holy Land, but they were not prepared to permit highwaymen to exact tribute from them. They declared a *jehad*, a holy war.

Baldwin IV was a shining light of Christendom; Raynald de Châtillon was one of those dark and inscrutable figures who leave on the pages of history the shadowy evidence of their many treacheries. Saladin attacked in force, and the army of Raynald and Guy de Lusignan was destroyed on the Horns of Hattin in a battle so terrible that it haunted the Crusaders throughout the remaining years of their occupation of the Holy Land.

On July 1, 1187, Saladin had captured the Crusader base at Tiberias on the Sea of Galilee. The Crusader army reached Sepphoris near Nazareth, determined to avenge the loss of Tiberias. The True Cross, ornamented with jewels, was brought from Jerusalem to lead the army to victory. Now at long last they believed they could destroy Saladin, who had so nearly been destroyed at Montgisard. In the expectation of a quick victory the Crusaders marched in the direction of the Sea of Galilee.

From the beginning there were omens of disaster, quarrels among the leaders, inexplicable treacheries. They left the sweet wells of Sepphoris behind them and in straggling columns entered the stony, barren, and parched hills of Jebel Turan, camping on the night of July 3 on the heights known as the Horns of Hattin, not far from a famous sanctuary dedicated to Jethro. On the foothills below Jesus was believed to have spoken to the multitudes.

All that night the Crusaders suffered from thirst, for it seemed that no one had troubled to bring water because the Sea of Galilee was so close. Saladin's army marched toward the Horns of Hattin and set up their camp not far from the Crusaders. That night the soldiers of both sides slept on the ground within earshot of one another, and in the morning the Saracens withdrew a little along the slopes, leaving the Crusaders on the high ground between the horns, thirsty, crying out for the water which never came, while the sun shone out of the pitiless blue sky and the lake beckoned. About ten o'clock in the morning five treacherous knights from the household of the Count of Tripoli rode to Saladin's headquarters with information about the plight of the Crusaders, and not long afterward the Count of Tripoli led his remaining knights down the hillside against a Saracen army, which merely parted to let the Crusaders pass through their lines, and then formed ranks again, cutting up that small detachment of cavalry at their leisure. Soon the Saracens were setting fire to the brush on the parched uplands, and the Crusaders were choking in the smoke and deafened by the roaring of the fire and the shouts of the Saracens, who spent the afternoon driving them into the flames. By nightfall the Saracens had captured the True Cross, the King of Jerusalem, Raynald de Châtillon, nearly all the treasure of the Crusaders, and their supply trains. Saladin had avenged Montgisard. On the Horns of Hattin an entire army lay dead, and no triumph could be sweeter.

The scene of the surrender has been brilliantly described by the Arab historian ibn-Sheddad. Raynald de Châtillon and the King of Jerusalem were brought to Saladin's tent. Because the king was suffering from thirst, Saladin offered him a bowl of sherbet made with iced rose water. The king drank a little and then handed the bowl to Raynald. Saladin, who was watching closely, saw that he had been placed at a disadvantage, for by immemorial custom he could not kill a guest who accepted food from his hands. He explained to the king that the bowl of rose water was intended for him, and for him alone; Raynald could expect no mercy. Then he dismissed the prisoners and deliberated with himself about their fate. Here is ibn-Sheddad's account of the next few moments:

At this time there were only a few servants in the tent. The King was ordered to stand at the tent-gate, but the Prince (Raynald) was summoned into the presence, and thereupon Saladin reminded him of what he had previously said, adding: "Behold, I will support Muhammad against thee!" He then called upon the prince to embrace Islam, and when the prince refused, he drew a sword and struck him a blow which severed the arm from the shoulder. This was the signal for the servants to despatch the prisoner, and God hurled his soul into hell.

And when the corpse was dragged away and thrown out of the tent-gate, the King saw how his companion had been treated and thought he would be the next victim, but the Sultan brought him into the tent and calmed his fears.

"It is not the habit of kings," said Saladin, "to kill kings. That man transgressed all bounds, and that is why he was killed."

And all that night the conquerors rejoiced and chanted the praises of God until the dawn came, and then the Sultan went down to Tiberias.[1]

For Saladin the victory was complete, and it remained only to capture the Crusader fortresses. In the following weeks one fortress after another fell—Acre, Nablus, Haifa, Caesarea, Sepphoris, Nazareth, Beirut. Failing to capture Tyre, Saladin marched on Askelon, and then turned his attention to Jerusalem, which fell on October 2. The Christians, who had expected the same treatment which was meted out to the Muslims and Jews when they conquered the city under Godfrey, were surprised to learn that by command of Saladin they would be allowed to go free. Each man paid a ransom of ten Tyrian dinars, each woman five dinars, each child one dinar. The penniless were allowed to go without paying. The huge gilded cross above the Dome of the Rock was thrown down, and in its place there rose the crescent of Islam.

History has dealt kindly with Saladin. It is remembered of him that he was often sweet-tempered, gentle, and chivalrous, and that he formed enduring friendships with the Crusader captains. That he rose to power by killing everyone in his path, and was capable of the same treacheries as the Crusaders was generally forgotten. What distinguished him from others was his calm, his physical beauty, and a certain adroitness of gesture; he could think largely; and he acted with terrible speed. When he died, his sword was placed beside his body and buried with him. "His sword," says the pious chronicler, "accompanied him to Paradise." He was the only Muslim who entered Paradise fully armed.

The wars continued. Though they had lost most of their fortresses in Syria and Palestine, Antioch, Tripoli, and Tyre remained in the possession of the Crusaders and served as strong points for the

[1] Beha Ed-din ibn Sheddad, *The Life of Saladin*, London, Palestine Exploration Fund, 1897, p. 115.

continuing adventure of reconquest. Because Acre lay only a few miles south of Tyre, it offered the most hopeful *point d'appui;* it was captured after a two years' siege. But the great days were already over. Isolated towns and fortresses would fall into their hands; Crusades would continue to be mounted with or without the approval of the pope; and vast amounts of treasure would be squandered to revive the lost fortunes of the Kings of Jerusalem, whose empty titles survived to remind the proud that even the most august titles were impermanent and in their nature beyond men's power to grasp.

The spiritual motive which lent nobility to the early years of the Crusades could not survive a century of wars. Commercial motives increasingly interfered, and human rivalries found full expression in the acquisition of lands and feudal estates. At no time were the Crusades directed by a single compelling idea; and in the play of extraneous forces the original motive was often lost to sight.

In July 1203 an army of Crusaders on their way to the Holy Land reached Constantinople, only to discover that the supplies promised to them were not yet available. They remained in the city, at odds with one another and the Greeks, in a state of prolonged frustration. Nine months passed, and then they decided that the eastern empire must pay for its errors. In March they decided to put into operation a plan which had been ripening for nearly a century: they would storm the city and divide the empire among themselves. It was an act of consummate treachery, and could have only one result— Constantinople would be so weakened that it would never again emerge as a great power. The city was sacked. Libraries were burned, the jeweled altar of Hagia Sophia was ripped up and divided among the looters, holy relics were pilfered, and the great palaces and churches were despoiled to make a Crusader's holiday. In vain the pope thundered: "The Latins have given an example only of iniquity and the works of darkness. These defenders of Christ, who should have turned their swords only against the infidels, have waded through Christian blood." The Crusade against the Christians proved to be successful beyond the wildest dreams of the Venetians who had instigated it, and as a result of this victory against a defenseless people the Venetians were able to proclaim that they were the inheritors of "a half and a quarter of the Roman Empire."

A Latin dynasty now ruled from Constantinople for fifty-seven years; six emperors with unlikely names exerted their imperial powers over a fast diminishing empire. Baldwin and Henry of Flanders, Peter and Robert de Courtenay, John of Brienne, and the luckless Baldwin II, who spent a good part of his life wandering across Europe in search of gratuities for the upkeep of his empire, selling holy relics to the highest bidder, maintained their precarious position only because the times were so turbulent that the Greeks were unable to mount an offensive. At last Constantinople fell to the Paleologi, and the short reign of the Latins came to an end.

The conquest and occupation of Constantinople drained away the energy of the Crusades. The Holy Land was starved of defenders; and where previously men had fought for the holy places, they now fought for the islands of the Aegean and the provinces of Greece and Rumania. For a little while longer obscure princes gloried in the title of King of Jerusalem, while retaining a small foothold in the Holy Land. While cavalcades of ghostly warriors roamed among the great fortresses of Syria, the final issue was no longer in doubt. On May 18, 1291, Acre fell to the Sultan al Ashraf, and with its fall the Crusades came to an end. Today in Palestine and Syria and in the surrounding deserts there can still be seen the gaunt castles which seem to have been built for eternity by a people who felt that no earthly power would ever remove them from the land. They are all that survives of the ancient Kingdom of Jerusalem now forever lost.

26 ✠ THE KING AND THE EMPEROR

IN THE thirteenth century a blinding light still hovered around the thrones of kings, and sometimes the light was more palpable than the occupant of the throne. These pools of light burned with a steady glow. Power streamed from them, words poured out of them, the histories of nations revolved around them, and the king himself was dazzled by their splendor. There was a mystery attached to kingship, which men rarely attempted to resolve. The ancient titles of the kings were often meaningless, bearing little relationship to the power they wielded. They claimed to rule by divine right, but in fact they ruled by overwhelming force and by the institution of an arduous tyranny. In their various ways they were all usurpers.

To the men of the thirteenth century the phenomenon of kingship was a fact of life, like birth and death. These concentrations of power had come into existence as a result of strange irreversible accidents, the misfortunes of war, the blunders of the nobility, the ambitions of women. There was always something inhuman in these kings who postured and assumed the aspects of divinity, uttering commands in voices charged with menace, reserving to themselves power over life and death. Christianity had not tamed them. Indeed it had given to kingship an even more exalted status than it possessed in pagan times, for the kings accepted the brilliant fiction that they had received their crowns directly from the hands of Christ. On edicts, coins, manuscripts, and mosaics they showed themselves to be especially favored by God. To this day the coins of Great Britain bear the inscription surrounding the head of the sovereign: DEI GRATIA.

The grace of God worked in curious ways to produce the medieval kings. Few were worthy, and fewer still fought off the corruptions of power. They were like highwaymen standing on a bridge that all men had to cross, and they looted at their pleasure. The privileges of kingship included the right to terrorize, to intimidate, to defraud, to debase the currency, to steal. Only in England, where the barons forced King John to sign the Magna Charta, were limitations imposed on the king's prerogatives. Throughout Europe, from Byzantium to the Pyrenees and from Norway to Sicily, the kings were absolute tyrants.

On very rare occasions it happened that a king arose, who sometimes reigned mercifully in the fear of God. Such a king was Louis IX of France, the son of a French father and a Spanish mother, Blanche of Castile. His father died when he was eleven years old. During the years of his minority the Queen Mother, a devout and determined woman, acted as regent. The boy became the creature of his mother's will, given to good works and contrite prayers, fasting and rigorous self-discipline. Blanche of Castile encouraged in her son an abject fear of sin, saying: "I would rather see you die than commit a mortal sin." Although the king retained a proper fear of mortal sin to the end of his life, joy kept breaking in. It was a quiet joy, as of one who was not given to demonstrative affections or outbursts of sudden excitement. Grave, sweet-tempered, strangely gentle in an age when kings were not expected to be gentle, he showed no signs of having suffered from his mother's harsh schooling.

He grew up into a lean, tall, contemplative man, more like a cleric than a reigning prince. He resembled the monks so much and was so often in their company that he was sometimes called "Friar Louis." Once an old woman mocked him, calling him king of the monks, and swearing that he should be chased from the throne. He answered gravely: "In all you say you are telling the truth, for I am unworthy to be king. Our Lord, if he had been so minded, would have put a better person in my place." It was an instructive answer, for it implied that he owed his crown to Christ and regarded himself as unworthy in relation to Christ; he did not regard himself as an unworthy king.

All commentators are agreed on his physical beauty, his easy grace of movement, his pallor, his quiet demeanor, the sweetness of his smile. He had a commanding presence, and did not suffer fools gladly. After hearing Mass in the chapel at Vincennes outside of Paris, he liked to walk in the woods, and there, sitting on the ground under an old oak, he would administer justice informally to the poor. At other times, wearing a taffeta cloak and with a peacock's plume in his hat, he liked to walk with the royal councilors in the garden of his palace in the Cité, and to the poor people who crowded round him, all shouting at once, he would cry, "Silence! One at a time!" and call for a carpet to be spread on the grass, and there, surrounded by his high officers of state, he would pass judgment more formally.

He was a man who hated ostentation, while insisting on appearing in sumptuous robes of state on very formal occasions. He was aware that the splendor of his court had to be maintained. To his sons he said: "You should clothe yourselves well and decently, so that your women will love you more and your household will respect you; for the wise men say we ought to dress and arm ourselves in such a manner that neither shall the good men of the world blame us for extravagance nor the young gallants blame us for meanness." Following his own advice he would appear on ceremonial occasions in a sumptuous vermilion surcoat edged with ermine, wearing his golden chains of office, an intricately decorated gold-hilted sword at his side.

Humility, not pride, was his besetting sin; he enjoyed humility unashamedly, and especially liked washing the feet of beggars, caring for lepers, and tending the sick. Once he asked one of his companions, Sieur Jean de Joinville: "Which would you rather be—a leper or in mortal sin?" "I would rather have committed thirty or forty sins than be a leper," Joinville replied. The king said nothing more until the next day when he summoned Joinville to sit at his feet. "Yesterday you spoke rashly," he said, "for all the ills of the body are cured in a little time when a man dies, but if the soul is tarnished and if you are uncertain whether God has pardoned you, the evil will last forever as long as God sits in Paradise." Then he asked Joinville whether he had ever washed the feet of poor men on Maundy Thursday, and Joinville answered: "Sire, far be it from me to wash the feet of poor men! No! Never will I do such a thing!" The king said kindly: "Then you are wrong again—thinking yourself too great to do what God himself did for our enlightenment. Now I pray you for the love of God and for the love of me, get yourself into the habit of washing poor men's feet."

Joinville, who tells the story himself, appears never to have succumbed to the passion of washing poor men's feet. He was a kindly, garrulous, intelligent man, ten years younger than the king whom he survived by nearly fifty years. He wrote his chronicles at the age of eighty-five—he died at the age of ninety-three. But there is no hint of the author's old age in his long and artless chronicles; he writes with a youthful and happy vigor about the king he loved.

While the king's humility gives him a peculiarly medieval character, there was in fact very little that was medieval in his national policy. He was determined to impose his rule over the large areas of France he had inherited, and he was equally determined to control the Church, even condemning the pope for his exactions on the people of France. He did not deny that the pope possessed "the fullness of power" (*plenitudo potestatis*), but he hinted that he too possessed this power, and would not abrogate it. Against the pope he continually insisted on his own prerogatives, claiming the right to dispossess all the churches and monasteries of their treasures at a time of national emergency. Related to most of the crowned heads of Europe, the king acted as the royal marriage-broker very much like Queen Victoria in another age, thus ensuring that the kings at least would be sympathetic to his aims. He allowed King Henry III of England to retain Périgord and Limousin as fiefs, even though he had ample strength to expel the English from France. He explained his action in a revealing phrase. "Our wives are sisters and our children are cousins-german, and for this reason it is important that there should be peace between us," he said, after signing a treaty of peace with the English king. "There is very great honor for me in this peace I am making with the King of England, since he is now my vassal, which before he was not."

Although Louis IX held steadfastly to the medieval concept of the honor that accrues to those who stand in a position of authority over their vassals, the real reasons for permitting the English to retain their dominion in France were far more complex. He used his royal relatives as levers for his own political ends. Kingship was a family business, which of necessity excluded the pope, the only power who could also claim the divided affection of the French. Standing in the center of the circle of European kings, Louis IX was in a position to lead a united front against the ambitions of the papacy.

He was no less a Catholic for being at times bitterly hostile to the pope. In matters of religion he was as absolute as in matters of gov-

St. Francis, by Cimabue, from the lower church at Assisi.

St. Clare, by Simone Martini, from the lower church at Assisi. (*Alinari*)

St. Louis, painted wooden portrait, now in the Musée de Cluny. (*Musée de Cluny*)

St. Thomas Aquinas, by Piero della Francesca, from the Poldi-Pezzoli Museum, Milan.

Boniface VIII, by Arnolfo di Cambio, from the Museum of the Duomo, Florence. (*Alinari*)

Descent from the Cross, by Giotto, in the Cappella Scrovegni in Padua. (*Anderson*)

Dante: a portrait by Giotto in the Bargello, Florence. Copy made by Seymour Kirkup before the repainting. (*Alinari*)

Deathmask of Dante in the Palazzo Vecchio, Florence. (*Brogi*)

Lucidato sul fresco di Giotto
da Seymour Kirkup, il primo
promotore della ricerca, primo
della restaurazione nel 1841.

ernment. He punished blasphemers and heretics mercilessly, and took comfort from the fact that he sent scores of heretics to the stake in Burgundy, Champagne, and Flanders. When the fagots were lit, Dominicans, who had pronounced their verdict, would step back to permit the royal sergeants the honor of superintending the burning. To the saintly Louis IX goes the dubious honor of being the man most responsible for organizing the Inquisition in France.

This thin and rather gangling king, with a broad forehead, high cheekbones, and finely sculptured lips, looking more Spanish than French, dedicated to good works, continually insisting that he had only one task, and that was to govern his people well, was a mystic who sometimes, like Francis and Thomas Aquinas, lost himself so completely in his devotions that he forgot where he was; and his companions, coming upon him at his midnight prayers with news of urgent business, would see him kneeling on the bare stones, saying in a dazed whisper: "Where am I?" Yet for the greater part of his life he knew exactly where he was, and what he was doing. He saw himself as king by divine right, *gratia dei,* in possession of "the fullness of power," only because he spent his life imitating Christ and followed the appointed pathways. He could not conceive of himself as other than a king whose whole life was an act of dedication to Christ.

He was twenty-five when he heard that the Latin emperor of Constantinople, Baldwin II, was contemplating the sale of the Crown of Thorns. The emperor had already borrowed heavily on the Crown, which reposed in a warehouse at Constantinople belonging to Nicola Quirino, the leading Venetian merchant. The price was 177,300 livres, amounting to nearly $5,000,000 of our money. Two Franciscans were dispatched to Constantinople to arrange the sale. At last a heavy down payment was made, and in slow stages the Franciscans returned to France with the relic. In August 1239 the king rode in state to Villeneuve-l'Archevêque, near Sens, together with his brother Robert of Artois. The Crown of Thorns, enclosed in a double casket of gold and silver, was solemnly escorted to Paris. In the whole course of his life the king probably never knew such pure and intense excitement again. The royal progress lasted for eight days. Paris was beflagged. Masses were held whenever they paused on the journey. In the eyes of the king he had become the possessor of the most valuable object in Christendom, beyond price.

The Crown of Thorns was the most perfect of talismans, the

most royal of gifts, not to be compared with any other holy relic. The bones of saints, the vials of the Virgin's milk, the holy girdles and slippers that had been handed down over the generations, all these were merely the decorations of the mystery, while the mystery itself was expressed in the Crown. A contemporary hymn celebrated the Crown as the very portrait of the Godhead. For Louis IX, the new acquisition represented a vast extension of "the fullness of power."

Two years later there came news that a substantial portion of the True Cross, the blade of the Holy Lance, and the sponge of the Passion were for sale. Once again there was a royal progress to receive the relics and carry them to Paris. The king was determined that these treasures should be housed worthily, and he accordingly ordered that a new chapel should be built for them within the palace precincts, to be known as *La Chapelle de la Sainte Couronne et la Sainte Croix*. The name of the architect is unknown. It is likely that Pierre de Montereau, already famous for his work at Saint Denis and the refectory and Lady Chapel of Saint Germain-des-Près, was called in as an adviser. Unlimited sums of money were placed at the disposal of the architect, the existing church of St. Nicholas was torn down, and the new chapel arose within three years. It was a crystal jewel box of rainbow colors, with the broken light of thousands upon thousands of fragments of colored glass falling upon the gold shrine containing the holy relics. The columns were so slender, the stained glass windows so large, that the entire chapel seems to be made of glass. In the sunlight the chapel glows in a fire of rainbows.

Even at Chartres there is nothing to compare with the massive jewel-like incandescence of the Sainte Chapelle. Here light is triumphant, pouring through the immense windows like a benediction. Vermilion, scarlet, yellow, white, many blues and greens and ochers fill the air with a vivid, trembling, and flowing light, never still. Under a green moon and a red sun an ocher Christ lies crucified on a green cross, while a Roman soldier in a vermilion cape pierces his side with a spear and another soldier offers him hyssop. So, from window to window, the colors change according to the whims of the artists and the availability of colored glass, but blue, vermilion, and ruby-red predominate. In the Sainte Chapelle it is always dawn and sunset. Something of the same effect is achieved in the Capella Palatina in Palermo, where the candlelight flickers on walls sheeted with mosaics, but even the most luminous mosaics retain a kind of heaviness. There is no heaviness in the Sainte Chapelle, where the air waves like banners.

Within a decade the king had amassed a treasury of relics such as existed nowhere else. He acquired the Nails, the Reed, the Purple Robe, a piece of the Holy Shroud, a portion of the Napkin used by the Magdalene to wash Christ's feet, a vial of the Virgin's milk and another of the Precious Blood, a stone from the Holy Sepulchre, and the inscription that surmounted the Cross, together with the blue mantle of the Virgin and the swaddling clothes worn by Christ in the manger. In time he even acquired the rod with which Moses struck the rock, for there was no end to the inventiveness of the Byzantines and the Venetians. It mattered little to the king whether the relics were authenticated; it was enough that they existed and that he could adore them in the holy light pouring through the colored glass.

Armed with this talismanic power, the king embarked on the first of his Crusades. Jerusalem had fallen to Baibars, the commander of the Egyptian army in Palestine and future Mameluke sultan of Egypt, and the king accordingly directed his army at the serpent's head—Cairo, which was known to the Crusaders as Babylon. On June 5, 1249, at dawn, when his flagship *Montjoie* lay at anchor outside Damietta, the king took a running jump and leaped in full armor into the sea. An army of some six thousand Egyptians faced him on shore. As Joinville tells the story, he would have gone on to charge the six thousand singlehanded if his knights had not prevented him. He was in an exalted and excited mood, and he seems to have thought that Egypt would fall like a ripe fruit.

Egypt did not fall. For strategic reasons Damietta was abandoned to the French, but the easy victory was only the beginning of a series of costly defeats, for the Nile was at its height and they made their way with difficulty along the canal banks in the direction of Babylon. Pestilence spread through the army. Communications with Damietta were cut off. The enemy was skillful, well armed, and well served by intelligence agents who spied on the French and sent accurate reports to their commanders. From the Byzantines the Egyptians had inherited the engines enabling them to burn their enemies with "Greek fire." At Mansura, which means "victory" in Arabic, the French were defeated in a pitched battle. The king's brother, Robert of Artois, was killed, and the king himself narrowly escaped capture. He was ill with dysentery, "to such an extent that it was necessary to cut away the lower part of his drawers." He ordered a retreat, and a week later, while floundering along the canal banks, the entire army, including the king, was surrounded and made prisoner.

For a while the Egyptians toyed with the thought of torturing the king to death. Finally, they decided that nothing was to be gained by torture, and that it was more profitable to demand a stupendous ransom. They demanded a million bezants in gold, corresponding to some $15,000,000. When this was paid, the tattered remnant of the army was allowed to go free. The Crusaders still possessed their powerful fortresses along the Palestinian coast, and instead of sailing back to France, the king decided to spend his remaining years in the Holy Land in the hope of reviving the Kingdom of Jerusalem from fortified positions in Acre, Tyre, Jaffa, and Sidon, leaving France in the hands of his mother, Blanche of Castile. Commentators have agreed a little too readily that the king was wasting his time. In fact he was shoring up the ruins of the kingdom, forming alliances, attacking Persian raiders, encouraging the tribes to live in peace. By his presence he was ensuring that the Crusade was not forgotten, and that in the fullness of time Jerusalem, which he never saw, would return to Christian hands.

He formed an alliance with Rashid el Din Sinan, who led the hashish-smoking Assassins and was known as the Old Man of the Mountains, sending him gifts and receiving in return some of the plunder acquired by the Assassins—an apple made of rock crystal, a crystal elephant, and a crystal giraffe, with the more convincing gift of a shirt which the powerful sheikh offered the king in testimony of affection, saying that it was proper to send something he had worn next to his skin. In return the king sent him his gold signet ring. Joinville describes the lawless Assassins with gusto, and reports that when the Old Man of the Mountains rode abroad, a herald strode before him with a Danish ax, the long haft covered with silver and decorated with knives, and the herald shouted: "Turn away before him who bears in his hands the death of kings."

Such dangerous alliances were necessary. It was an age of dangerous expedients, for the Crusaders possessed scarcely more than a toehold on the Palestinian coast. Of knights at arms under the king's command there were no more than fourteen hundred according to Joinville, who enjoyed a position of great authority under the king and was likely to know the exact figure. Battles therefore were avoided, unless absolutely necessary. No pitched battles were fought. Small raiding parties inflicted heavy damage. After one such raiding party at Sidon, the king helped to bury the dead. "He himself carried the putrid and stinking corpses to the trenches where they were to be buried," writes Joinville, "and never once held his nose as the others did."

After four years in Palestine, the king learned of the death of his mother, Blanche of Castile, and returned to France. Sixteen years later he led his second Crusade, an expedition against the bey of Tunis. The Crusade was successful, but success was bought at a terrible price, for the Crusaders were struck with plague soon after they landed on the Tunisian shore and the king was among the first casualties. He died on a bed covered with ashes on August 25, 1270. He had time to murmur "Jerusalem, Jerusalem," and to utter the prayer of St. James: "Keep, Lord, Thy people, and sanctify them, that fortified with the help of Thine apostle St. James they may please Thee in their works and serve Thee with a quiet heart. Amen."

Such was Louis IX, the only French king who achieved sainthood, a quiet, courteous, determined, and sometimes generous, man, whose successors were unworthy of him.

Quietness was not a characteristic that can be attributed to the Emperor Frederick II, who was the contemporary of Louis IX. On the contrary he was strident, urgent, and demanding, passionately absorbed in himself rather than in God, determined to wield power for the joy it gave him rather than to impose any particular beliefs on the world, having faith only in himself. Half German, half Norman, he acted throughout his life as though the world were his pleasure garden, and people were chessmen to be moved about at his pleasure. In his own lifetime he was known as *Stupor Mundi,* the Stunner of the World.

Louis IX was a tall scholarly man with stooped shoulders and lank flaxen hair. Frederick II was red-haired, with blazing blue eyes, a firm chin, a hard mouth, an air of consummate intelligence. He had the body of a wrestler. He became bald as he grew older, but this was no hardship, for he remembered that Caesar was also bald; and he was bow-legged from long riding, and this too was no hardship, for he was accustomed to wear the long brocaded gowns worn by Byzantine emperors. In his capital at Palermo he lived in oriental luxury, surrounded by eunuchs and harem women, with Muslim attendants serving as secretaries and officers of state, rejoicing in the best of both worlds, the East and the West. His mother died when he was four years old. He spent his wild youth at Palermo as a ward of the pope, and in that subtropical city with its rose-red cupolas among the palms, the mosques jostling the Norman churches, the narrow streets filled with traders from all the ports of the Mediterranean, he was perfectly at home.

Through his mother he was descended from the Norman kings of Sicily, and his paternal grandfather was Frederick Barbarossa, the Holy Roman Emperor. Frederick's task was to retain his hereditary possessions, Sicily and vast areas of Italy, Germany, and Burgundy; and there was no limit to his ambitions, for he hoped to rule the world. He was four years old when he was crowned king of Sicily. Thereafter he was to acquire the crown of Charlemagne at Aachen, the crown of the Holy Roman Empire in Rome, and the crown of the Kingdom of Jerusalem, which he placed on his own head in the Church of the Holy Sepulchre. He inherited these crowns by virtue of his descent and inheritance, but all had to be fought for. His weapons were cunning, silence, boundless ambition. With his cool intelligence he was a match for all his enemies, including the pope, who placed him under a ban of excommunication.

He was eighteen when he crossed the Alps with only sixty knights to take possession of his German empire, entering the town of Constance three hours before it was due to be occupied by the Emperor Otto IV. The German princes flocked to the banner of the young king who proclaimed himself emperor; and with the defeat of Otto at the battle of Bouvines two years later, Frederick emerged as the undisputed claimant to the imperial throne. Crowned at Aachen on the marble throne of Charlemagne, he proceeded to proclaim the Crusade, following his grandfather Barbarossa and the even more exalted Charlemagne, whom he regarded as an imperial ancestor. Charlemagne had butchered the tribes into accepting Christianity, and Frederick, ruling over an empire which consisted of a Joseph's coat of imperial fiefs, surrounded by unruly princes who regarded their emperor with veneration and his lands with cupidity, seems to have hoped in the first flush of his new powers that he could unite a dying empire by leading its subjects to Jerusalem. On the day following his coronation he listened from early morning to night to a succession of

Crusade sermons. Then he forgot the Crusade. He was too busy with his own problems to spend time over the problems of Palestine.

Five years later he was crowned in Rome, receiving the *sacrum imperium* from the hands of the pope. Clad in the imperial vestments Frederick knelt beside the tomb of St. Peter and received the miter, the crown, and the sword, which he brandished three times, crying out that he had now become a soldier in the service of St. Peter, and a few moments later he received the scepter and the orb, the last of the five tokens of imperial power. The choir sang: "To Frederick ever glorious, of the Romans the unconquered Emperor, be life and victory!" He showed his subservience to the Church by holding the pope's stirrup and leading him a few paces before mounting his horse. Then the emperor rode off to his encampment on Monte Mario, which was safer than Rome.

For Frederick, twice crowned, possessor of vast estates in Germany, Italy, and Sicily, absolute power still remained for the future. Such power as he possessed was limited to Sicily and southern Italy, which he administered with the help of an efficient civil service recruited from all over Europe. The officials of his treasury were Muslims; the medical services were in the hands of Jews; the architects and mosaicists were Byzantines. Frederick spoke Arabic, Hebrew, Italian, German, Greek, and Latin. His court was a microcosm of the East and West, and he saw himself as the superb arbiter of the destinies of Europe and the coasts of Asia. At his coronation he promised the pope he would soon embark on a Crusade. The promise remained unfulfilled while he put down a Muslim rebellion in Sicily and set about strengthening his small and highly organized kingdom. In 1224 he founded the University of Naples, the first secular university, with the deliberate object of training men for the civil service. By the summer of 1227 the pope's patience was exhausted. Frederick was continually talking about his Crusade, and doing nothing. He set sail at last from Brindisi, only to return two days later to port when an epidemic broke out. For his failure in advancing the Crusade, the pope summarily excommunicated him. There were to be many more excommunications. Frederick seems to have regarded excommunication as a legitimate weapon to be employed by the pope whenever confronted with recalcitrant princes. As emperor, he felt immune from such pinpricks, for he possessed more powerful weapons: an army, an efficient government, and resources of treasure greater than those possessed by any king or sultan.

At last in the summer of 1228 he set out for the Holy Land to fulfill the promises made so often and so unwisely. He was already in correspondence with al-Kamil Muhammed, the Sultan of Egypt, and his aim from the beginning was to acquire possession of Jerusalem by treaty rather than by force of arms. His army was small, consisting of about six hundred knights and a few thousand foot soldiers. With these pathetically small forces the emperor set out to reconquer the Holy Land and to crown himself King of Jerusalem.

To the surprise and bafflement of the pope, Frederick succeeded in accomplishing exactly what he set out to do. He was on excellent terms with al-Kamil Muhammed, and he was able to negotiate a settlement with the Muslim prince by which Nazareth, Bethlehem, and Jerusalem, with a strip of territory connecting Jerusalem and Acre, were all ceded to him. It was a vast, an astonishing triumph. Previously he had claimed the title of King of Jerusalem through his marriage to the fourteen-year-old Isabelle de Brienne, titular heiress of the Kingdom of Jerusalem. Now he was king in fact. The excommunicated emperor strode up to the altar of the Church of the Holy Sepulchre, seized the crown, placed it on his own head, and announced that he was the Emperor of Peace, thus comparing himself with Jesus, and that he had accomplished his destiny without chariots or horses or brave men, quietly working a great wonder, thus comparing himself with God. "More by the power of my wonders than by men's courage," he declared, "I have caused the work to be accomplished which for long times past many princes and many mighty of the earth with the multitude of their peoples have all essayed in vain." It was no more than the truth.

For fifteen years, until 1244, Frederick could claim that the holy places of Palestine were under his sovereign protection. Never again were they to be owned by a Christian. The student of medieval history is confronted by a stupendous irony: the only western emperor ever to claim sovereignty over Jerusalem since the time of the Arab invasion was a man under a ban of excommunication. Frederick had no sooner sailed for the Holy Land than the pope ordered a Crusade against his Italian territories.

A month after his coronation in Jerusalem Frederick returned to his beloved Sicily, to reassert his independence of the pope and to attempt the plan that had been maturing in his mind since he was a youth. All of Italy, he hoped, would be united under his imperial rule. In this he was less successful than in his conquest of the holy places, for the Vicar of Christ was ruthlessly determined to raise up enemies against him, and soon most of Italy was in a state of civil war, with some communes taking up arms for Frederick and others for the pope. Every city was a house divided against itself. The war between the State and the Church was now in the open, and Frederick's skill in diplomacy was strained to the utmost as he attempted to weld together a network of cities and communes at war with their neighbors. All was confusion. Jerusalem, Bethlehem, and Nazareth had fallen like ripe plums into his hands, but it was no easy matter to take possession of the warring cities of Italy.

Meanwhile he maintained himself as though he were in fact as well as in name the Roman Emperor, inheritor of the earthly possessions of Augustus and Justinian. Like Justinian, he produced a resounding code of laws, which he called the *Liber Augustalis*. Like Augustus, he minted beautiful gold coins bearing his imperial effigy on one side and the Roman eagle on the other. When he traveled, he was always accompanied by a vast retinue of officials, judges, jesters, and executioners; and to the horror of the pope his bodyguard consisted of infidel Muslims. These processions were accompanied by his treasury and his menagerie, which included leopards, lions, panthers, bears, ostriches, an elephant, and a giraffe. His harem also accompanied him. Suppliants at his court would see him sitting on a high throne, a huge crown suspended above his head, a purple carpet laid before him. On this carpet the suppliants would crawl toward the throne, inching their way, not daring to look up at him. The voice of the emperor was rarely heard. Instead the *logothete* would utter the emperor's command, and the emperor himself would make a slight gesture with his hand to indicate that the audience was over. Louis IX would throw himself down at the foot of a tree in the park of Vincennes and administer justice with casual informality. Frederick, following the example of the Persian and Byzantine courts, administered justice as though he were God.

The pope thought Frederick was Antichrist, the Beast of *The Book of Revelation,* and went to some pains to insist on the correspondence between Frederick and the Beast. Pope Gregory IX had as great a passion for rhetoric as Frederick, whom he denounced with soaring invective:

> *Out of the sea rises up the Beast, full of the names of blasphemy, raging with the claws of the bear and the mouth of the lion and the limbs and likeness of the leopard, opening its mouth to blaspheme the Holy Name and ceasing not to hurl its spears against the tabernacle of God and against the saints who dwell in heaven. With fangs and claws of iron the Beast seeks to destroy everything and to trample the world to fragments beneath its feet.*[1]

Frederick appears to have been amused by these tremendous trumpetings, but he took their implications seriously. The war between the emperor and the Church was to be prolonged indefinitely, but it was most violent in those early beginnings. No quarter was given. Frederick's armies dealt mercilessly with the cities which sided with the pope.

The Franciscans, who detested panoply, had little sympathy for Frederick, and proved to be excellent propagandists. They spread stories of Frederick's impiety far and wide. Salimbene, a Franciscan friar, described Frederick at length, leaning heavily on his vices, known and imaginary. It is Salimbene who tells the story of how Frederick invited two men to dinner, and then sent one to bed and the other to the hunt; in the evening he had both of them disemboweled in his presence in order to learn which of them had digested his food better. There was perhaps an element of truth in the story. Frederick was continually conducting scientific experiments. He delighted in the new sciences, in the learning of Arabic doctors and the encyclopedists of Spain, studied astronomy, astrology, mathematics, botany, and physics with passionate interest, and compiled long lists of questions which he expected his scholars to answer. He was not satisfied with easy answers. His library was full of treatises in Arabic, Hebrew, Greek, and Latin. He wrote a book on falconry which testifies to his spirit of scientific inquiry. He was skeptical on all matters, including religion, and it seems never to have occurred to him that there was any harm in skepticism.

He was the first of the modern emperors, but his roots lay in the

---

[1] Ernst Kantorowicz, *Frederick the Second*, London, Constable and Company, 1931, p. 498.

remote and dangerous past. He was the brother of the ancient Sumerian sun kings. He would make wise and intelligent observations about the nature of the winds or of submarine volcanoes, and in the next breath he would wonder aloud why the pope dared to oppose him, the descendant of kings. Who was the pope's father? By what sign had the pope come into his inheritance? Was the pope christened in a royal robe and crowned with a royal crown? It was not so much that he was a skeptic in matters of religion, as wholly ignorant. For him Christ was a blaze of majesty and power; and there were no Beatitudes.

Farseeing in matters of scientific inquiry, he was also astonishingly adept in manipulating people. Yet he had little understanding of the political forces at work. He was blind to the emerging power of the city states, which defied emperor and pope alike. Regarding the Milanese, who placed the highest price on their freedom, with special loathing, he determined to destroy them. With the help of his German knights he destroyed their army at Cortenuova. The Milanese fought around the *carroccio*, the high-masted chariot bearing the crucifix and the standard of the commune. The *carroccio* was the symbol of their freedom. Frederick captured it, roped the *podesta* of Milan, Pietro Tiepolo, to the lowered mast, and had it drawn through the streets. The once powerful Pietro Tiepolo, the son of a Doge of Venice, was left dangling in mid-air while the people shouted in derision. Trumpeters from the back of an elephant blew triumphal blasts. Frederick went on to hang Tiepolo on the shores of the Ionian Sea, and the sacred *carroccio* was drawn by a team of mules from Milan to Rome, where it was mounted on five marble pillars on the Capitol with an effusive description of the greatness of the conqueror and a promise of a similar fate for *carroccios* that dared to offend the emperor.

He was fighting a losing battle. He built a triumphal arch in his own honor at Capua, but his triumphs were curiously short-lived. The Sultan al-Kamil Muhammed died in 1238; his successors showed no desire to bind themselves by treaty with Frederick; and soon Jerusalem fell. Again and again the pope called for a Crusade against Frederick, and at last, losing all patience, he sentenced him for the second time to be excommunicated as a heretic and a perjurer who had wantonly broken the peace between himself and the Church. Frederick replied: "I have been the anvil long enough; now I shall play the hammer."

It was an empty boast, for the hammer had lost its cunning. He attacked Parma, intending to raze the city to its foundations and to build a new city, to be called Vittoria in his own honor. Parma held out. Frederick amused himself by planning the new city, building a temple to St. Victor, and minting coins. He was hunting with his beloved falcons when he heard an uproar in the distance and saw the first flames. A desperate sortie from Parma had led to the rout of his camp. With barely fourteen men he escaped encirclement and fled to the south. Fifteen hundred of his men were slain, and twice that number taken prisoner. His treasury—all his ceremonial robes, his scepter, his royal seal, the giant crown which hung suspended over his head during his audiences, and all his wealth of gold and silver—fell into the hands of the enemy. Two years later he died as he had lived, unreconciled to the Church, leaving to his successors only a heritage of conflict. He was buried in Palermo Cathedral in a shroud of Arabian silk. His sarcophagus of dark red porphyry supported by four lions gleams like blood.

His sarcophagus bears an inscription which tells us little about the man:

> Si probitas, sensus, virtutem gratia, census,
> Nobilitas orti possent resistere morti,
> Non foret extinctus Fridericus qui jacet intus.

> *If probity, understanding, grace of virtue, wealth,*
> *Nobility of birth were able to resist death,*
> *Frederick, who lies within, would not have died.*

The epitaph might have been applied with greater truth to Louis IX. Frederick possessed wealth, noble birth, and understanding, but he was too treacherous and murderous to claim the virtue of probity. His power passed with him. Eighteen years after his death the last of his line, the boy king Conradin, was captured by Charles of Anjou and executed in the market square of Naples. There is a legend that when the boy's head fell to the ground an eagle swooped down, dipped its wing in the blood, and then mounted to heaven.

27 ✠ THOMAS AQUINAS

THERE lies in the Basilica of Saint Sernin in Toulouse a mottled brown skull wrapped in a faded napkin, exhibited in a gilded glass case. There is an inscription in florid eighteenth century handwriting, reading simply: S. *Thomas d'Aquin*. The brow is broad, the chin is firm, and there is nothing remarkable about the skull. What is remarkable is that it is not remarkable, for there is little doubt that this is the authentic skull of the most learned and angelical of the doctors of the Church, the man who singlehandedly wrote the massive tablets of the law.

While he was alive, they called him the Dumb Ox, but there was nothing ox-like about him except his monumental patience. To us, living so many centuries later, he was larger than life, larger than the popes, larger than his century, which he dominated by the power of his genius. No one ever before or since has written so well about the laws of the Christian life. His *Summa theologica*, which he wrote over a period of seven years, is exactly what it professes to be: a summary of all the theology known or contemplated up to his time. He died at the age of forty-nine, and no one will ever know how in so short a life he was able to accomplish so much.

He was born in the castle of Roccasecca near Naples, the seventh and last son of Count Landulf of Aquino and Theodora of Theate, early in the year 1225. His father belonged to the Lombard nobility; his paternal grandmother was a sister of Frederick Barbarossa; his mother descended from Norman nobility. The blood of the Hohenstaufens flowed through his veins, and inevitably his family was caught up in the wars of succession. He was about twenty when his

elder brothers took part in an uprising against Frederick II. One
brother, Raynaldo, was tortured and executed by the emperor, and the
family was compelled to take refuge in the papal Campagna. Thomas
showed no interest in earthly wars. Throughout his life one subject
interested him to the exclusion of all other subjects. The subject was
God.

He was five years old when he was offered to the abbey of
Monte Cassino, the offering being a kind of penance by his father
who had only the previous year ravaged the abbey at the command
of Frederick II. In this way Count Landulf sealed his peace with the
monks and provided his son with a future benefice. In time the boy
would become the abbot of Monte Cassino, rich, powerful, and respected. But the boy decided otherwise. He was fifteen or sixteen
when he announced that he would become a preacher. Instead he became a theologian, a mystic, and a law-giver.

At the age of nineteen he received the habit, and was showing
himself so much in love with scholarship that it was decided to send
him to the University of Paris. His mother had other ideas and ordered him to return home to manage the family estates. He refused,
and set out for the north, only to be kidnaped by his brother Raynaldo, who forced him to obey his mother's wishes and sent him
under guard to the castle of Roccasecca. There he remained for little
more than a year, still wearing his habit, sullenly determined upon
disobedience, reading the Bible and contemplating the sacred mysteries, living the life of a recluse. At last, realizing that nothing was to
be gained by keeping him a prisoner, his mother relented. Once more
he set out for Paris.

On the way he stayed briefly in Rome in order to have an audience with the pope. It was at this time that he composed the greatest,
as it is the simplest, of his prayers:

*Lord Jesus Christ, I pray that the fiery and honey-sweet power
of Thy love may detach my soul from everything under heaven, so
that I may die from love of Thy love, Who out of love for my people
didst die upon the tree of the Cross. Amen.*

It is perhaps worth remembering when we read the *Summa theologica*, that interminable lawyer's brief on behalf of God, that
Thomas was perpetually conscious of "the fiery and honey-sweet
power."

Above all he was a mystic, counting scholarship and theological argument as no more than minor props of devotion. He threw his whole soul into his prayers, weeping and sighing and waving his arms, or standing motionless, completely unconscious of the world around him, on the steps of the altar. The calm of his prose is delusory, for it conceals violent emotions. He was a violent man, who believed strongly in taking heaven by storm. The *Summa theologica* was only one of his many weapons.

Poetry was another of his weapons, for he wrote some of the greatest of medieval hymns, including the hymns for the Office of Corpus Christi and the famous *Pange, lingua, gloriosi corporis myste-rium*. Argument and debate were other weapons. He cultivated them with a proper sense of a strategical need of massing his ideas and then pouring them out in a flood on the unwary adversary; he preferred to fight with heavy artillery than with a rapier. The character of the man resembled his appearance. He was tall and thickset, unbending, stern, and sweet-tempered. It was remembered that he had one enormous eye that looked out upon the world, while the other eye was smaller and seemed to look inward.

There was something formidable in Thomas's appearance, his ungainliness, his lumbering stride. He looked a little like an ancient Roman emperor conscious of his imperial dignity, and he did not suffer fools gladly. Once he leaned out of a window when some students shouted that there was a winged ox flying over the monastery. When the students roared with laughter to find him searching the skies for the winged ox, he snapped: "I was not so simple as to believe that an ox could fly, but I never imagined that a religious man could stoop to falsehood." Thereafter he was called the Dumb Ox, and the name stuck to him.

There are other stories told about him; all of them reveal the flavor of the man. Once, when he was teaching in Paris, he returned from St. Denis with his students. He was lost in thought, oblivious of the city rising before him in all its glory of towers and pinnacles. One of the students said, "Master, do you not see how beautiful Paris is?" Thomas shrugged his shoulders: "Oh yes, very beautiful." "Master," said the student, "I would to God the city was yours." Thomas turned to him slowly: "What do you think I could possibly do with it?" "You could sell it to the King of France," the student laughed, "and with the money build convents for the Order of Preachers."

Thomas thought for a moment. "There is only one thing I want now—the homilies written by St. Chrysostom on the Gospel according to St. Matthew." Then, ponderously, he walked on toward Paris.

At any moment of the day he might lose himself in thought and become oblivious of his surroundings. Once he was summoned to dine with King Louis IX, the future saint. At the dinner table he completely forgot where he was, followed a thought to its conclusion, and suddenly hammered the table with his huge fist, exclaiming: "Ah, there's an argument which will destroy the Manichees!" There was consternation round the table; someone whispered that he should ask pardon of the king for his unseemly behavior, but the king observed kindly: "Our friar has been thinking. Summon the secretary to take down the thought before it escapes."

Thomas liked to have three or four secretaries around him; like Jerome he kept them busy. The story is told that when he was dictating into the night, holding the candle so that the secretary could see what he was writing, he continued dictating even when the candle had burned down to his hand and did not stop until he smelled the burning flesh. In his lifetime he wrote or dictated thirty books, many of them voluminous.

His first work was a treatise called *On Being and Essence*, being an examination of some ideas in Aristotle's *Metaphysics*. He went on to write a *Commentary on the Sentences of Peter Lombard*, and while passing through Brabant on his way to Cologne he compiled for Adelaide, Duchess of Brabant, a treatise *On the Government of the Jews*. This was the mere beginning; afterward came the torrent.

The wonder is that he was able to write with such outward calm when he was perpetually involved in bitterly waged doctrinal disputes. In Paris he taught every day at the Convent of Saint Jacques on the Left Bank, as holder of one of the two chairs of theology reserved for the Preachers. As a Dominican, a member of a mendicant order, he incurred the attacks of the seculars, who professed to believe that nothing was so dangerous as the preaching of a mendicant. Thomas was preaching on Palm Sunday at Saint Jacques when a proctor marched into the church and read out a long letter from Guillaume de Saint-Amour, in which the crimes of the mendicant orders were discussed at length. They were false apostles, uncommissioned adventurers, precursors of Antichrist. What right had they to preach when they were given over to so many heresies, so many incongruities of thought? Let them be removed, or at the very least let their influence be restricted. When the proctor had finished reading the letter, Thomas made no reply; he simply went on with his sermon. But the issue was now joined. The matter engaged the attention of the pope, who had to decide whether the Dominicans and Franciscans were to be allowed to teach in the schools, and especially at the University of Paris, which prided itself on being the greatest and most brilliant college in the world. For a moment Rome was won over by the seculars; the pope announced that the secular independence of the university was to be maintained, and the privileges of the religious were to be abolished. But such self-denying ordinances were doomed to be reversed, and new orders went out against the seculars. Guillaume de Saint-Amour replied with a vitriolic pamphlet, *On the Dangers of the Present Time*. Thomas replied with his carefully written treatise *Contra impugnantes*, in which there was no trace of vitriol. Guillaume's book was condemned and ceremonially burned in the court of Rome, and the king banished him from France.

From this unpleasant encounter Thomas emerged as the defender of the mendicant orders, and their right to teach. From Rome, where he defended his cause, he returned to Paris to receive the cap and ring, the outward signs of his doctorate. He lectured, became a member of the king's privy council, and there began in those years the immense correspondence which he carried on till his death. He also began to write the *Summa contra Gentiles*, the first of those voluminous works which were intended to cover all aspects of the problem under discussion with such completeness that the enemy, ignorance, would never find any orifice to enter. There is no flashing of wings. He writes with studied calm, unhurrying in his hunt after the quarry. He followed the precept of St. Chrysostom, who wrote in one of his homilies on St. Matthew: "The full measure of philosophy is to be simple with prudence: such is the angelic life." But simplicity and prudence were abandoned when he wrote on the margins of the manuscript, in his crabbed and scarcely legible medieval handwriting, those despairing cries which punctuate his text, "I pray to Thee, O Lord, or else I am lost," or more simply, "*Ave Maria.*"

In 1261 he was summoned to Italy by Pope Urban IV, and for the next eleven years he was continually traveling. He taught for short periods in Rome, Pisa, and Bologna, and when the General Chapter of the order met in London at Pentecost in the year 1263, he accompanied them, staying in the priory at Holborn, receiving a new white and black habit from King Henry III, and taking part in the election of Albertus Magnus as the new Vicar-General. He returned to Rome by way of Paris and Milan, and it was there that he composed the office of Corpus Christi, in which there was so great a marriage of doctrine and song that Urban IV presented him with a large silver dove containing the sacred species. Shortly afterward, amid a host of other occupations, he began to compose the *Summa theologica.*

He was now at the height of his powers, and every kind of position was offered to him. He refused them all, content, as he said, "to remain a humble religious." He grew heavier as he grew older, and when he walked in the fields the peasants would gaze open-mouthed in astonishment at this man who was so tall and so heavy that he moved like a kind of lumbering tower, dwarfing his companions. He had a large head like a pumpkin, and was growing bald. They said his skin was "the color of new wheat," his nose strong and aquiline, his mouth firm and well carved, and he had heavy jowls. William of Tocco tells us that his skin was unusually delicate and tender, so that the least scratch caused a sore, and if, as sometimes happened, he had to undergo a bleeding or a cauterization, the instruments left his skin fearfully blemished, though he felt no pain. Meditation was his anesthetic. He would simply close his eyes and meditate; at such times he was lost to the world. According to Aristotle a delicate, easily bruised skin is characteristic of great intellects.

Thomas was so often lost in meditation that a special companion, Reginald of Piperno, was deputed to sit by him and see that he ate the food presented to him. He was always falling into long meditative trances. He saw visions. Once he entered his cell to find Christ standing among his tumbled manuscripts written on odd scraps of paper. On another occasion St. Paul came quietly into his room to explain a problem of interpretation. Toward the end of his life he spoke frequently of seeing the Virgin. On one occasion she revealed to him that his station in life would never be changed; it was a revelation he received with an outburst of joy, for he dreaded elevation to the prelacy. William of Tocco describes him as a man marvelously contemplative, *vir miro modo contemplativus.* In him the pure intelligence assumed the colors of mystical fire.

Though he lumbered like an elephant there was nothing earthy in him. The ordinary everyday world had no interest for him; he took no pleasure in art, which he dismissed in the *Summa contra Gentiles* in three brief sentences. What interested him was "the fiery and honey-sweet power," the presence of God. When he described the appearance of the Virgin in his cell, he said she was like "the brightest of bright mirrors, more polished and pure than the Seraphim, of such purity that nothing purer can be imagined except it were God." He called God "the intelligible light," and like the perpetual opening of windows the words "light" and "shining" flow through his work.

To the very end he remained the aristocrat, never smiling overmuch, inflexibly resolved on the study of God. He said he could never understand how anyone conscious of mortal sin could laugh or be merry. When his sister Theodora inquired how to become a saint, he replied with one word, *Velle* (Resolve), thus perhaps testifying to the strength of his Norman character. When giving sermons, he threw back his head, closed his eyes, and gripped the handrail so tightly that his knuckles shone white; and this strange posture gave him the appearance of an admiral on the bridge of his ship ordering an attack. His favorite ejaculation was, *Tu Rex gloriae, Christe: Tu Patris sempiternus es Filius,* and perhaps it was characteristic of the man who was related to half the kings of Europe that he should have praised the King of Glory and omitted the Holy Ghost.

He spent the remaining years of his life at Naples, suffering from toothache and malaria, seeing visions and talking to the dead. He once saw the devil as a Negro, but that was a commonplace vision shared by every neurotic nun who saw an inexplicable black shadow. A more convincing vision occurred when he saw Father Romanus, the man to whom he had vacated his chair at the University of Paris. Romanus was dead. Seeing him, Thomas said, "How do I stand with God, and are my works pleasing to Him?" "Thou art in good state," Romanus replied, "and thy works are pleasing to God." Thomas then asked: "How do the Blessed see God, and do our acquired habits abide with us in Heaven?" It was a question which had long tormented him, and he hoped at last to receive some illumination, but Romanus gave the impression of being bound to secrecy. "It is enough if I tell you that I see God," he answered. "Ask me no more. As we have heard, so we have seen, in the city of the Lord of Hosts." He vanished, leaving Thomas as perplexed as ever about whether the Blessed retained their habits in heaven, but with the assurance that they retained their powers of sight. Shortly afterward Thomas wrote in his notebook: "Therefore it is by specular vision that the blessed see God."

Toward the end of his life these visions came in increasing numbers. In the feast of St. Nicholas in December 1273 he fell into a long ecstasy while celebrating Mass. He told no one what happened to him during the ecstasy, but from that hour, in the words of William de Tocco, his biographer, "he hung up his writing instruments." His secretary Reginald of Piperno urged him to resume writing, but he said: "I cannot. Such things have been revealed to me that all I wrote before was no more than straw." It was observed that he now spoke with the strange gentleness and gravity of the dying.

The feast of St. Nicholas occurs early in December. A few days later Thomas went to visit his sister Marietta, Countess of Severino, but left just before Christmas. He spoke very little, and it was remembered that his few words were concerned with the joys of life in heaven. He was like a man who had prepared all his luggage and was ready to leave the earth.

He was very ill when he returned to Naples, hoping to spend his last days there, but the pope suddenly summoned him and bade him attend the Council of Lyons. Accordingly, toward the end of January, accompanied by two friars, he set out on what was to be his last journey.

There was a time when he marched across the Alps without any difficulty, but that time was long since gone. His body weakened by fasting and mortifications, he was in no shape to make the arduous journey across the mountain passes in the depth of winter. On a mountain road near Terracina he stumbled and fell. He was too weak to continue the journey, and when his secretary reminded him that he should exert all his remaining energy in order to attend the Council because the pope would surely grant him a cardinal's hat, Thomas answered: "What has that to do with me? Please understand that I shall never be anything but a simple religious for the rest of my life."

Not far from Terracina stood the castle of his niece, Countess Francesca Ceccano, and there he was taken on muleback. A doctor was summoned, and thinking to pamper the patient, he asked whether there was any food which he would specially like. Thomas said he would like some herring, which he had enjoyed in France, though it was rarely found in Italy. It so happened that a fisherman had just found some herring in his creel, and this was brought to him. "Where does it come from?" Thomas asked, and his secretary answered, "It comes from God."

A few days later Thomas had revived sufficiently to continue his journey to Lyons. He was in good spirits, and no longer had the look of a dying man. But they had gone only a few miles when he collapsed again near the Cistercian Abbey of Fossa Nuova. It was February 10, 1274. As he was carried through the cloisters, he knew he would never leave the place and murmured the words of the Psalmist: "This is my rest forever: here I shall dwell, for I have chosen it." They laid him down in the abbot's cell, heaped small fires of fagots round him, and were silent when he complained: "Why should holy men carry wood for my fire?"

He survived for nearly a month, growing weaker each day. At his request they read to him the *Song of Solomon,* and according to his practice he dictated a commentary on the verses, but it was clear that he was no longer in full possession of his faculties. He rambled, and for long periods remained silent. One day they read to him the verse: "Come, my beloved, let us go forth to the fields," and he fainted. The viaticum was brought to him. Lying in the arms of his secretary, he murmured: "I receive Thee, ransom of my soul. For love of Thee have I studied and kept vigil, toiled, preached, and taught. Never have I said word against Thee." And thinking of the shortness of his life, he went on: "If I have received more graces and lights than other doctors who have lived long lives, it is because the Lord wished to shorten the days of my exile, and to take me the sooner to be the sharer of His glory, out of a pure act of mercy. If you love me sincerely, be content and comforted, for my own consolation is perfect." He died in the early morning of March 7, 1274, having survived the long winter into the spring.

Nine years before his death Thomas began work on his masterpiece, the *Summa theologica,* which was intended to be nothing less than the sum of all theological knowledge. Nothing would be left out; every conceivable theological problem would be resolved, or at least stated in such a way that resolution would be implied. Even questions which could not be answered were argued and debated to the point of exhaustion, so that it was inconceivable that any further arguments could be brought to them. It was as though in the eyes of Thomas, Christianity had developed to a point beyond which it could not go; and the *Summa theologica* was clearly intended to be the capstone of the entire edifice.

To those who set eyes on it for the first time it is a bewildering work, consisting of an endless series of closely reasoned arguments, appeals to authorities, interpretations of texts, and arguments deduced from these interpretations, all gathered together in the form of an extensive lawyer's brief: objections, conclusions, refutations. Thomas sails into each argument with astonishing ease; he gives the impression that there is scarcely a single theological problem which will not submit to the discipline of reason. Almost he has the mind of a computer; texts are fed to him, then they are weighed, and if found wanting they are discarded, but as the reasoning machine works on the vast assemblage of texts, which includes the whole of the Bible and all the great theological texts written up to this time and the more eloquent pagan writers, there is heard the humming of invisible machinery, lights flash on fluorescent panels, and the final answer is handed down as effortlessly as if it were produced electronically. Very minor questions, as for example, whether it is possible for a blessed angel to sin, are submitted to the same process as very weighty questions. There is something relentless in the steady march of Thomas's mind as he goes out to conquer the entire field of theology as it was known in his time.

The physical dimensions of the work are stupefying, for it is considerably longer than the Bible. Altogether 512 theological propositions are discussed at length, with sobriety and precision. The first book (*God in Himself and as Creator*) demonstrates and analyzes the proofs of God's existence, the nature of the Trinity, the six days of Creation, the Angels, and man. All this is set forth in 119 propositions subdivided in 584 articles covering 851 double-columned pages in one of the more easily accessible editions. The second book (*God as the End of All Things*) is further subdivided into two books, *The First of the Second* and *The Second of the Second*, each of these two books being as long as the first. The third book (*God as Redeemer*) was never completed. It treats of Christ, Redemption, Incarnation, Baptism, Confirmation, the Eucharist, and Penance. After ninety propositions have been discussed, the Oxford manuscript bears the note: "Here Thomas died. O death, thou art accursed."

Just as the *Divine Comedy* offers the sum of Christian experience, so the *Summa theologica* offers the sum of Christian theory. Everything that could possibly be thought about God and Creation at that time was included in it, set down in the proper order, and expounded with appropriate skill. There are no half-measures. Like

Dante, Thomas was bent on the conquest of a universe.

To understand the *Summa* best one should bear in mind that it is a deliberate act of conquest requiring a clear knowledge of the weapons involved, a careful disposition of forces, and a command of strategy, tactics, and logistics. Thomas attacked from a position of strength because he was armed with the authority of the Church and a prodigious knowledge of Christian texts. The war is fought with invisible reserves which can be brought up whenever desired, and when the enemy territory is occupied, it is not destroyed but made to serve the purpose of further conquests, further sallies into the country of ignorance.

Sometimes the argument is merely an excuse for Thomas to state his most intimate thoughts, and at such times the chiseled perfection of the lawyer's brief gives way to flashes and coruscations of excitement. An anthology derived from Thomas would be as exciting as one gathered from Augustine. There are moments when he is the pure humanist. "Man," he says, "is bound by a kind of natural debt to live with others merrily (*ut aliis delectabiliter convivat*)." He notes in passing that even in the state of innocence there would be enjoyment of sex. He offers no fundamental objection to sexual pleasure; the pleasures of the innocent will be all the greater. "Some say they would have less pleasure; I answer that the purer the nature, the greater the pleasure." He is superb when he talks about the nature of love:

He who wills to enjoy the gift of loving is perfect when he loves as much as he can. For then the whole heart of a man is borne toward God, and this is the perfection of the love of heaven (caritas patriae), unattainable here by reason of life's infirmities which do not permit us to meditate on God all the time. So too by loving a man may strive to keep himself free for God and things divine, putting other matters aside, save as life's needs require, and this is the perfection of love, possible in this life, yet not for all who love. Then there is the way of loving which consists of habitually setting one's heart on God, so that one thinks and wills nothing contrary to divine love; and this grace is common to all who love.

(*Summa theologica*, II, ii, xxiv, 8)

This is not exactly as Thomas wrote it. I have stripped away the terrible little phrases: *In the first place, in the second place, in the third place.* They add nothing, and they conceal the poetry which lies at the heart of all his arguments.

Poetry, indeed, is always breaking through. He could not escape from the cadences of the Psalms, and they can be heard throughout his work, breaking across the formal precision of the schoolman who proposes to solve every question by an appeal to logic. There are times when logic fails, and poetry provides the only viable solution. In his sermon *On the Body of Our Lord* Thomas declares: "God gave us the bread of angels for the refreshment of our souls. . . . On the breaking of the bread Thou art not broken, nor art Thou divided. Thou art eaten, and like the Burning Bush Thou art not consumed." The poetry of the angelic hierarchies delighted him, and he was continually discussing the angelic presences. He asked whether angels grieve over the errors of men, and anwered:

> *Angels grieve neither over the sins nor the punishment of men. For, as says Augustine, punishment and grief arise only from what contravenes the will, but nothing happens in the world contrary to the will of the angels and the blessed. Their will is entirely fixed upon divine justice, and nothing takes place in the world save what takes place according to their command. And so, in brief, nothing takes place in the world contrary to the will of the blessed.*
>
> (*Summa theologica*, I, cxiii, 7)

Like all the great Fathers of the Church, Thomas stands out at a time of crisis. His task, as he saw it, was to shore up a faith in danger of ruin from lack of logic; and as Dante summoned the pagan Virgil to his side, so Thomas summoned Aristotle to be his companion through the mountainous landscapes of theology.

Today the *Summa* has come back into fashion, for it describes a world which is singularly complete, rounded off, plausible. If the original causes are accepted, their effects must be as Thomas stated them; every cause and effect is woven into an inescapable web of logic. He wrote at the beginning of the *Summa*: "In the sacred science everything is contemplated from the standpoint of God, and the content of this science is in part God Himself, and in part other beings inasfar as they are ordained unto God as unto their beginning and end." So he went on to describe a universe worth living in, rich in audacious meanings, and illuminated by the presence of a divine fire coursing through all things.

28 ✛ TRIUMPH AND TRAGEDY

O F ALL the popes who ever reigned the strangest and unhappiest was Celestine V, who never wanted to be pope. Dante consigned him to Hell; the Church, more merciful, made him a saint. He was one of those men who seem destined for martyrdom, at the mercy of the world's discords. He reigned for four months, and spent the remaining two years of his life in the prison of his successor, dying at the age of eighty-two in abject misery. Between Celestine V and Boniface VIII, his successor, there could be no common ground. One was a pious hermit devoted to prayer and good works, the other was a prince devoted to earthly power.

The story of Celestine's pontificate provides an object lesson in the dangers of sanctity confronted by princely ambitions. He wanted no part of power, assumed the papacy only because it was forced on him, and when at last he was forced to step down from his throne, hoping to return to a life of contemplation, he may have know that Boniface VIII would give him no peace. He was doomed to be extinguished, and he died like a candle that is snuffed out.

Peter of Murrone was born in 1214, the eleventh child of a peasant family in Perugia. As a youth he joined the Benedictine order, and lived a life of renunciation in the mountains above Sulmone. Soon others followed him, and at the Council of Lyons in 1274 he asked Pope Gregory X for authorization to create an Order known as "the Spirituals" in honor of the Holy Ghost, the *Sanctus Spiritus*. In time some twenty communities of contemplative monks came into existence, but once he had brought the Order into being, Peter of Murrone returned to the contemplative life, living in a mountain cave on herbs and water, wearing only a homespun shirt, passing his days alone with the Alone. There was scarcely anyone in Italy with so great a reputation for sanctity.

Many had prophecied the coming of a pope who would deliver Christendom from the politics of power. The abbot Joachim of Flora, who claimed the gift of prophecy, had stated categorically that an angel-pope would usher in a new age. Roger Bacon had prophecied the coming of a *pastor angelicus*. Between 1276 and 1292, no less than seven popes had reigned, some of them for only a few months, and in the popular imagination these brief reigns were the punishments of a wrathful God on simoniacal intriguers. When Nicholas IV died in 1292 after a reign of four years, Cardinal Latino Malabranca, bishop of Ostia, solemnly put forward the claims of Peter of Murrone to the papacy. He hinted that he had received a divine revelation. Quarrels over the succession had lasted for two years. The cardinals had been continually deadlocked. The Conclave, meeting in Perugia, had come to no conclusions, and during the long summer of 1294 the cardinals, who felt they were dying of interminable arguments, malaria, and boredom, decided that Peter of Murrone would make an acceptable pope, if only because all the other alternatives were unthinkable. The Savelli, Orsini, and Colonna candidates were at each others' throats. It was believed that a truly holy pope, remote from all factional quarrels, would restore stability to the papacy. Accordingly Peter of Murrone was asked to present himself to the cardinals at Perugia.

Although he was elected pope by acclamation, Peter of Murrone had no knowledge of and little interest in the papacy. He disliked his ceremonial robes, complained bitterly about the hundreds of documents laid before him every day, and asked that a narrow cell should be built for him within the papal palace. "Has God raised me up in order to cast me down?" he asked. "What have I to do with the world's quarrels? I wish I was back in my poor cell!" He had reason to fear his exalted position, for, being in Naples when he was elevated to the papacy, he had become the prisoner of Charles of Anjou, the brilliant and resourceful younger brother of Saint Louis of France.

Peter of Murrone was wax in the hands of Charles of Anjou. When Charles asked him to appoint nine new cardinals, all French or Neapolitan, Peter obliged. When Charles asked that his second son Louis be appointed Archbishop of Lyons, Peter obliged again.

Charles was an audacious and cunning tyrant; he even succeeded in forging documents to grant the whole of the Church tithes to the King of France.

The old hermit became pope under the title of Celestine V. He rode to his coronation on a donkey, his hands folded in prayer, his eyes downcast, while Charles of Anjou and his son Charles Martel, recently crowned King of Hungary, walked beside him, holding the bridle. Palms were laid at his feet, hosannas were chanted, the bells rang to announce the coming of a new Saviour. A strange, bent man with a wild beard and a face of icy pallor was being greeted as the *pastor angelicus* promised by Joachim of Flora, who had prophecied that with the coming of the holy pope a reign of peace would descend upon earth. After the angelic pastor there would come three more, who would be known as the Angelic Shepherds. There would be a century of holiness.

"What will you do now, Peter of Murrone?" asked the Franciscan poet Jacopone da Todi. "You are put to the test, and we shall see the work for which a life of contemplation has prepared you. If you disappoint the hopes of the world, there will be a curse upon you!"

For all his simplicity and holiness Celestine V seems to have known he was doomed. He prayed for the apostolic renewal of the Church, and found only intrigues. The wiles of Charles of Anjou wearied him, but the wiles of Cardinal Benedetto Gaetani proved more pleasing. The cardinal belonged to a noble family of the Campagna. He was strong-willed, intelligent, deeply versed in canon law, and serenely indifferent to holiness. Far from being an angelic pastor, he was an intriguer of extraordinary attainments. He had been the close adviser of two popes, and had been sent as papal legate to England and France. He decided to remove Celestine V from his throne and to become pope.

On December 13, 1294, after a reign of only four and a half months, Celestine V was induced to abdicate. At a secret consistory he appeared in full pontificals and read out the bull in which he declared himself divested of his pontificate, which he described as a burden too heavy to be borne. He spoke of his ignorance of papal affairs and the greater ignorance and sinfulness of the Christian people. He gave the cardinals full authority to elect a successor. Then he descended from his throne, stripped himself of his insignia, lifted the tiara from his head and removed from his finger the Fisherman's ring.

In the midst of the cardinals he sat on the ground like a beggar.

There were many who said that Cardinal Gaetani had written the bull. Others spoke of a mysterious speaking tube that reached down into the pope's cell and through which there came strange voices at night, urging him to abandon himself to God's will and then insisting it was God's will that he should renounce his pontificate. On Christmas Eve Cardinal Gaetani became pope, choosing the name Boniface VIII. The hermit saint was succeeded by the worldly jurist and politician, riddled with ambition and determined upon power.

Dante described Celestine V as one who through cowardice made the great refusal—*che fece per viltate il gran rifiuto*. The accusation was unjust: not cowardice, but the determination of his enemies, led to his downfall; and his enemies included at their head the ruthless aristocrat who became his successor.

The new pope decreed that the old pope should be kept a prisoner of the papal state. By some miracle Peter of Murrone escaped the vigilance of the police and succeeded in boarding a ship bound for Greece. Unfortunately a storm drove the ship back to the Italian coast. He was arrested and sent under guard, with two brothers of his Order, to Fumone, a mountain castle in the Campagna, where he died two years later, worn out by old age and the rigors of imprisonment.

Boniface VIII was a portent and a mirror of his times, a harsh, brutal, and superbly intelligent man who knew exactly what was needed to restore the primacy of the Church. He knew when to strike, but he was too inflexible to know when not to strike. He made mistake after mistake, and brought the Church close to ruin.

His enemies ranged from the Franciscans, who had hoped to see a *pastor angelicus* on the throne, to the kings of Europe and the feudal princes of Rome. He could do little to influence the Franciscans, and he seems to have despised the kings and emperors of Europe too much to know how to behave toward them. Against the feudal princes, and especially the two Colonna cardinals, he acted vigorously. The cardinals Jacopo and Pietro Colonna were simply deprived of their offices and dignities. "I will root out this accursed family and its diseased blood, which time after time raises its arrogant head," he proclaimed, and he would have destroyed the Colonnas root and branch if it had been possible. He was a man of furious energy, with a high color, fond of sweeping gestures, and absolutely intolerant of opposition. He was about sixty years old when he was elected, and his temper did not improve with the years. He suffered from painful attacks of the stone. We have seen in our own age the effects of physical disease on dictators.

Boniface VIII was a dictator: one of those harsh, interfering, opinionated men who believe they have a mission to order people about. He issued streams of orders to the Church and regarded kings as his obedient servants. He looked like a dictator. As we see him in Arnolfo's extraordinary elongated statue now in the Museum of the Duomo in Florence, he was one of those heavy men who yet move nimbly, tall and well proportioned, bristling with an air of natural authority and conscious of his intellectual superiority. He wears a tiara shaped like a bullet, and though one hand is raised in blessing, the gesture seems oddly out of place: he is altogether too commanding a figure to offer a gentle blessing on the world. He looks like a lawyer, and in fact he spent the early years of his pontificate struggling with a massive compendium of canon law. But though he was accustomed to the intricacies and subtleties of canon law, he recognized only one law. It was a very simple law: it stated that the pope's authority extended over the whole earth. The simplicities of this law concealed many complexities, and he was sometimes aware of them.

When the King of France, Philip le Bel, decided to tax the clergy, Boniface VIII replied immediately with the decretal *Clericis Laicos* forbidding the king to raise any revenues from the clergy without the express permission of the pope. A similar decretal was sent to King Edward I of England. There was uproar. The English king was incensed and outlawed all clerics who sided with the pope, thus giving them the choice between apostasy and treason. The French king decided upon the less barbarous expedient of refusing to grant export licenses to bullion leaving France and ordering all foreign merchants out of the kingdom, thus depriving the pope of his French revenues. The war of nerves between the pope and the kings of England and France had begun.

It was a long war, fought without mercy by irresponsible autocrats, none of whom had the least intention of surrendering his position. If the pope stepped back a little, it was only in order to advance further. He backed down over the question of taxes, permitting the kings to tax the clergy at times of emergency, and in order to ensure the flow of French gold and to please Philip le Bel, he canonized Louis IX, the saintly king who had died a martyr to the faith. He had not however changed his purpose. The supremacy of the pope was to be maintained at all costs, even at the cost of losing his throne.

At Christmas 1299 the crowds flocked to St. Peter's tomb in unparalleled numbers. From all over Christendom pilgrims came to seek the solace of the Church. Pondering the sudden revival in religious feeling, Boniface decided that it was due to his leadership of the Church, and that he would be able to reinforce his leadership by instituting a new and hitherto undreamed of ceremony to celebrate the new century. The ceremony took the form of a papal Jubilee. For the first time in its history the Church, speaking through the mouth of Boniface, announced a plenary indulgence for the remission of punishment due to sin. The faithful were promised full remission of Purgatory if they visited the seven basilicas. Those who could not undertake the pilgrimage were promised the same heavenly reward on payment to the Church of the traveling expenses they would have incurred if they had gone on pilgrimage. The Jubilee was a great success. Prices in Rome were deliberately kept low; thirty thousand pilgrims went in and out of the city daily; two hundred thousand people crowded into the inns and lodging places. The festival lasted a whole year, to the glory of Boniface and the financial advantage of the Church. Only one cloud darkened the horizon; among the countless pilgrims there were no kings.

From all over Europe men gathered in Rome as though to a feast. The pilgrims were good-tempered and law-abiding, and they were filled with kindness and charity for one another. They carried children, the sick, and the aged on their shoulders to the tomb of the Apostle; they beggared themselves with gifts to the Church. The peace of God reigned in the crowded streets. The chronicler Giovanni Villani tells the strange story of how the pope himself would sometimes appear in the streets, a tall commanding figure, wearing a double crown, while heralds strode before him with two uplifted swords, crying: "I am Caesar! I am Emperor!"

He was neither caesar nor emperor, and he was not long to be pope. The quarrel with King Philip broke out afresh over a matter that seemed unlikely to have great consequences. Within Languedoc lay the town of Pamiers, recently made into a bishopric by Boniface. The new bishop was Bernard Saisset, a personal friend of the pope, a man of wild speech. Saisset loved Boniface and detested Philip le Bel. He declared his love and detestation to anyone who cared to listen to him, and his behavior came to the notice of the king. In July 1301 Saisset was arrested and accused of insulting the king's majesty, of pursuing heretical doctrines, and of making defamatory remarks on the pope, the last two charges being added to demonstrate that the French court was perfectly capable of inventing purely imaginary charges. The arrest of a bishop by a civil court being contrary to canon law, Saisset appealed to the pope. Boniface replied with a bull denouncing King Philip for arresting a bishop and ordered the king to present himself in Rome to answer for his crimes. This bull had the strange effect of introducing a primitive form of parliamentary democracy into France, for in order to defend himself the king summoned a general assembly at Rheims to include all classes of the nation including the Third Estate; this general assembly was in fact the first meeting of the States General.

There was now open war between the pope and the king, a war all the more tragic because it was fought with the weapons of subversion and fraud. The pope commanded the king to submit, employing the contemptuous and arrogant language of a master to a slave. At a full consistory he declared: "If the King of France does not behave himself, I shall have the unpleasant duty of deposing him like a little boy." In the bull he said the same thing in more decorative language, and denounced the king as an infidel for rejecting the supreme authority of the Church. Pierre Flotte, the chancellor, replied with a ruse. He published the papal bull in a pamphlet distributed in Paris, with additions that made it even more insulting and intolerable. The quasi-forgery was designed to strip the pope of his pretensions and to show him as a grasping and incompetent potentate suffering from overweening pride. It was a masterly stroke. At the States General Pierre Flotte delivered a bill of particulars designed to make the pope appear even more incompetent, grasping, and proud. His life was vile; he was a murderer, a heretic, a practitioner of black magic, a monster who deserved only to be killed. The pope wanted all the world's revenues in order to further his private ambitions. Moreover, he was not the pope but a usurper, and it was the duty of "the very Christian King of France" to avenge the crime committed on the body of the Church. Lies, half-truths, and innuendoes filled the bill of particulars, and Boniface VIII was depicted as though he were some predatory insect. King Philip replied to the pope in a letter even more extraordinary than the original bull. "Philip, by God's grace King of the

French, to Boniface, who pretends to be Pope, little or no greetings!"
The rest of the letter was in the same tone of derisive comment.

The States General was called in the spring of 1302. In the following autumn Boniface VIII summoned four French archbishops,
thirty-five bishops, and six abbots to Rome, and castigated them for
permitting the French King to denounce the supreme pontiff, and
once more delivered himself of an inflexible statement of papal authority. The bull *Unam Sanctam* claimed that there was only one
Church and only one authority: the pope, who as Vicar of Christ and
successor of St. Peter, wielded both the temporal and spiritual swords
for the good of all souls. The temporal sword was subject to the spiritual; and while dominion over the earth was entrusted to kings, it
was only in order to work God's will on earth under the pope's direction. Both swords were in the power of the Church and received their
ultimate sanction from the pope. The infinite extent of papal authority was repeatedly emphasized. "We declare, proclaim, and define
that subjection to the Roman Pontiff is absolutely necessary for the
salvation of every human creature."

"Maleficus, non Bonifacius!" said the king, and one of his ministers said: "My master's sword is of steel, the Pope's is made of
words." Though the king was shaken by the new bull, his ministers
calmly went on measuring steel against words. One of the leading figures at court, William de Nogaret, a lawyer from Languedoc with
bitter memories of the Inquisition, had by this time become chancellor. His grandfather had been burned at the stake as a heretic, and he
was determined upon revenge. The form of revenge was very simple:
he would assassinate the pope, or at the very least render him harmless
in the same way that Boniface had rendered his predecessor harmless.

The conspiracy against the pope was carefully prepared in a
manner which has become more familiar in recent years than it was in
the Middle Ages. First, the pope must be stripped of his dignity. It
was thought necessary to accuse him of even more monstrous crimes
than he had committed; he was to be accused of so many evils that
people would be forced to believe him guilty. At a Council of State
held in the Louvre in the summer of 1303 William de Plasian declared
that Boniface had caused the loss of the Holy Land, that he was a
heretic and a simoniac, that he had murdered many priests and had
seduced many people into idolatry, that he had turned his back on the
altar during Mass, that he did not believe in transubstantiation or the

immortality of the soul, and that he erected silver statues of himself in the churches to his own glory. These were sinister charges, and they were designed to have a sinister effect.

Meanwhile William de Nogaret made his way to Italy under pretext of taking part in a mission of reconciliation. Some weeks were spent in forming a powerful coalition of allies. On September 7, 1303, a small but well-armed group of rebels marched on the family estate of the Gaetani family at Anagni, where the pope was staying. There was fierce fighting in the streets. Boniface took refuge in the cathedral, where the rebels found him standing before the altar in full pontificals, wearing his double crown, holding the Cross and the Gospels in his upraised hands. He was prepared for martyrdom, but Nogaret, though determined on the pope's downfall, was under strict orders to capture him alive and bring him to Lyons for public trial. He placed the pope under arrest, and then hesitated after hearing that the townspeople were determined to release the captive. His hesitation proved to be his undoing. The people of Anagni rose in revolt, aided by the arrival of troops of the Orsini. The pope's palatial mansion was set on fire, and it was remembered that the pope blessed the people from the balcony of the burning palace. Captured by the troops of the Orsini, he was brought to Rome and lodged in the Lateran. Thereafter he was never seen again except as a dim shape behind the windows. He had gone mad. He died a month later, three years after he celebrated his papal Jubilee and seven years after the death of Celestine V in the prison of Fumone. He was about eighty-four years of age.

His contemporaries said of Boniface VIII that "he crept in like a fox, reigned like a lion, and died like a dog." They said that Celestine V had cursed him, saying, *"Morietur ut canis!"* and the curse was now fulfilled. Yet in the eight years and nine months of his pontificate he demonstrated a powerful talent for exalting the Church; and the claims he made for the two swords were to haunt Europe for generations to come.

The bull *Unam Sanctam* came as the culmination of a long process of development. Boniface's manner of declaring the supremacy of the Church was offensive, but he was saying what Thomas Aquinas had already declared. The quarrel that began when an obscure priest became Bishop of Pamiers ended with the "Babylonian Captivity" of the papacy, which was not fully to end for over a century. Of the nine popes who followed Boniface VIII, eight ruled from Avignon in

France; and the vast hulk of the Palace of the Popes on the banks of the Rhône is mute testimony to the downfall of the supreme pontiff, who was pontiff only in name.

By ordering the kings of the earth to submit to him, Boniface was assuming the role of spiritual and temporal emperor over the whole world. He saw himself as another Augustus, another Constantine. He was determined to pit the authority of the Church against the authority of the kings in an age of growing nationalism, and he failed precisely because the people were no longer capable of enduring his arrogance. The bull *Unam Sanctam* was a cry of triumph at a moment of defeat.

The downfall of Boniface changed the nature of the papacy. Though the popes would continue to declare that they were the divinely privileged arbiters of the world's destinies, they no longer carried conviction. They were seen to be human—all too human. They suffered from mortal frailties, and were not strangers to self-will, treachery, and violence; the evil they sometimes committed was not forgiven by people with long memories. Dante consigned Boniface to hell among the simoniacs, and at the sight of "the whore that sitteth upon the waters," fouling even hell with its presence, Dante seems to be choking at the mouth. The rage is naked, but it is not directed against the papacy. It is directed against the person of the pope who nearly ruined the Church by his willfulness.

Once the pope had been defied by the secular power, there would be no end to it. Having humbled the pope, the king turned his attention to the Knights Templar, whose wealth and influence survived the loss of the Latin kingdom in the East. The Order had endured for nearly two hundred years since it was founded by Hugh de Payens to guard the Christian sanctuaries and the approach roads in the Holy Land. St. Bernard had given the Knights Templar his blessing and an oath based on the primary vow of the Cistercians. The knights were dedicated to poverty, chastity, and obedience. Poverty, however, had proved to be elusive, for the safeguard of so much property involved the knights in banking. The accumulated wealth of the Order was prodigious, and very tempting to the king, who had no scruples in offering to protect the Order while secretly making plans to destroy it. He set about seizing the wealth of the Order with the same cold-bloodied determination with which he set about the destruction of Boniface VIII.

The king's relations with the Order were close and outwardly friendly. Once when attacked by a Paris mob, he had taken refuge in the Temple; he showed his gratitude by becoming an *ex-officio* visitor to the Order, attending its ceremonial functions, sometimes being present at the introduction of new candidates for knighthood. He knew its leading members intimately, and was therefore in a position to hatch the plot more effectively. With the help of William de Nogaret, a man of stupendous daring and astonishing criminality, the king set about destroying the Order.

Over the years the Order had become aristocratic and exclusive, with no roots among the people, who feared its wealth and power. For perhaps half a century rumors had been current of the strange practices of the knights. It was whispered that on the day of initiation the candidates for knighthood were ordered to spit on the Cross, that they adored the image of Baphomet, who was clearly Muhammad in a thin disguise, and that they indulged in homosexual practices. Even worse crimes were attributed to them, for it was said that they were in league with the devil and could conjure up his presence at will. They were also charged with being dishonest speculators, and this charge was probably true. Yet their greatest crime in the eyes of the people was that they ostentatiously displayed their wealth. The people had no sympathy for them. When the blow fell, no one defended them. On October 12, 1307, the Grand Master Jacques de Molay attended the funeral of Catherine de Courtenay, the wife of Charles de Valois, the brother of the king. On the following night the king gave orders for the arrest of all the Templars known to be in France. Jacques de Molay and sixty others were arrested in Paris and some eighty more Templars were arrested elsewhere in France. The Templars were doomed; no pity would be shown to them, and they died miserably, denying up to the last moment that they had committed any crimes.

The trial of the Templars was a lengthy and devious one, for like other tyrants who came after him, King Philip desired abject confessions before sentencing them to death. It was not enough to pronounce them guilty; they must recognize their own guilt and thank him for permitting them to die. They were all tortured. Thirty-eight of the knights died in the torture chambers. The survivors were often so paralyzed with fear that they confessed to any charges, however grotesque. The most damning confession came from the Grand Master himself. On October 25, less than two weeks after his arrest, he signed a confession in which he declared that he was guilty of denying Christ and of spitting on the Cross. The confession was embodied in a letter ostensibly to be sent to all the Templars of France.

The trials continued, more Templars were rounded up, the torture chambers echoed with the cries of the knights who had fought the Saracens bravely, but were powerless against the king's men. The new pope, Clement V, a creature of Philip le Bel, issued a bull calling on the kings and princes of Europe to arrest the Templars wherever they could be found. There ensued a long quarrel between the pope and the French king as to who should control the lives and properties of the imprisoned Templars, and how they should die, and by what law they should be condemned. The quarrel came to a temporary end in the early summer of 1310 when the Archbishop of Sens at the king's orders placed fifty-four Templars on trial and condemned them to be burned at the stake as relapsed heretics for daring to retract their confessions.

On the following day the knight Aimery de Villiers-le-Duc, a man of fifty, who had spent more than half his life in the Order, was brought before the inquisitorial commission. Ordered to plead, he said: "I confessed to these accusations because the tortures inflicted upon me were too great to be borne, and my confessions were false. Yesterday when I saw fifty-four of my brothers driven away in carts to be burned at the stake because they had refused to confess our alleged sins, I thought I would not be able to overcome my fear of fire. I should now be able to confess everything. I feel this. I would confess that I killed the Lord if this were demanded of me." Then he turned to the commissioners and begged them not to repeat to the guards what he had just said, forgetting that it was the commissioners, not the guards, who had the power to send him to the stake.

The fifty-four Templars had been burned in the open country outside the Porte St. Antoine. They were roasted on slow fires, all protesting their innocence to the last. Two days later six more Templars were sent to the stake at the Place de Grève. Meanwhile the ecclesiastical commissioners continued their grim work of terror.

The last act of the tragedy took place early in 1314 when the Grand Master Jacques de Molay and with him Gaufrid de Charney, the preceptor of Normandy, were brought to a scaffold erected in front of Notre Dame. There in front of the people and the papal legates they were ordered to repeat their confessions, with the promise that if they did so they would not be burned, but sentenced to prison for life. De Molay, who had been cowed by terror and torture, now flung aside all his hesitations and in a loud voice confessed his guilt, but it was not the confession which the king wanted from him. "I do confess my guilt," he said. "It consists in having, to my shame and dishonor, through the pain of torture and fear of death, suffered myself to utter falsehoods, imputing scandalous sins and iniquities to an illustrious Order which nobly served the cause of Christianity. I disdain to seek a wretched and disgraceful existence by engrafting another lie on an original falsehood." In this way Jacques de Molay replied to the king's charges after more than six years of torture. The king acted swiftly. On his own responsibility he ordered the Grand Master and the preceptor of Normandy to be sent to the stake. That same night they were burned to death on the little island of the Seine known as the Isle of Trellises.

The proudest, bravest, and richest Order in Christendom now came finally to an end, its members burned at the stake or scattered to the four corners of the earth, its vast properties confiscated, its wealth purloined by the king. The Order, which had deserved well of the Church, was sacrificed by the Church to the secular power for the sake of an accommodation. Within the Church there had always been a civil war, the dangerous rivalries tending to weaken the fabric of autocratic rule. Under Celestine V, Boniface VIII, and their successors the Church proved to be powerless; and while repeating the formulas of autocracy, it bowed before the French king, who made it his captive.

Among the burning fagots on the Isle of Trellises the dream of a Christian empire ended. With the Knights Templar died the hope of reviving the Crusades against the advancing Turks. Once the Church had given its blessing to the knights who stood on guard at the frontiers of Christianity. Now, with the surrender of the knights to the secular power, the Church showed that it was indifferent to its own frontiers and to the ideals of chivalry.

The Church, not Christianity, was in danger. The fact that the distinction could be made showed to what an extent the Church had forfeited its historical role, how much it had contributed to its own downfall. Dante, who lived through those perilous times, prayed for the swift coming of an avenger. In his lifetime no avenger appeared.

In exile the Church continued to live in error: error was in the air it breathed and the landscapes it walked. Claiming sovereignty over all men, it was sovereign over none; and the pope from his huge fortress prison in Avignon merely stirred the air delicately with his hands, having abandoned all hope of influencing the world.

It was the end of Christendom. Never again would it be possible to dream of a true Christian empire embracing the whole of Europe. In time an avenger would appear in the shape of an obscure pilgrim climbing the steps of the Scala Santa in Rome, that marble stairway reputed to have been removed from the palace of Pontius Pilate in Jerusalem, and having reached the fourth or fifth stair he would tell himself and later the world that the Church had drowned in its own panoply.

Meanwhile in Avignon the Church dragged on its slow, useless existence, remote from the people, remote from the scholars, and remote from Christ. By an act of suicide the Church brought the Christian centuries to an end.

29 ✠ DANTE

At VERY rare intervals in history it happens that a man emerges who sums up the experience of ages. He is born, goes to school, marries, has children, quarrels with his fellows, suffers the same defeats which afflict his contemporaries, and dies. There is nothing in his conduct or behavior to suggest that he bears the burden of the centuries, and no one living at the time of his death would guess that a whole age had passed away. He goes through life quietly; at his death the lightning strikes, and the thunder echoes from the mountains.

Such a man was Dante Alighieri, who towers above the people of his time because he accomplished the final act which brought the Middle Ages to an end. The *Divine Comedy* was the crown and seal of all that went before; in that long and arduous epic, in which comedy has no place, he created what was at once the ultimate justification for medieval Christianity and its sentence of death. Beyond the *Divine Comedy* it would be impossible for any man to go.

Out of visions, legends, and the accumulated knowledge of centuries Dante constructed a vast shimmering edifice unlike any constructed up to his time. It extended over the whole reach of human and divine experience, and demanded of its author an extraordinary sensitivity to Christian faith in its manifold forms. The epic was not concerned with this world, but with all worlds; not with this time, but with all time; and it was rooted in a single event which included within its circumference all the events that have ever taken place and all that will ever take place. Its purpose, like the purpose of *Paradise Lost,* was to "assert eternal providence and justify the ways of God to men," but the scope was so vast that it seemed to escape altogether from anything so mundane as purpose. It was as though a Gothic cathedral had acquired voice and color and movement, and was singing.

Never again was there to be heard a voice which sang so sweetly or so uncompromisingly about the Christian mystery. In the *Divine Comedy* faith is absolute; there is no holding back; no doubts are expressed. The vision is pursued unrelentingly. Though he speaks often of trembling before the vast enormity of the scenes which open out to him, he writes with an assurance which suggests that he never trembled in his life. He walks through Hell, Purgatory, and Heaven with perfect composure and a steady tread. Boccaccio tells the story of the poet wandering one day through the streets of Verona and overhearing some women discussing him. "Look at him!" said a woman at a doorway. "There is a man who goes down to hell and returns whenever he likes and brings us tidings of those who are down below." Another woman replied: "No doubt you are saying the truth, for do you not see how his hair is black and singed, and his face bronzed with all the heat and smoke down below?" Boccaccio tells us that Dante was pleased with the words and smiled to himself as he went on his way.

In his lifetime he was regarded with supernatural awe; after his death he acquired the reputation which had long been enjoyed by Virgil—he was believed to be a magician, a man who could conjure up the dead. He became a legend during his lifetime. After his death the legend assumed such towering proportions that he almost disappears under its weight.

Of the man himself we know disappointingly little; not that there were many mysteries in his life, but he held himself in such reserve that he never completely acquires a recognizable human personality. We know that he was born toward the end of May 1265, the son of a notary, Alighieri degli Alighieri, and his young wife, Bella degli Abati, who descended from the nobility. We know that his mother died when he was very young, that his father remarried, and that he was orphaned in adolescence. We know that at the age of nine he attended a May feast given by a certain Folco Portinari, and there for the first time, while in the company of his father, caught a glimpse of Beatrice Portinari wearing a crimson gown, and remained for the rest of his life under her spell. Beatrice had just passed her ninth birthday; Dante was approaching his tenth. He saw her again nine years later when she was accompanied by two gentlewomen, and her greeting moved him so deeply that he was like someone stricken with a fever and dreamed a strange dream in which she appeared to be cradled in the arms of the Lord of Terrible Aspect, shrouded in a bloody cloth. In one hand the Lord held up a burning heart, which was Dante's own, and the heart was fed to the lady who vanished heavenward. As Dante relates the dream in the *Vita Nuova*, there is no doubt that he regarded it as a forewarning of her death, which took place seven years later. Out of the greeting and the terrible dream came the *Divine Comedy*.

For the remaining years of his life Dante was to walk in the bright shadow of Beatrice, a strange, withdrawn, and lonely man who found salvation only in her guiding presence. He was wedded to her more absolutely than he was wedded to his wife, who bore him three children.

We know Dante's appearance so well that if he entered a room we would recognize him instantly. The long face, the aquiline nose, and the protruding lower lip have become familiar from innumerable paintings and sculptures. One painting, executed by Giotto during Dante's lifetime, has survived on the walls of the chapel of the Palazzo del Podestà in Florence. When the chapel was transformed into a prison for condemned prisoners, the fresco depicting God reigning over the Blessed in Paradise was understandably covered with plaster, and so it remained for centuries. In 1850 it was decided to remove the plaster, and Dante was discovered among the many portraits of Florentine citizens depicted on the fresco. One eye had been damaged by a nail, but otherwise the painting was remarkably preserved. Dante is seen in profile in a contemplative mood, wearing the *lucco* and *berretta* of the Florentine magistrate, with a book under one arm, and holding a pomegranate, symbol of life and suffering, in his hand. He was clothed in garments of red, white, and green, the colors in which Beatrice appears in the Earthly Paradise. For some reason the whole figure was repainted shortly after its discovery, and the original green became chocolate. Yet there emerges an astonishingly vivid portrait of the poet in his young manhood, and there is no doubt of its authenticity; nor is there any doubt of the authenticity of the death mask preserved in the Signoria at Florence. The soft features have become cragged with age, the beaked nose is more hawk-like, the sharply sculptured lips are now turned down at the edges; it is the mask of a dead warrior. These are the only renderings of his features known to have been made in his time.

His contemporaries saw him as a man apart, harsh and bitter in features and in soul alike, lost in visions and scornful of the world around him. The Florentine chronicler Giovanni Villani described him as "presumptuous, hard, and disdainful," and noted that he scarcely deigned to converse with ordinary men. Boccaccio, who was eight years old when Dante died, says that he seldom spoke unless directly addressed, and when he did speak it was with a voice and manner exactly measured and adapted to the occasion. He had the scholar's fastidious reserve, and an aristocratic temper, longing, as Boccaccio says, "for honor and fame perhaps more than was altogether consistent with the nobility of his character." There was iron in him, and great pride, and a deep vein of sensuality. Boccaccio describes him as "dark-skinned, his hair thick, black, and curling like his beard," and he was slightly hump-backed from long studying. Sometimes the gentle scholar appears as a satyr, and the thoughtful melancholy expression gives place to naked rage.

Of Dante's manuscripts none have survived; no scrap of paper bearing any words written by him has been handed down, though there are contemporary documents relating to him. Yet we know what his handwriting looked like. Boccaccio saw his manuscripts and informs us that "he wrote a finished hand, making thin, long, and perfectly formed letters," adding that he had more than an ordinary talent for drawing. No doubt he sketched the scenes of the *Divine Comedy*, for they have a pictorial frieze-like quality and almost demand to be drawn; and indeed such drawings, of astonishing delicacy and firmness, were made by Botticelli during the last years of his life. The *Divine Comedy* is like a Chinese scroll that opens slowly on the towering landscape of the universe.

No one knows how long he labored over the epic, or when its first tentative beginnings emerged. He seems to have worked at it for many long years, for there are many changes of mood and alterations of feeling. The famous letter of Can Grande della Scala, lord of Verona, to whom he sent the first cantos of the *Paradiso* and explained that the work must be understood on many levels of meaning, seems to have been composed in 1318. By this time the *Inferno* and *Purgatorio* would appear to have been completed. Work on the *Paradiso* went on slowly. At some time in 1320, the year before his death, he spoke of the *Paradiso* to his friend Giovanni del Virgilio, giving him to believe that it was still unfinished. At his death the last cantos were missing, and according to Boccaccio they were only discovered eight months later when Dante's son Jacopo had a dream in which it was revealed to him that the last thirteen cantos could be found in a little niche in the wall where Dante had concealed them. Then at last, with the crowning entry of the poet into the eternal light and the flame of love, the *Divine Comedy* comes to the end that had long been foreseen; and in the visions of those nearly lost posthumous cantos he achieved heights of poetry never reached before.

In his letter to Can Grande, Dante wrote that the whole work was undertaken not for a speculative but for a practical end. "The purpose of the whole and of this portion (the opening cantos of the *Paradiso*) is to remove those who are living in this life from the state of wretchedness and to lead them to the state of blessedness." He claimed to be the appointed guide to heaven, a new St. Paul leading the faithful to the heavenly vision, a new Aeneas marking the stages of the journey from fallen Troy to spiritual Rome. In fact the task that Dante gave himself was far more than to be the guide to blessedness. He claimed the power to pass judgment on the dead, to question them, and to demand answers from them. Throughout the *Inferno* and the *Purgatorio* he appears as a Grand Inquisitor. So he says in his letter to Can Grande: "Taken literally the subject is the state of the soul after death, simply considered. But taken allegorically the subject is man, according as by his good or ill deserts he renders himself liable to the reward or punishment of Justice." Justice, indeed, is the major theme of the *Inferno* and the *Purgatorio*. The judge in all his panoply visits judgment on those who are already judged.

As Dante stalks over the bodies of the damned, recognizing now one and now another as they appear in the pits, the smoking sands and the rivers of boiling blood, we are made aware that we are entering a world so far from our own preoccupations that it is almost beyond our power to understand. Hell is painted in romanesque colors, stark with a purely human horror. There is nothing here to frighten a generation that has known Auschwitz. The torments are physical; the damned suffer in body, while their minds are remarkably disengaged; they proclaim in happy defiance the enormity of their sins. Farinata thrusts himself upright from his blazing tomb "as though he had all

Hell in deep despite." Francesca confesses her sin—a single kiss. Pier delle Vigne, like the son of Priam in Virgil's *Aeneid*, becomes transformed into a tree and speaks through the tree's wounds, swearing by the roots of the tree that he never broke faith with his lord, the Emperor Frederick II. Men have their faces scorched, hang head-down in mud, are flayed and pummelled and torn to pieces, but their torments are incomparably less terrible than the torments living men have suffered today. The anguish that feeds on itself, the hopelessness and despair brought on by diabolical intelligence are rare. Dante is describing a Hell that is almost too easy.

This pleasant and rather enviable Hell, with its machinery of steep cliffs, wild woods, and blood-red lakes, resembling the Apennines on a stormy night, is essentially theatrical. With every canto a new backcloth appears; the spotlight wavers and settles on some remembered crime, some injury committed on history or on Dante. Sometimes we see the sinners in their full dimensions, but always briefly. They may be seen as briefly as Minos, the gaunt judge of the underworld, whose brutish shape is conjured up in a single stupendous line: "*Stavvi Minos orribilmente, e ringhia*" (There sits the awful Minos, grinning). Or they may simply pass in review, only their names being mentioned in catalogues that read like litanies. Or else Dante will linger over them, inquiring into the nature of the crime like a father confessor who seeks even in Hell to grant absolution against a penance. Francesca da Rimini, murdered by her husband, confesses her love for her husband's brother:

> *Noi leggiavamo un giorno per diletto*
> *di Lancialotto come amor lo strinse:*
> *soli eravamo e sanza alcun sospetto.*
>
> *Per più fiate li occhi ci sospinse*
> *quella lettura, e scolorocci il viso;*
> *ma solo un punto fu quel che se vinse.*
>
> *Quando leggemmo il disiato riso*
> *esser baciato da contanto amante,*
> *questi, che mai da me non fia diviso,*
>
> *la bocca mi baciò tutto tremante.*
> *Galeotto fu il libro, e che lo scrisse:*
> *quel giorno più non vi leggemmo avante.*

One day for pastime we read of Lancelot,
and how he was caught in the toils of love:
we were alone and suspected nothing.

Many times this reading caused us to gaze
into each other's eyes, our faces drained;
but only one moment overcame us.

When we read of how the longed for smile
was kissed by such a lover, then he
who will never be torn away from me

kissed me on the mouth all trembling.
Galeotto was the book, and he who wrote it:
that day we read in it no more.

(Inferno V, 127–138)

These lovers who slip so quietly into sin scarcely deserve their place in Hell, and Dante seems to have been perfectly aware that he was doing violence to the scheme of Hell by placing them in the second circle in the company of Semiramis, Cleopatra, Helen, Achilles, Paris, and Tristan. Francesca was no heroic and commanding figure leaving a trail of ruin behind her; she fell into love as others fall into sleep; her crime was in being killed by her husband. There is some ambiguity in her presence in Hell, for she belongs elsewhere. Her punishment is to wander eternally with her lover, flying light upon the wind like thistledown: an enviable torment. Dante wept with pity and fell to the ground in a dead faint when he heard her story: it was pity for her death, not for her sin.

These ambiguities are present throughout the *Inferno* and *Purgatorio*. Dante is not always the judge; nor is he always the lonely, friendless ghost wandering through the dark roads of Hell. Friendship, indeed, will sometimes permit him to color his verdicts; it was his friendship for Guido da Polenta, lord of Ravenna and father of Francesca, that enabled him to deal gently with her. He loved Guido this side of idolatry, and it was Guido who protected him during the last years of his life when he was staying in Ravenna.

Throughout the *Divine Comedy* the harsh medieval world of the bestiaries conflicts with the clear and trembling world of Beatrice. Romanesque wages war with Gothic, winter with spring. The ravening or stately beasts who appear at intervals, that strange menagerie of gryphons, leopards, lions, and she-wolves, derive from the same sources of the imagination which produced the contorted romanesque carvings. The lion at Moissac, threatening to devour everyone who enters the church, walks by Dante's side. Romanesque, too, are the grotesque tyrants who are held up for execration. Ugolino, Count of Donoratico, is thrown into prison with his sons and grandsons, and the prison key is tossed in the Arno. Ugolino's sons and grandsons die; to live a few days longer Ugolino eats their flesh, and when Dante finds him in Hell he was still gnawing on a skull, "his teeth as strong as a dog's upon a bone." Ugolino, seen in the dim light of his prison cell, belongs to nightmare. He is one of those who suffer excruciating torment while alive, and merely repeats the habitual punishment in Hell. He belongs to a world already vanishing, while Francesca, singing of earthly love as sweetly as Beatrice sings of heavenly love, belongs to a more gentle age.

Yet always there is the sense of a judgment being passed, of the ceremonies of justice being performed in a court which is continually on the move. Dante never forgot that he had been a magistrate. His verdicts are clear-cut; there is no appeal; every crime fits neatly into its appointed category. It is not only that he is never overwhelmed by doubts or hesitations, but it is unthinkable that doubts should arise or that he should ever hesitate. Even on Hell he imposes order. There is something breathtaking in the inevitability of his progress from one circle to the next. Never again were the categories to be differentiated so neatly. After his death the map would be rolled up, and a new and far more complicated map of the human spirit would replace it.

What is disturbing in Dante is his intellectual pride, his titanic assurance. He is not only the judge of the underworld, but he is also monarch, high priest, and executioner. Once Leonardo da Vinci spoke with envy and approval of the eastern kings who showed themselves only when hidden by masks and veils; with Dante we feel we are in the presence of someone who is continually veiled, whose features are never revealed, an intellect so proud that we are almost surprised that he did not meet himself and curse himself during his voyage through Hell. He is *l'uomo universale*, master of all arts and sciences, closer to Aristotle than to Virgil, having read all the books and penetrated all the secrets of the universe. Pride dogs his footsteps, and there is some significance in the fact that his first encounter in Hell was with a strange tribe of angels of his own invention, for they are unknown to theology. These were "the angels that were not rebels, unfaithful to God, faithful only to themselves":

Angelli che non furon ribelli,
nè fur fideli a Dio, ma per sè foro.

(*Inferno* III, 38)

When Dante comes to describe the proud, the violent against God and nature, those who have attempted to scale the uttermost heights, there is always something curiously relenting in him. Almost he pardons the proud; his greatest fury is directed against the covetous. The proud rebellious Nephilim, "the mighty men of old," who made war on Heaven, are seen in the fading light like distant fortress towers, and although Dante places them resolutely in Hell, he permits them to retain their ancient grandeur, as though it was theirs by right. Indeed, throughout the *Inferno* the evil retain their grandeur and their sharp outlines against the midnight sky, while the tenants of Purgatory and Heaven become more and more diffuse as they approach the blinding light of God.

Dante was perfectly aware of his own pride, and his disdainful soul, *alma sdegnosa*, took what small comfort it could from the contemplation of himself. He speaks of "those sorry souls who live without infamy and without renown, displeasing to God and his enemies," and he was clearly not to be counted among them. For himself he would have renown or infamy, whatever the cost. Behind the clean façade of the *Divine Comedy*, polished like marble, there lurk more terrors than he ever hinted at. His Hell is child's play compared to the Hell he knew. His calm is superficial, and the steady rhymes conceal, and therefore make tolerable, the searing violence of his spirit.

In this, of course, Dante resembles his mentor Virgil, the violent contemplative who was asked to compose an epic on the Augustan peace and wrote instead an epic of legendary wars. There is no sun in the *Aeneid*. All is tempest, flashes of lightning, wounded soldiers in moonlight, funeral pyres—the Gothic horrors piled up in monstrous evocation of the discords in the Roman soul. Virgil begins and ends in grief. The speech of Aeneas sitting over the dead deer by the light of cauldron flames, a speech that Dante was to transform into a statement of abounding faith, sets the major theme—the grief of conquest. Dante's theme is a more modest one. It is the grief of living on this earth.

So Dante presents himself as the stranger, remote from the pre-occupations of this world, rejoicing in Hell, rejoicing even more in Purgatory, and still more in the perfect peace of Heaven. Yet, strangely, he writes best about this world; and when he writes of Heaven he employs the imagery of jewels and flowers and running streams, the same images he had introduced into his love poems. Heaven is the rose window of a Gothic cathedral. When he writes of the world, the artificial images are abandoned, and we see how closely he studied the people he disdained. Especially in the *Inferno* we are made aware of the ordinary events of everyday life as they break through the murk of Hell. Writing of those who are traitors to their kin, he devises a suitable punishment for them—they are to be immersed in ice with only their faces peering above the surface. Although he clearly hates these people, images of another and more familiar world enter his thoughts, and we are introduced to the familiar village pond where the bullfrogs croak, the storks chatter among the reeds, and the farm-girls dream their lives away. Here he describes the traitors frozen in the ice of the lowest circle:

> *E come a gracidar si sta la rana*
> *col muso fuor dell' acqua, quando sogna*
> *di spigolar sovente la villana:*
>
> *livide, insin la dove appar vergogna,*
> *eran l'ombre dolenti nella ghiaccia,*
> *mettendo i denti in nota di cigogna.*
>
> *And as the croaking bullfrog lies*
> *with muzzle above the surface of the water,*
> *what time the farm-girl dreams of harvesting,*
>
> *livid, to the place where shame appears,*
> *the sorrowing shades transfixed in ice*
> *set their teeth like storks chattering.*
>
> (*Inferno* XXXII, 31-36)

Here the seasons are reconciled; harvest time, summer, and winter disturb the poet from his dreams of Hell, and the insistent world demands to be present. It could hardly be otherwise; the disdainful poet loved the world too much. He was altogether too sensual, too demanding, to be free of the world's pleasures. Ultimately he wanted what all men want: power, women, a corner he could call his own.

Though the composition of the *Divine Comedy* seemed to remove him from the preoccupations of ordinary men, those same preoccupations were continually felt, and they were all the more present when he was least conscious of them. In Hell, too, there must be bullfrogs, storks, and farm-girls.

For nature he had a special tenderness; for women he had more than tenderness. His love affairs were numerous, and it would seem that they were brief, unhappy, and violent. He was continually wandering and seems never to have entered upon a permanent liaison. We learn from Boccaccio that "the vice of lustfulness found no small place in him, not only in his youth but also in the years of his maturity," and Beatrice herself in the *Purgatorio* accuses him of hurling himself into the arms of another woman as soon as he learned of her death. His poetry is raw with unregenerate passion, and when in his lofty fashion he speaks of love in the abstract, physical love is never far away. He knew love's treacheries and women's helpless tears:

> *il nudo bracchio, di dolor colonna,*
> *sente l'oraggio che cade dal volto*

"The naked arm, the column of grief, felt the flood of tears falling down her face." When he sees through a torn skirt "that part of her which it is courteous to be silent about," the woman pleads that she is helpless and must offer herself because "our nature commands us to come to you." But it was also the nature of Dante to console himself with women, and when they refused him, he could be merciless. In the *Pietra Sestina*, named perhaps after a young woman called Pietra, of the noble Paduan family of the Scrovigni, he abandoned the sweet *dolce stil nuovo* for a powerfully harsh utterance, a chilling exhibition of controlled fury:

> *To the dim day and the large circle of shade*
> *I have come, alas, and to the whitening hills,*
> *Where there is no more color on the leaves,*
> *And yet my longing has not changed its green,*
> *Embedded as it is in the flinty stone,*
> *Which speaks and hears as though it were a woman.*
>
> *So in this fashion does the fair young woman*
> *Stay frozen in the snow that lies in shade—*
> *For she is no more moved than is a stone*
> *When the sweet season comes that warms the hills,*

And changes them again from white to green
By strewing them with flowers and with leaves.

When on her hair she sets a wreath of leaves,
She drew our thoughts from every other woman:
For then she mingled golden curls with green
So well that Love came nestling in her shade:
Love has imprisoned me among low hills
More closely than in walls of limestone.

Her beauty has more virtue than a stone,
The wound she deals may not be healed by leaves:
For I have fled through plains and over hills
Seeking refuge from so dangerous a woman,
And from her light there is for me no shade
In hill or under wall or where the leaves are green. . . .

In such a poem he shows himself subdued by some unobtainable woman, and giving way to his grief with more venom than he knew. The granite face is misleading. Sometimes he shows the angry, contorted face of a child who knows no panacea for his terrible griefs. There is a famous fragment on a wandering scholar in the St. Polten Register: "I am a wanderer, almost a beggar, revealing against my will the wounds inflicted by fortune, a ship without sail or rudder drifting in dry winds." These were dangerous winds, and they carried Dante across the length and breadth of Italy, like an autumn leaf.

The authoritarian temper of his mind was sharpened by exile. When the French under Charles of Valois marched into Florence and established his political enemies in power, he was condemned *in absentia* to pay a heavy fine, and when the fine remained unpaid, he was condemned to death by fire. It is not a fate that a man regards with equanimity. Dante went into exile because there was no alternative, because the consequences of being captured were too terrible to contemplate. The sentence was passed in March 1302, when he was thirty-seven years old. For the remaining nineteen years of his life he was to live in dread of capture or betrayal.

A lonely, embittered man, with a price on his head and without means, for the Florentine government had sequestered his entire property, he behaved as political refugees often behave: his one consuming thought was the overthrow of the Florentine government, whatever the cost in human lives and in human hopes. When the Holy Roman Emperor Henry VII crosses the Alps with the aim of reuniting Germany and Italy and restoring the empire of the Hohenstaufen, Dante welcomed him as the preordained successor of the Caesars, the hammer which would destroy the power of the papacy and the city states. In 1311 "the divine and the triumphant Henry" was crowned in Milan with the iron crown of Lombardy, so named because the plate lining the crown was fashioned, according to tradition, from a nail of the Cross. Dante, who was present at Milan, swore an oath of fealty to the emperor and kissed his feet. In the *Paradiso* an even greater honor was reserved for Henry: alone among the emperors he was given a place in heaven marked by a crown. Henry VII proved to be an incompetent strategist; and though to Dante's joy he laid siege to Florence—never was the poet more vehement than when he prophecied the awful fate awaiting the Florentines if they refused to accept the German as their rightful king—the king was unable to conquer the city, and he died obscurely a few years later, having failed to accomplish his grand design. Henry VII proved to be an improbable candidate for the throne of Augustus.

Yet for a brief period there were bright hopes in the air. The dream of a united Italy, with both the emperor and the pope ruling from Rome, haunted Dante as long as he lived. Many years after the death of Henry VII he composed his Latin treatise *De Monarchia*, at once a tribute to the dead monarch and a plea for the revival of the ancient Roman Empire. The treatise is closely argued. Had not the Roman Empire acquired divine sanction from the birth of Christ? God had singularly blessed the Roman people by granting them dominion over the earth. Had not Augustus ruled by God's command? The will of God had manifested itself throughout Roman history, and it was therefore the duty of men to perpetuate Roman rule and to obey the appointed emperor in all matters concerning government, and the pope in all matters concerning the spiritual life. In this way the powers of heaven and earth would be held in a perfect balance, and peace would be granted to all mankind. Rome with its two thrones would become the fountain of all blessings.

In the *Divine Comedy* Dante portrayed an ordered universe; in *De Monarchia* he portrayed an ordered empire; and both were dreams. The world he knew was profoundly disordered and agitated, and he was himself uprooted and alienated from the society he lived in, the eternal wanderer in search of a lodging house. He despised the earthly Church, which could give him no shelter, and found no comfort in the intrigues of the city states. While he protested against the vices of his age, the leaping pride and individualism which were making a mockery of order, he was himself the victim of pride and the most individual of men. He was caught in a trap which he described at length in the *Inferno* and the *Purgatorio*. In the *Paradiso* and *De Monarchia* he showed the way out of the trap, having discovered that the most perfect freedom lay in submission to the supreme authority of God and emperor. But it was already too late for dreams. Never again was there to be a Holy Roman Emperor capable of dominating an empire; and man, not God, stood in the center of the universe.

The tragedy of the *Divine Comedy* lay in the imperfection of man, his refusal to submit himself completely to authority, his impudence and self-reliance, enabling him to disregard the established dogmas of the Church and the traditions of his own past. Dante came on the scene just at the moment when the entire fabric of Christian civilization was being questioned by men who no longer felt any profound loyalty to the Church, and still less did they feel any loyalty to the emperor. The great continuous questions of man's essence and existence were being asked anew by men determined to discover the truth for themselves. Dante, too, asked these questions, but he answered them according to the traditions of an earlier age. He dreamed of being a great innovator, one of those men who accomplish God's purpose in new ways, but his thoughts centered about the events of the past. Authority, the Roman Empire, Augustus Caesar, Virgil, the *pax romana*, the virtues inherent in order and conformity, to these he paid tribute in a long backward glance. But the future was of little interest to him. He summed up the experience of thirteen centuries, and found them wanting.

One day a certain Friar Ilario, a humble monk of the monastery of Corvo, was wandering in the mountains in search of a night's lodging, when he came upon a stranger who was gazing fixedly and with a great yearning at a monastery. The stranger was like a man in a trance. Friar Ilario, a bold man, went up to him and said: "Tell me, what are you looking for?" There was no answer, and he repeated the question. Then at last the stranger turned away from the monastery, gazed at Friar Ilario, and said: "Peace." Some moments passed, and then the stranger removed from his bosom a small book, saying: "Here is part of a poem I am writing, and I give it to you as a keep-

sake, so that you may remember me." The small book contained the
opening cantos of the *Inferno*, beginning:

> *Nel mezzo del cammin di nostra vita*
> *mi ritrovai per una selva oscura,*
> *Che la diritta via era smarrita.*

> *Midway upon the journey of our life*
> *I found myself within a gloomy wood,*
> *For the straight way was utterly lost.*

The story told by Friar Ilario offers one of the few glimpses we
have of Dante in his wanderings through the gloomy wood, searching
for the straight way and finding it only in his dreams. A somber man,
given to sudden acts of generosity, searching beyond the monastery
walls for the peace that is not of this earth, violent and humble by
turns, he seemed to include within himself all the conflicting forces of
his age. Once he described Henry VII as "an eagle, terrible in gold,"
upheld by the angelic hosts as he swooped across the sky from the
Pyrenees to the Caucasus, but he was himself that eagle. To the end
there was something terrible and fearful about Dante Alighieri, whose
name means "the enduring and the winged."

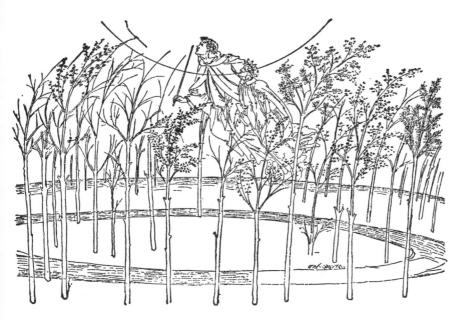

30 ✠ THE END OF CHRISTENDOM

ABOUT the time of the death of Dante the traditional world which was born of the marriage of Christianity and the surviving remnants of the Roman Empire came to an end. The old preoccupations gave place to new; old habits were being abandoned; the ancient faith was being questioned; the earthly horizons of men were vastly expanded. Quite suddenly the world seemed to change color and texture, becoming a different world altogether. Where before Christ stood at the center of the universe, now once again for the first time since the age of Pericles man saw himself at the center of the universe, resplendent in his new-found powers.

Those powers were awe-inspiring, for they involved nothing less than man's discovery of himself by his own native intelligence without benefit of dogma. He was no longer terrified by the powers of the Church; the papacy had submitted to the temporal power and was living out its long "Babylonian captivity" in Avignon, no longer presiding over the mainstream of human thought. Men were free to invent, to experiment, to follow ideas to their ultimate and dangerous conclusions. A new music was being heard, stronger, coarser, and more violent than anything heard previously; and the world was being orchestrated anew.

It was not only that the city states were emerging as powers in their own right and that nationalism was becoming a force to be reckoned with, ultimately to break the power of the papacy, but the intellectual leadership of Europe was now firmly in the hands of the universities. Paris, Padua, and Bologna, not Rome, had become the centers where the new dogmas were being discovered. While Latin

His shadow over the earth, His body no longer ethereal, glittering with the diamond-points of mosaics, but heavy with human weight and rounded with human form. The frescoes of the Arena Chapel at Padua were painted about 1305. In them he showed decisively that religious emotion can be conveyed in three-dimensional forms in bright colors that accurately represent the colors of the earth, not the colors of an imagined heaven. The dawn rises, dusk falls, men and women move about the earth, and their movement is also a part of divinity. The frescoes are remarkably well preserved, and we can still see the gleaming freshness of the design and the glowing colors in those panels reaching up to the roof, transforming the entire chapel into a jewel box; yet the jewels do not dazzle; a calm light pours down from the walls; there is the sense of a mystery revealed in human terms; God walks in the noonday, and feels the sun's heat on his face.

The stupendous achievement of Giotto lies in his imaginative vision and the sense of continuing movement he gives to his painted figures. In some thirty-seven panels he depicts the life of Christ with the precision of a man who was present and saw it with his own eyes. The Scriptures and the apocryphal Gospels provide the theme, but Giotto follows his own visionary way, painting what he saw, stripping from his design everything that was merely glimpsed or seen in passing. He sees steadily, in memorable blocks of color, the scenes set against the pervading blue of the sky in an architectural framework of rocks and houses. He gives depth and grandeur to the parade of figures streaming across the whole length of the chapel.

The Byzantine artists knew exactly how to represent the Pieta. They painted the Virgin and St. John beside the livid Christ lying at the foot of the Cross, while Mary Salome and Mary the mother of St. John hover in the background. In this way they had represented the traditional theme in innumerable frescoes and mosaics in a manner sanctified by custom and convention. Giotto saw it differently. He painted a wandering yellow wall and a dead tree, a broken hillside beneath a clouded sky, and in the shelter of the wall the Virgin holding the dead Christ on her knees. Christ is calm in death, the Virgin expresses the agony of grief. The long sloping wall, the gray hills, the dead tree, and the huddled figures around the body of Christ express the torrent of grief ebbing and flowing across the painting. Angels hover in the sky, and they too are weeping. All are lamenting over the dead Christ—all except one. In the center of the painting we see

St. John in a voluminous red robe, leaning forward and gazing down at Christ. His face is lit with a smile of adoration, his arms are flung back in wonderment, youthful energy pours through him, and he is caught up into a heaven of exultation. There is no grief in him. He stands there in the attitude of a man who has known no greater joy than the sight of the dead Christ, for to him alone there is given the knowledge of the resurrection.

In that splendid and majestic painting Giotto has succeeded in conveying a sense of divinity working through the very human mourners and the exultant St. John. Human flesh is portrayed as it is, human gestures are depicted with a profound knowledge of human emotion, and always there is the sense of movement toward some mysterious end. Cennino Cennini said that "Giotto translated the art of painting from Greek to Latin, and made it modern," but this is to underestimate his contribution to sensibility. He translated Byzantine painting into the language of the human heart, and in so doing poured life into a decaying tradition. Like Dante, who was his friend, he assumed the visionary's right to interpret Christian ideas according to his own light, which was not the light of the Church. He committed the supreme heresy of transforming God into man.

It was a heresy which was to continue over the centuries, gathering strength with every advance in human knowledge. The theologians might deplore the new place given to man; they could not prevent him from occupying it. To the Neoplatonists of Florence, man with his creative forces stood at the center of the universe, taking command of his own destiny. Pico della Mirandola, the youthful "earl of Mirandolle and lord of Italy," stated the case for man's supremacy in his *Most Elegant Oration on the Dignity of Man* in which he announces that man belongs neither to earth nor to heaven, but to some special region in between. From this command post he surveys his destiny. The Creator speaks to man:

I have made thee neither heavenly nor earthly, neither mortal nor immortal, and like a judge appointed for being honorable thou art made the moulder and maker of thyself; thou mayest knead thyself into whatever shape thou desirest. Thou mayest sink into a beast, or be born anew in a divine likeness. The brutes bring forth from the mother's body what they will carry with them as long as they live; the higher spirits are from the beginning, or soon after, what they will be for ever. To thee alone is given a growth and a development depending on thine own free will. Thou bearest in thee the seed of universal life.

Man, endowed with an angelic intelligence and a divine body, the master of creation, the superb artificer of his own destiny, no longer needed the consolations of religion. He was free to do as he pleased, and possessed no use for moral restraints. The measure of the change can be seen in Michelangelo's heroic Christ in the Sistine Chapel, a figure of elemental power and youthful authority, more Apollo than Christ, with no stain of suffering on his broad brow, unwounded and beautiful. The torment and the fierce hopes belong to the forgotten past; the Crucifixion took place in another dispensation of time; and man arises at last in his new splendor.

For Marsilio Ficino, the contemporary of Pico della Mirandola, the destiny of man was even more exalted. Man was the vicar of God, who had planted a divine intelligence in his rational soul; and just as all things were possible to God, so all things were possible to man. According to Ficino, life circulates from the earth to the stars "in order to constitute the uninterrupted tissue of the whole of nature": man upon earth commands, or at least possesses the power to command, the whole universe. The proper task of man was therefore the heroic conquest of the universe, his mastery of all space and time. "As for our desire for victory," wrote Ficino, "we can easily recognize the immeasurable splendor of our soul from the fact that even dominion over this world will not satisfy it, if after having subdued this world, it learns that there is another which is still unsubdued."

A soul so immeasurably splendid, so like to God, had little need of God's favor. Faith, grace, penitence, and prayer were, in the eyes of Ficino, no more than the decorations of the religious life; he preferred a world in which all the decorations were stripped away so that man in his nakedness and pride could make his triumphant assault on the universe. Man, made in the likeness of God, no longer had need of God, for he was himself divine.

We who come later, recognizing the illimitable powers of human ingenuity and the wayward strength of men to dominate their environment, find ourselves in a quandary. We have learned long ago that conquest is not enough and that the insatiable hunger for dominion gives no comfort to the soul. Human sorrow and grief, the miracles of birth and death, remind us of our insufficiency and powerlessness; none of our ills are exorcised by dominion; and the vision of Ficino ends in despair. Men in their troubled lives need a more nourishing food. They need mercy and loving-kindness, justice and peace, the hope of blessedness. The widow's tears, the child's loneliness, the old man's fear of death, the sick man's terror of his wounds—these remain, and will remain, to remind us of our weakness. We learn in the end that we are not godlike, and we are far from being able to recognize the immeasurable splendor of our souls. Pico della Mirandola spoke of men having the power to sink to the level of the beasts or to be born anew in a divine likeness. We have learned to our sorrow that we are more like beasts than divinities.

When Caesar was all-powerful and the world lay at the feet of his merciless legionaries, Christ brought mercy into the world. He pleaded against the rule of force, the arbitrary judgments of tyrants, the pomp and majesty of this world, saying that all men were their brothers' keepers and should love one another. He proclaimed the kingdom of love, more powerful and enduring than imperial Rome. In search of this kingdom men followed in their multitudes and attempted to build a Christian empire to establish his rule over the earth, and when this earthly empire faded, he was more powerful than ever. His kingly power was not manifested from the thrones of the mighty, but in the mysterious solitudes of the human heart, the heart speaking to the heart. As long as there is suffering and death men will listen to the voice by the lakeside, saying: "Come unto me, all ye that labor and are heavy laden, and I will give you rest."

✠ CHRONOLOGICAL TABLE ✠

A.D.

c. 460   Dionysius the Areopagite's writings are in circulation
527-65   Reign of Justinian
529   Closing of Schools in Athens; extinction of Platonic philosophy
532   Nika riots; beginning of building of Hagia Sophia
537   Dedication of new Hagia Sophia
540   Birth of St. Gregory the Great
546   Rome taken by Goths
570   Birth of Muhammad
604   Death of St. Gregory the Great
622   Flight of Muhammad to Medina
635-41   Arabs conquer Palestine, Persia, and Egypt
713-34   Arabs conquer all Spain except Asturias
732   Arabs defeated by Charles Martel
742   Birth of Charlemagne
778   Roncesvalles
800   Coronation of Charlemagne in Rome
814   Death of Charlemagne
c. 843   Norse raiders sail up French rivers
862   Foundation of Russian empire by Rurik
888   Dismemberment of Charlemagne's empire
c. 900   Norsemen have encircled Europe
c. 989   Vladimir, Grand Prince of Kiev, baptised
1003   Raoul Glaber describes French churches
c. 1031   Birth of Roger I of Sicily
1061-91   Normans settle in Sicily
1066   William the Conqueror invades England
1078   Death of Jean de Fécamp
1094   Birth of Hugo of St. Victor
1095   Urban II summons council at Clermont and launches First Crusade
1096-99   First Crusade
1098   Founding of Cistercian Order; death of Roger I
1110   Birth of St. Aelred
1113   Royal portal at Chartres
1123   Birth of Richard of St. Victor
1128   Founding of Order of Templars
1130   Suger appointed abbot of St. Denis
c. 1131   Completion of tympanum at Moissac
1147-49   Second Crusade
1153   Death of St. Bernard
1182   Birth of St. Francis
1187   Horns of Hattin
1189   Death of King William the Good of Sicily
1189-92   Third Crusade
1194   Birth of Frederick II
1200   Catharism flourishes
1202-04   Fourth Crusade
1204   Sack of Constantinople by Crusaders
1216   Death of Innocent III
1224   St. Francis receives the stigmata
c. 1225   Birth of St. Thomas Aquinas

A.D.

1226	Death of St. Francis
1244	Montségur captured; end of Cathar resistance
1250	Death of Frederick II
1261	Constantinople recovered by the Greeks
1265	Birth of Dante
1270	Death of St. Louis
1274	Death of St. Thomas Aquinas
1294	Celestine V deposed; Boniface VIII succeeds him
1303	French attack on Anagni; Boniface VIII captured
1305	Giotto paints frescoes in Arena Chapel at Padua
1314	Jacques de Molay burned at the stake
1316	Mondini de Luzzi compiles the first anatomical survey
1321	Death of Dante
1326	Brass cannon manufactured in Florence

✠ BIBLIOGRAPHICAL NOTE ✠

THE literature of Christianity is so vast and so fearfully comprehensive that sometimes one wishes another St. Francis of Assisi would arise to throw all the books out of the window. Every aspect of Christ's life on earth has been studied and minutely examined until it would seem that the world must grow weary of so many hairs split in so many microscopic ways. But the books will always continue to be written, because every age demands its own understanding of him, and its own reassurance. Meanwhile, the best are always those which some unknown author begins tomorrow night.

Since mercifully it is beyond anyone's capacity to compile a comprehensive bibliography of Christianity, I have thought it better to omit the books I consulted in libraries and to concentrate on the books that were near at hand, on my shelves: the old second-hand books and the new paperbacks and the very few which came fresh from the press. So this is simply a list of books from a working library, well-thumbed and dog-eared.

THE CHRIST

EISLER, ROBERT. *The Messiah Jesus and John the Baptist*. New York, The Dial Press, 1931.

GOGUEL, MAURICE. *Jesus and the Origins of Christianity*. New York, Harper & Brothers, 1960.

GUIGNEBERT, CHARLES. *Jésus*. Paris, La Renaissance du Livre, 1933.

MEREJKOWSKI, DMITRI. *Jesus Manifest*. New York, Charles Scribner's Sons, 1934.

————. *Jesus the Unknown*. New York, Charles Scribner's Sons, 1934.

THE PLACE AND THE TIME

DUNKERLEY, RODERICK. *Beyond the Gospels*. Harmondsworth, Penguin Books, 1957.

GEIKIE, CUNNINGHAM. *The Holy Land and the Bible*. New York, James Pott, 1888.

MERRIL, SELAH. *Galilee in the Time of Christ*. London, The Religious Tract Society, 1891.

NEWMAN, JOHN P. *From Dan to Beersheba*. New York, Hunt and Eaton, 1892.

PICK, BERNHARD. *Paralipomena: Remains of Gospels and Sayings of Christ*. Chicago, Open Court Publishing Company, 1908.

THE TEACHING

COWPER, B. HARRIS. *The Apocryphal Gospels*. London, Williams and Norgate, 1867.

HITCHCOCK, ROSWELL D. and BROWN, FRANCIS. *Teaching of the Twelve Apostles*. New York, Charles Scribner's Sons, 1885.

ST. PAUL

NOCK, ARTHUR DARBY. *St. Paul*. London, Thornton Butterworth, 1938.

THE EARLY FATHERS

DANIÉLOU, JEAN. *Origen*. New York, Sheed and Ward, 1955.

FARRAR, FREDERICK W. *Lives of the Fathers*. London, Adam and Charles Black, 1907.

WILSON, WILLIAM (translator). *The Writings of Clement of Alexandria*. Edinburgh, T. & T. Clark, 1867.

THE MARTYRS

DANIEL-ROPS, HENRI. *The Church of Apostles and Martyrs*. New York, Image Books, 1962.

EUSEBIUS. *The History of the Church*. Harmondsworth, Penguin Books, 1965.

CONSTANTINE

BURCKHARDT, JACOB. *The Age of Constantine the Great*. New York, Anchor Books, 1949.

JONES, A. H. M. *Constantine and the Conversion of Europe*. New York, Collier Books, 1962.

THE EARLY SONGS

MEAD, G. R. S. *The Hymn of Jesus*. London, John M. Watkins, 1963.

ST. AUGUSTINE

BOURKE, VERNON J. *The Essential Augustine*. New York, American Library, 1964.

HEALEY, JOHN (translator). *The City of God*. London, J. M. Dent, 1957.

WATTS, WILLIAM (translator). *St. Augustine's Confessions*. London, William Heinemann, 1922.

THE ROMAN FATHERS

PAYNE, ROBERT. *Fathers of the Western Church*. New York, Viking Press, 1951.

ST. JOHN CHRYSOSTOM

PALLADIUS. *The Dialogue Concerning the Life of Chrysostom.* New York, The Macmillan Company, 1921.
PAYNE, ROBERT. *The Holy Fire.* London, Skeffington, 1958.

THE CAPPADOCIAN FATHERS

CLARKE, W. K. L. *The Ascetic Works of St. Basil.* London, Society for Promoting Christian Knowledge, 1925.
DANIÉLOU, JEAN. *From Glory to Glory: Texts from Gregory of Nyssa's Mystical Writings.* New York, Charles Scribner's Sons, 1961.
FOX, SISTER MARGARET. *The Life and Times of St. Basil.* Washington, Catholic University Press, 1939.
GOGGIN, SISTER THOMAS AQUINAS. *The Times of St. Gregory of Nyssa.* Washington, Catholic University Press, 1947.

GREGORY THE GREAT

DUCKETT, ELEANOR SHIPLEY. *Monasticism.* Ann Arbor, University of Michigan Press, 1961.

JUSTINIAN

URE, PERCY NOBLE. *Justinian and his Age.* Harmondsworth, Penguin Books, 1951.

THE EMPIRE OF MUHAMMAD

IBN-ISHAQ. *The Life of Muhammad.* (translated by A. Guillaume) London, Oxford University Press, 1955.

CHARLEMAGNE

EINHARD. *The Life of Charlemagne.* (translated by Samuel Epes Turner) Ann Arbor, University of Michigan Press, 1960.
FICHTENAU, HEINRICH. *The Carolingian Empire.* New York, Harper Torchbooks, 1964.
HINKS, ROGER. *Carolingian Art.* Ann Arbor, University of Michigan Press, 1962.
LUQUIENS, FREDERICK BLISS (translator). *The Song of Roland.* New York, The Macmillan Company, 1962.

THE COMING OF THE NORTHMEN

BRØNDSTED, JOHANNES. *The Vikings.* Baltimore, Penguin Books, 1965.

THE FIERY COLORS

DEMUS, OTTO. *The Mosaics of Norman Sicily.* New York, The Philosophical Library, 1950.
DIEZ, ERNST, and DEMUS, OTTO. *Byzantine Mosaics in Greece: Daphni and Hosios Lucas.* Cambridge, Harvard University Press, 1931.

MATHEW, GERVASE. *Byzantine Aesthetics*. London, John Murray, 1963.
RICE, DAVID TALBOT. *The Art of Byzantium*. New York, Harry N. Abrams, 1959.

THE ROMANESQUE POWER

CHAGNOLLEAU, JEAN. *Moissac*. Paris, Arthaud, n.d.
GANTNER, JOSEPH. *Romanesque Art in France*. London, Thames and Hudson, 1956.
VIDAL, MARGUERITE. *Quercy Roman*. Paris, Zodiaque, 1959.

THE GOTHIC SPLENDOR

FRANKL, PAUL. *The Gothic*. Princeton, Princeton University Press, 1960.
JOHNSON, JAMES ROSSER. *The Radiance of Chartres*. London, Phaidon Press, 1964.
MALE, EMILE. *The Gothic Image*. New York, Harper & Brothers, 1958.

THE MYSTICAL EMPIRE

AELRED, SAINT. *On Jesus at Twelve Years Old*. (translated by Geoffrey Webb and Adrian Walker) London, A. R. Mowbray, 1956.
HUGH OF ST. VICTOR. *The Divine Love*. (translated by a Religious of C.S.M.V.) London, A. R. Mowbray, 1956.
JAMES, BRUNO S. *Saint Bernard of Clairvaux*. New York, Harper & Brothers, 1957.
UNDERHILL, EVELYN. *Mysticism*. New York, Noonday Press, 1955.

THE HERETICS

NELLI, RENÉ. *Écritures Cathares*. Paris, Editions Denoël, 1959.
NIEL, FERNAND. *Albigeois et Cathares*. Paris, Presses Universitaires de France, 1959.
RUNCIMAN, STEVEN. *The Medieval Manichee*. New York, Viking Press, 1961.

ST. FRANCIS

BONAVENTURE, SAINT. *The Life of St. Francis*. London, J. M. Dent, 1905.
JÖRGENSEN, JOHANNES. *St. Francis of Assisi*. New York, Image Books, 1955.

THE CHOIRS OF SONG

LINDSAY, JACK. *Song of a Falling World*. London, Andrew Dakers, 1948.
WADDELL, HELEN. *Mediaeval Latin Lyrics*. Harmondsworth, Penguin Books, 1962.

THE CRUSADES

BARKER, ERNEST. *The Crusades*. London, Oxford University Press, 1923.
HILL, ROSALIND (editor). *The Deeds of the Franks*. London, Thomas Nelson and Sons, 1962.
RUNCIMAN, STEVEN. *A History of the Crusades*. New York, Capricorn Books, 1964.

THE KING AND THE EMPEROR

KANTOROWICZ, ERNST. *Frederick II*. New York, Frederick Ungar, 1957.
MAILLET, GERMAINE. *La Vie Religieuse au temps de Saint Louis*. Paris, Robert Lafont, 1954.
VILLEHARDOUIN and DE JOINVILLE. *Memoirs of the Crusades*. New York, E. P. Dutton, 1958.

ST. THOMAS AQUINAS

COPLESTON, F. C. *Aquinas*. Baltimore, Penguin Books, 1965.
MARITAIN, JACQUES. *St. Thomas Aquinas*. New York, Meridian Books, 1958.

TRIUMPH AND TRAGEDY

BAINVILLE, JACQUES. *Histoire de France*. Paris, Arthème Fayard, 1924.
DANIEL-ROPS, HENRI. *Cathedral and Crusade*. New York, Image Books, 1963.

DANTE

BARBI, MICHELE. *Life of Dante*. Berkeley, University of California Press, 1954.
BRANDEIS, IRMA. *The Ladder of Vision*. New York, Anchor Books, 1962.
TOYNBEE, PAGET. *Dante Alighieri, His Life and Works*. New York, Harper Torchbooks, 1965.

THE END OF CHRISTENDOM

BAKER, HERSCHEL. *The Image of Man*. New York, Harper & Brothers, 1961.

✠ INDEX ✠